Ultimate Venus

Takako Shigematsu

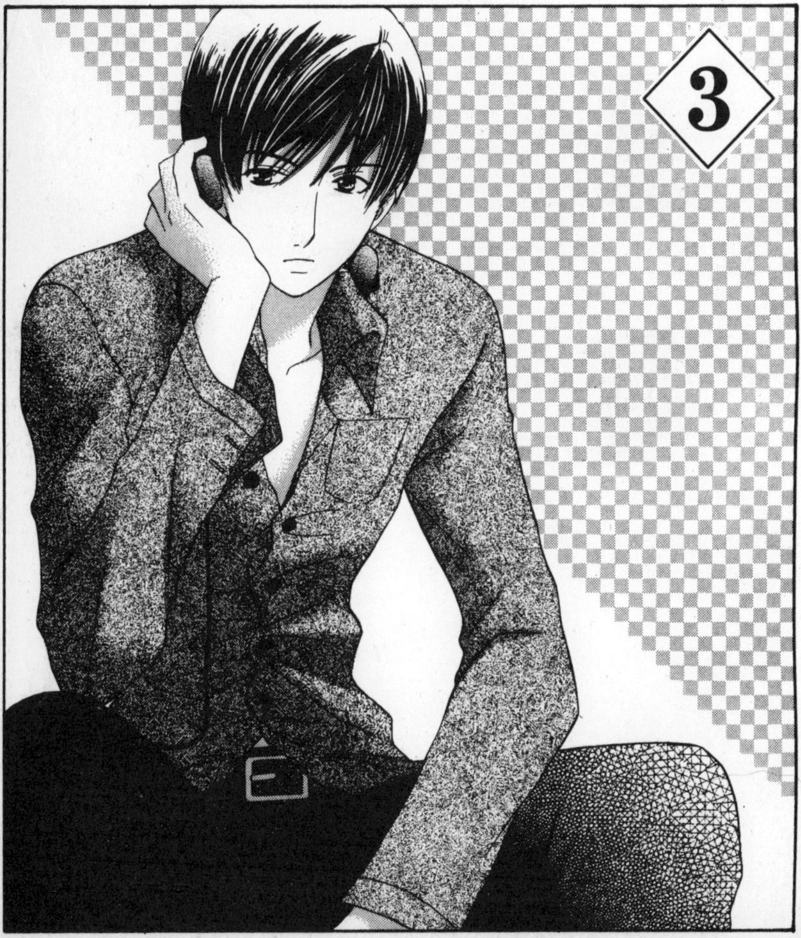
3

Translation –Christine Schilling
Adaptation – Brynne Chandler
Lettering & Retouch – Erika T.
Production Assistant – Suzy Wells
Editorial Assistant – Mallory Reaves
Production Manager – James Dashiell
Editor – Brynne Chandler

A Go! Comi manga

Published by Go! Media Entertainment, LLC

Kyukyoku Venus Volume 3
© TAKAKO SHIGEMATSU 2007
Originally published in Japan in 2007 by Akita Publishing Co., Ltd., Tokyo.
English translation rights arranged with Akita Publishing Co., Ltd.
through TOHAN CORPORATION, Tokyo.

Visit us online at www.gocomi.com
e-mail: info@gocomi.com

ISBN 978-1-933617-90-9

First printed in December 2008

1   2   3   4   5   6   7   8   9

Manufactured in the United States of America

by

Takako Shigematsu

Volume 3

go!comi

VOLUME:3
CONTENTS

* Story so far *

When Yuzu Yamashita's mother passed away, she thought she was all alone in the world. Then she met Hassaku Kagami and found out she had a grandmother who lives in a castle and is the president of the multinational Shirayuki Group! Once Yuzu becomes a candidate to be the family heir, her life is filled with bizarre dangers, like an attempted kidnapping! Though she starts going out with her Elite Class A classmate and bodyguard, Iyo Hayashibara, Yuzu's afraid she's really falling for Hassaku!

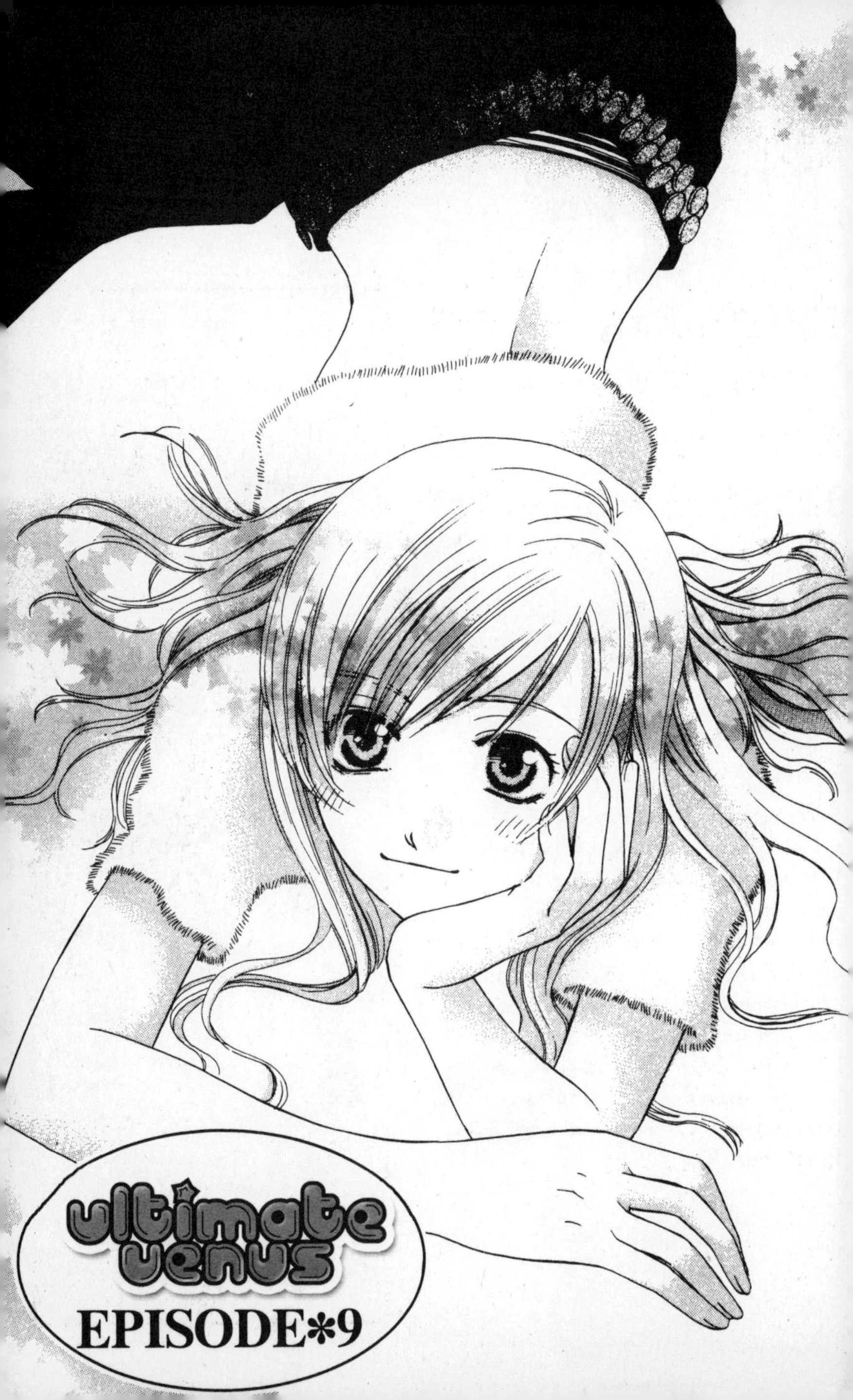
ultimate venus
EPISODE*9

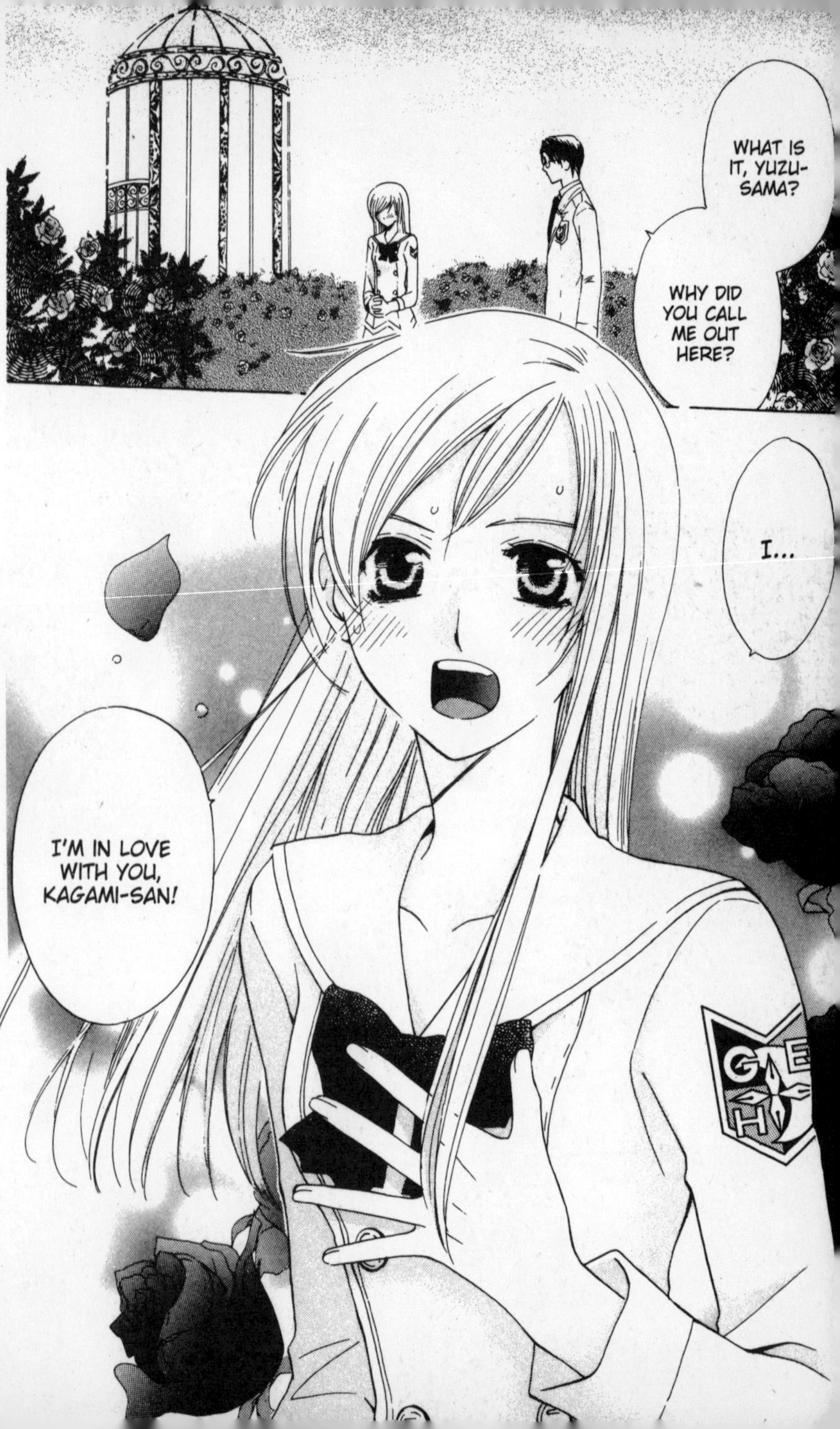
WHAT IS IT, YUZU-SAMA?
WHY DID YOU CALL ME OUT HERE?
I...
I'M IN LOVE WITH YOU, KAGAMI-SAN!
GEH

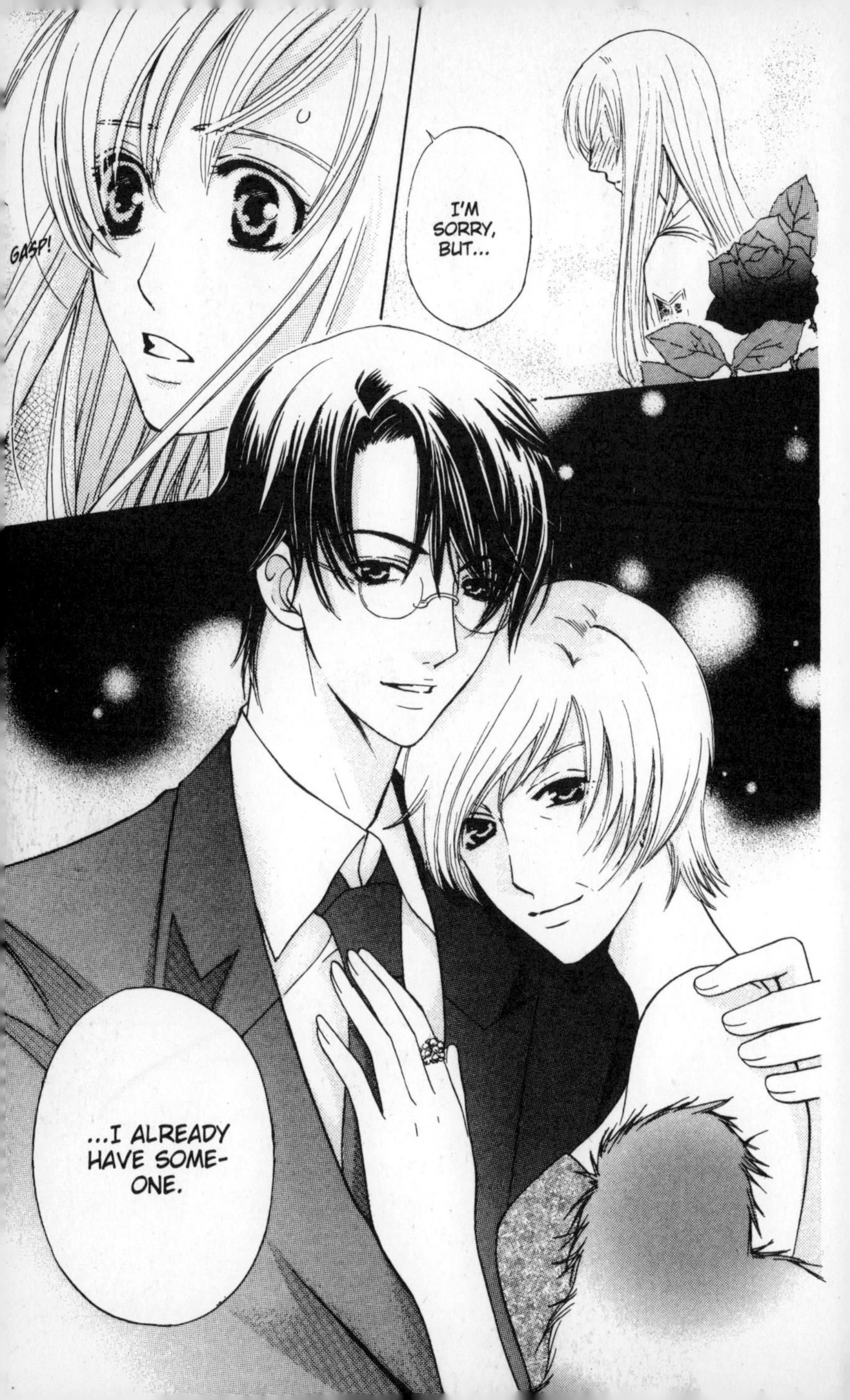
I'M SORRY, BUT...
GASP!
...I ALREADY HAVE SOME-ONE.

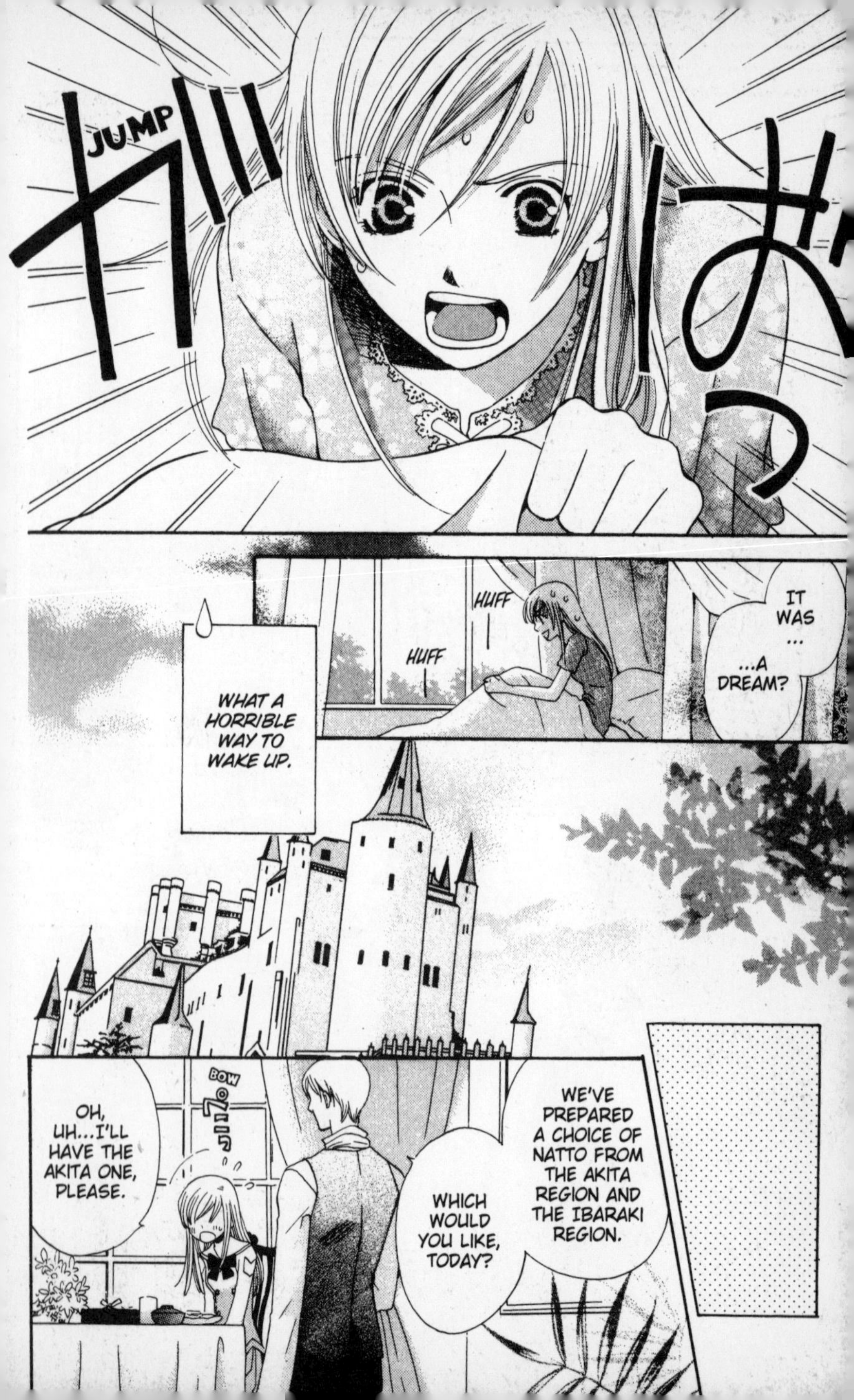
JUMP
IT WAS...
...A DREAM?
HUFF
HUFF
WHAT A HORRIBLE WAY TO WAKE UP.
WE'VE PREPARED A CHOICE OF NATTO FROM THE AKITA REGION AND THE IBARAKI REGION.
WHICH WOULD YOU LIKE, TODAY?
BOW
OH, UH...I'LL HAVE THE AKITA ONE, PLEASE.

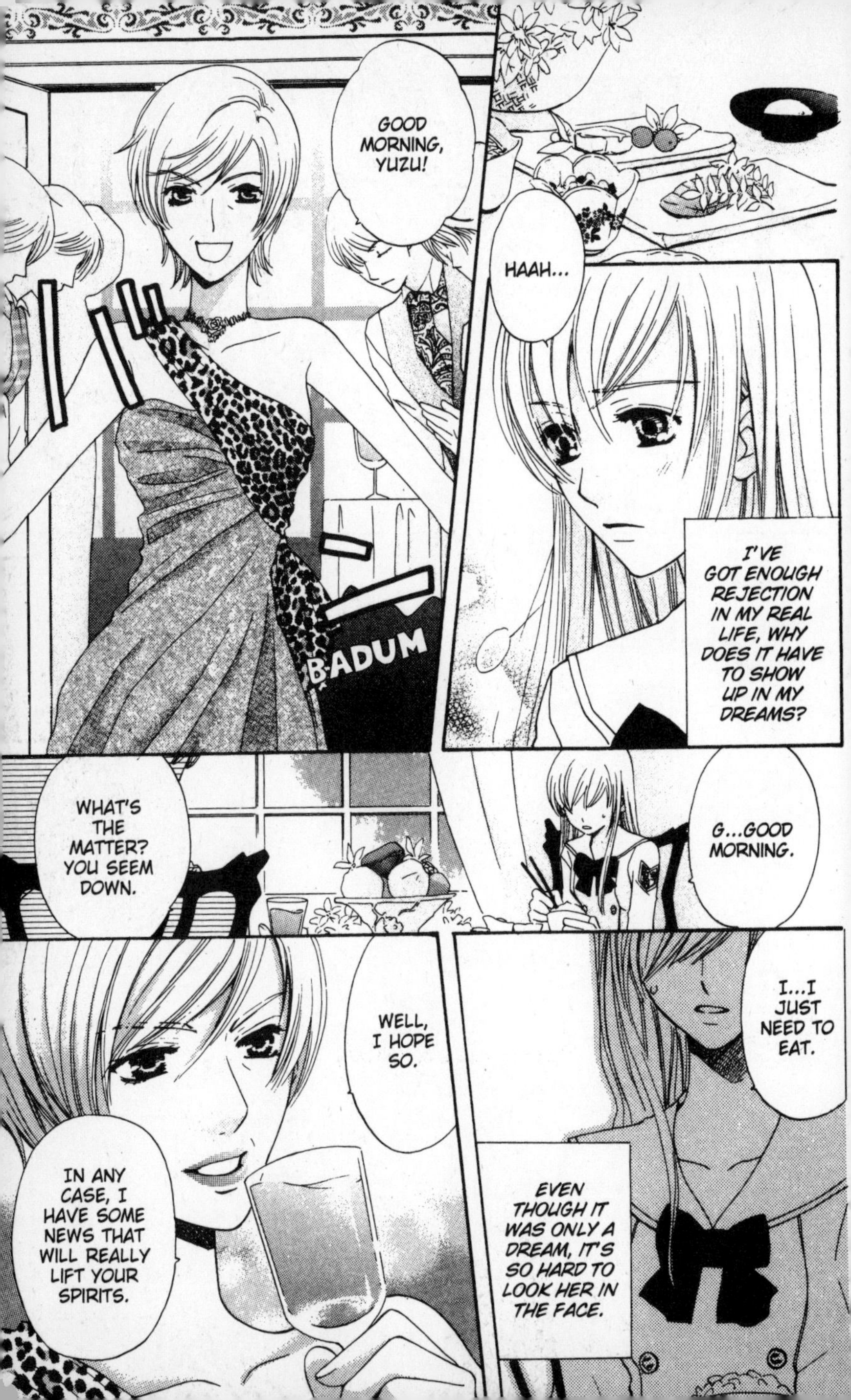
HAAH...
I'VE GOT ENOUGH REJECTION IN MY REAL LIFE, WHY DOES IT HAVE TO SHOW UP IN MY DREAMS?
GOOD MORNING, YUZU!
B-ADUM
G...GOOD MORNING.
WHAT'S THE MATTER? YOU SEEM DOWN.
I...I JUST NEED TO EAT.
EVEN THOUGH IT WAS ONLY A DREAM, IT'S SO HARD TO LOOK HER IN THE FACE.
WELL, I HOPE SO.
IN ANY CASE, I HAVE SOME NEWS THAT WILL REALLY LIFT YOUR SPIRITS.

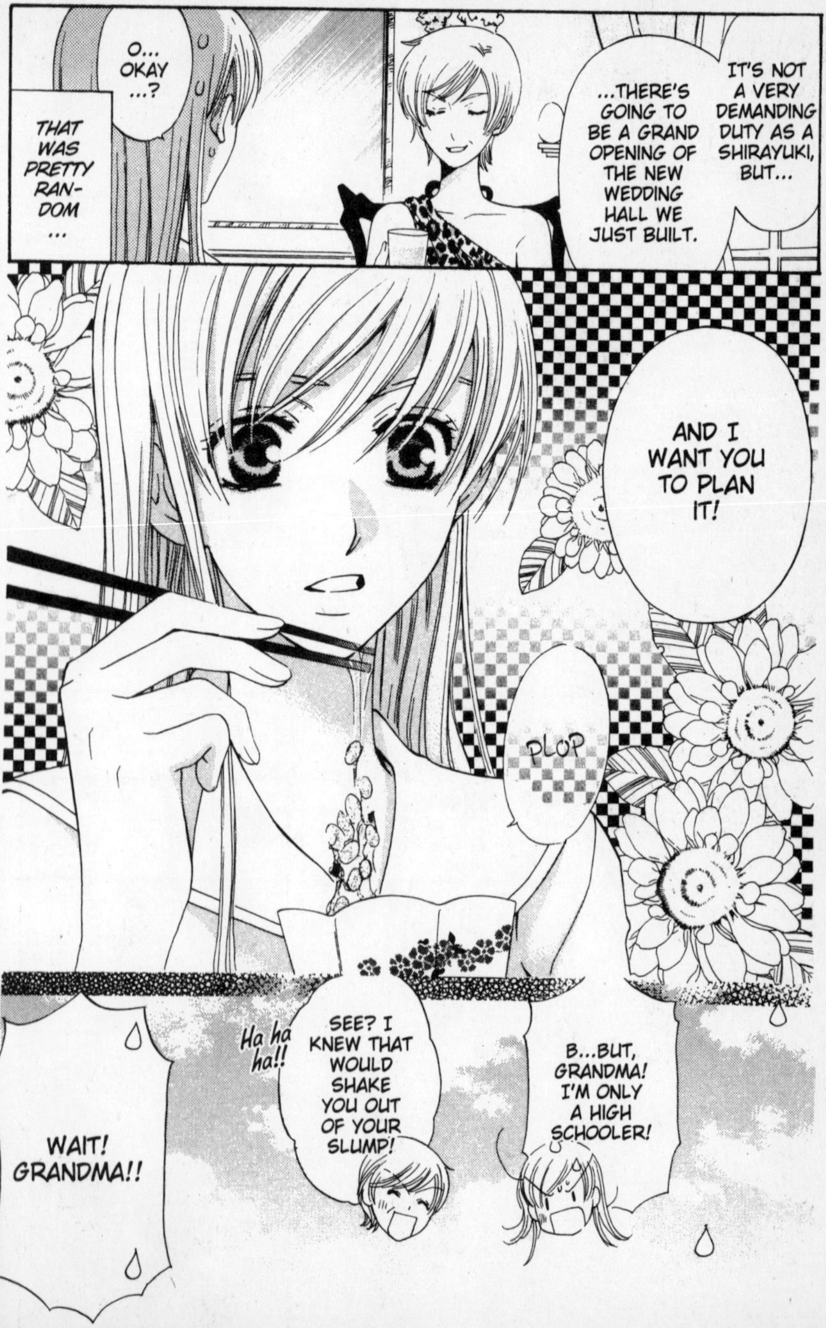
IT'S NOT A VERY DEMANDING DUTY AS A SHIRAYUKI, BUT...
...THERE'S GOING TO BE A GRAND OPENING OF THE NEW WEDDING HALL WE JUST BUILT.
O... OKAY ...?
THAT WAS PRETTY RAN-DOM ...
AND I WANT YOU TO PLAN IT!
PLOP
B...BUT, GRANDMA! I'M ONLY A HIGH SCHOOLER!
SEE? I KNEW THAT WOULD SHAKE YOU OUT OF YOUR SLUMP!
Ha ha ha!!
WAIT! GRANDMA!!

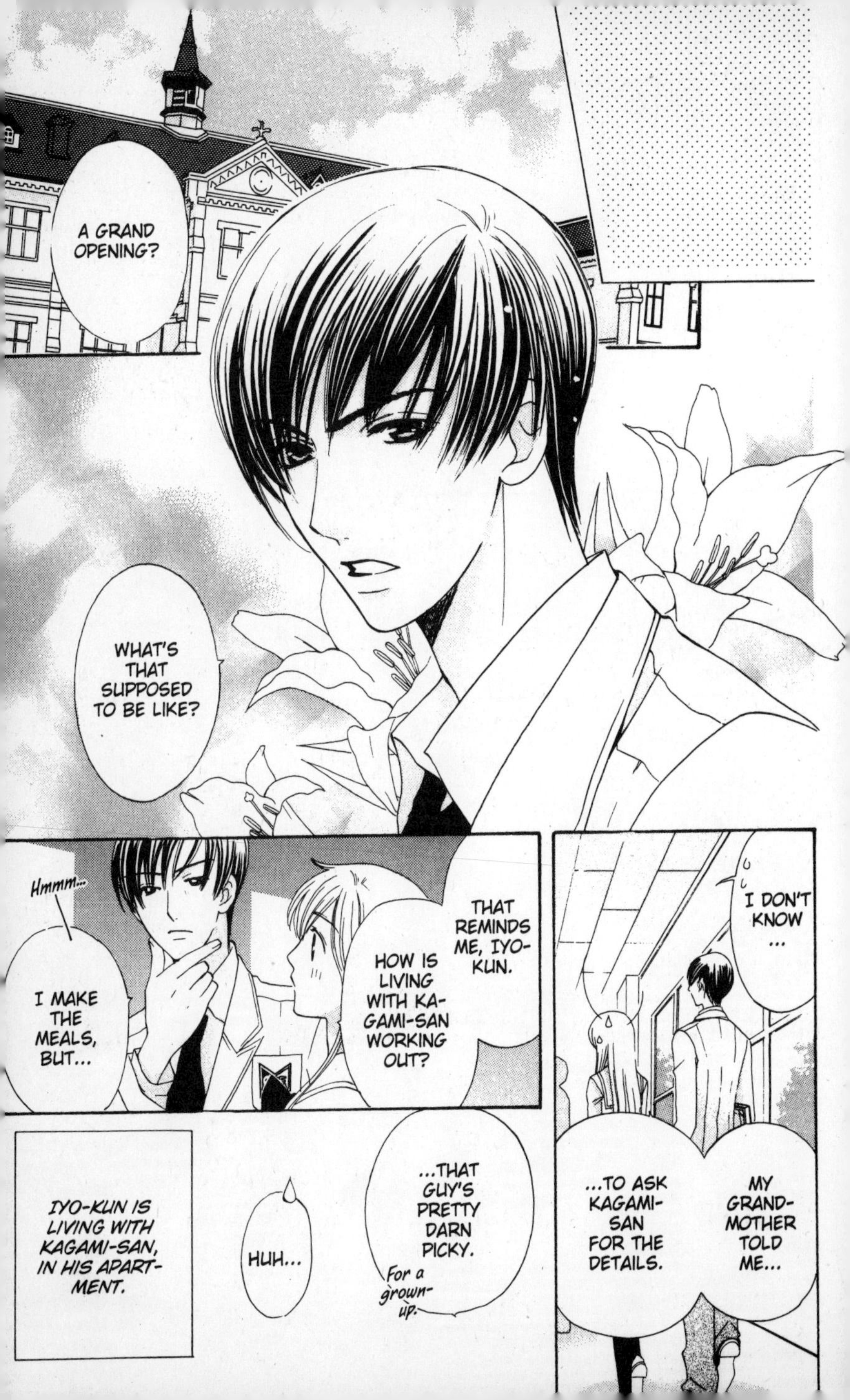
A GRAND OPENING?
WHAT'S THAT SUPPOSED TO BE LIKE?
I DON'T KNOW ...
MY GRANDMOTHER TOLD ME...
...TO ASK KAGAMI-SAN FOR THE DETAILS.
THAT REMINDS ME, IYO-KUN.
HOW IS LIVING WITH KA-GAMI-SAN WORKING OUT?
Hmmm...
I MAKE THE MEALS, BUT...
...THAT GUY'S PRETTY DARN PICKY.
For a grown-up.
HUH...
IYO-KUN IS LIVING WITH KAGAMI-SAN, IN HIS APART-MENT.

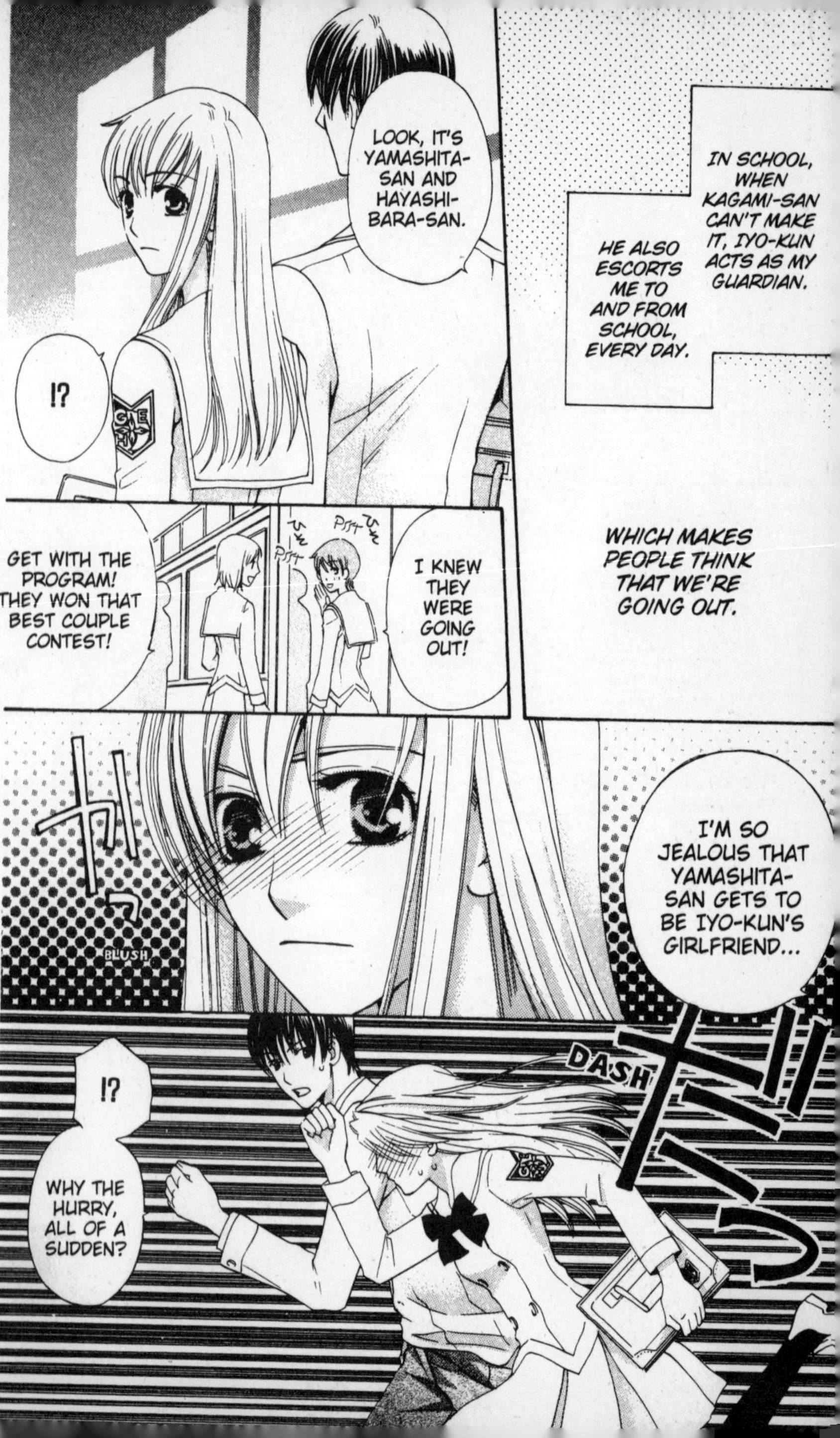
IN SCHOOL, WHEN KAGAMI-SAN CAN'T MAKE IT, IYO-KUN ACTS AS MY GUARDIAN.
HE ALSO ESCORTS ME TO AND FROM SCHOOL, EVERY DAY.
LOOK, IT'S YAMASHITA-SAN AND HAYASHI-BARA-SAN.
!?
WHICH MAKES PEOPLE THINK THAT WE'RE GOING OUT.
I KNEW THEY WERE GOING OUT!
PSST
PSST
GET WITH THE PROGRAM! THEY WON THAT BEST COUPLE CONTEST!
I'M SO JEALOUS THAT YAMASHITA-SAN GETS TO BE IYO-KUN'S GIRLFRIEND...
BLUSH
DASH
!?
WHY THE HURRY, ALL OF A SUDDEN?

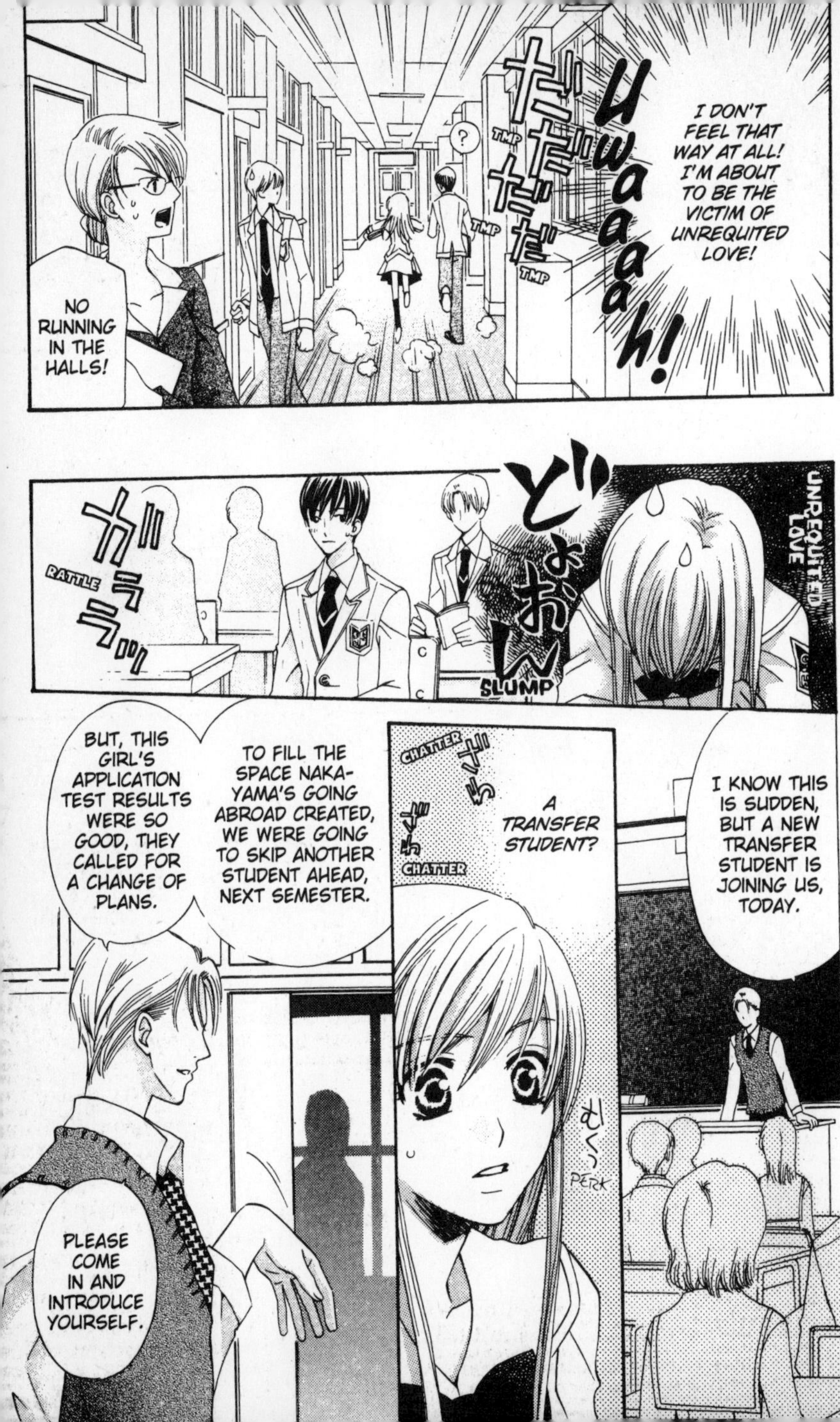
I DON'T FEEL THAT WAY AT ALL! I'M ABOUT TO BE THE VICTIM OF UNREQUITED LOVE!
Uwaaaah!
TMP
TMP
TMP
?
NO RUNNING IN THE HALLS!
UNREQUITED LOVE
SLUMP
RATTLE
I KNOW THIS IS SUDDEN, BUT A NEW TRANSFER STUDENT IS JOINING US, TODAY.
CHATTER
CHATTER
A TRANSFER STUDENT?
PERK
TO FILL THE SPACE NAKA-YAMA'S GOING ABROAD CREATED, WE WERE GOING TO SKIP ANOTHER STUDENT AHEAD, NEXT SEMESTER.
BUT, THIS GIRL'S APPLICATION TEST RESULTS WERE SO GOOD, THEY CALLED FOR A CHANGE OF PLANS.
PLEASE COME IN AND INTRODUCE YOURSELF.

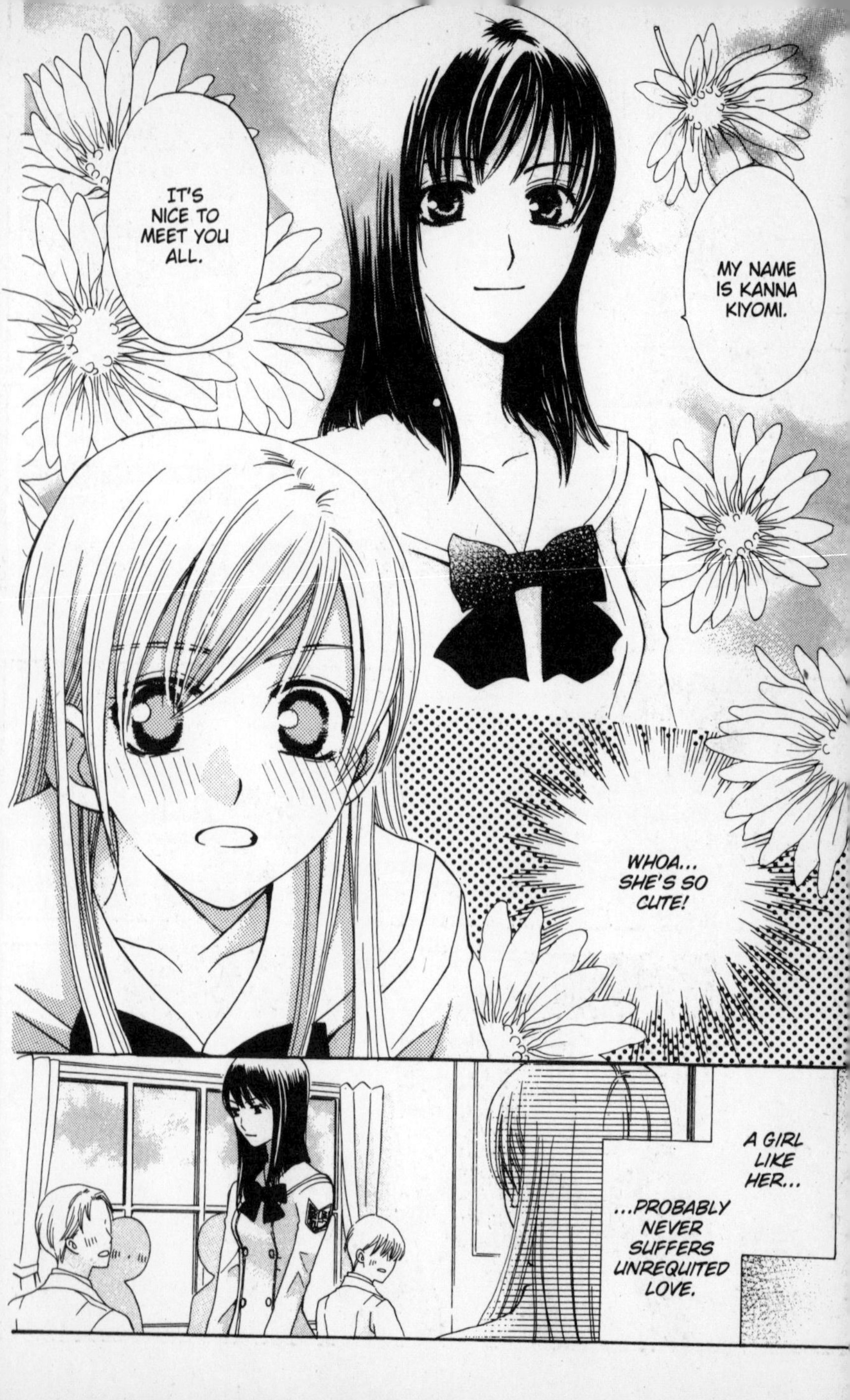
MY NAME IS KANNA KIYOMI.
IT'S NICE TO MEET YOU ALL.
WHOA... SHE'S SO CUTE!
A GIRL LIKE HER...
...PROBABLY NEVER SUFFERS UNREQUITED LOVE.

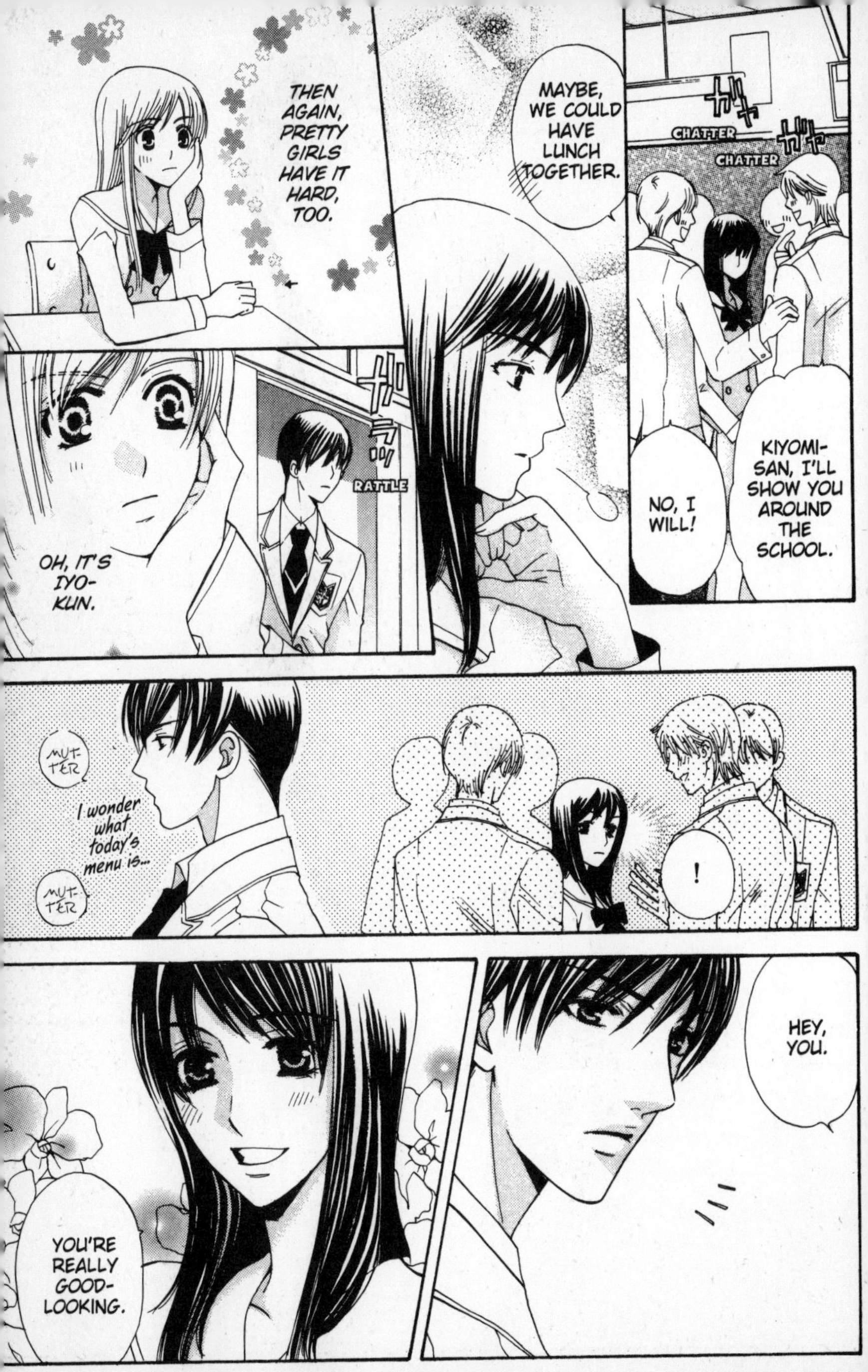
CHATTER
CHATTER
KIYOMI-SAN, I'LL SHOW YOU AROUND THE SCHOOL.
NO, I WILL!
MAYBE, WE COULD HAVE LUNCH TOGETHER.
THEN AGAIN, PRETTY GIRLS HAVE IT HARD, TOO.
RATTLE
OH, IT'S IYO-KUN.
!
MUTTER
I wonder what today's menu is...
MUTTER
HEY, YOU.
YOU'RE REALLY GOOD-LOOKING.

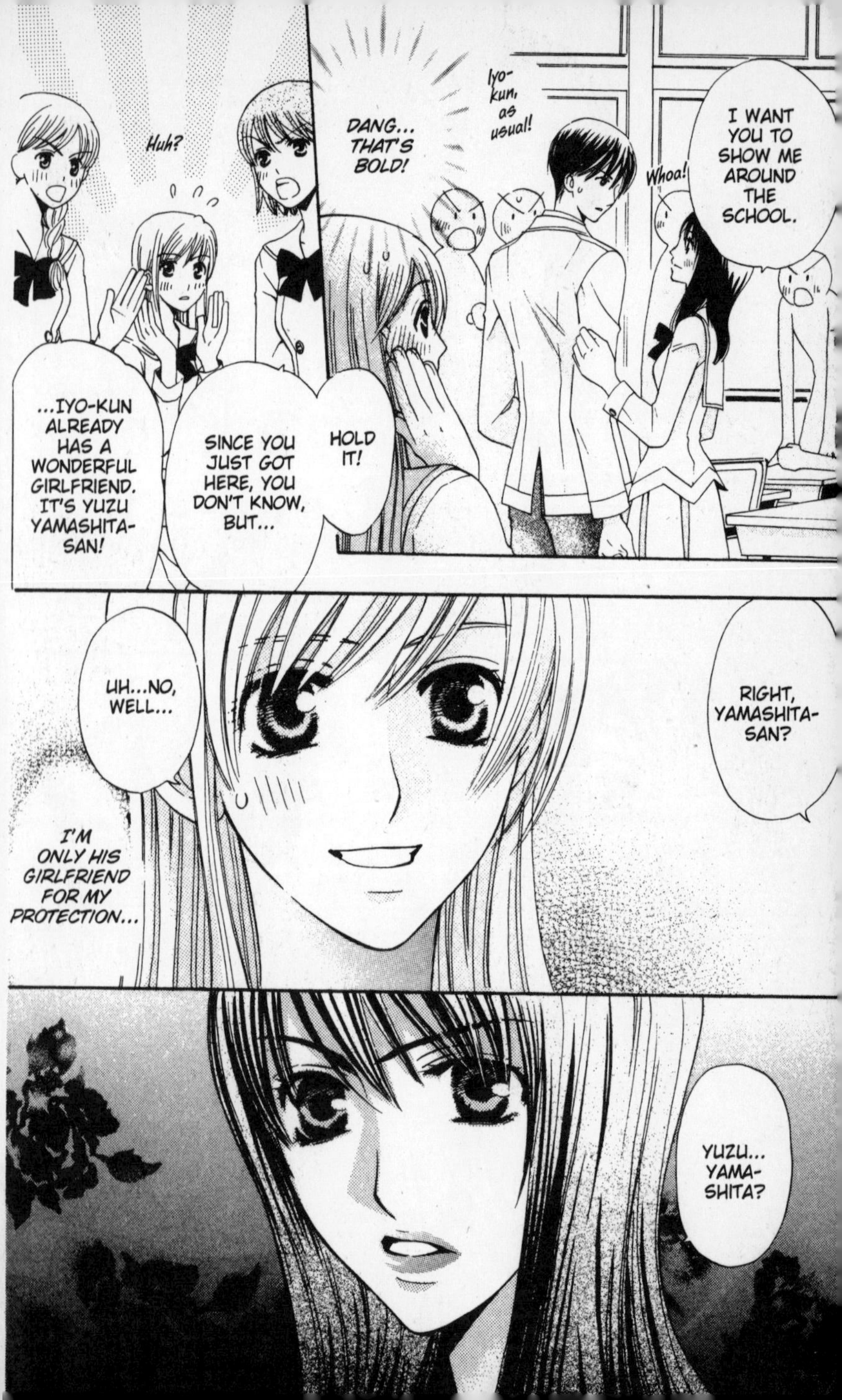
I WANT YOU TO SHOW ME AROUND THE SCHOOL.
Whoa!
Iyo-kun, as usual!
DANG... THAT'S BOLD!
HOLD IT!
Huh?
SINCE YOU JUST GOT HERE, YOU DON'T KNOW, BUT...
...IYO-KUN ALREADY HAS A WONDERFUL GIRLFRIEND. IT'S YUZU YAMASHITA-SAN!
RIGHT, YAMASHITA-SAN?
UH...NO, WELL...
I'M ONLY HIS GIRLFRIEND FOR MY PROTECTION...
YUZU... YAMASHITA?

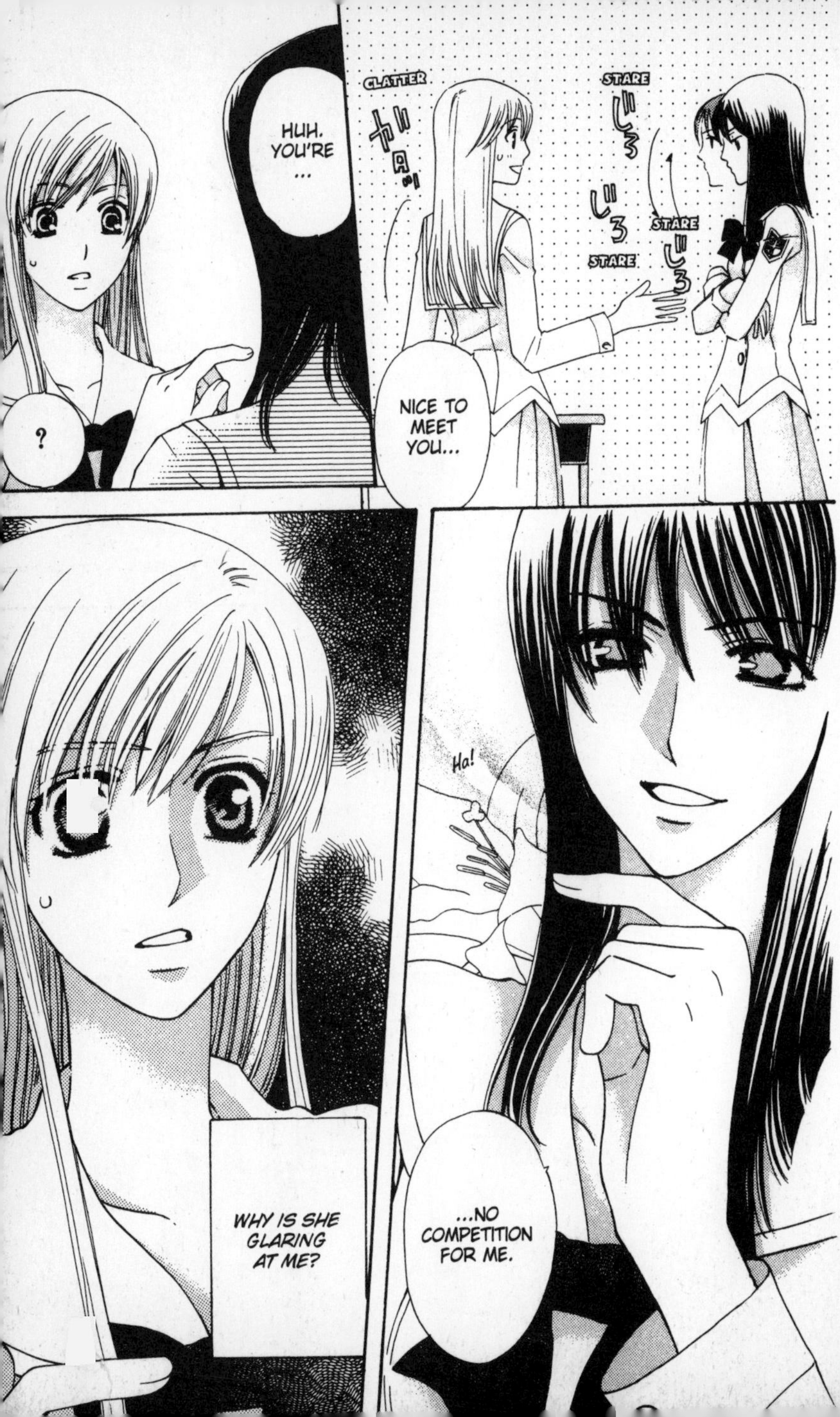
STARE
じろ
STARE
じろ
STARE
じろ
CLATTER
NICE TO MEET YOU...
HUH. YOU'RE ...
?
Ha!
...NO COMPETITION FOR ME.
WHY IS SHE GLARING AT ME?

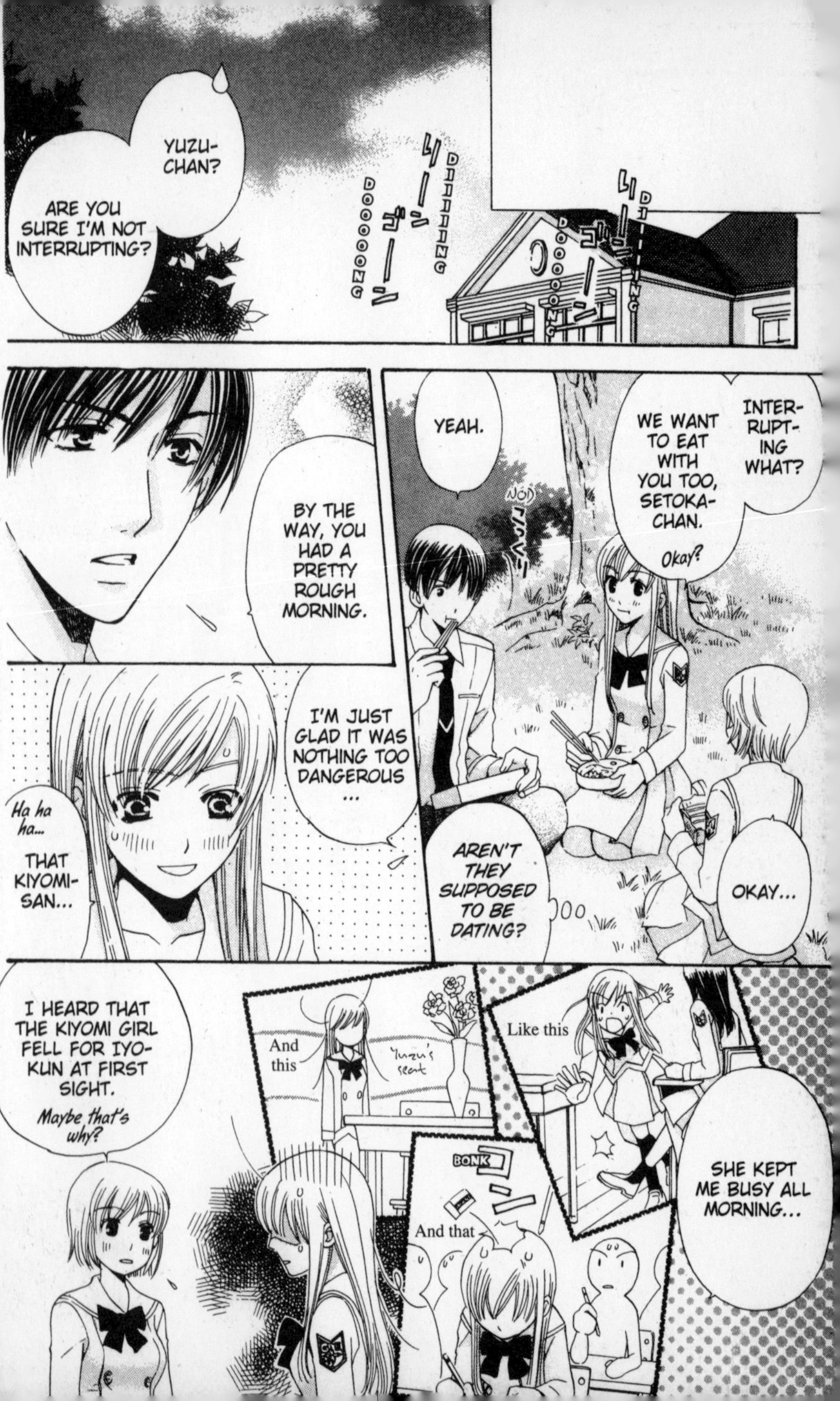
DIIIING
DOOOOONG
DIIIING
DOOOOONG
YUZU-CHAN?
ARE YOU SURE I'M NOT INTERRUPTING?
INTERRUPTING WHAT?
WE WANT TO EAT WITH YOU TOO, SETOKA-CHAN.
Okay?
YEAH.
NOD
OKAY...
AREN'T THEY SUPPOSED TO BE DATING?
BY THE WAY, YOU HAD A PRETTY ROUGH MORNING.
I'M JUST GLAD IT WAS NOTHING TOO DANGEROUS...
Ha ha ha...
THAT KIYOMI-SAN...
SHE KEPT ME BUSY ALL MORNING...
Like this
And this
Yuzu's seat
BONK
And that
I HEARD THAT THE KIYOMI GIRL FELL FOR IYO-KUN AT FIRST SIGHT.
Maybe that's why?

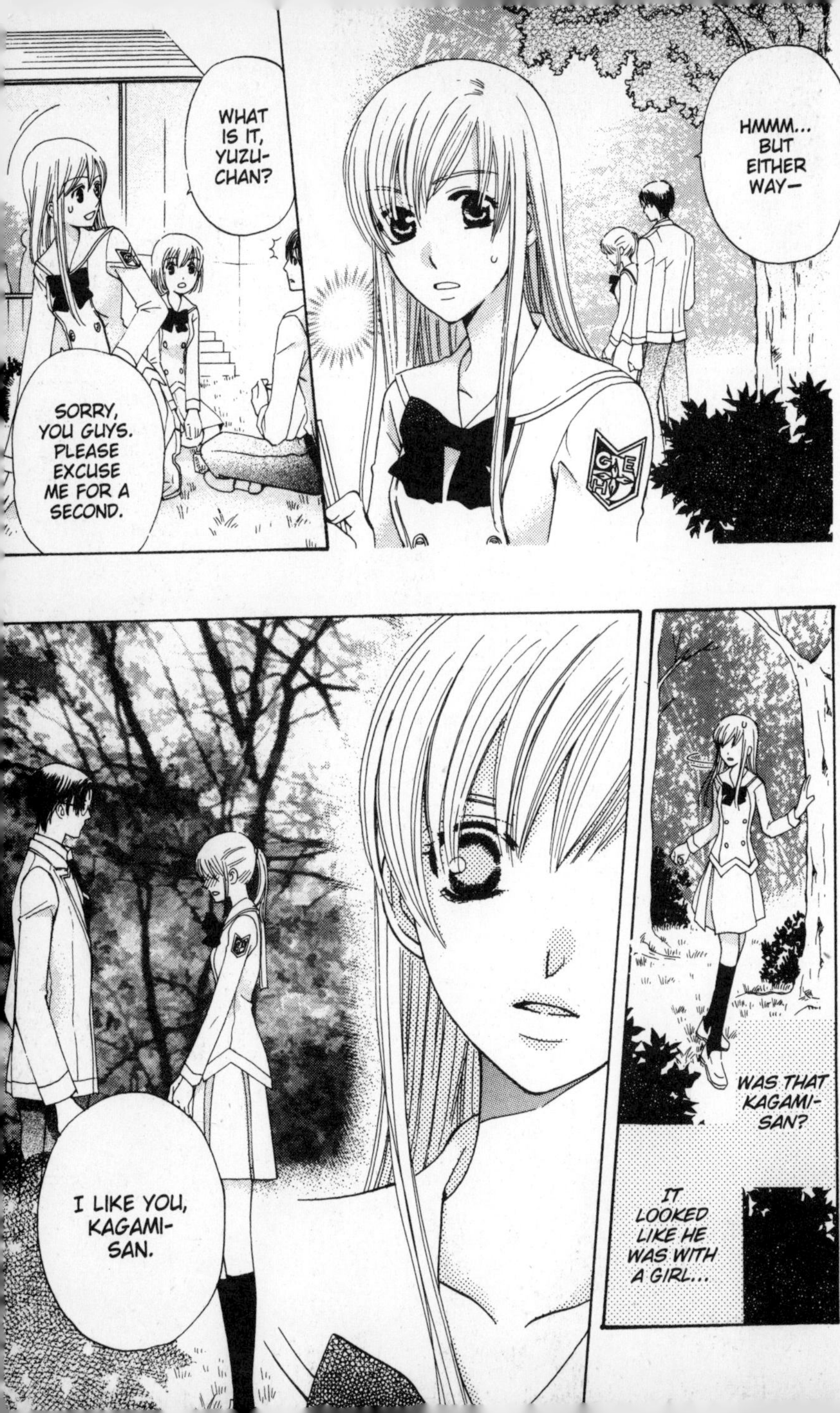
HMMM... BUT EITHER WAY—
WHAT IS IT, YUZU-CHAN?
SORRY, YOU GUYS. PLEASE EXCUSE ME FOR A SECOND.
WAS THAT KAGAMI-SAN?
IT LOOKED LIKE HE WAS WITH A GIRL...
I LIKE YOU, KAGAMI-SAN.

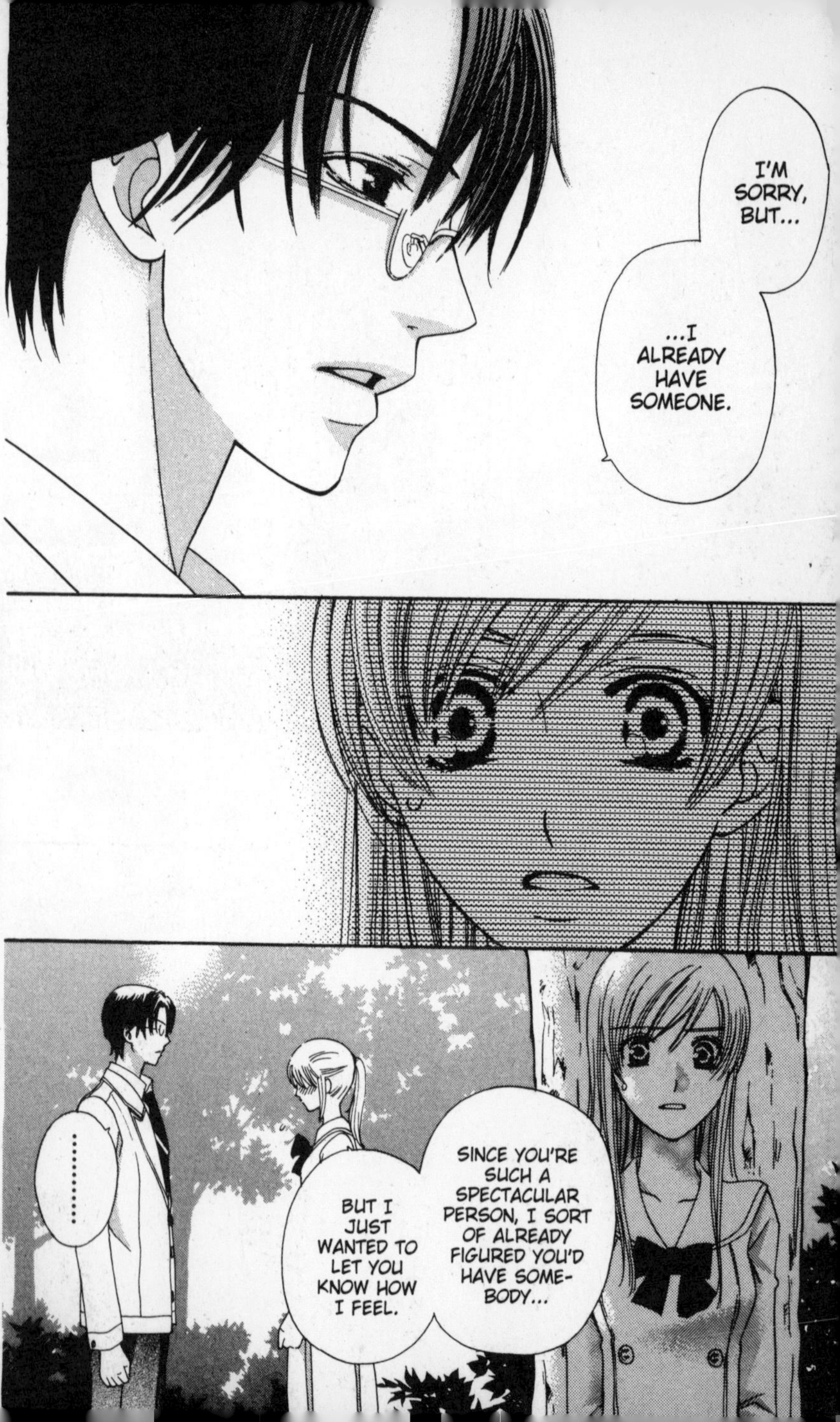
I'M SORRY, BUT...
...I ALREADY HAVE SOMEONE.
SINCE YOU'RE SUCH A SPECTACULAR PERSON, I SORT OF ALREADY FIGURED YOU'D HAVE SOME-BODY...
BUT I JUST WANTED TO LET YOU KNOW HOW I FEEL.
....

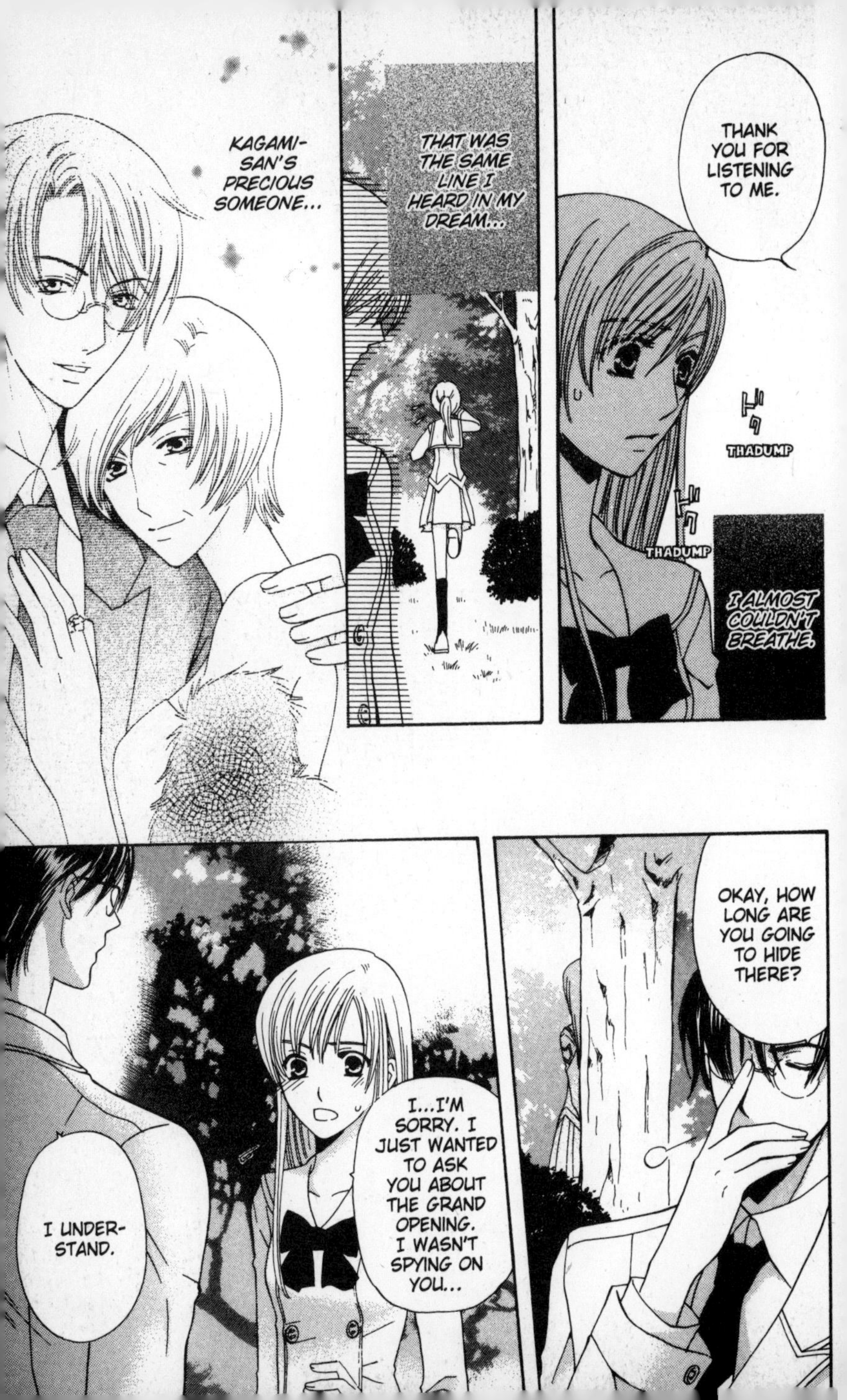
THANK YOU FOR LISTENING TO ME.
THADUMP
THADUMP
I ALMOST COULDN'T BREATHE.
THAT WAS THE SAME LINE I HEARD IN MY DREAM...
KAGAMI-SAN'S PRECIOUS SOMEONE...
OKAY, HOW LONG ARE YOU GOING TO HIDE THERE?
I...I'M SORRY. I JUST WANTED TO ASK YOU ABOUT THE GRAND OPENING. I WASN'T SPYING ON YOU...
I UNDER-STAND.

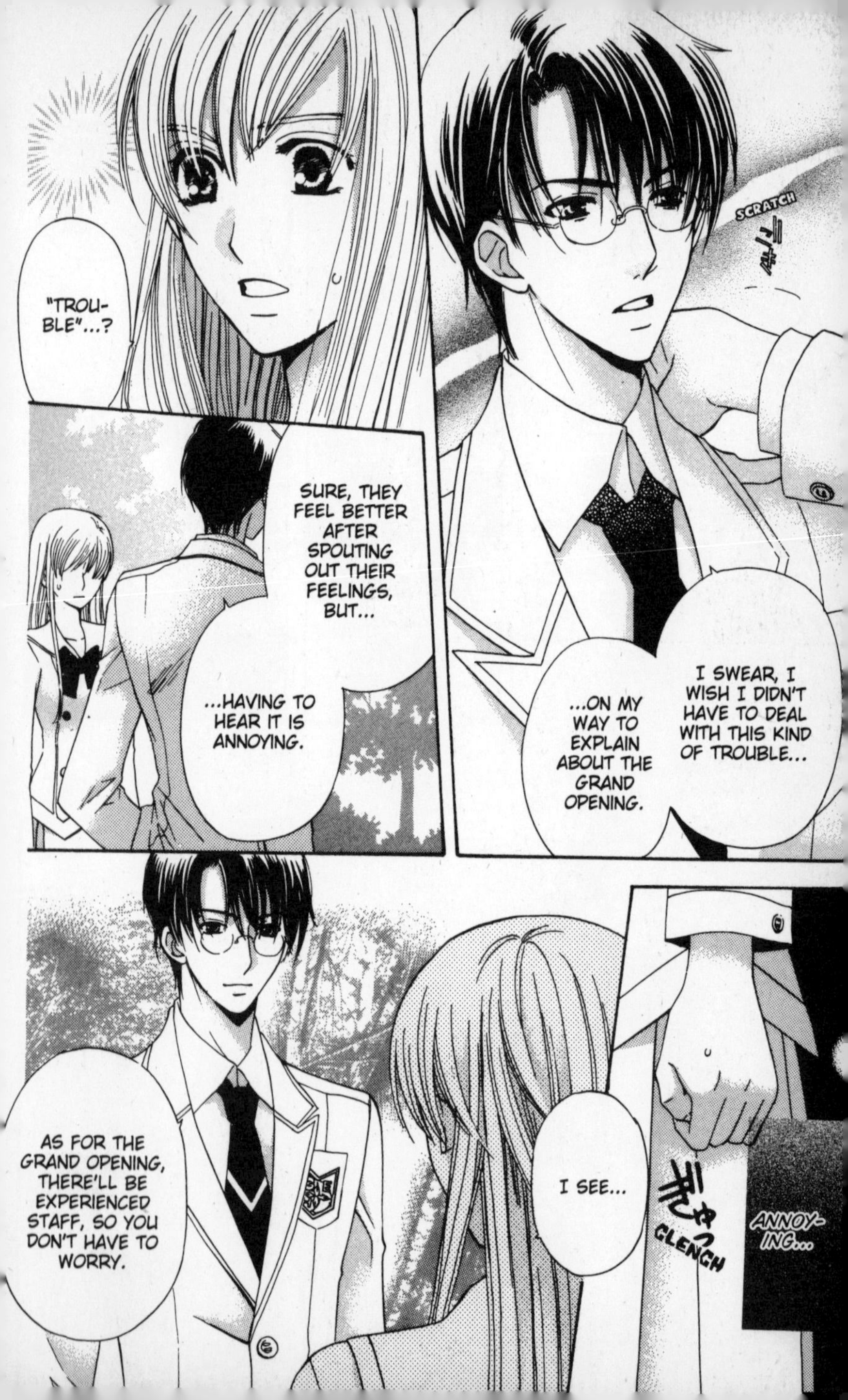
SCRATCH
I SWEAR, I WISH I DIDN'T HAVE TO DEAL WITH THIS KIND OF TROUBLE...
...ON MY WAY TO EXPLAIN ABOUT THE GRAND OPENING.
"TROUBLE"...?
SURE, THEY FEEL BETTER AFTER SPOUTING OUT THEIR FEELINGS, BUT...
...HAVING TO HEAR IT IS ANNOYING.
ANNOY-ING...
CLENCH
I SEE...
AS FOR THE GRAND OPENING, THERE'LL BE EXPERIENCED STAFF, SO YOU DON'T HAVE TO WORRY.

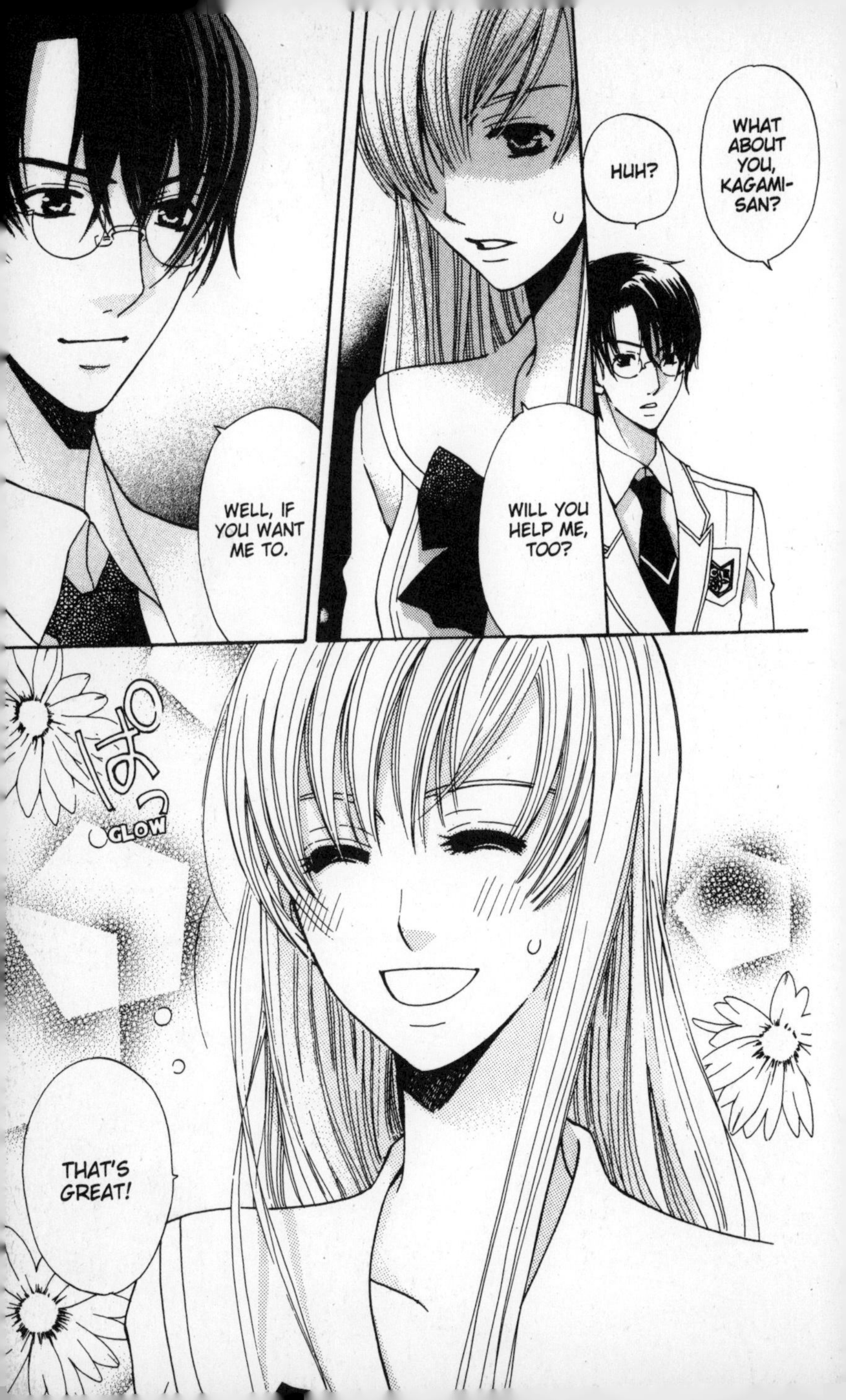
WHAT ABOUT YOU, KAGAMI-SAN?
HUH?
WILL YOU HELP ME, TOO?
WELL, IF YOU WANT ME TO.
ぱっ
GLOW
THAT'S GREAT!

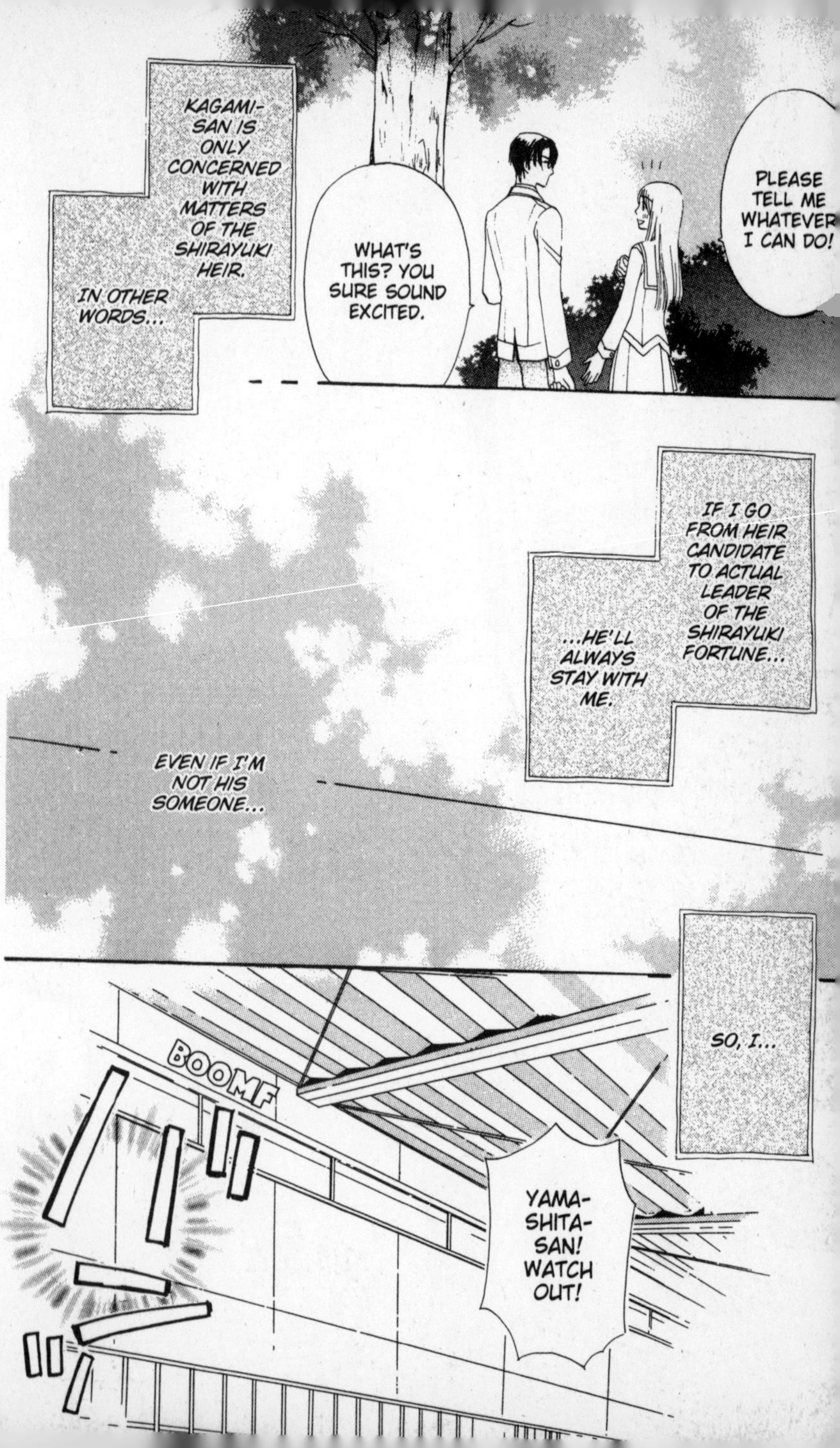
PLEASE TELL ME WHATEVER I CAN DO!
WHAT'S THIS? YOU SURE SOUND EXCITED.
KAGAMI-SAN IS ONLY CONCERNED WITH MATTERS OF THE SHIRAYUKI HEIR.
IN OTHER WORDS...
IF I GO FROM HEIR CANDIDATE TO ACTUAL LEADER OF THE SHIRAYUKI FORTUNE...
...HE'LL ALWAYS STAY WITH ME.
EVEN IF I'M NOT HIS SOMEONE...
SO, I...
YAMA-SHITA-SAN! WATCH OUT!
BOOMF

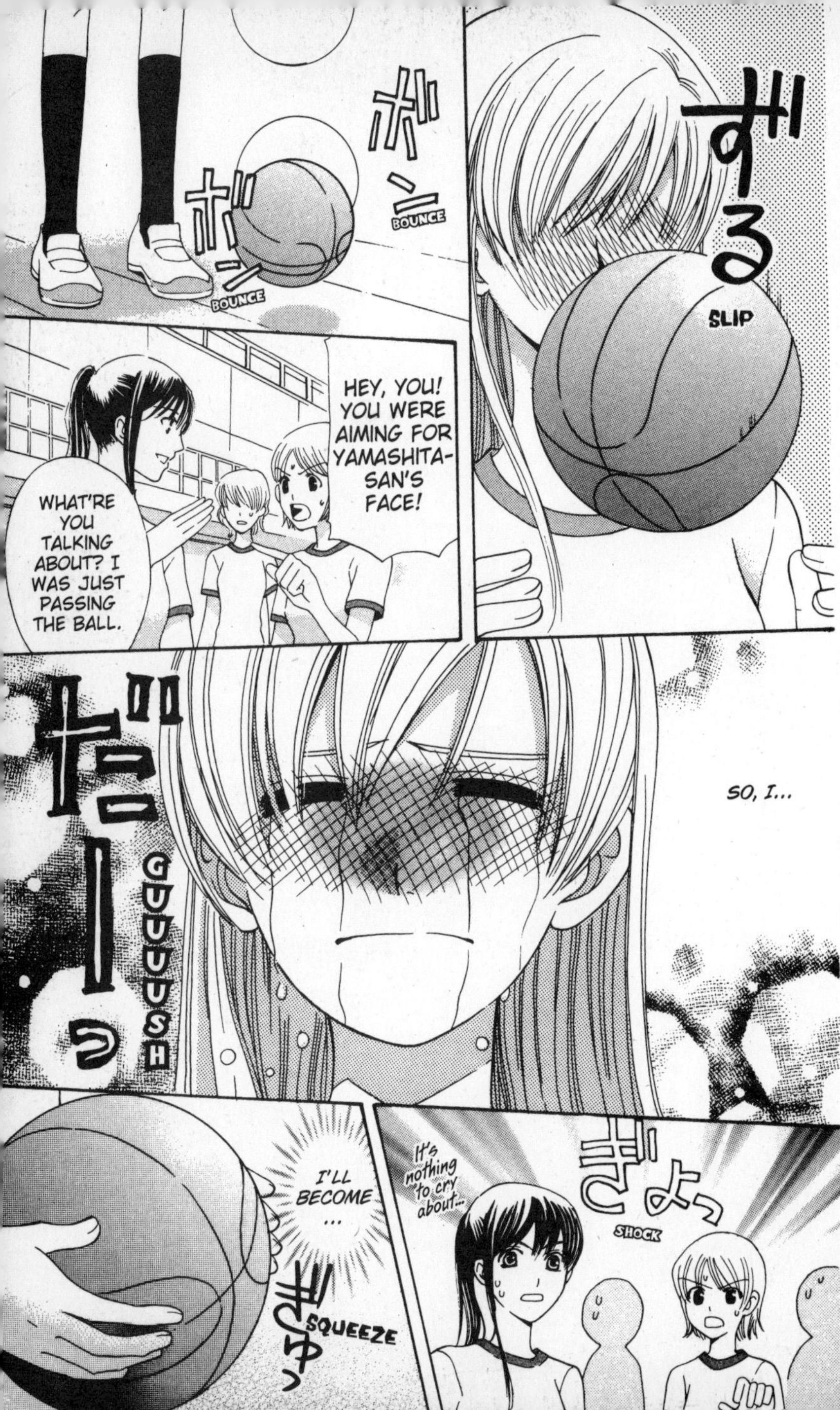

ずる
SLIP
ボーン
BOUNCE
ボーン
BOUNCE
HEY, YOU! YOU WERE AIMING FOR YAMASHITA-SAN'S FACE!
WHAT'RE YOU TALKING ABOUT? I WAS JUST PASSING THE BALL.
SO, I...
ぎゅーっ
GUUUUSH
ぎょっ
SHOCK
It's nothing to cry about...
I'LL BECOME ...
ぎゅっ
SQUEEZE

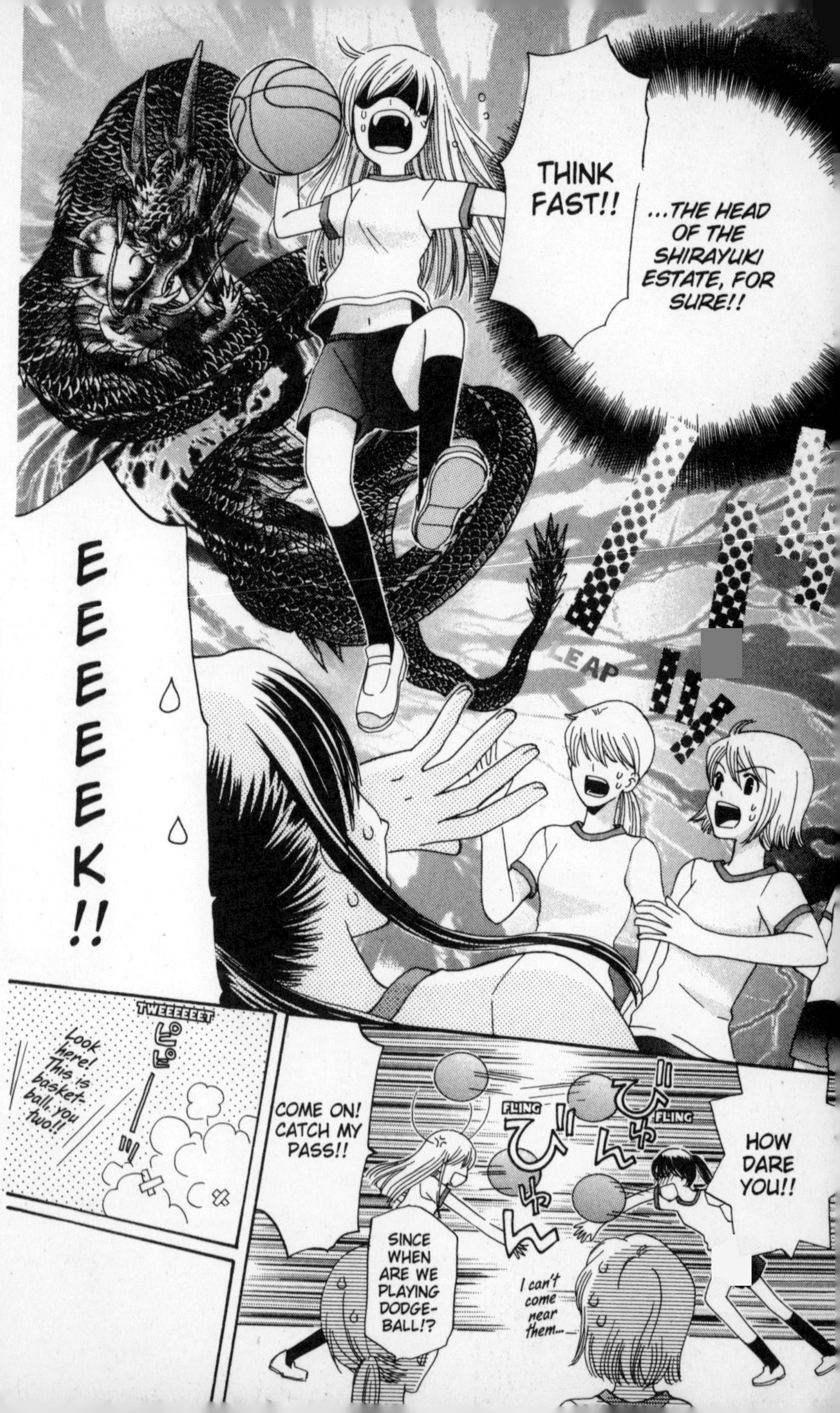
...THE HEAD OF THE SHIRAYUKI ESTATE, FOR SURE!!
THINK FAST!!
LEAP
EEEEEEK!!
HOW DARE YOU!!
FLING
FLING
COME ON! CATCH MY PASS!!
SINCE WHEN ARE WE PLAYING DODGE-BALL!?
I can't come near them...
TWEEEEEEET
Look here! This is basket-ball, you two!!

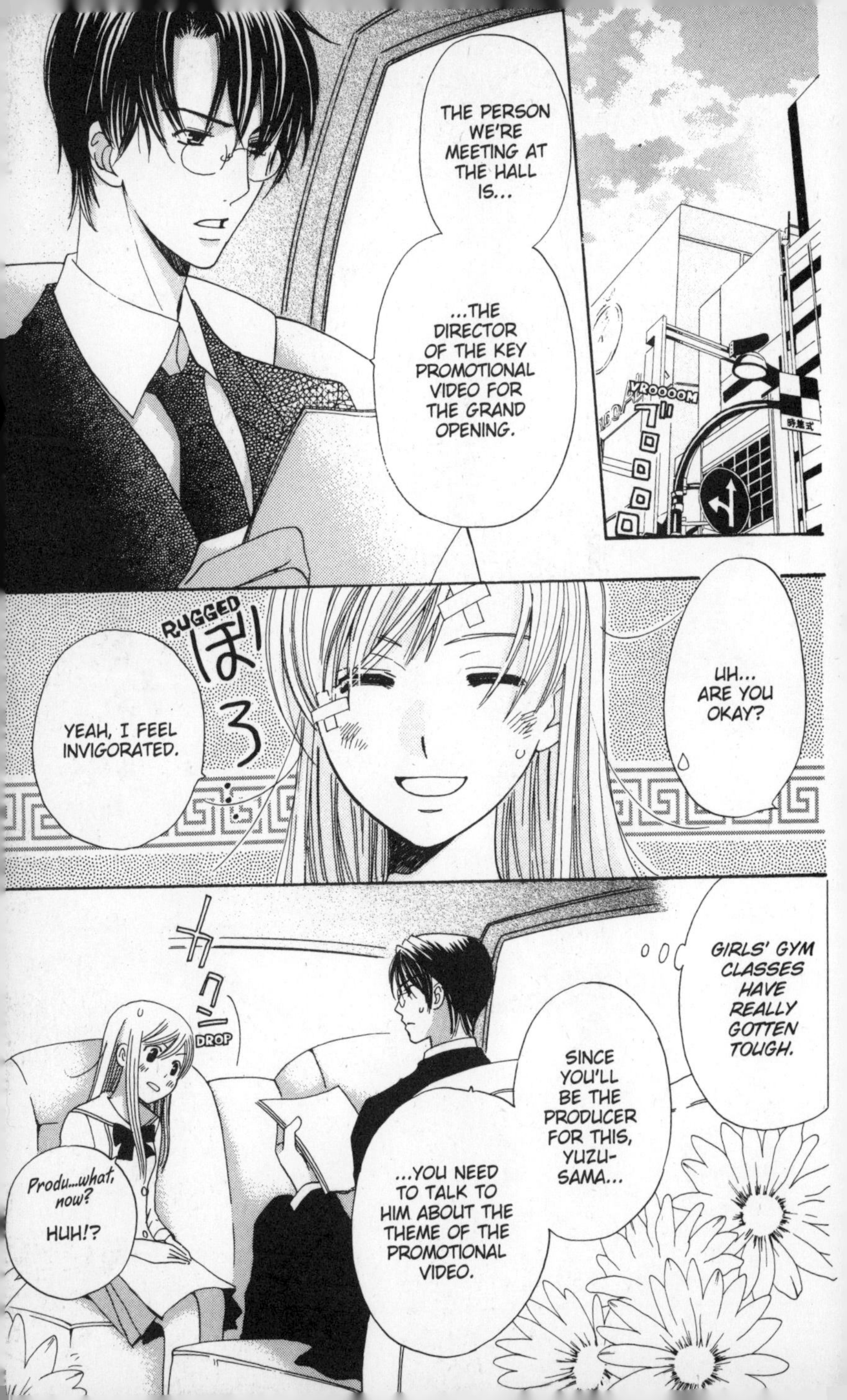
VROOOOM
THE PERSON WE'RE MEETING AT THE HALL IS...
...THE DIRECTOR OF THE KEY PROMOTIONAL VIDEO FOR THE GRAND OPENING.
UH... ARE YOU OKAY?
RUGGED
YEAH, I FEEL INVIGORATED.
GIRLS' GYM CLASSES HAVE REALLY GOTTEN TOUGH.
SINCE YOU'LL BE THE PRODUCER FOR THIS, YUZU-SAMA...
...YOU NEED TO TALK TO HIM ABOUT THE THEME OF THE PROMOTIONAL VIDEO.
DROP
Produ...what, now?
HUH!?

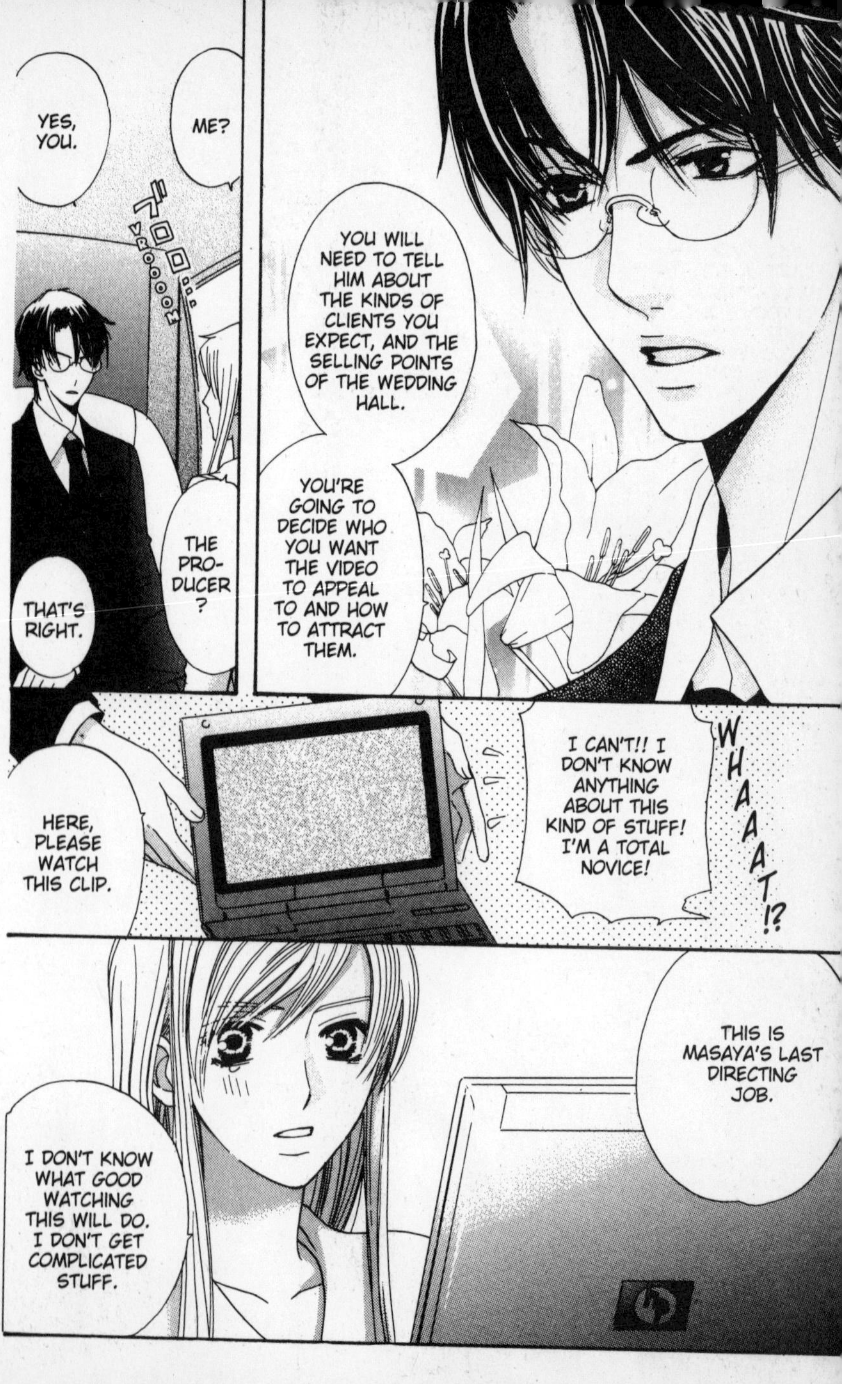
YOU WILL NEED TO TELL HIM ABOUT THE KINDS OF CLIENTS YOU EXPECT, AND THE SELLING POINTS OF THE WEDDING HALL.
YOU'RE GOING TO DECIDE WHO YOU WANT THE VIDEO TO APPEAL TO AND HOW TO ATTRACT THEM.
ME?
YES, YOU.
VROOOOOM
THE PRODUCER?
THAT'S RIGHT.
WHAAAT!?
I CAN'T!! I DON'T KNOW ANYTHING ABOUT THIS KIND OF STUFF! I'M A TOTAL NOVICE!
HERE, PLEASE WATCH THIS CLIP.
THIS IS MASAYA'S LAST DIRECTING JOB.
I DON'T KNOW WHAT GOOD WATCHING THIS WILL DO. I DON'T GET COMPLICATED STUFF.

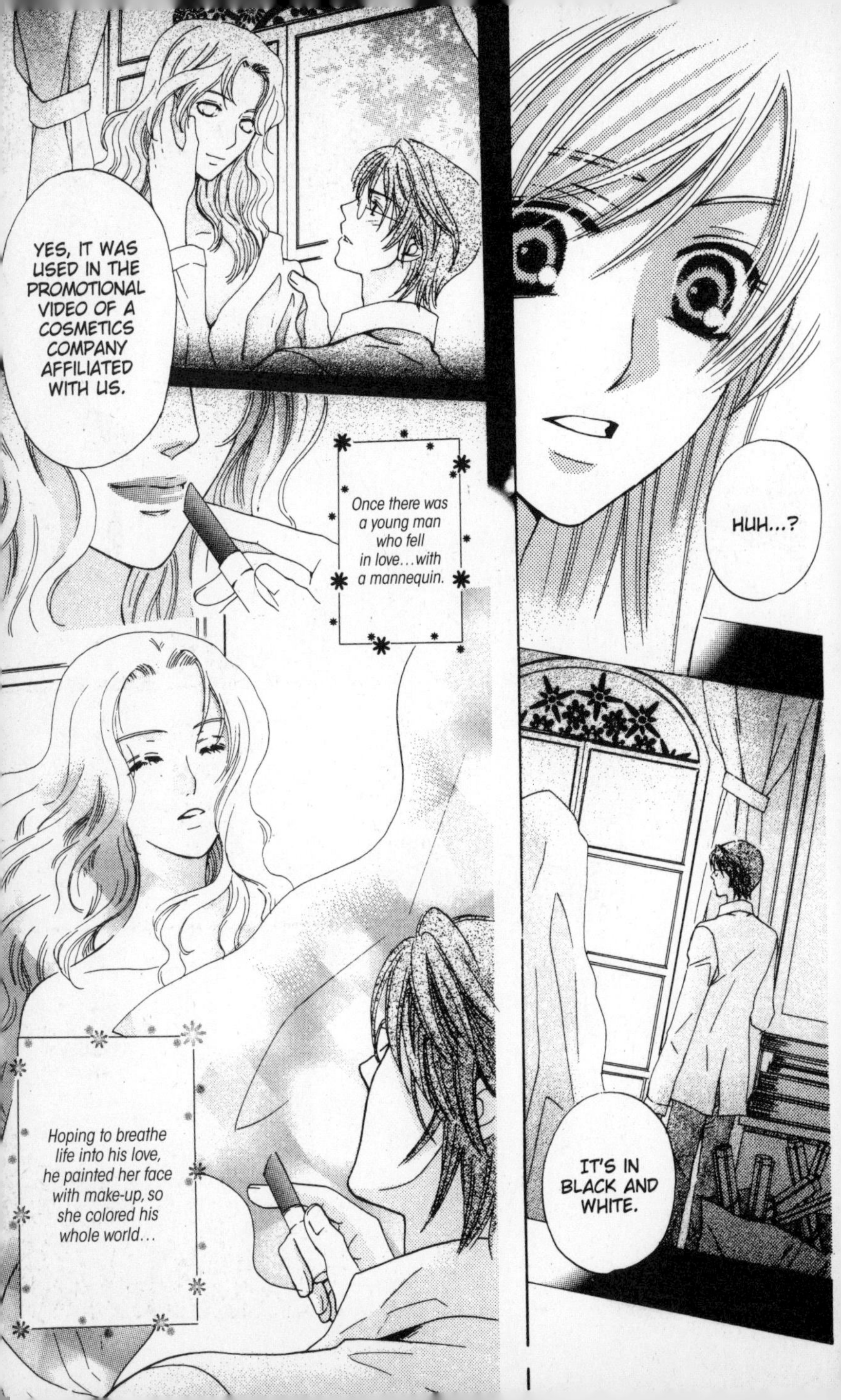

HUH...?
IT'S IN BLACK AND WHITE.
YES, IT WAS USED IN THE PROMOTIONAL VIDEO OF A COSMETICS COMPANY AFFILIATED WITH US.
Once there was a young man who fell in love...with a mannequin.
Hoping to breathe life into his love, he painted her face with make-up, so she colored his whole world...

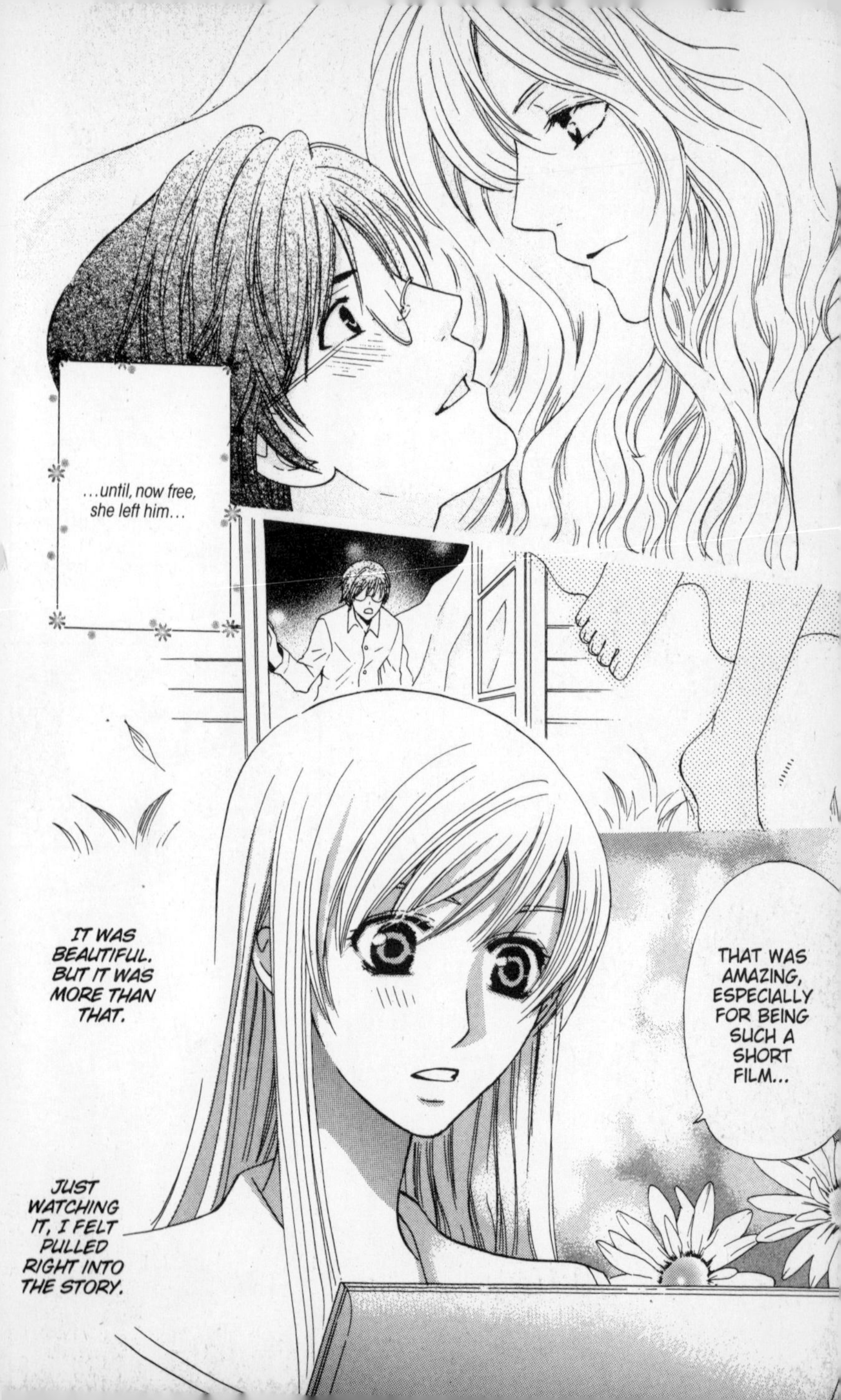
...until, now free, she left him...
THAT WAS AMAZING, ESPECIALLY FOR BEING SUCH A SHORT FILM...
IT WAS BEAUTIFUL. BUT IT WAS MORE THAN THAT.
JUST WATCHING IT, I FELT PULLED RIGHT INTO THE STORY.

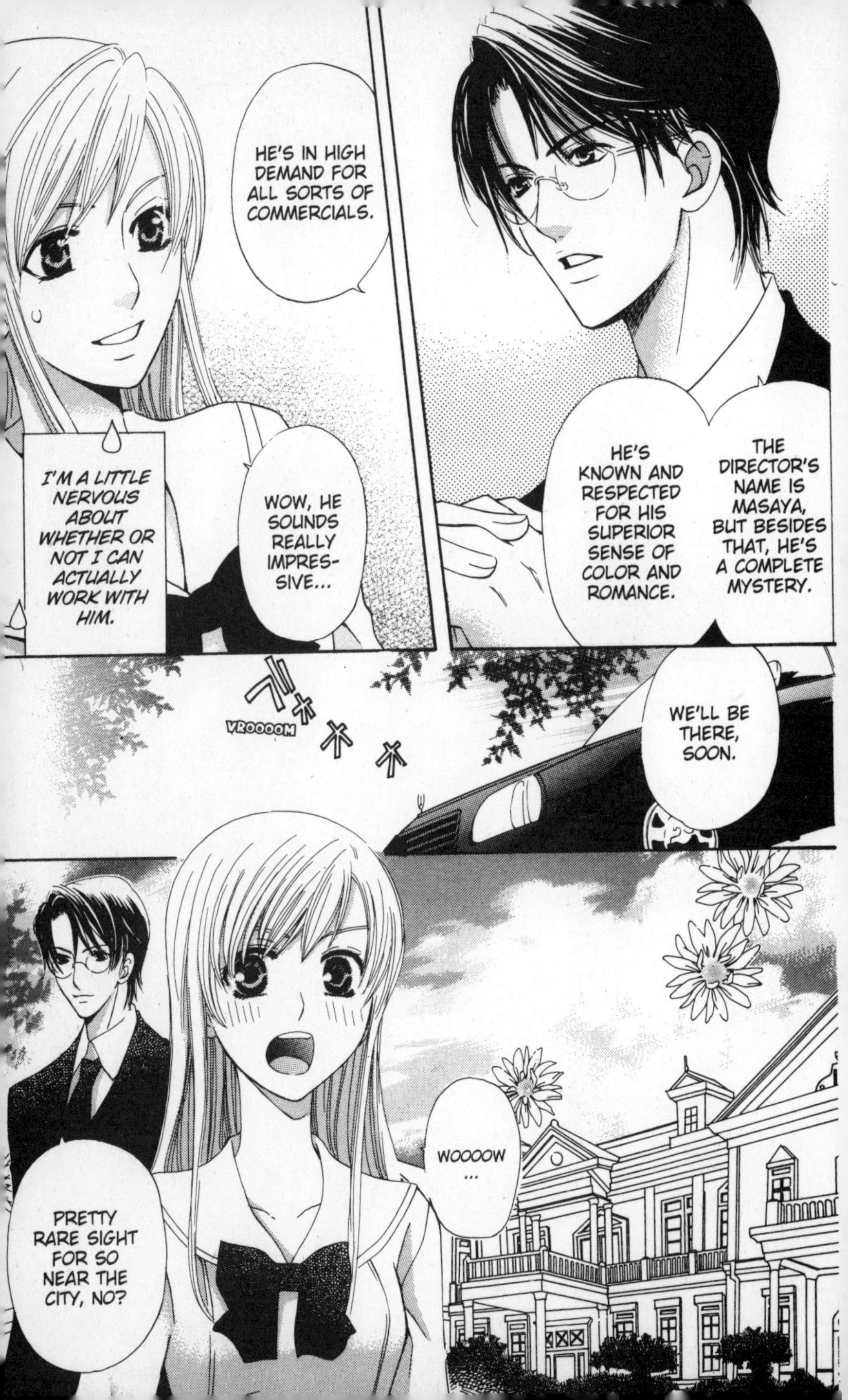
THE DIRECTOR'S NAME IS MASAYA, BUT BESIDES THAT, HE'S A COMPLETE MYSTERY.
HE'S KNOWN AND RESPECTED FOR HIS SUPERIOR SENSE OF COLOR AND ROMANCE.
HE'S IN HIGH DEMAND FOR ALL SORTS OF COMMERCIALS.
WOW, HE SOUNDS REALLY IMPRES-SIVE...
I'M A LITTLE NERVOUS ABOUT WHETHER OR NOT I CAN ACTUALLY WORK WITH HIM.
WE'LL BE THERE, SOON.
VROOOOM
WOOOOW ...
PRETTY RARE SIGHT FOR SO NEAR THE CITY, NO?

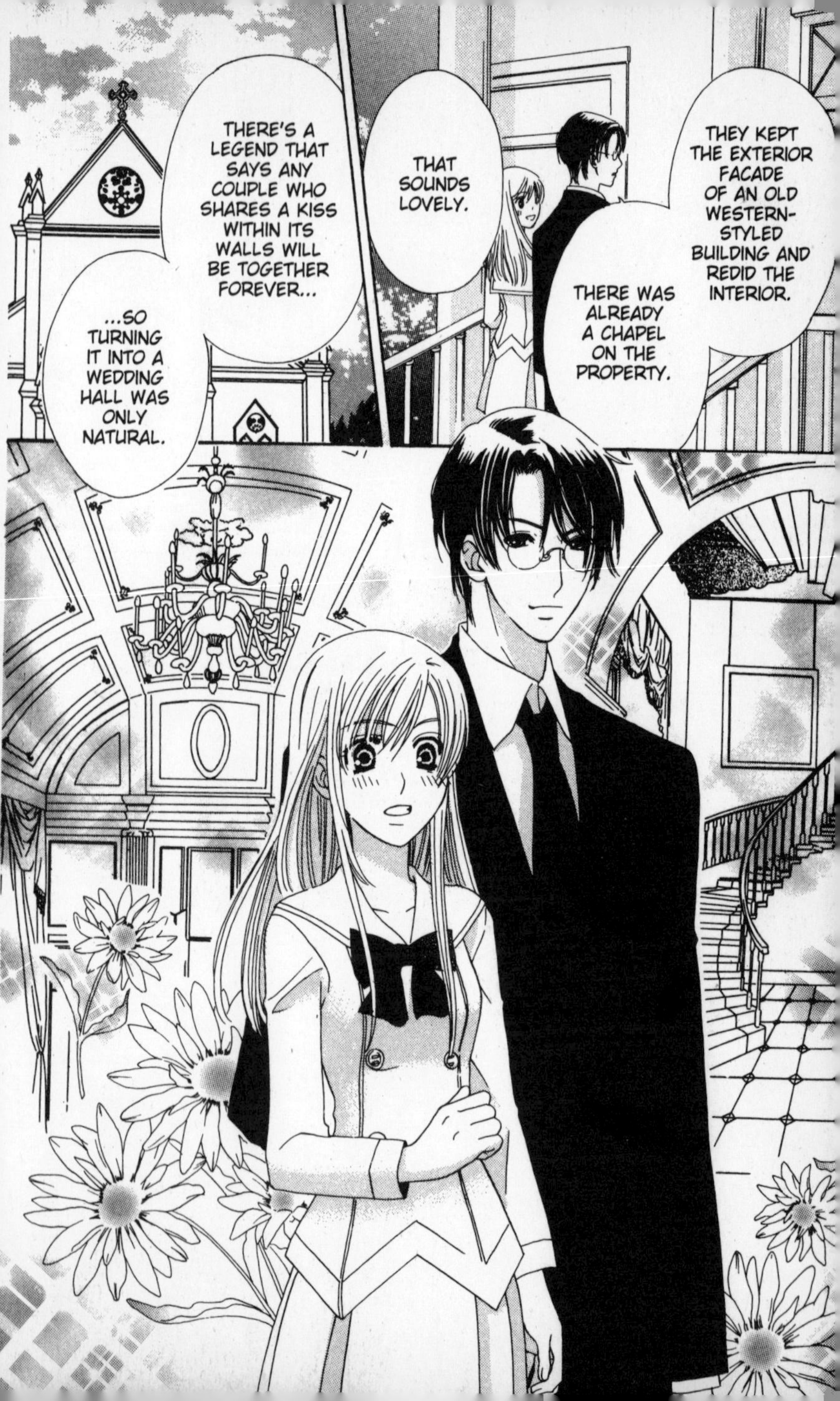
THEY KEPT THE EXTERIOR FACADE OF AN OLD WESTERN-STYLED BUILDING AND REDID THE INTERIOR.
THERE WAS ALREADY A CHAPEL ON THE PROPERTY.
THAT SOUNDS LOVELY.
THERE'S A LEGEND THAT SAYS ANY COUPLE WHO SHARES A KISS WITHIN ITS WALLS WILL BE TOGETHER FOREVER...
...SO TURNING IT INTO A WEDDING HALL WAS ONLY NATURAL.

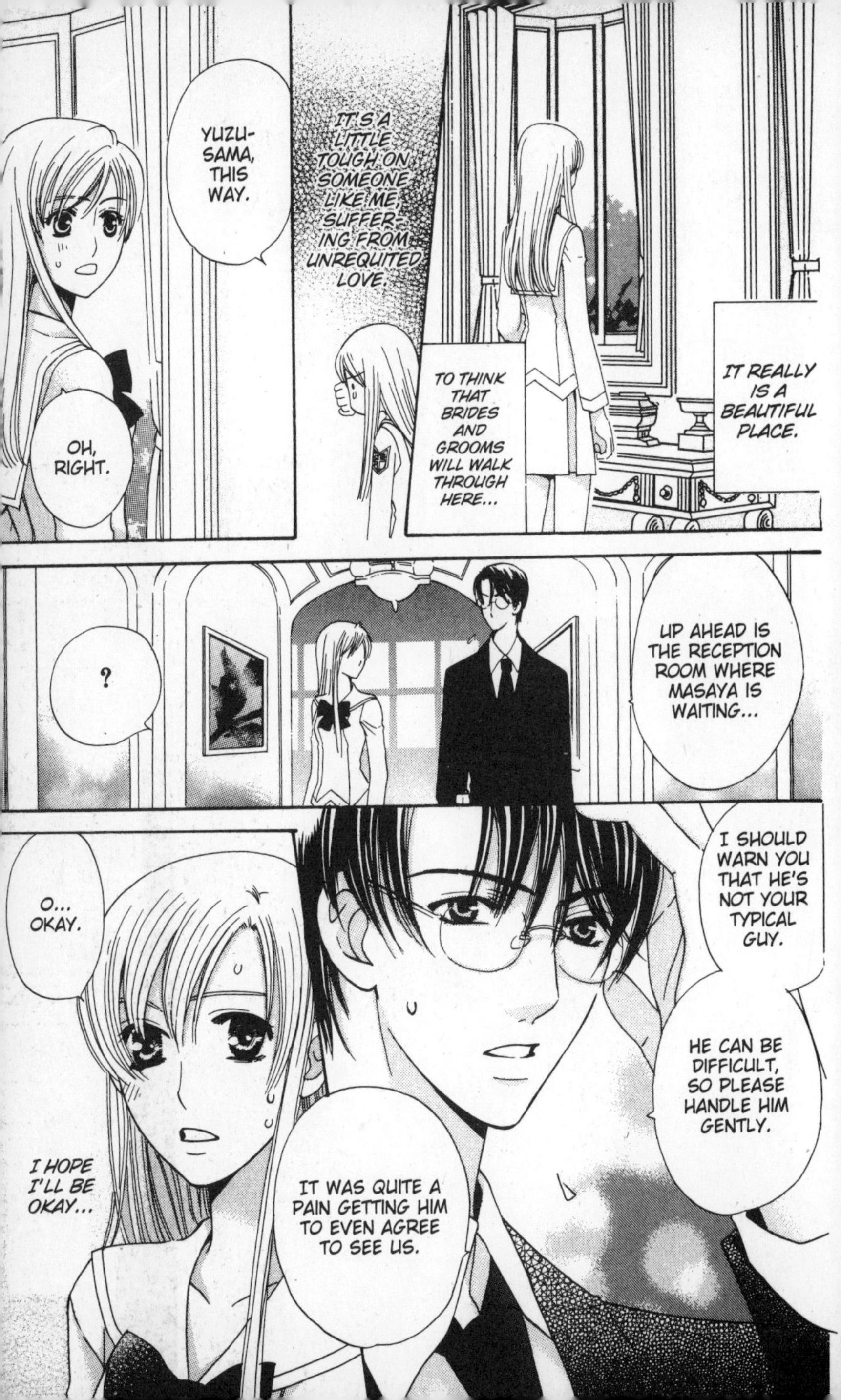
IT REALLY IS A BEAUTIFUL PLACE.
TO THINK THAT BRIDES AND GROOMS WILL WALK THROUGH HERE...
IT'S A LITTLE TOUGH ON SOMEONE LIKE ME, SUFFERING FROM UNREQUITED LOVE.
YUZU-SAMA, THIS WAY.
OH, RIGHT.
UP AHEAD IS THE RECEPTION ROOM WHERE MASAYA IS WAITING...
?
I SHOULD WARN YOU THAT HE'S NOT YOUR TYPICAL GUY.
HE CAN BE DIFFICULT, SO PLEASE HANDLE HIM GENTLY.
IT WAS QUITE A PAIN GETTING HIM TO EVEN AGREE TO SEE US.
O... OKAY.
I HOPE I'LL BE OKAY...

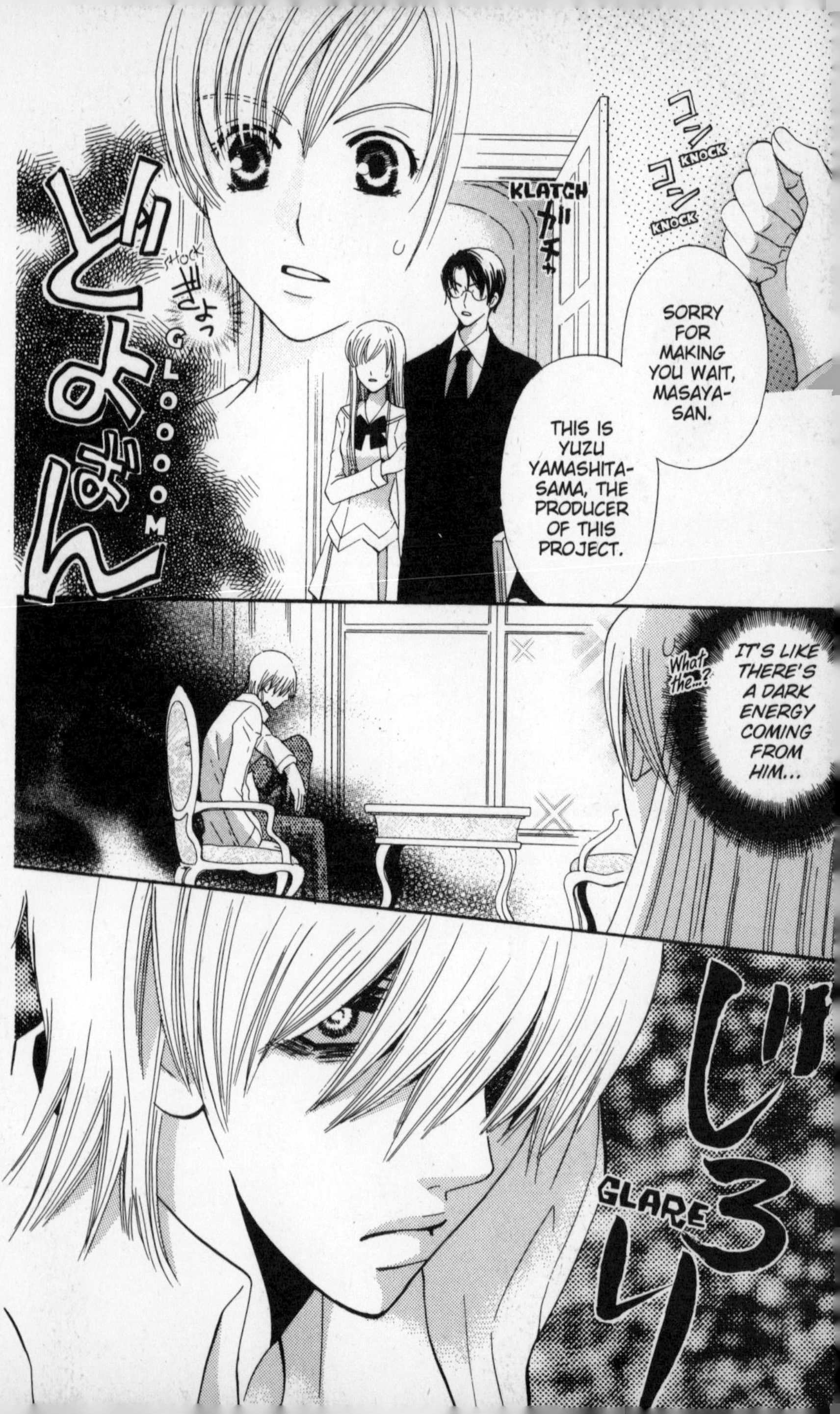

KNOCK
KNOCK
KLATCH
SORRY FOR MAKING YOU WAIT, MASAYA-SAN.
THIS IS YUZU YAMASHITA-SAMA, THE PRODUCER OF THIS PROJECT.
SHOCK
GLOOOOOM
IT'S LIKE THERE'S A DARK ENERGY COMING FROM HIM...
What the...?
GLARE

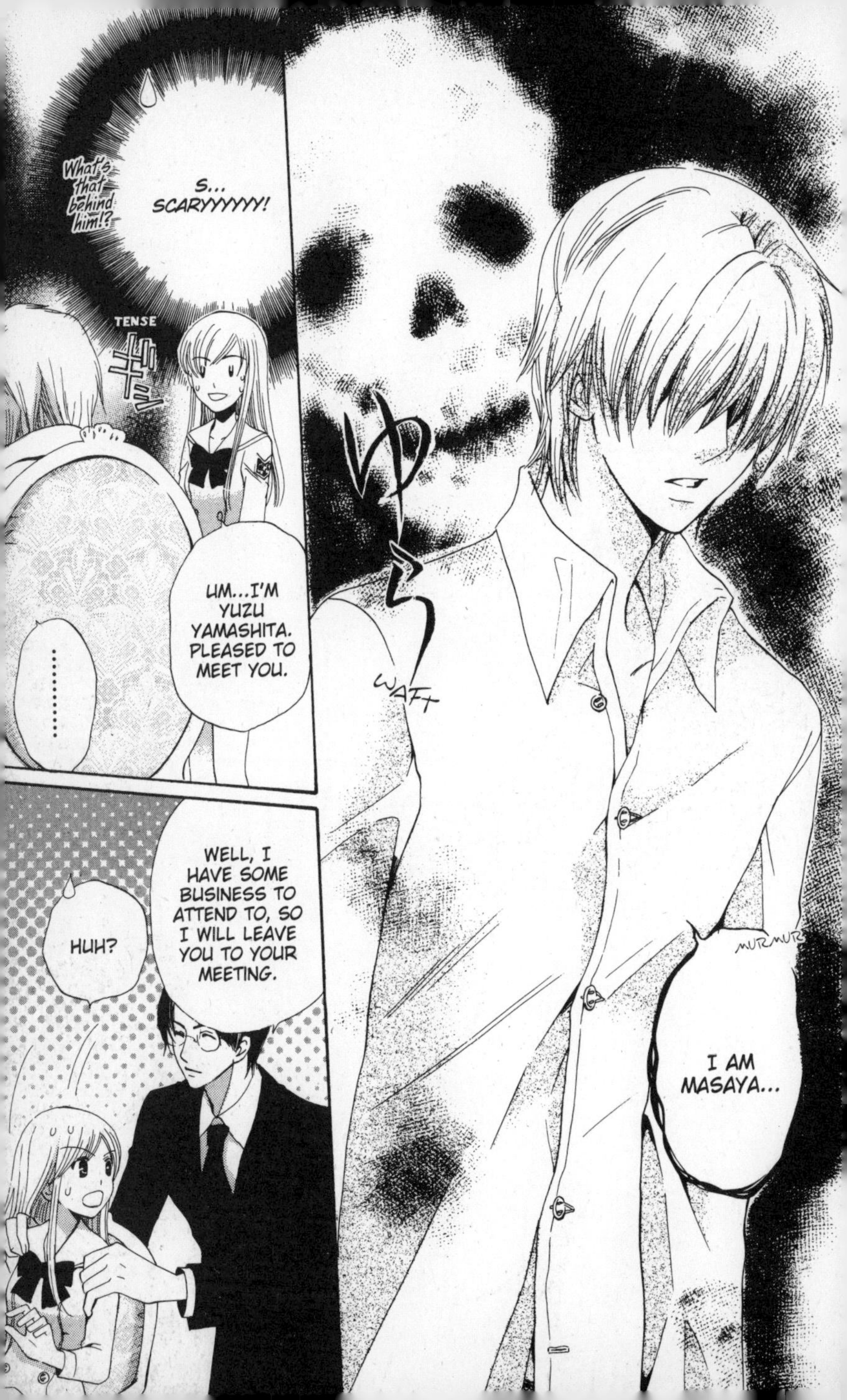
WAFT
MURMUR
I AM MASAYA...
What's that behind him!?
S... SCARYYYYYY!
TENSE
UM...I'M YUZU YAMASHITA. PLEASED TO MEET YOU.
......
WELL, I HAVE SOME BUSINESS TO ATTEND TO, SO I WILL LEAVE YOU TO YOUR MEETING.
HUH?

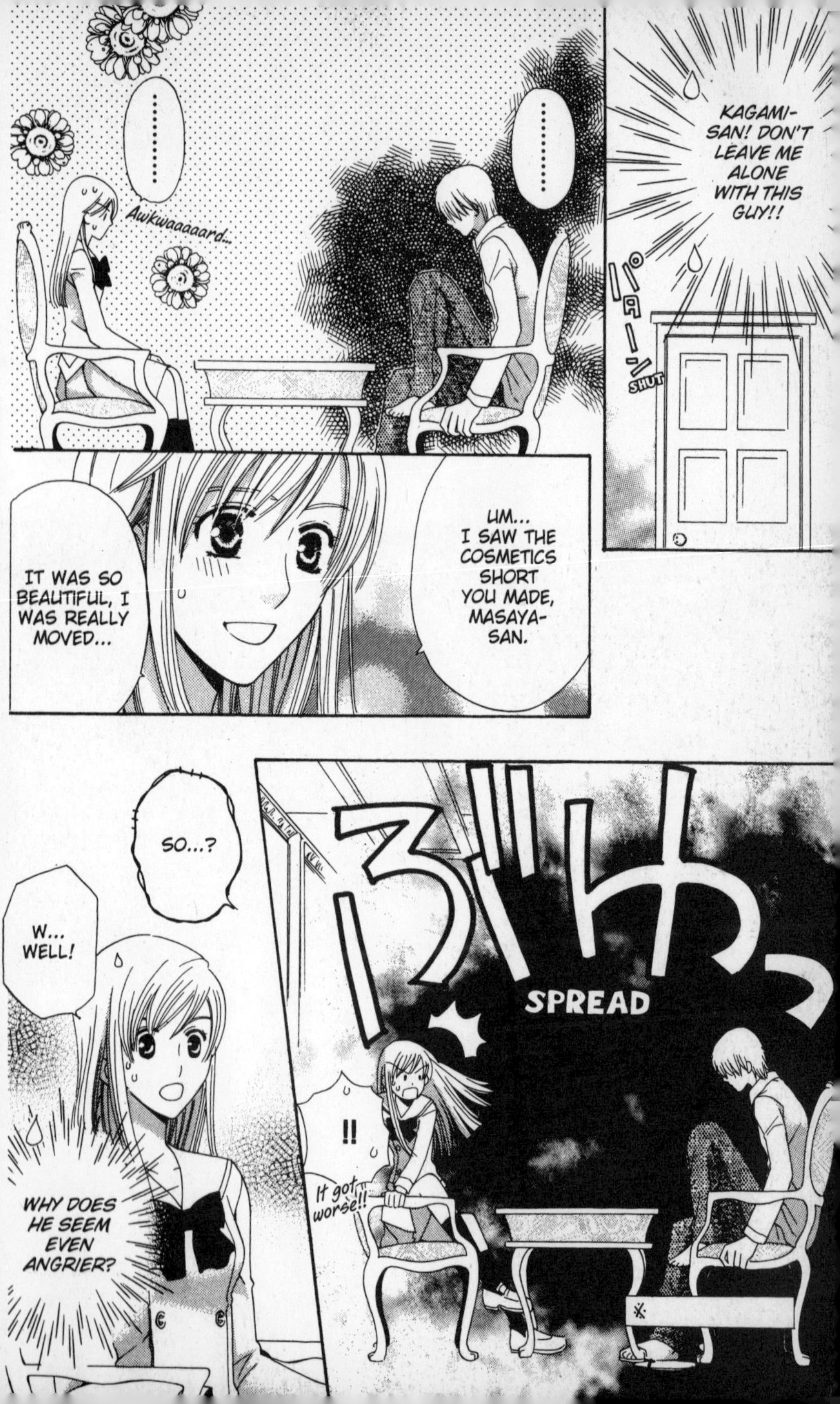
KAGAMI-SAN! DON'T LEAVE ME ALONE WITH THIS GUY!!
SHUT
......
......
Awkwaaaaard...
UM... I SAW THE COSMETICS SHORT YOU MADE, MASAYA-SAN.
IT WAS SO BEAUTIFUL, I WAS REALLY MOVED...
SPREAD
!!
It got worse!!
SO...?
W... WELL!
WHY DOES HE SEEM EVEN ANGRIER?

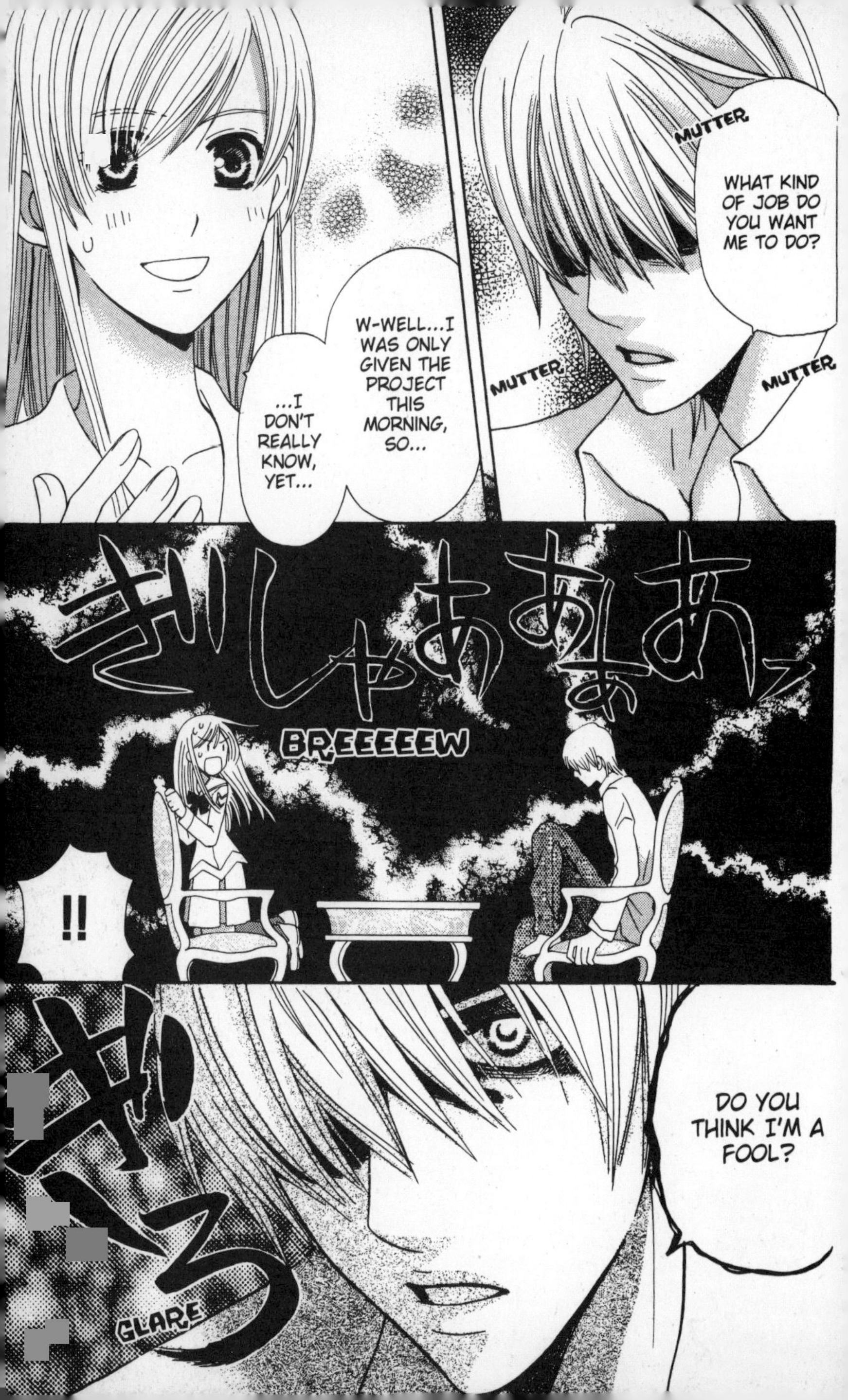
MUTTER
WHAT KIND OF JOB DO YOU WANT ME TO DO?
MUTTER
MUTTER
W-WELL...I WAS ONLY GIVEN THE PROJECT THIS MORNING, SO...
...I DON'T REALLY KNOW, YET...
BREEEEEEW
!!
DO YOU THINK I'M A FOOL?
GLARE

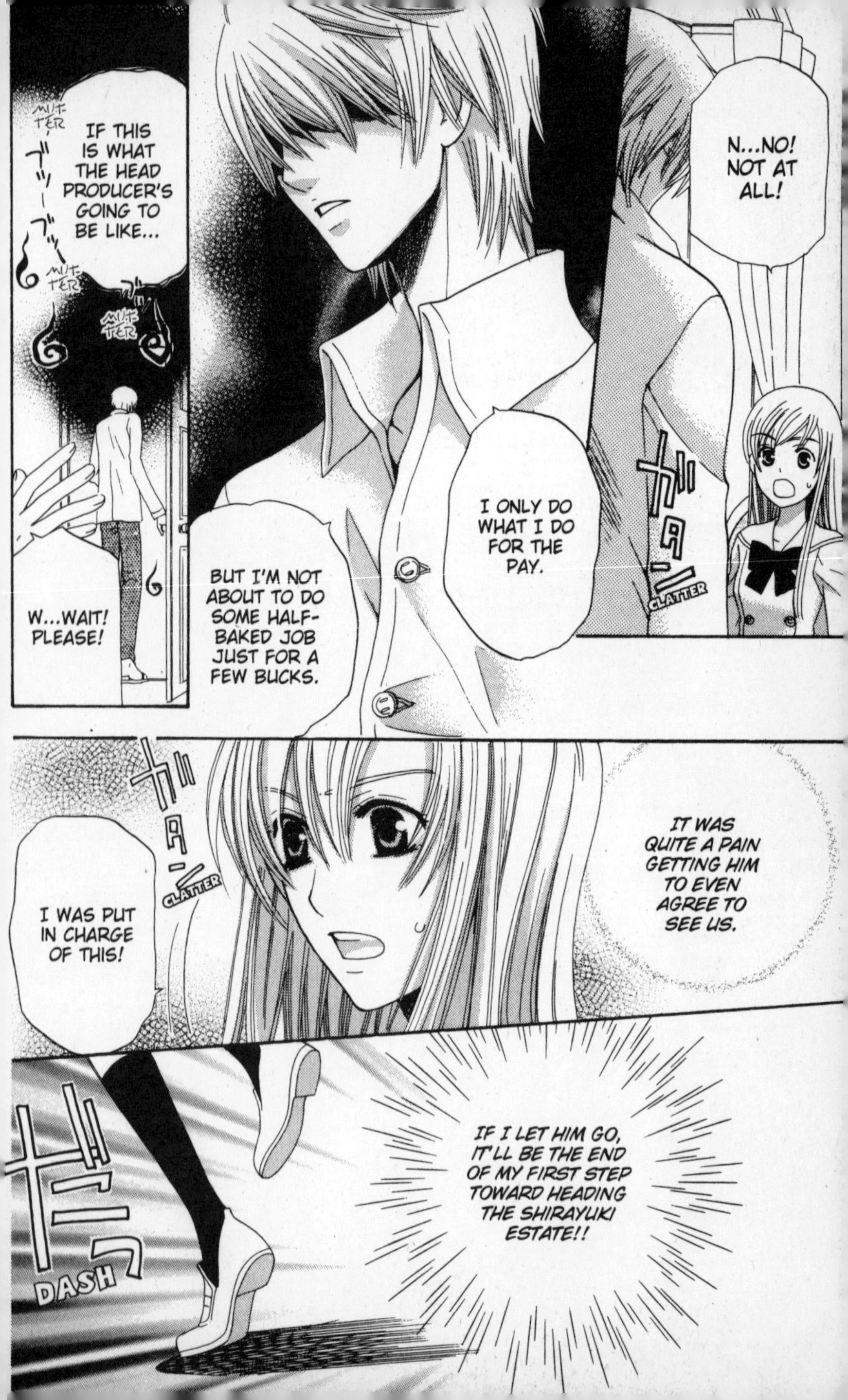
N...NO! NOT AT ALL!
CLATTER
I ONLY DO WHAT I DO FOR THE PAY.
BUT I'M NOT ABOUT TO DO SOME HALF-BAKED JOB JUST FOR A FEW BUCKS.
MUTTER
IF THIS IS WHAT THE HEAD PRODUCER'S GOING TO BE LIKE...
MUTTER
MUTTER
W...WAIT! PLEASE!
IT WAS QUITE A PAIN GETTING HIM TO EVEN AGREE TO SEE US.
CLATTER
I WAS PUT IN CHARGE OF THIS!
IF I LET HIM GO, IT'LL BE THE END OF MY FIRST STEP TOWARD HEADING THE SHIRAYUKI ESTATE!!
DASH

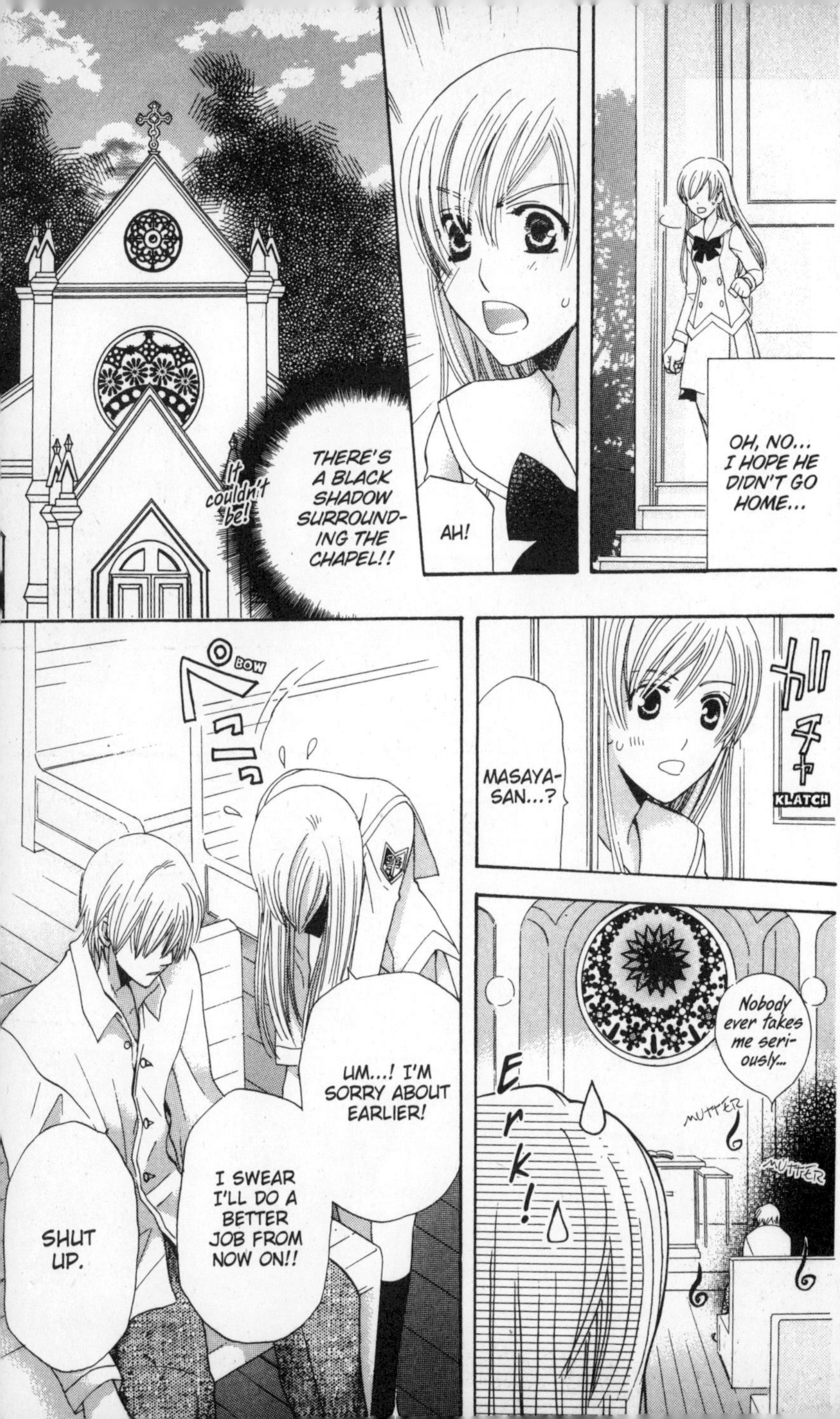
OH, NO... I HOPE HE DIDN'T GO HOME...
AH!
THERE'S A BLACK SHADOW SURROUNDING THE CHAPEL!!
It couldn't be!
KLATCH
MASAYA-SAN...?
Nobody ever takes me seriously...
MUTTER
MUTTER
Erk!
BOW
UM...! I'M SORRY ABOUT EARLIER!
I SWEAR I'LL DO A BETTER JOB FROM NOW ON!!
SHUT UP.

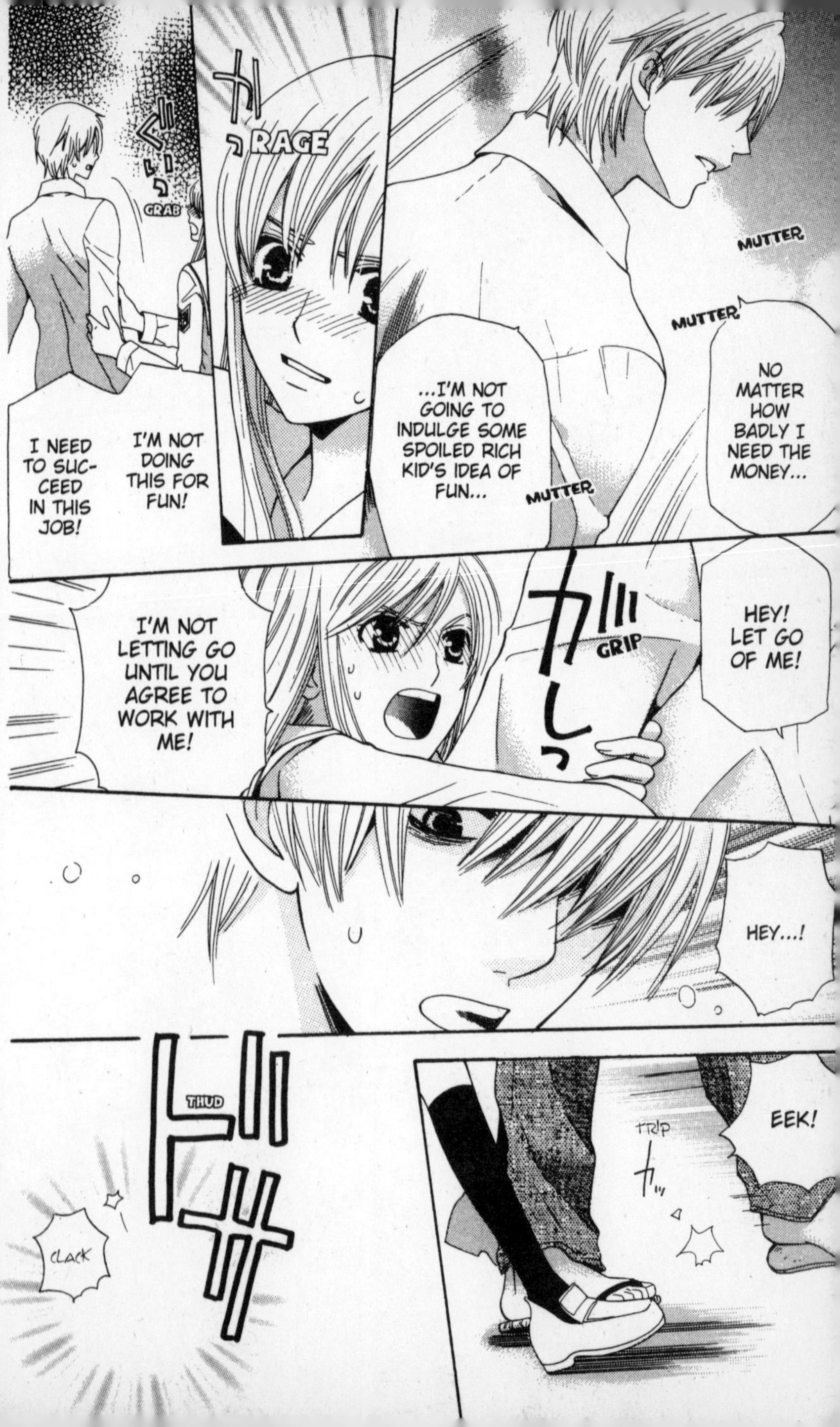
MUTTER
MUTTER
NO MATTER HOW BADLY I NEED THE MONEY...
...I'M NOT GOING TO INDULGE SOME SPOILED RICH KID'S IDEA OF FUN...
MUTTER
カッ
RAGE
ぐいっ
GRAB
I'M NOT DOING THIS FOR FUN!
I NEED TO SUC-CEED IN THIS JOB!
HEY! LET GO OF ME!
がしっ
GRIP
I'M NOT LETTING GO UNTIL YOU AGREE TO WORK WITH ME!
HEY...!
EEK!
ガッ
TRIP
ドサッ
THUD
CLACK

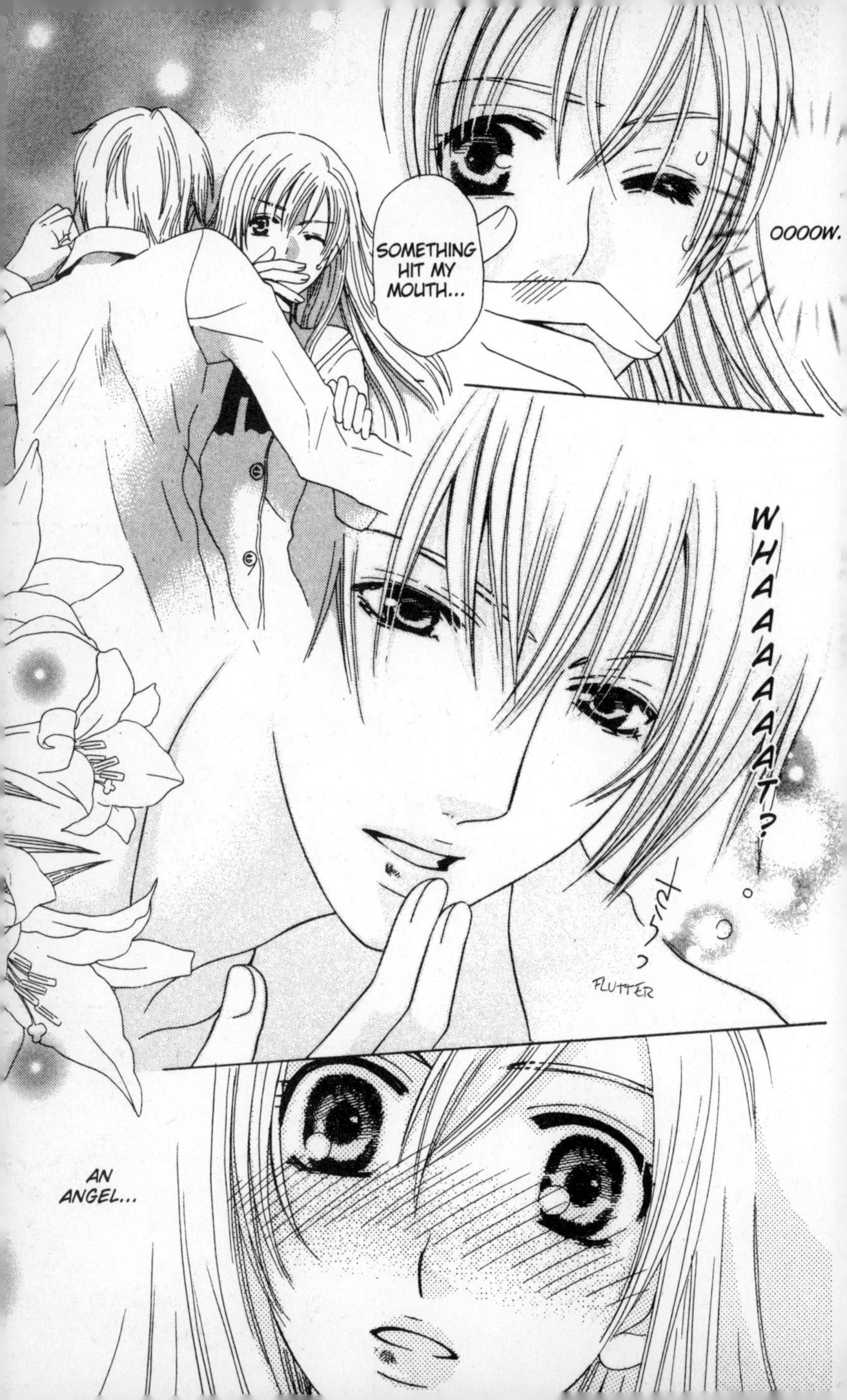
OOOOW.
SOMETHING HIT MY MOUTH...
WHAAAAAAT?
FLUTTER
AN ANGEL...

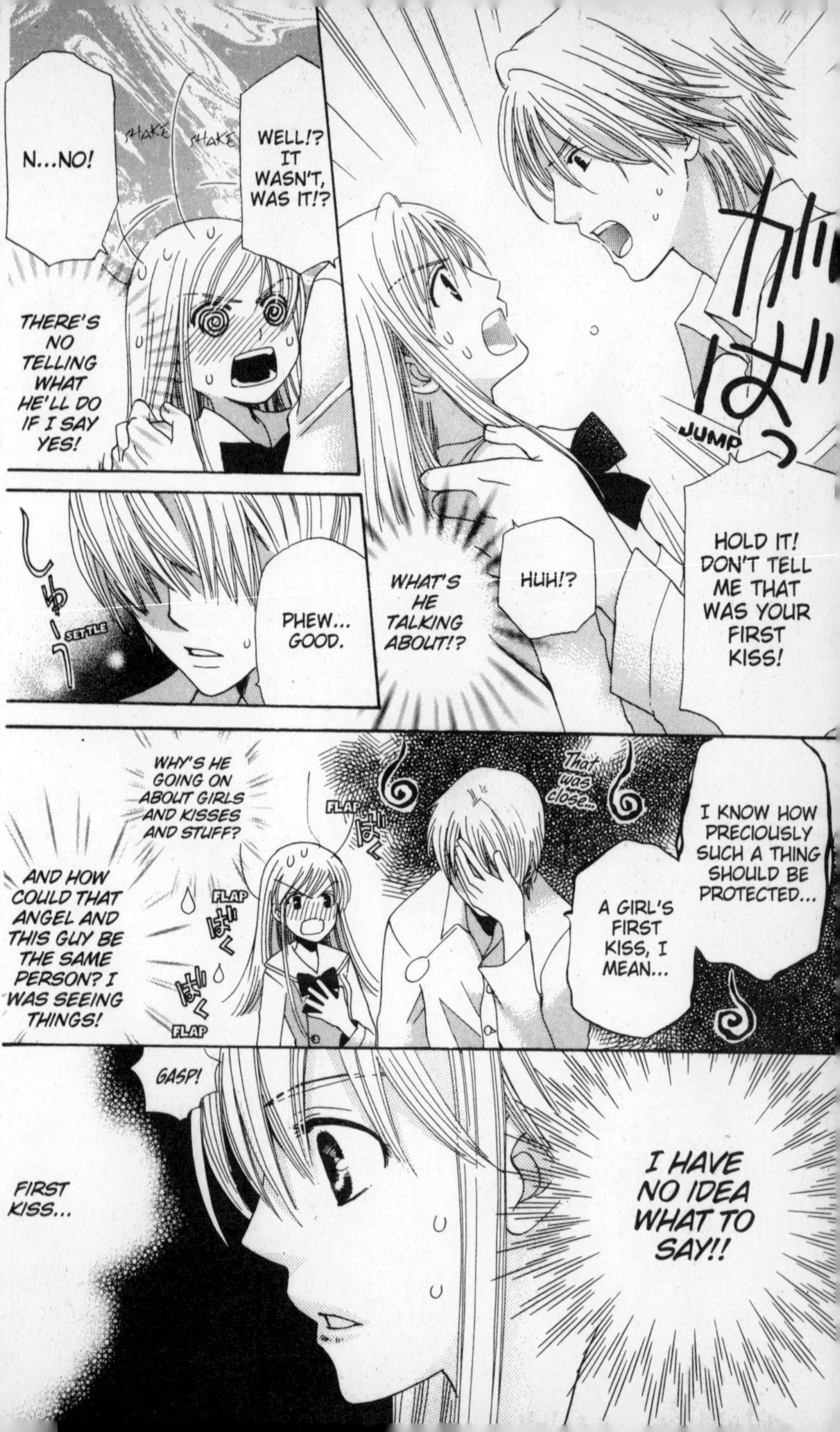

がばっ
JUMP
HOLD IT! DON'T TELL ME THAT WAS YOUR FIRST KISS!
HUH!?
WHAT'S HE TALKING ABOUT!?
WELL!? IT WASN'T, WAS IT!?
SHAKE
SHAKE
N...NO!
THERE'S NO TELLING WHAT HE'LL DO IF I SAY YES!
PHEW... GOOD.
SETTLE
I KNOW HOW PRECIOUSLY SUCH A THING SHOULD BE PROTECTED...
A GIRL'S FIRST KISS, I MEAN...
That was close...
FLAP
WHY'S HE GOING ON ABOUT GIRLS AND KISSES AND STUFF?
FLAP
FLAP
AND HOW COULD THAT ANGEL AND THIS GUY BE THE SAME PERSON? I WAS SEEING THINGS!
I HAVE NO IDEA WHAT TO SAY!!
GASP!
FIRST KISS...

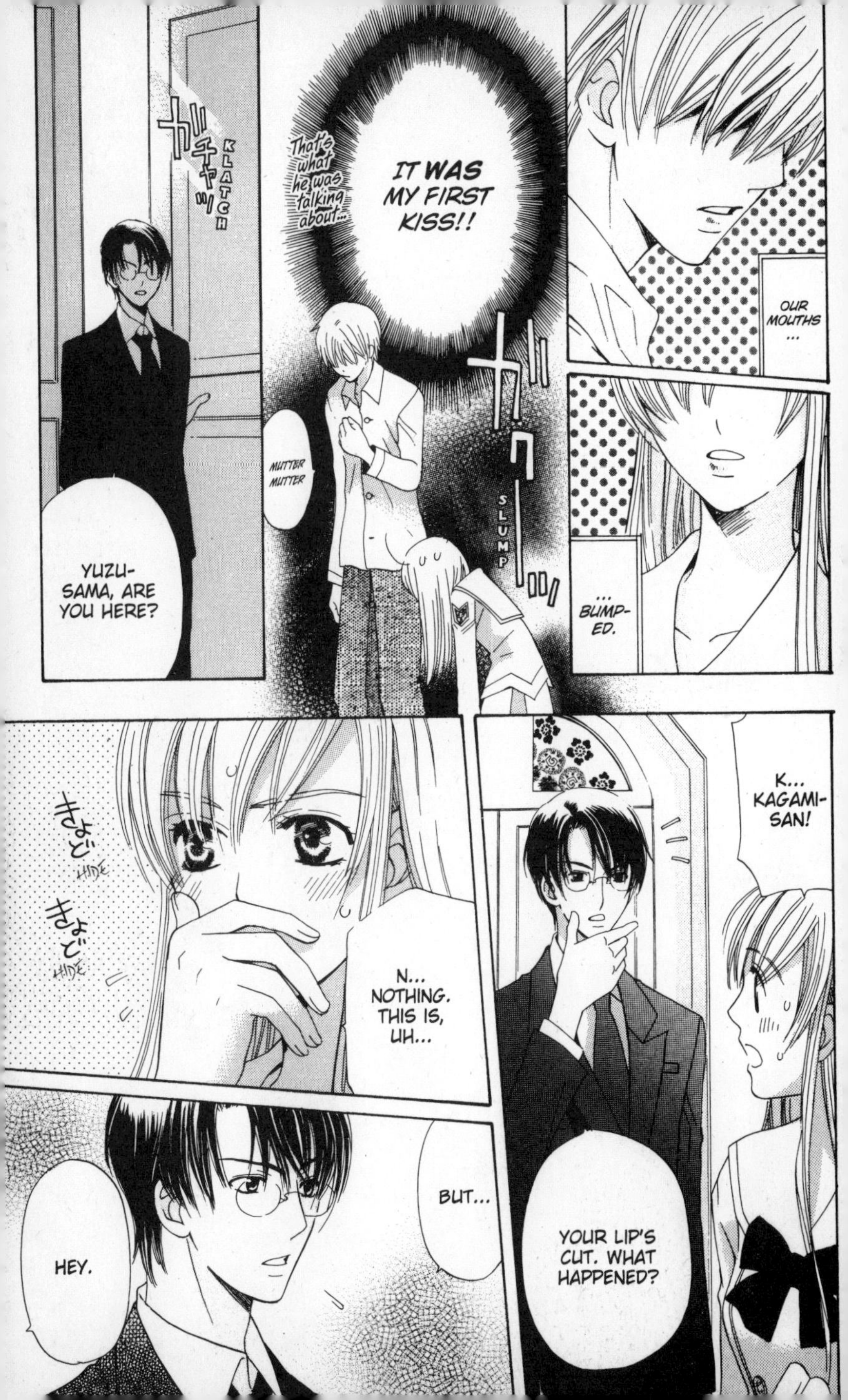
OUR MOUTHS ...
... BUMPED.
That's what he was talking about...
IT WAS MY FIRST KISS!!
MUTTER MUTTER
ガクー
SLUMP
カチャッ
KLATCH
YUZU-SAMA, ARE YOU HERE?
K... KAGAMI-SAN!
YOUR LIP'S CUT. WHAT HAPPENED?
きょど
HIDE
きょど
HIDE
N... NOTHING. THIS IS, UH...
BUT...
HEY.

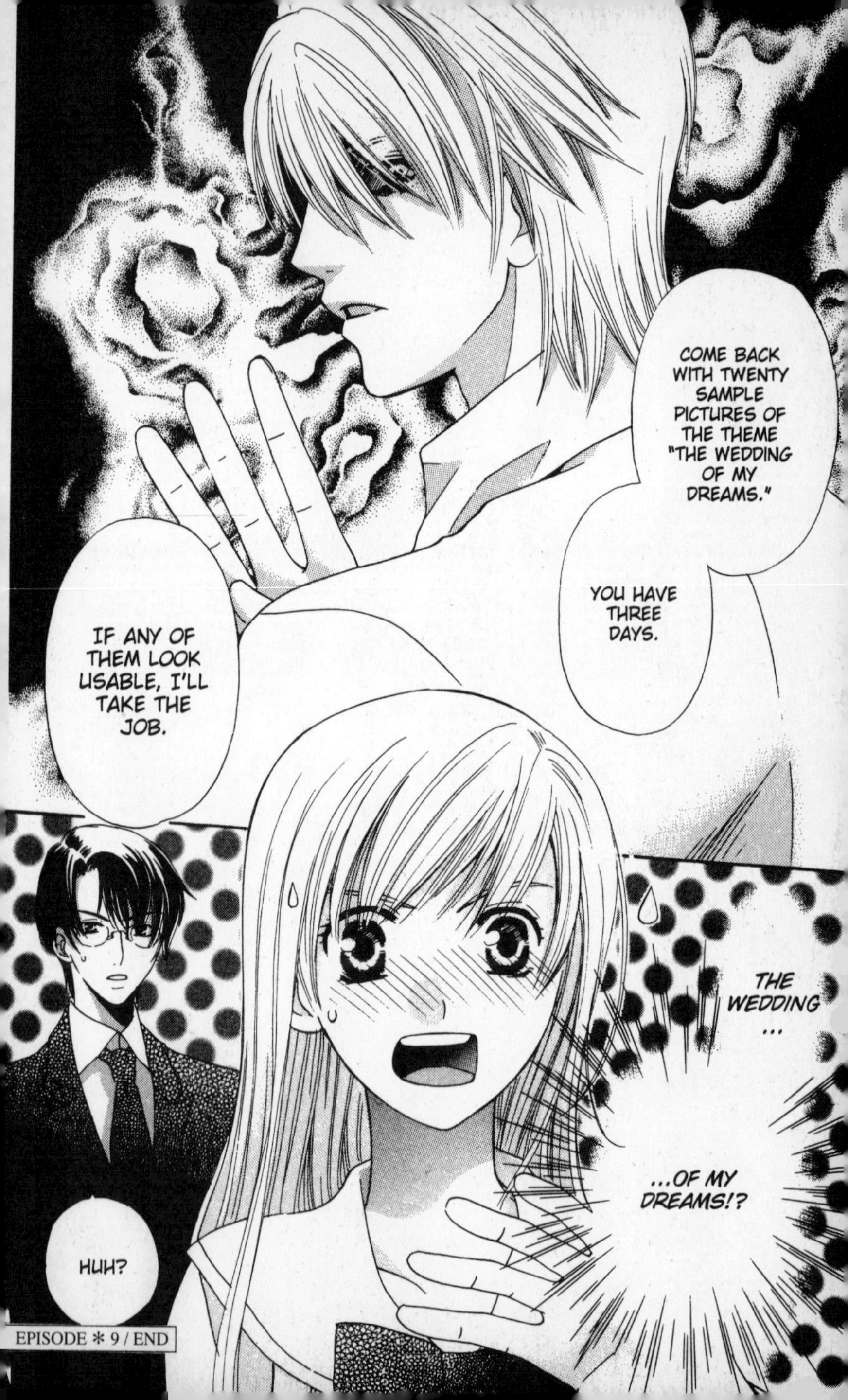
COME BACK WITH TWENTY SAMPLE PICTURES OF THE THEME "THE WEDDING OF MY DREAMS."
YOU HAVE THREE DAYS.
IF ANY OF THEM LOOK USABLE, I'LL TAKE THE JOB.
THE WEDDING ...
...OF MY DREAMS!?
HUH?
EPISODE * 9 / END

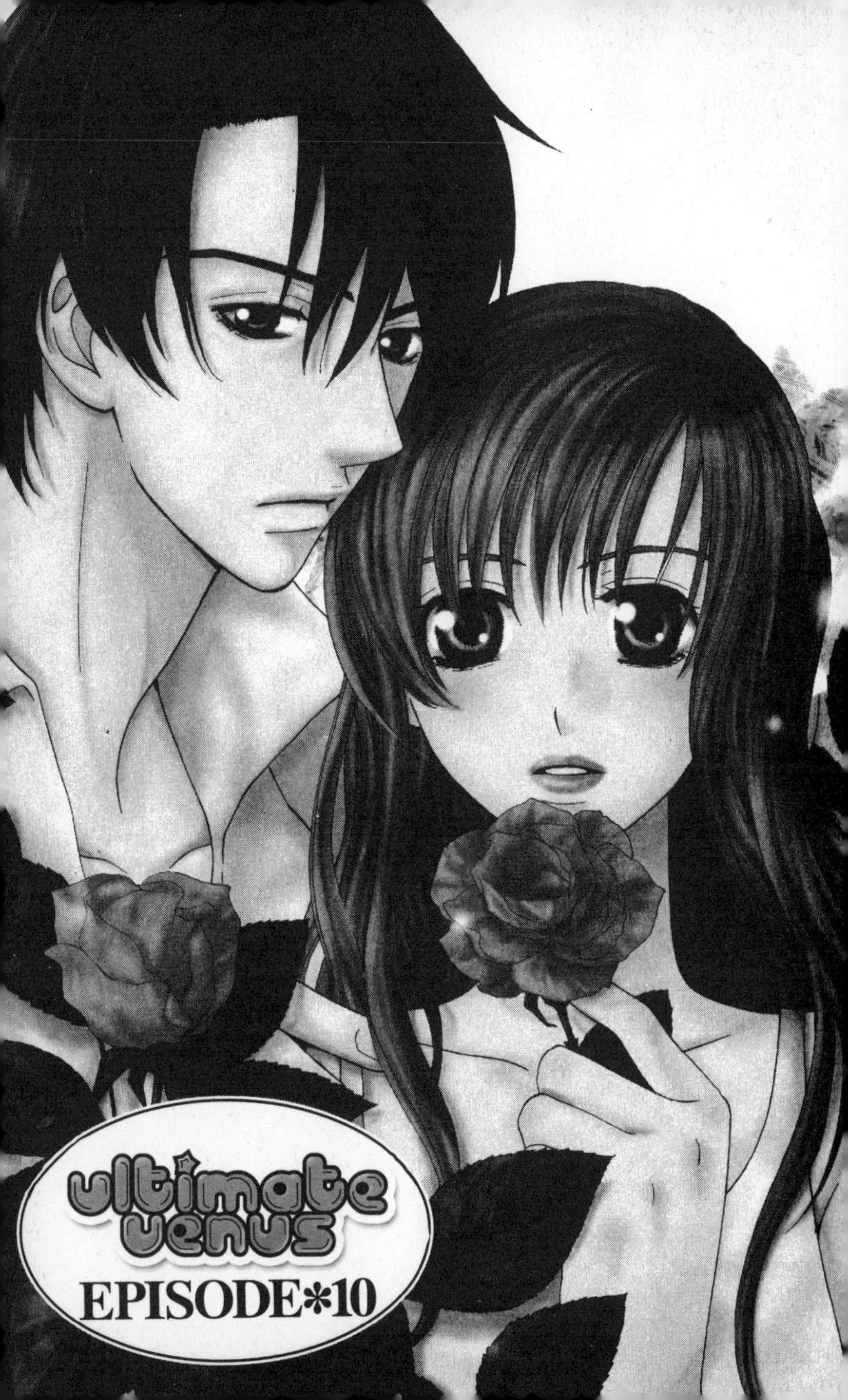
ultimate venus
EPISODE*10

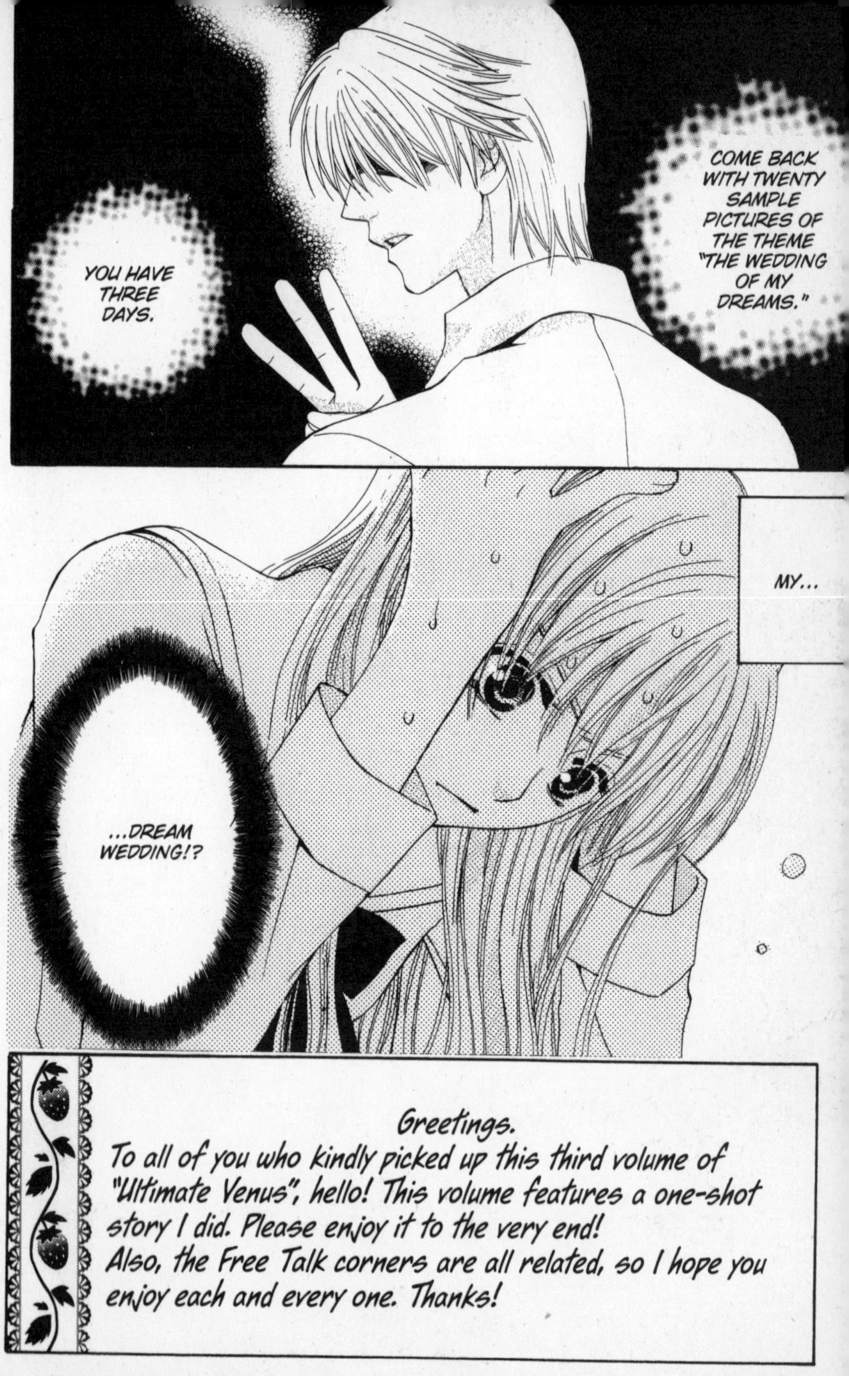
COME BACK WITH TWENTY SAMPLE PICTURES OF THE THEME "THE WEDDING OF MY DREAMS."
YOU HAVE THREE DAYS.
MY...
...DREAM WEDDING!?

Greetings.

To all of you who kindly picked up this third volume of "Ultimate Venus", hello! This volume features a one-shot story I did. Please enjoy it to the very end!
Also, the Free Talk corners are all related, so I hope you enjoy each and every one. Thanks!

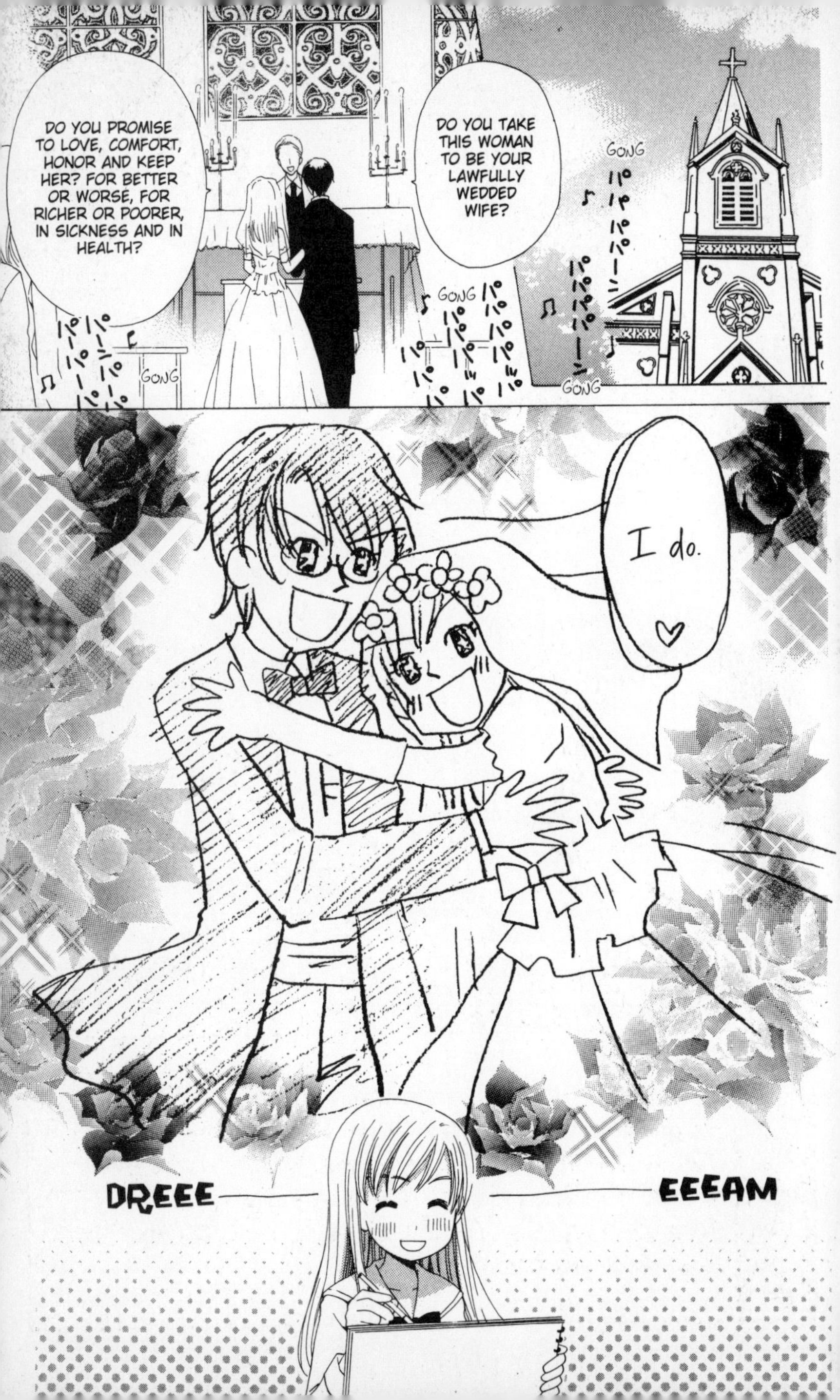
GONG
DO YOU TAKE THIS WOMAN TO BE YOUR LAWFULLY WEDDED WIFE?
GONG
DO YOU PROMISE TO LOVE, COMFORT, HONOR AND KEEP HER? FOR BETTER OR WORSE, FOR RICHER OR POORER, IN SICKNESS AND IN HEALTH?
GONG
GONG
I do. ♥
DREEE——
——EEEAM

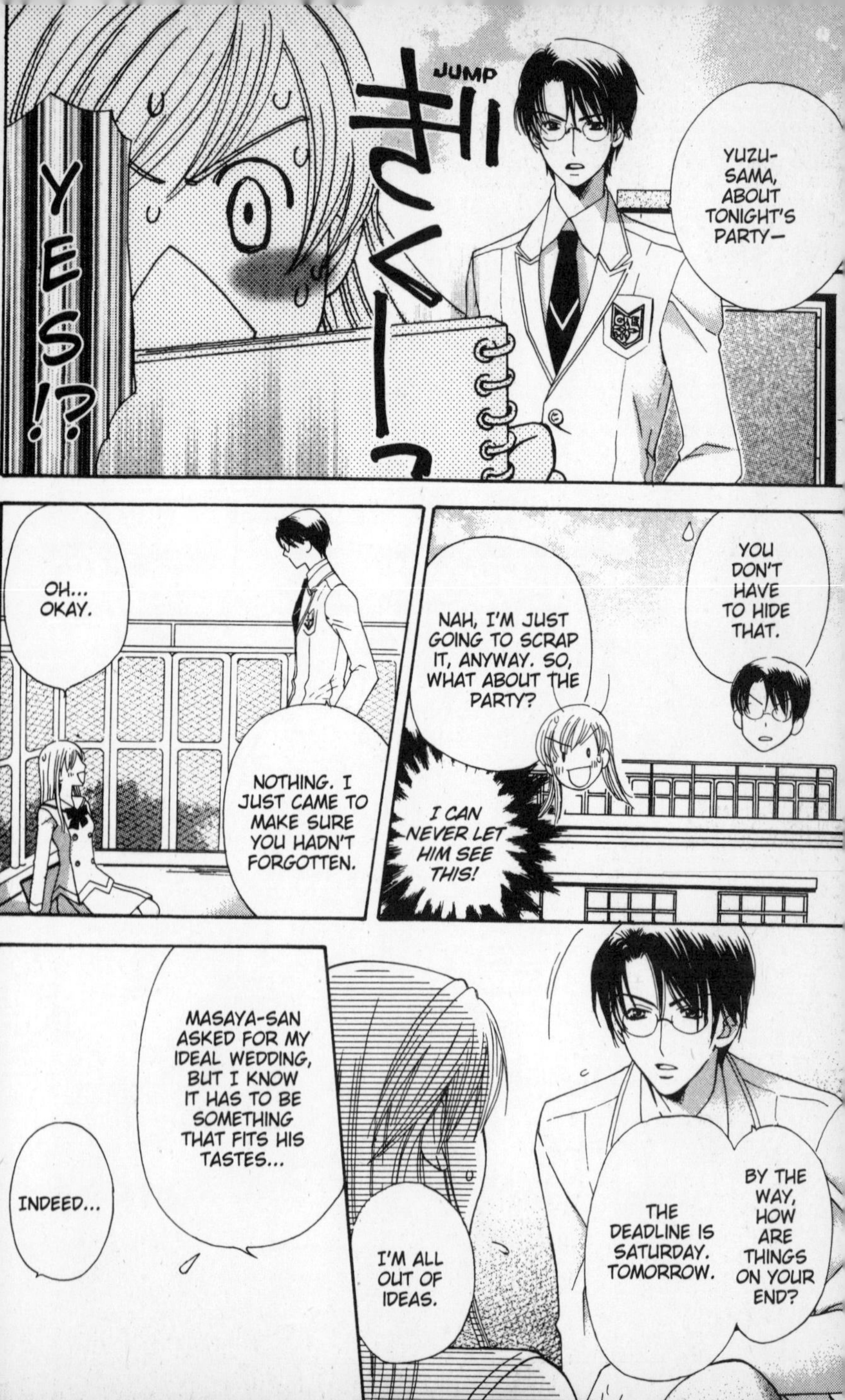

YUZU-SAMA, ABOUT TONIGHT'S PARTY—
JUMP
ぎくーっ
YES!?
YOU DON'T HAVE TO HIDE THAT.
NAH, I'M JUST GOING TO SCRAP IT, ANYWAY. SO, WHAT ABOUT THE PARTY?
I CAN NEVER LET HIM SEE THIS!
NOTHING. I JUST CAME TO MAKE SURE YOU HADN'T FORGOTTEN.
OH... OKAY.
BY THE WAY, HOW ARE THINGS ON YOUR END?
THE DEADLINE IS SATURDAY. TOMORROW.
I'M ALL OUT OF IDEAS.
MASAYA-SAN ASKED FOR MY IDEAL WEDDING, BUT I KNOW IT HAS TO BE SOMETHING THAT FITS HIS TASTES...
INDEED...

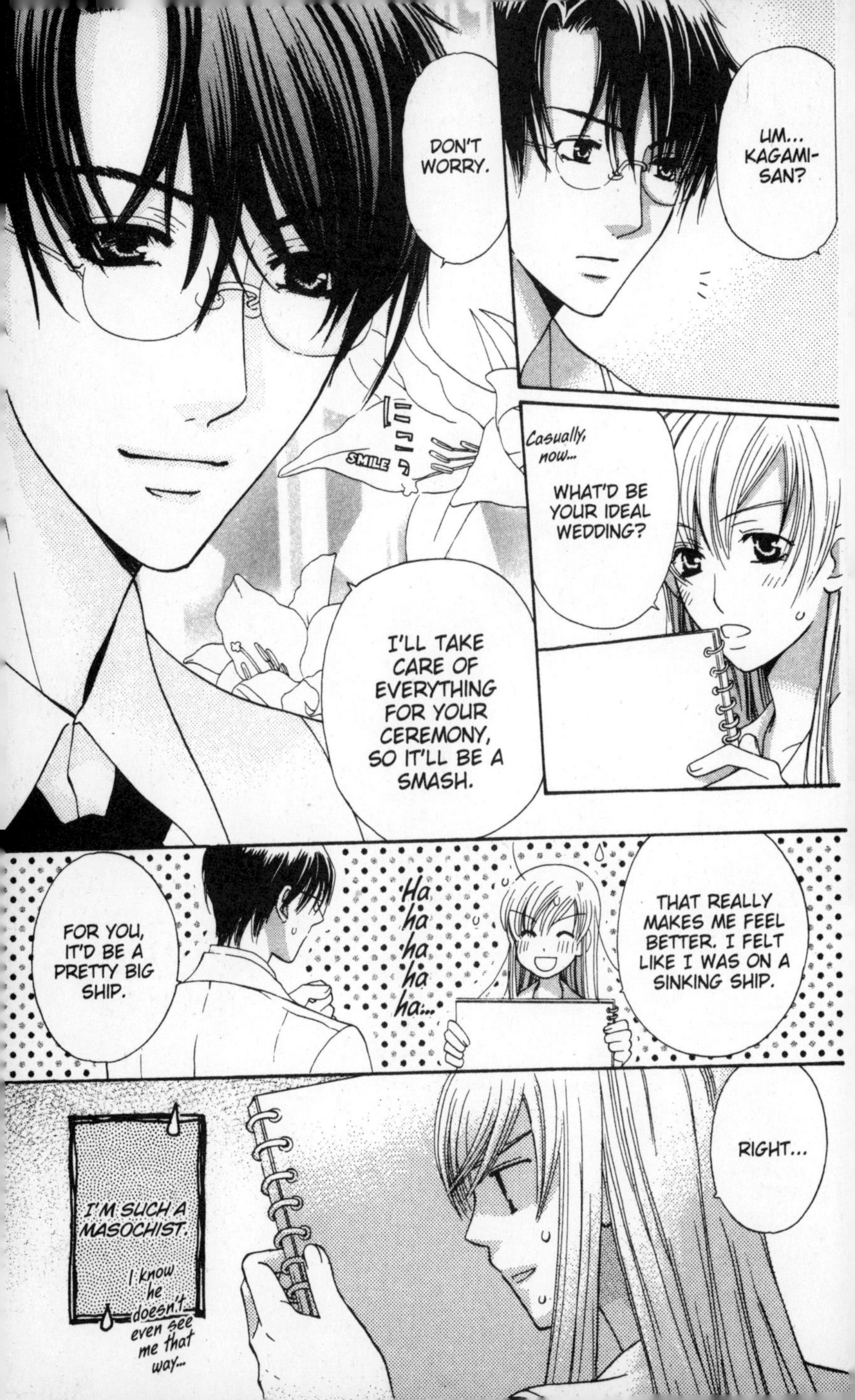
UM... KAGAMI-SAN?
Casually, now...
WHAT'D BE YOUR IDEAL WEDDING?
DON'T WORRY.
SMILE
I'LL TAKE CARE OF EVERYTHING FOR YOUR CEREMONY, SO IT'LL BE A SMASH.
THAT REALLY MAKES ME FEEL BETTER. I FELT LIKE I WAS ON A SINKING SHIP.
Ha ha ha ha ha...
FOR YOU, IT'D BE A PRETTY BIG SHIP.
RIGHT...
I'M SUCH A MASOCHIST.
I know he doesn't even see me that way...

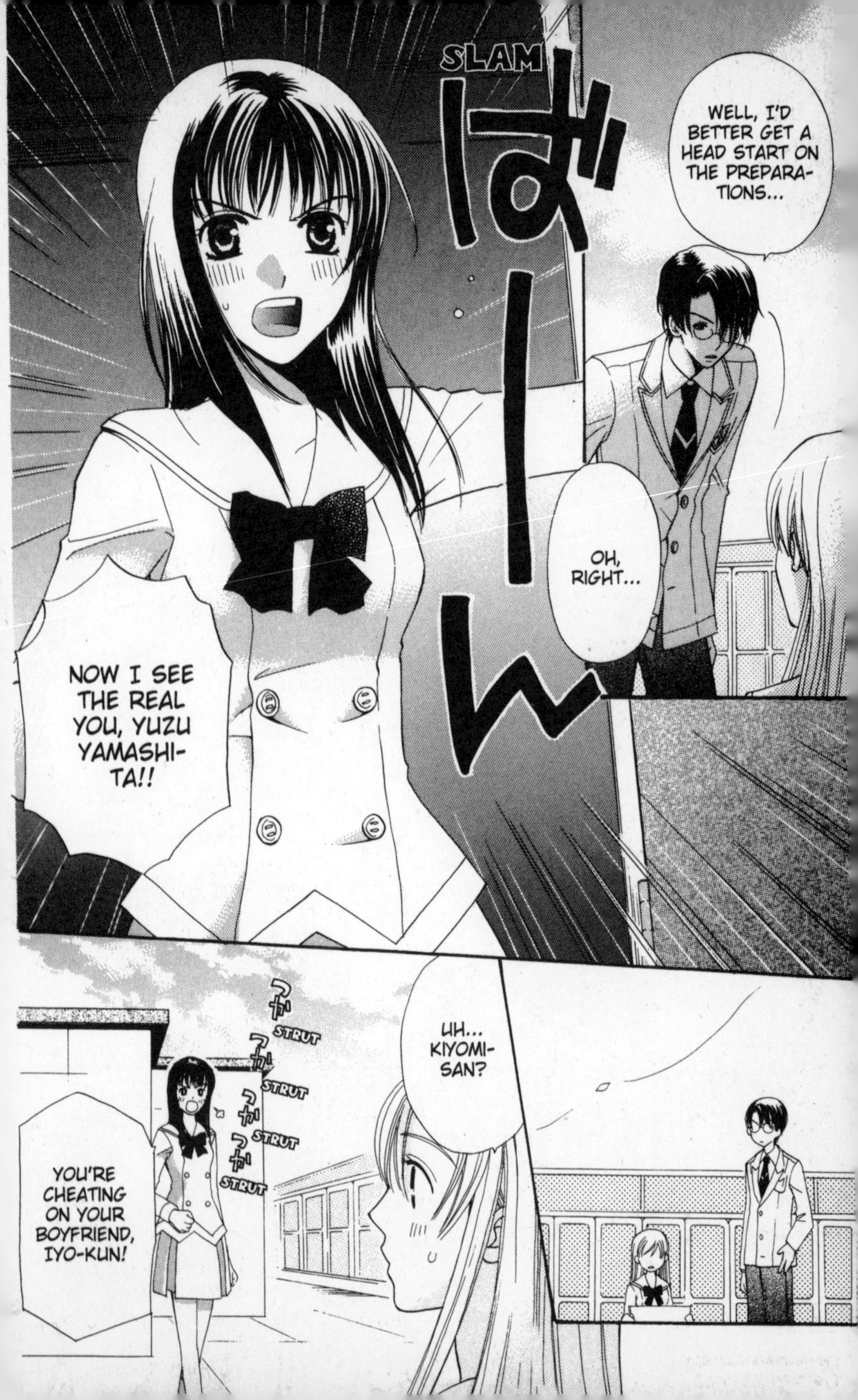
WELL, I'D BETTER GET A HEAD START ON THE PREPARATIONS...
OH, RIGHT...
SLAM
ばーん
NOW I SEE THE REAL YOU, YUZU YAMASHITA!!
UH... KIYOMI-SAN?
つか STRUT
つか STRUT
つか STRUT
つか STRUT
YOU'RE CHEATING ON YOUR BOYFRIEND, IYO-KUN!

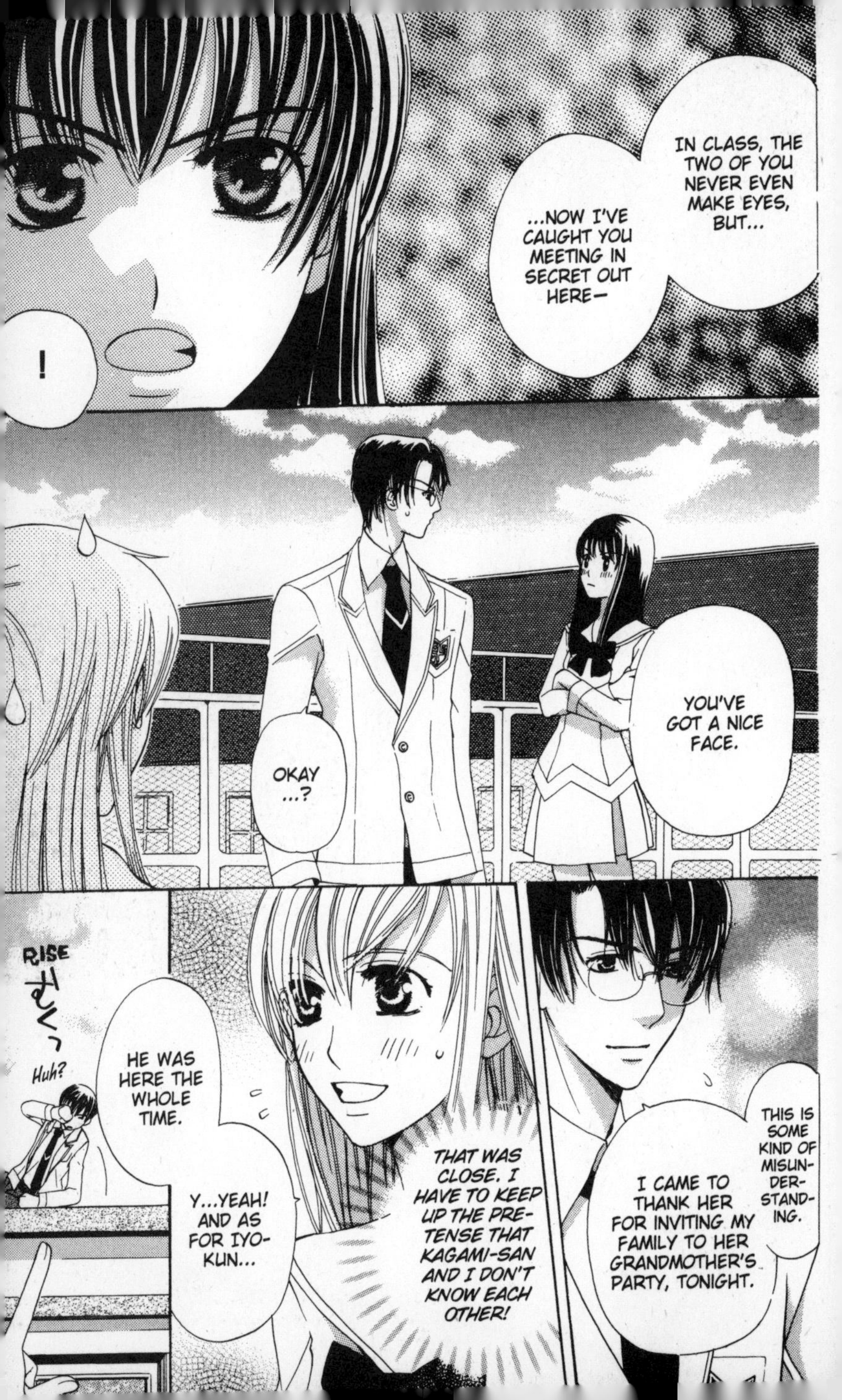
IN CLASS, THE TWO OF YOU NEVER EVEN MAKE EYES, BUT...
...NOW I'VE CAUGHT YOU MEETING IN SECRET OUT HERE—
!
YOU'VE GOT A NICE FACE.
OKAY ...?
THIS IS SOME KIND OF MISUNDERSTANDING.
I CAME TO THANK HER FOR INVITING MY FAMILY TO HER GRANDMOTHER'S PARTY, TONIGHT.
THAT WAS CLOSE. I HAVE TO KEEP UP THE PRETENSE THAT KAGAMI-SAN AND I DON'T KNOW EACH OTHER!
Y...YEAH! AND AS FOR IYO-KUN...
HE WAS HERE THE WHOLE TIME.
RISE
むくっ
Huh?

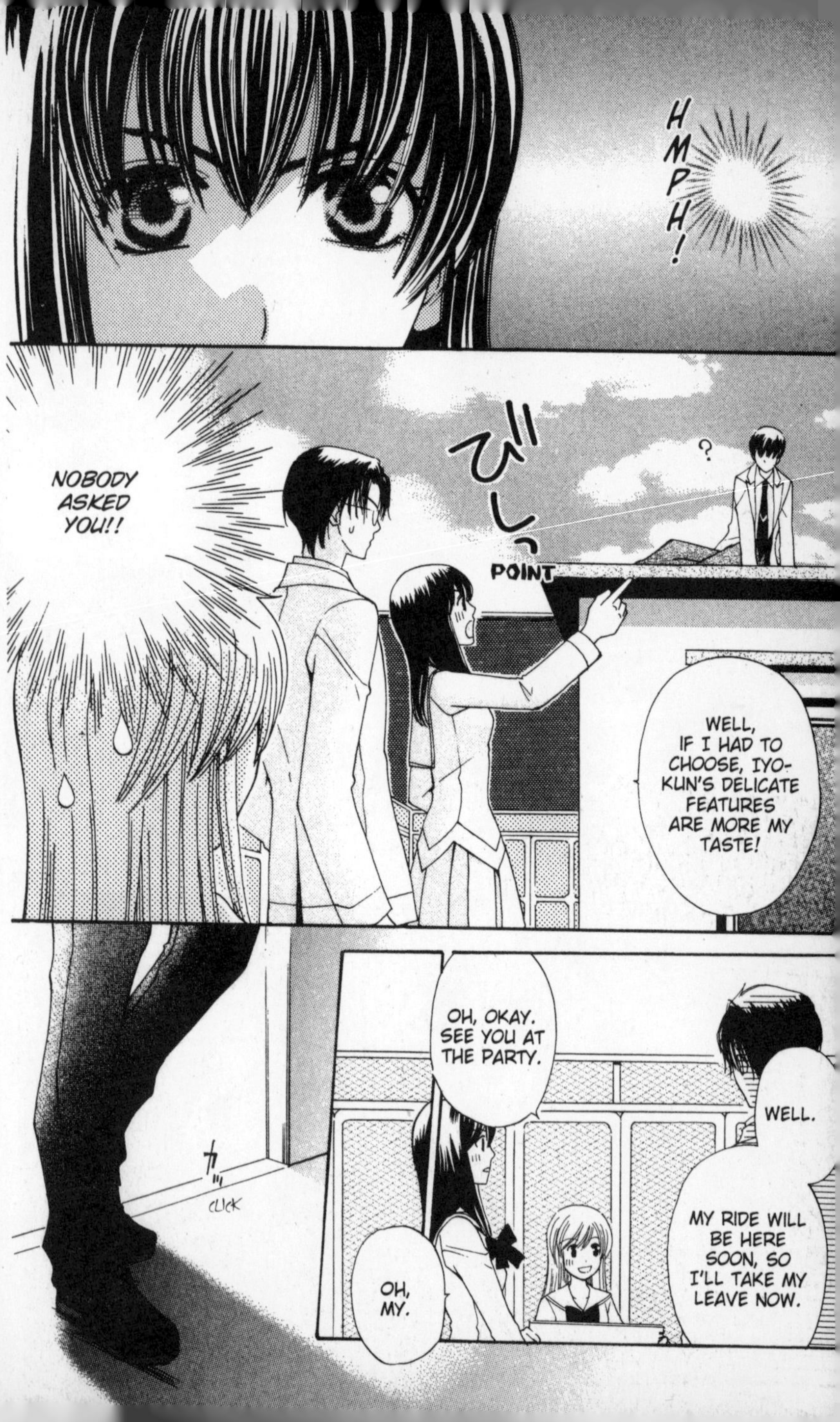
HMPH!
WELL, IF I HAD TO CHOOSE, IYO-KUN'S DELICATE FEATURES ARE MORE MY TASTE!
ぴしっ
POINT
?
NOBODY ASKED YOU!!
WELL.
MY RIDE WILL BE HERE SOON, SO I'LL TAKE MY LEAVE NOW.
OH, OKAY. SEE YOU AT THE PARTY.
OH, MY.
ガッ
CLICK

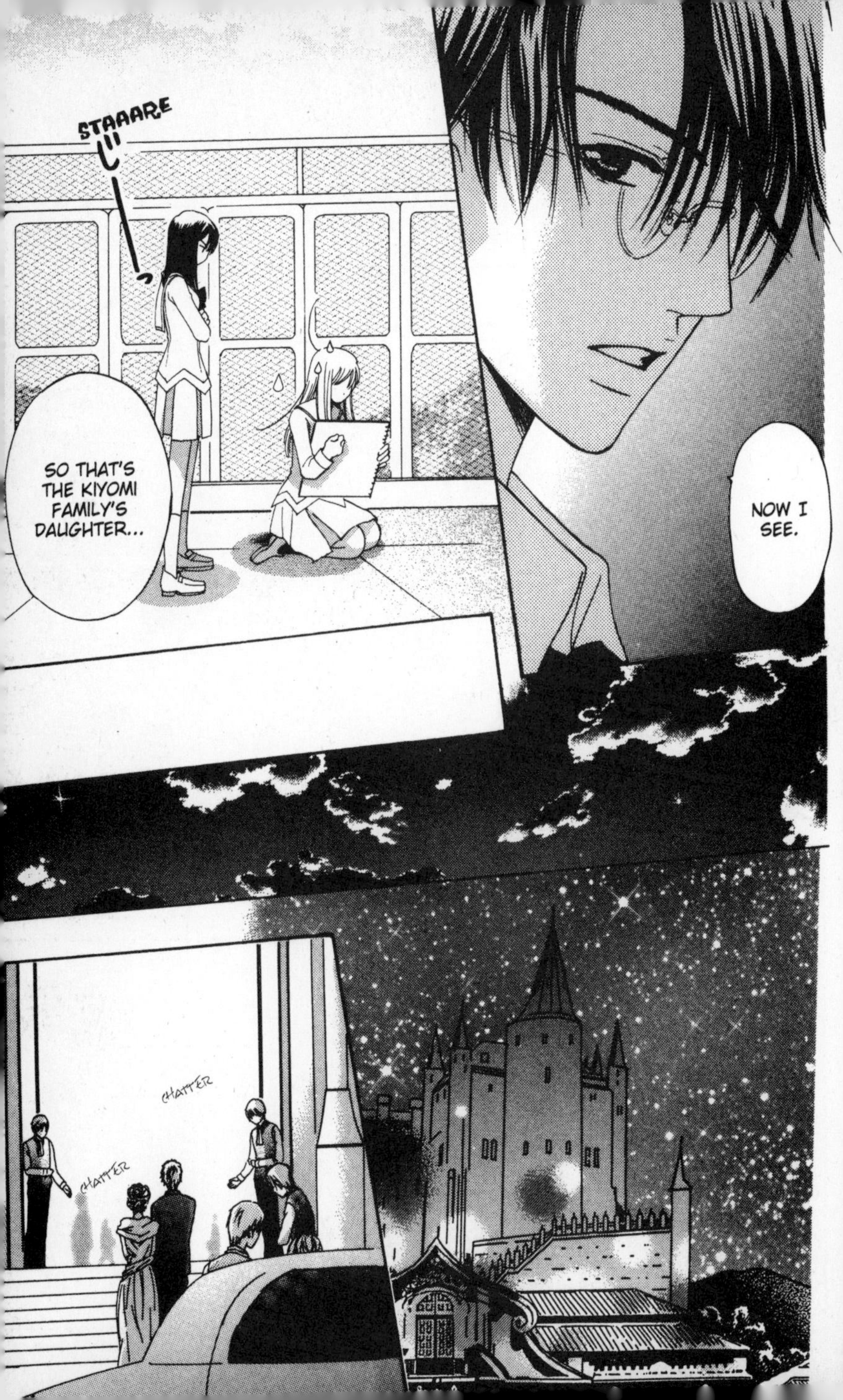
NOW I SEE.
STAAARE
じー
SO THAT'S THE KIYOMI FAMILY'S DAUGHTER...
CHATTER
CHATTER

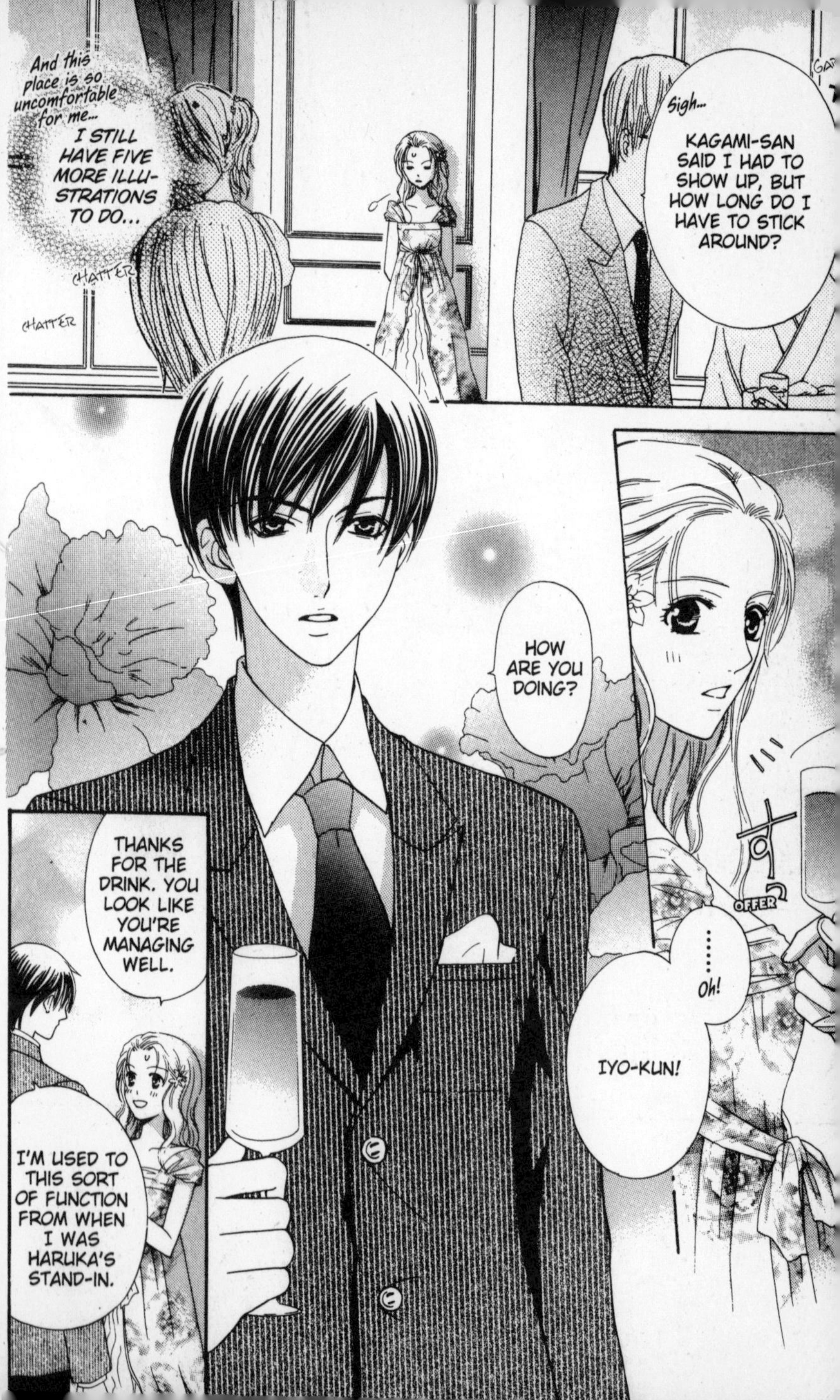

Sigh...
KAGAMI-SAN SAID I HAD TO SHOW UP, BUT HOW LONG DO I HAVE TO STICK AROUND?
And this place is so uncomfortable for me...
I STILL HAVE FIVE MORE ILLU-STRATIONS TO DO...
CHATTER
CHATTER
OFFER
......
Oh!
IYO-KUN!
HOW ARE YOU DOING?
THANKS FOR THE DRINK. YOU LOOK LIKE YOU'RE MANAGING WELL.
I'M USED TO THIS SORT OF FUNCTION FROM WHEN I WAS HARUKA'S STAND-IN.

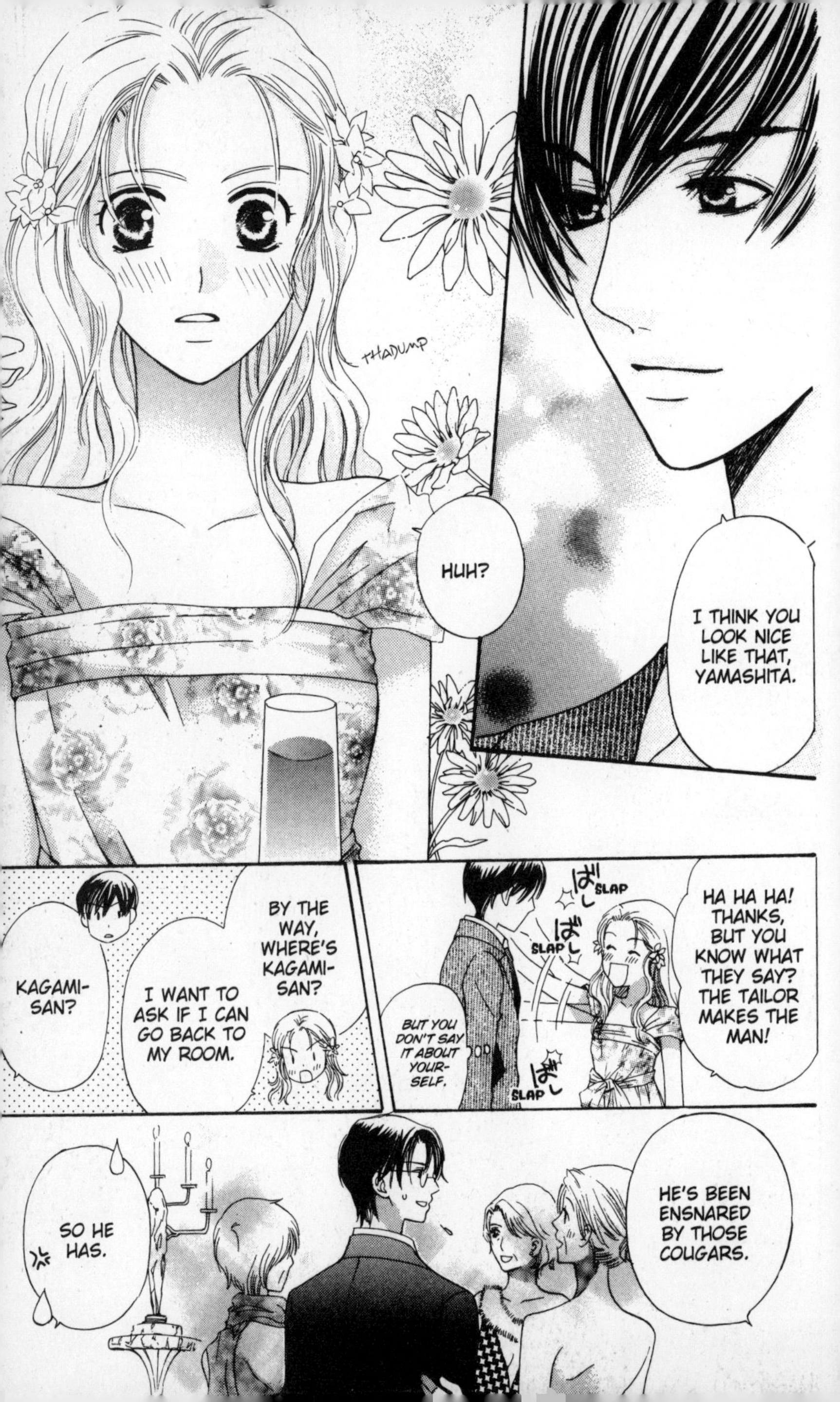

I THINK YOU LOOK NICE LIKE THAT, YAMASHITA.
HUH?
THADUMP
HA HA HA! THANKS, BUT YOU KNOW WHAT THEY SAY? THE TAILOR MAKES THE MAN!
ばし SLAP
ばし SLAP
ばし SLAP
BUT YOU DON'T SAY IT ABOUT YOURSELF.
BY THE WAY, WHERE'S KAGAMI-SAN?
I WANT TO ASK IF I CAN GO BACK TO MY ROOM.
KAGAMI-SAN?
HE'S BEEN ENSNARED BY THOSE COUGARS.
SO HE HAS.

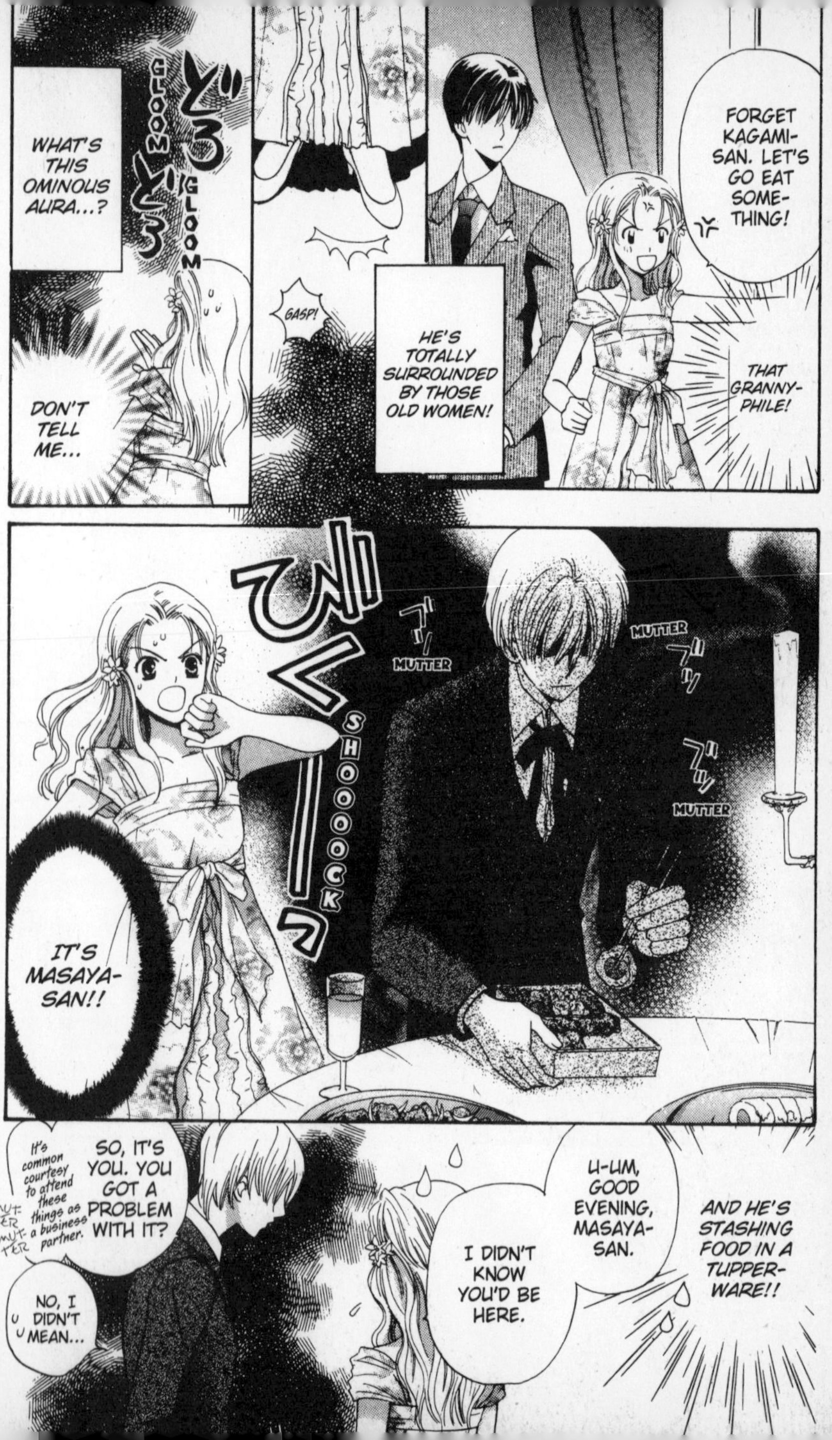
FORGET KAGAMI-SAN. LET'S GO EAT SOMETHING!
THAT GRANNY-PHILE!
HE'S TOTALLY SURROUNDED BY THOSE OLD WOMEN!
GASP!
GLOOM GLOOM
WHAT'S THIS OMINOUS AURA...?
DON'T TELL ME...
SHOOOOOCK
MUTTER
MUTTER
MUTTER
IT'S MASAYA-SAN!!
AND HE'S STASHING FOOD IN A TUPPERWARE!!
U-UM, GOOD EVENING, MASAYA-SAN.
I DIDN'T KNOW YOU'D BE HERE.
SO, IT'S YOU. YOU GOT A PROBLEM WITH IT?
It's common courtesy to attend these things as a business partner.
MUT-TER MUT-TER
NO, I DIDN'T MEAN...

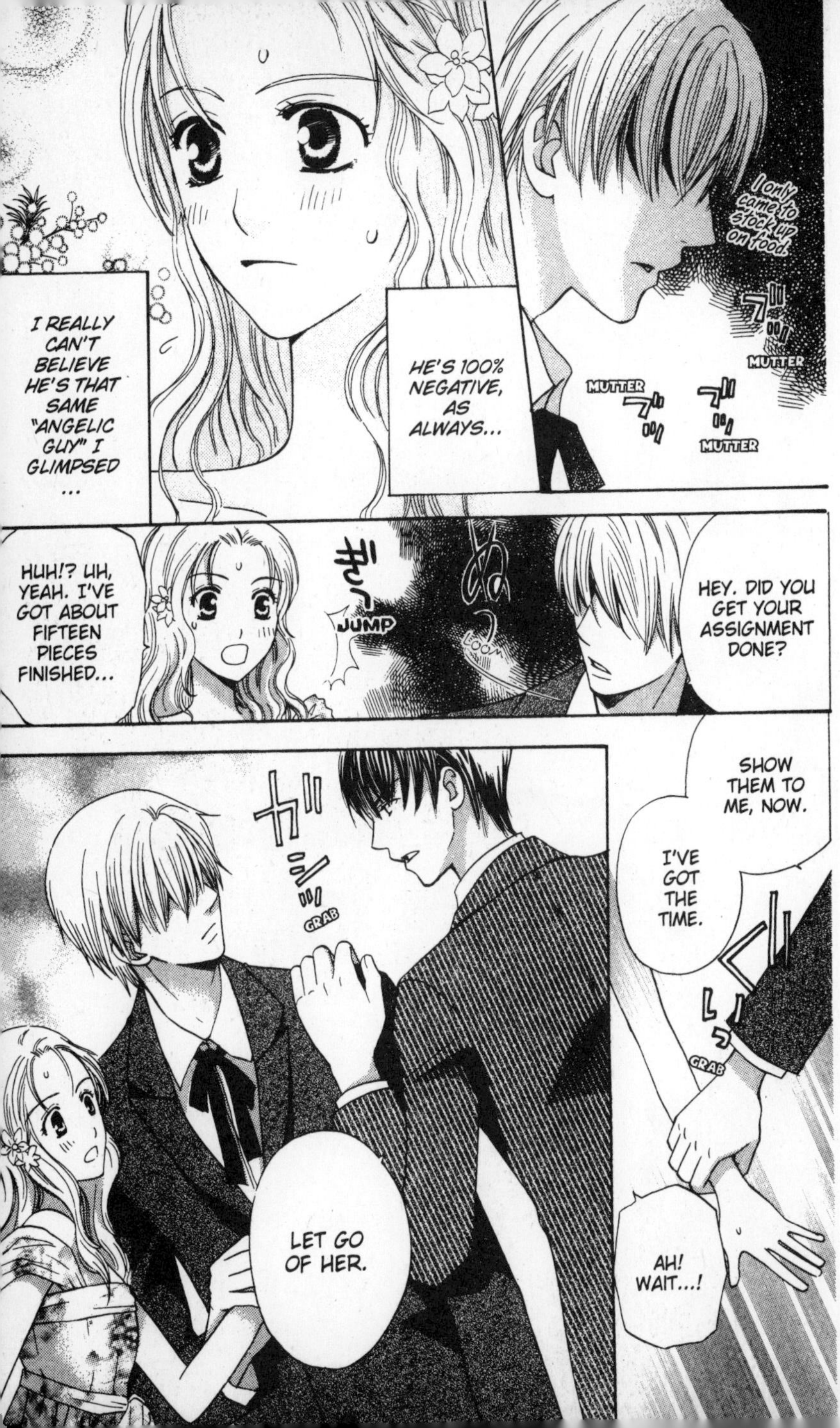

I only came to stock up on food.
MUTTER
MUTTER
MUTTER
HE'S 100% NEGATIVE, AS ALWAYS...
I REALLY CAN'T BELIEVE HE'S THAT SAME "ANGELIC GUY" I GLIMPSED ...
HEY. DID YOU GET YOUR ASSIGNMENT DONE?
LOOM
JUMP
HUH!? UH, YEAH. I'VE GOT ABOUT FIFTEEN PIECES FINISHED...
SHOW THEM TO ME, NOW.
I'VE GOT THE TIME.
GRAB
AH! WAIT...!
GRAB
LET GO OF HER.

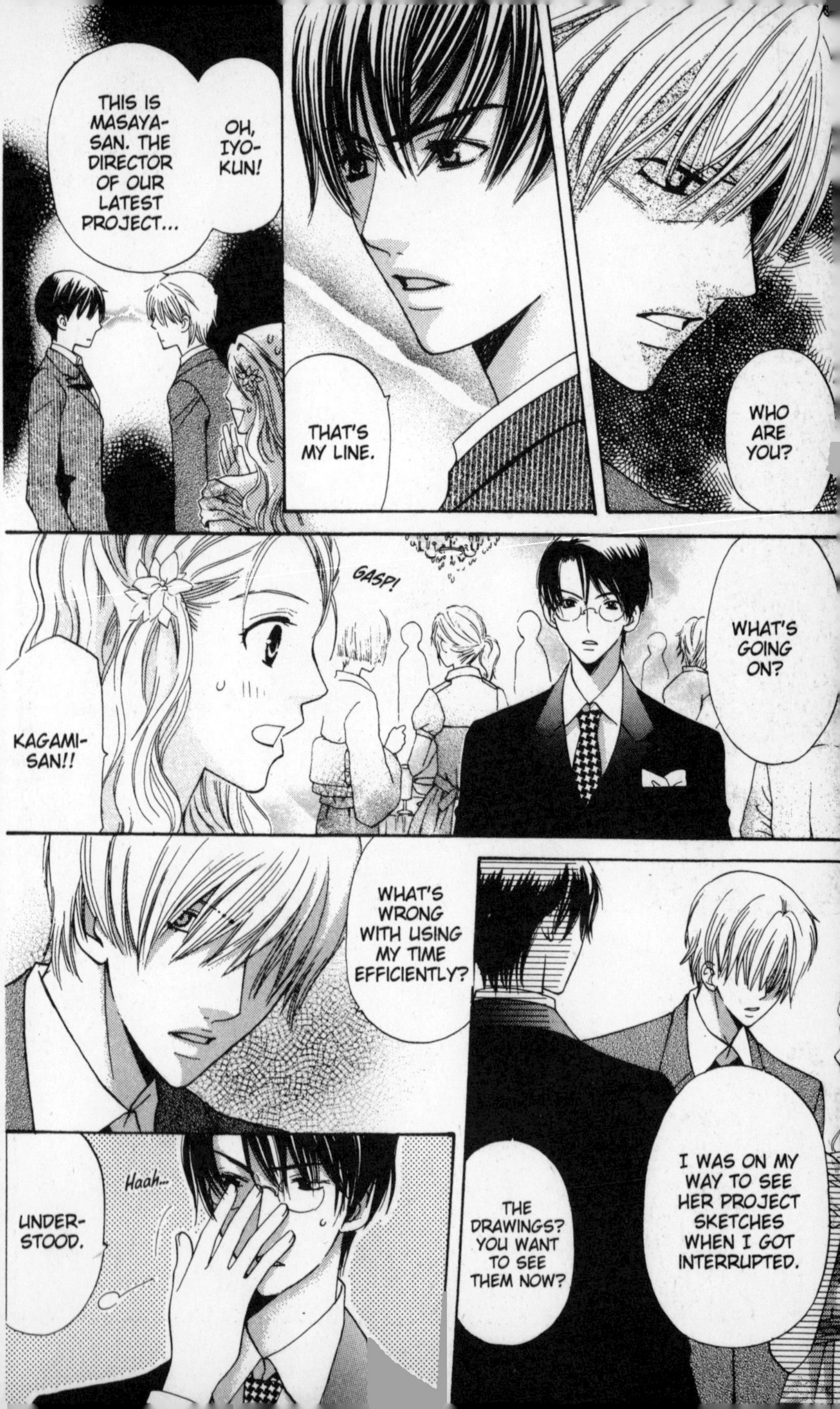
WHO ARE YOU?
THAT'S MY LINE.
OH, IYO-KUN!
THIS IS MASAYA-SAN. THE DIRECTOR OF OUR LATEST PROJECT...
WHAT'S GOING ON?
GASP!
KAGAMI-SAN!!
WHAT'S WRONG WITH USING MY TIME EFFICIENTLY?
I WAS ON MY WAY TO SEE HER PROJECT SKETCHES WHEN I GOT INTERRUPTED.
THE DRAWINGS? YOU WANT TO SEE THEM NOW?
Haah...
UNDER-STOOD.

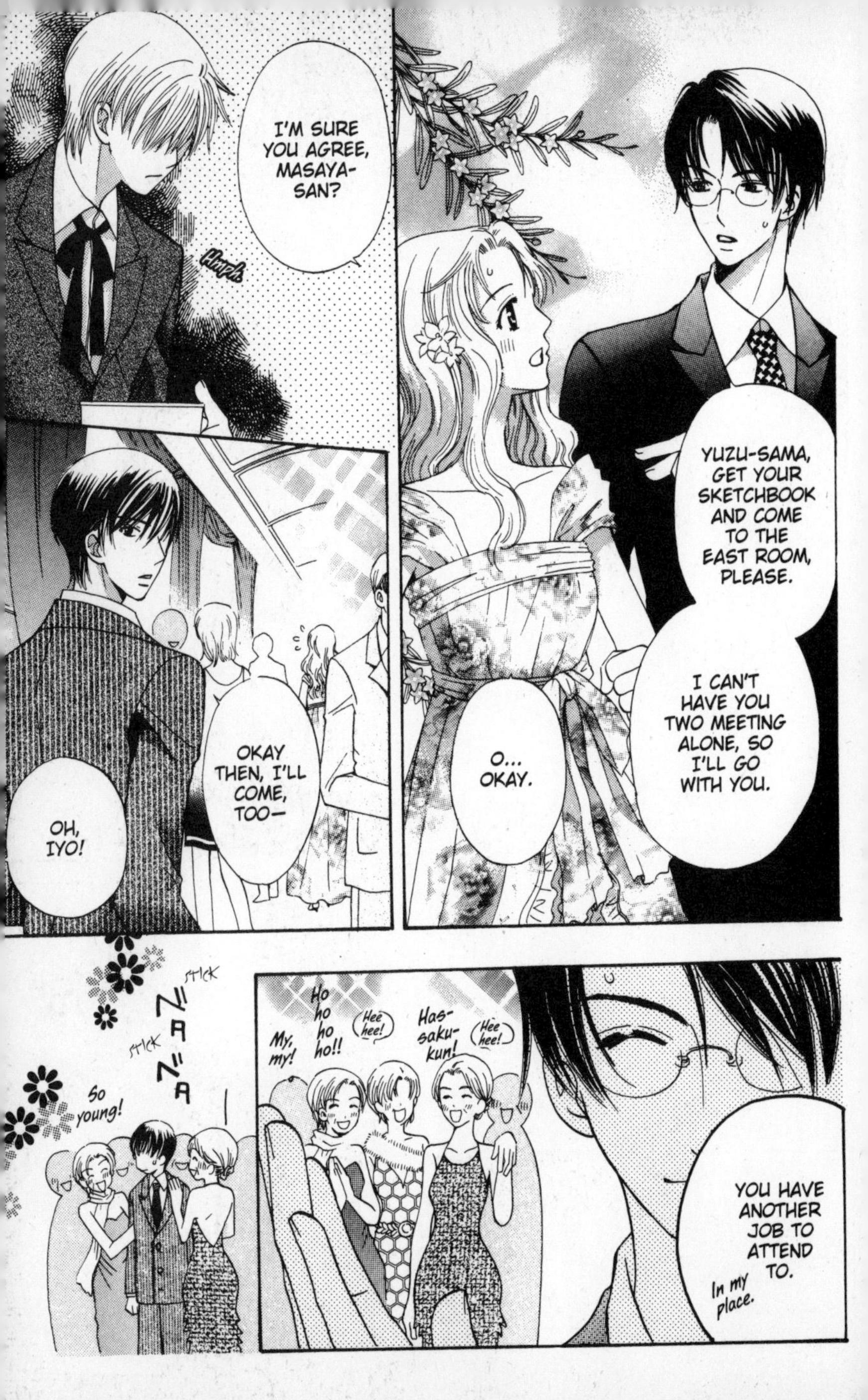
YUZU-SAMA, GET YOUR SKETCHBOOK AND COME TO THE EAST ROOM, PLEASE.
I CAN'T HAVE YOU TWO MEETING ALONE, SO I'LL GO WITH YOU.
O... OKAY.
I'M SURE YOU AGREE, MASAYA-SAN?
Hmph.
OKAY THEN, I'LL COME, TOO—
OH, IYO!
YOU HAVE ANOTHER JOB TO ATTEND TO.
In my place.
Hee hee!
Has-saku-kun!
Hee hee!
Ho ho ho ho!!
My, my!
STICK
STICK
So young!

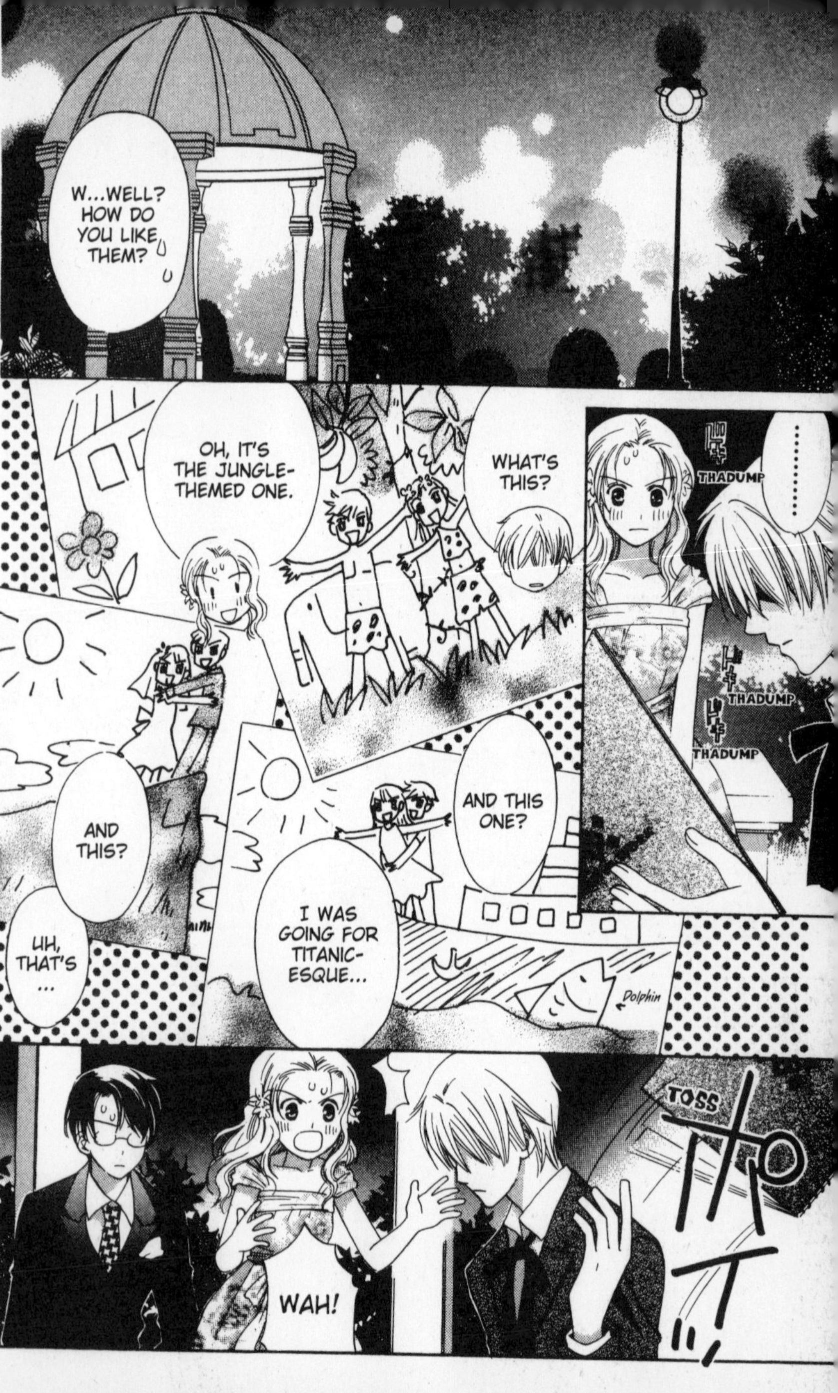
W...WELL? HOW DO YOU LIKE THEM?
......
THADUMP
THADUMP
THADUMP
WHAT'S THIS?
OH, IT'S THE JUNGLE-THEMED ONE.
AND THIS ONE?
I WAS GOING FOR TITANIC-ESQUE...
Dolphin
AND THIS?
UH, THAT'S ...
TOSS
WAH!

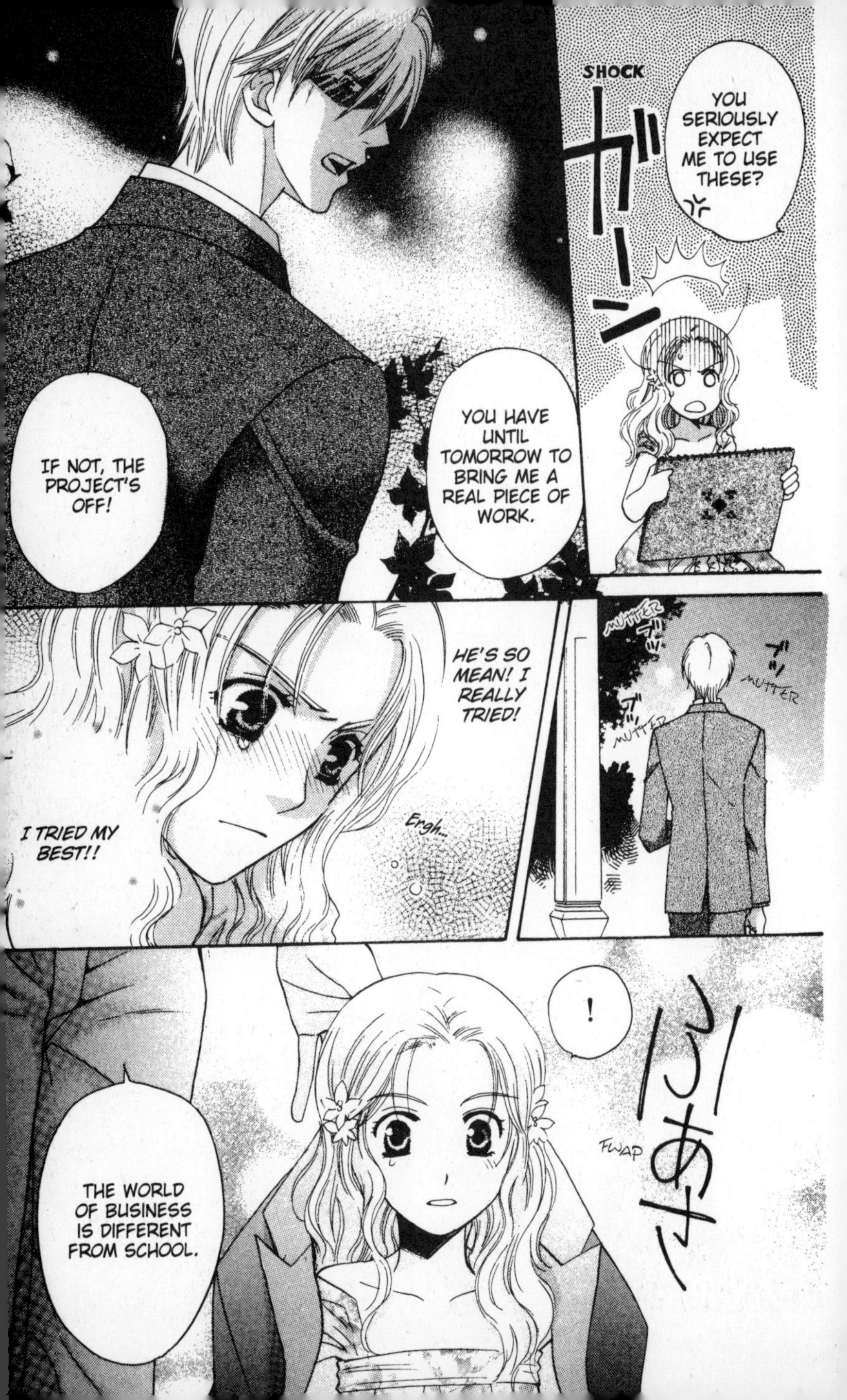
SHOCK
YOU SERIOUSLY EXPECT ME TO USE THESE?
YOU HAVE UNTIL TOMORROW TO BRING ME A REAL PIECE OF WORK.
IF NOT, THE PROJECT'S OFF!
MUTTER
MUTTER
MUTTER
HE'S SO MEAN! I REALLY TRIED!
Ergh...
I TRIED MY BEST!!
!
FWAP
THE WORLD OF BUSINESS IS DIFFERENT FROM SCHOOL.

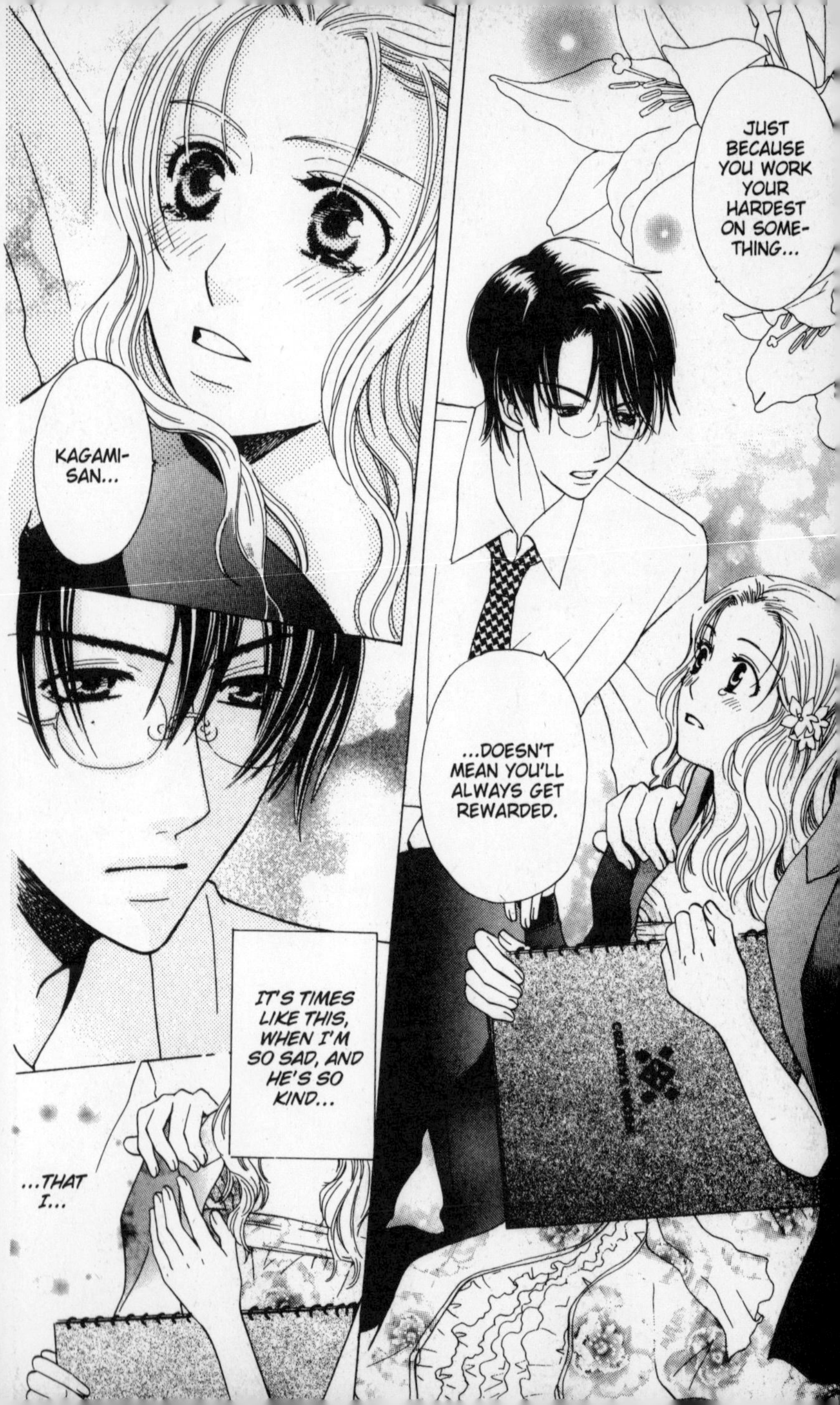
JUST BECAUSE YOU WORK YOUR HARDEST ON SOME-THING...
...DOESN'T MEAN YOU'LL ALWAYS GET REWARDED.
KAGAMI-SAN...
IT'S TIMES LIKE THIS, WHEN I'M SO SAD, AND HE'S SO KIND...
...THAT I...

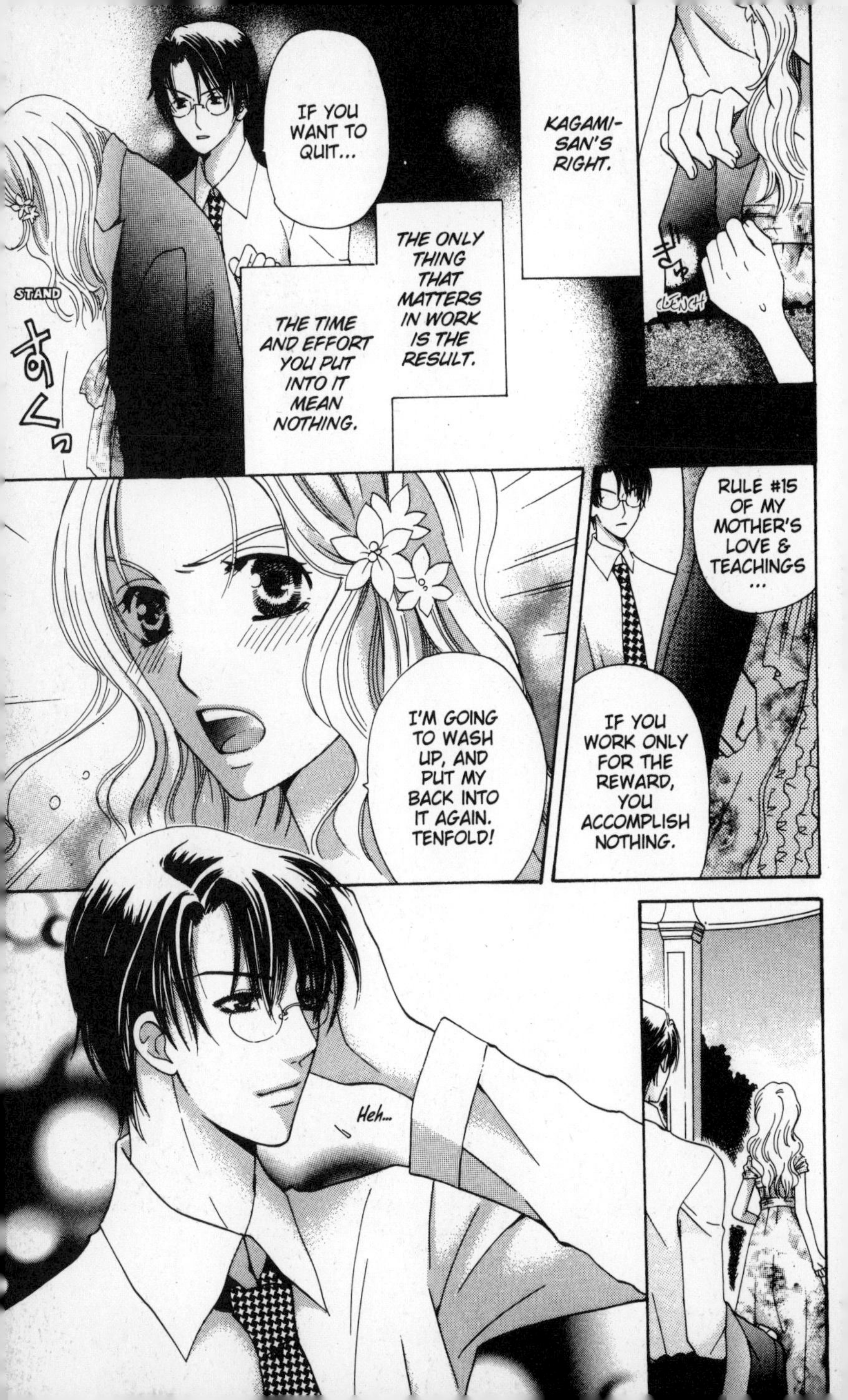
ぎゅ
CLENCH
KAGAMI-SAN'S RIGHT.
THE ONLY THING THAT MATTERS IN WORK IS THE RESULT.
THE TIME AND EFFORT YOU PUT INTO IT MEAN NOTHING.
IF YOU WANT TO QUIT...
STAND
すくっ
RULE #15 OF MY MOTHER'S LOVE & TEACHINGS ...
IF YOU WORK ONLY FOR THE REWARD, YOU ACCOMPLISH NOTHING.
I'M GOING TO WASH UP, AND PUT MY BACK INTO IT AGAIN. TENFOLD!
Heh...

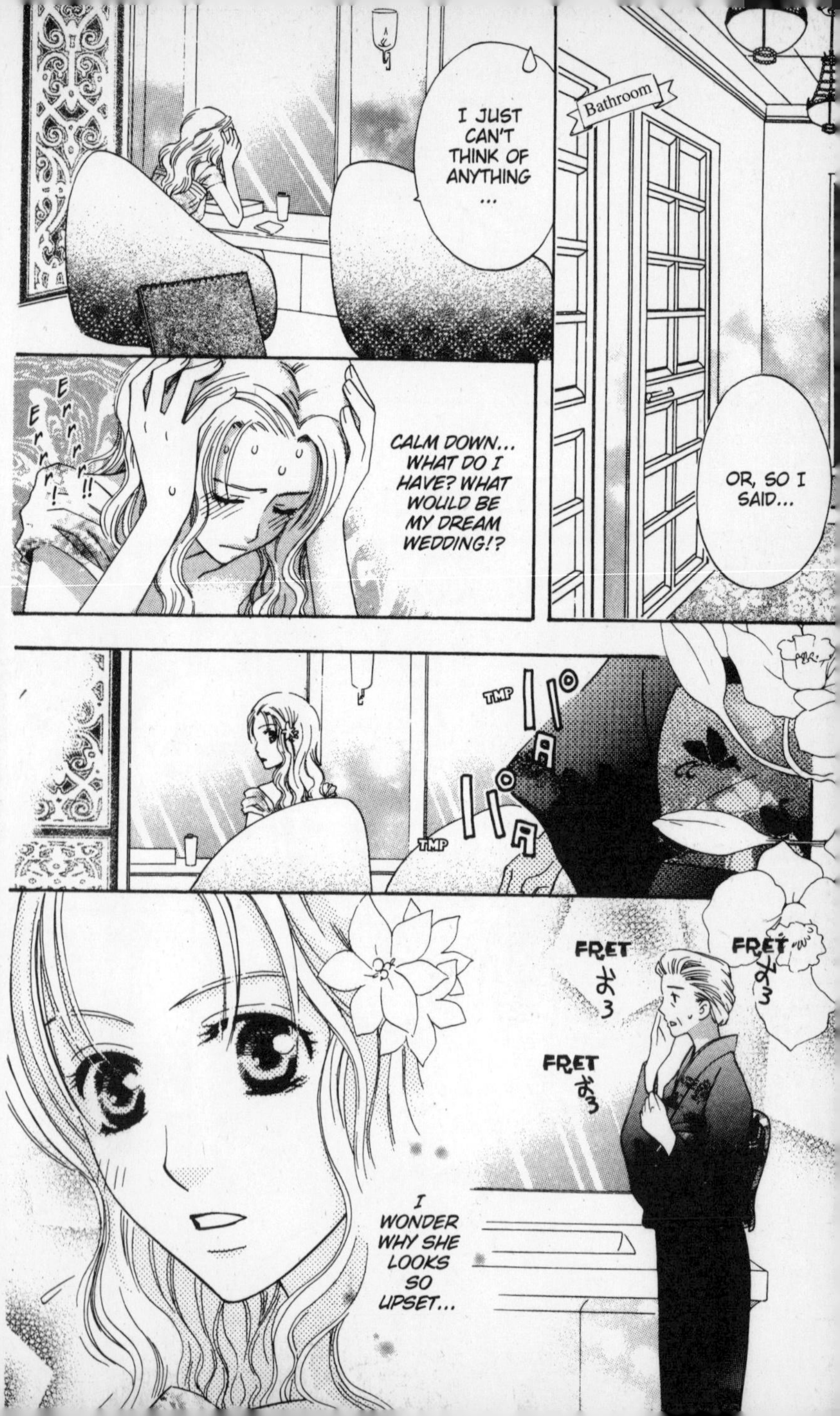

Bathroom
OR, SO I SAID...
I JUST CAN'T THINK OF ANYTHING...
Errrr!!
Errrr!
CALM DOWN... WHAT DO I HAVE? WHAT WOULD BE MY DREAM WEDDING!?
TMP
TMP
FRET
FRET
FRET
I WONDER WHY SHE LOOKS SO UPSET...

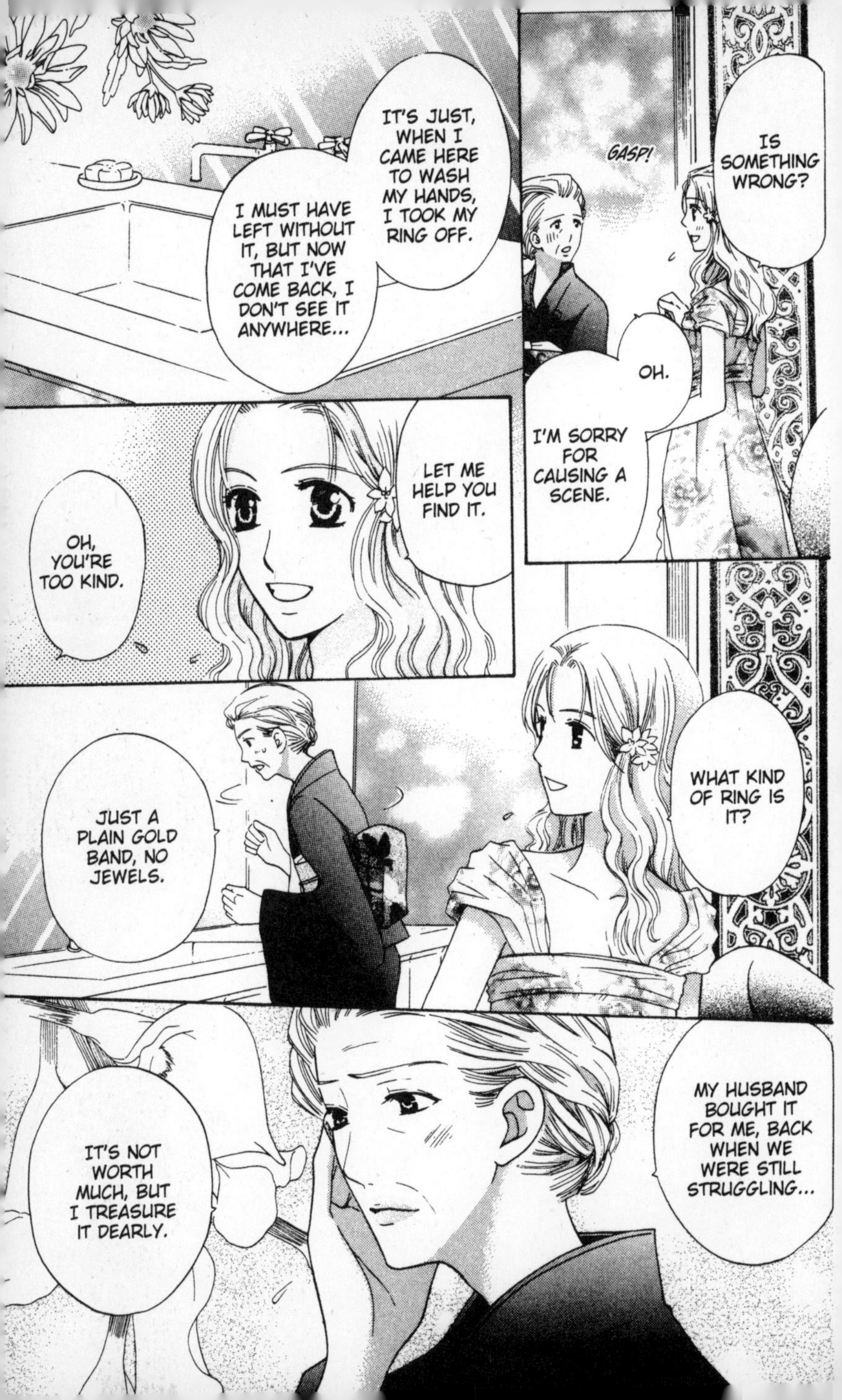
IS SOMETHING WRONG?
GASP!
OH.
I'M SORRY FOR CAUSING A SCENE.
IT'S JUST, WHEN I CAME HERE TO WASH MY HANDS, I TOOK MY RING OFF.
I MUST HAVE LEFT WITHOUT IT, BUT NOW THAT I'VE COME BACK, I DON'T SEE IT ANYWHERE...
LET ME HELP YOU FIND IT.
OH, YOU'RE TOO KIND.
WHAT KIND OF RING IS IT?
JUST A PLAIN GOLD BAND, NO JEWELS.
MY HUSBAND BOUGHT IT FOR ME, BACK WHEN WE WERE STILL STRUGGLING...
IT'S NOT WORTH MUCH, BUT I TREASURE IT DEARLY.

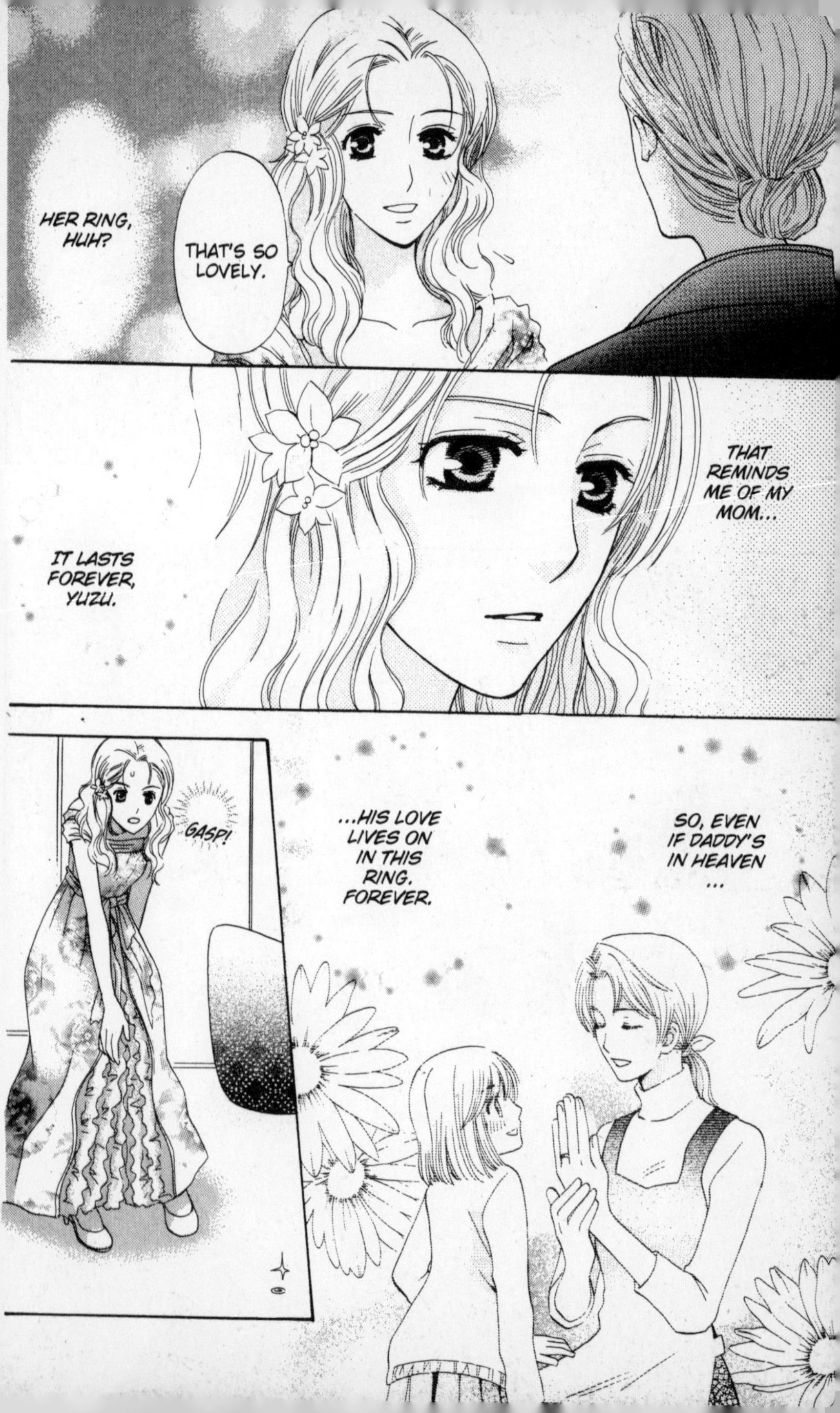
THAT'S SO LOVELY.
HER RING, HUH?
THAT REMINDS ME OF MY MOM...
IT LASTS FOREVER, YUZU.
SO, EVEN IF DADDY'S IN HEAVEN ...
...HIS LOVE LIVES ON IN THIS RING. FOREVER.
GASP!

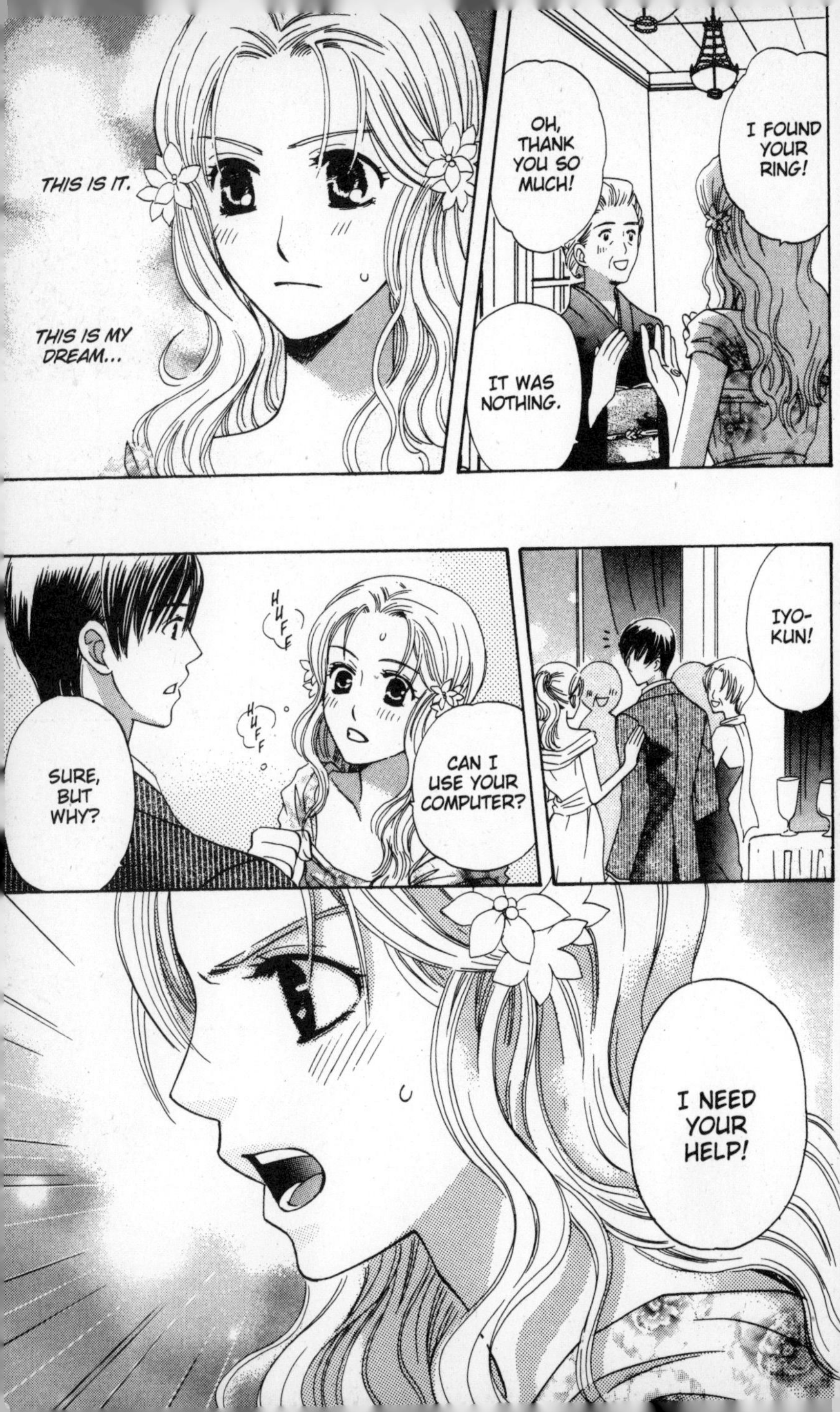
I FOUND YOUR RING!
OH, THANK YOU SO MUCH!
IT WAS NOTHING.
THIS IS IT.
THIS IS MY DREAM...
IYO-KUN!
HUFF
HUFF
CAN I USE YOUR COMPUTER?
SURE, BUT WHY?
I NEED YOUR HELP!

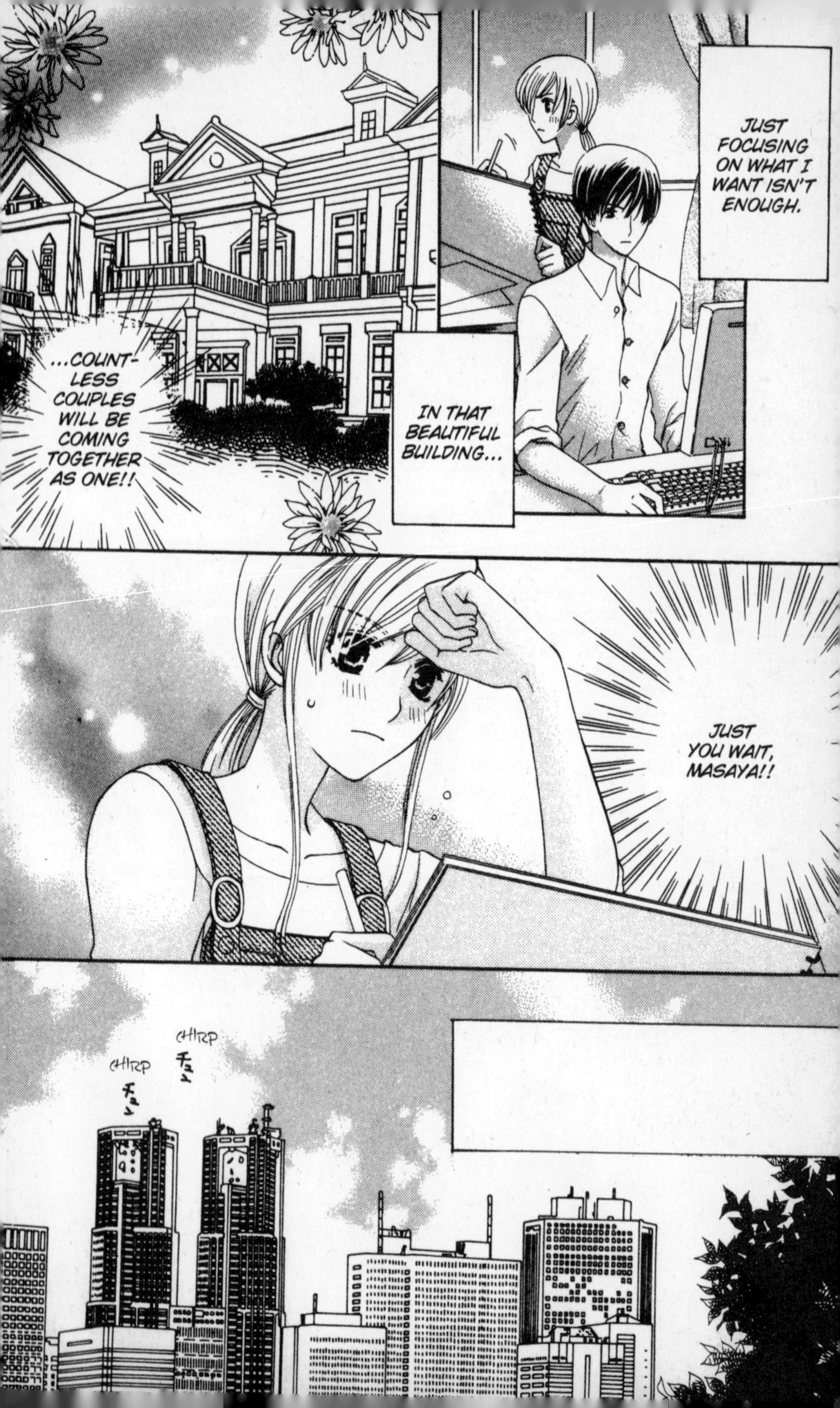

JUST FOCUSING ON WHAT I WANT ISN'T ENOUGH.
IN THAT BEAUTIFUL BUILDING...
...COUNT-LESS COUPLES WILL BE COMING TOGETHER AS ONE!!
JUST YOU WAIT, MASAYA!!
CHIRP
チュン
CHIRP
チュン

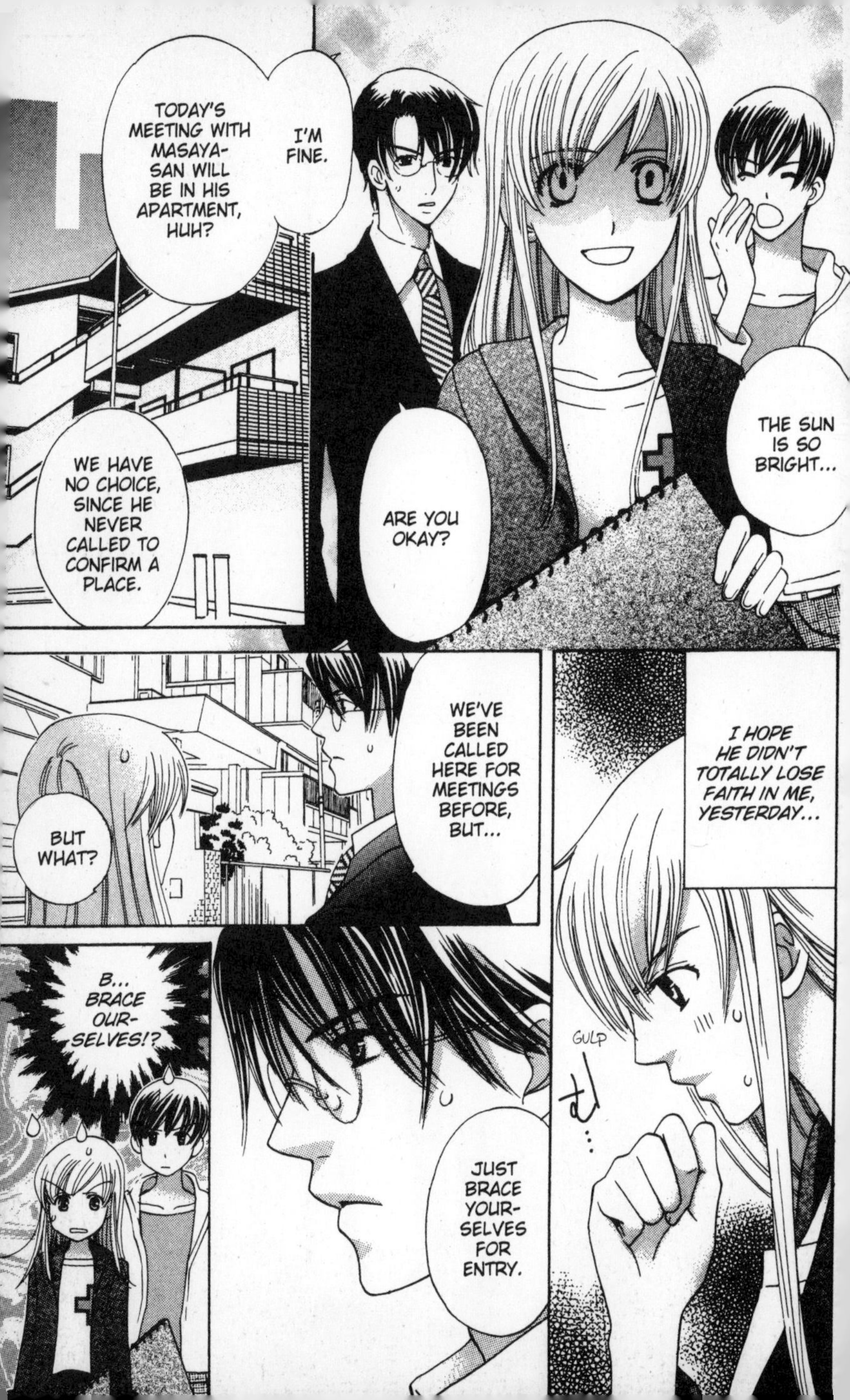

THE SUN IS SO BRIGHT...
ARE YOU OKAY?
I'M FINE.
TODAY'S MEETING WITH MASAYA-SAN WILL BE IN HIS APARTMENT, HUH?
WE HAVE NO CHOICE, SINCE HE NEVER CALLED TO CONFIRM A PLACE.
I HOPE HE DIDN'T TOTALLY LOSE FAITH IN ME, YESTERDAY...
GULP
WE'VE BEEN CALLED HERE FOR MEETINGS BEFORE, BUT...
BUT WHAT?
JUST BRACE YOURSELVES FOR ENTRY.
B... BRACE OURSELVES!?

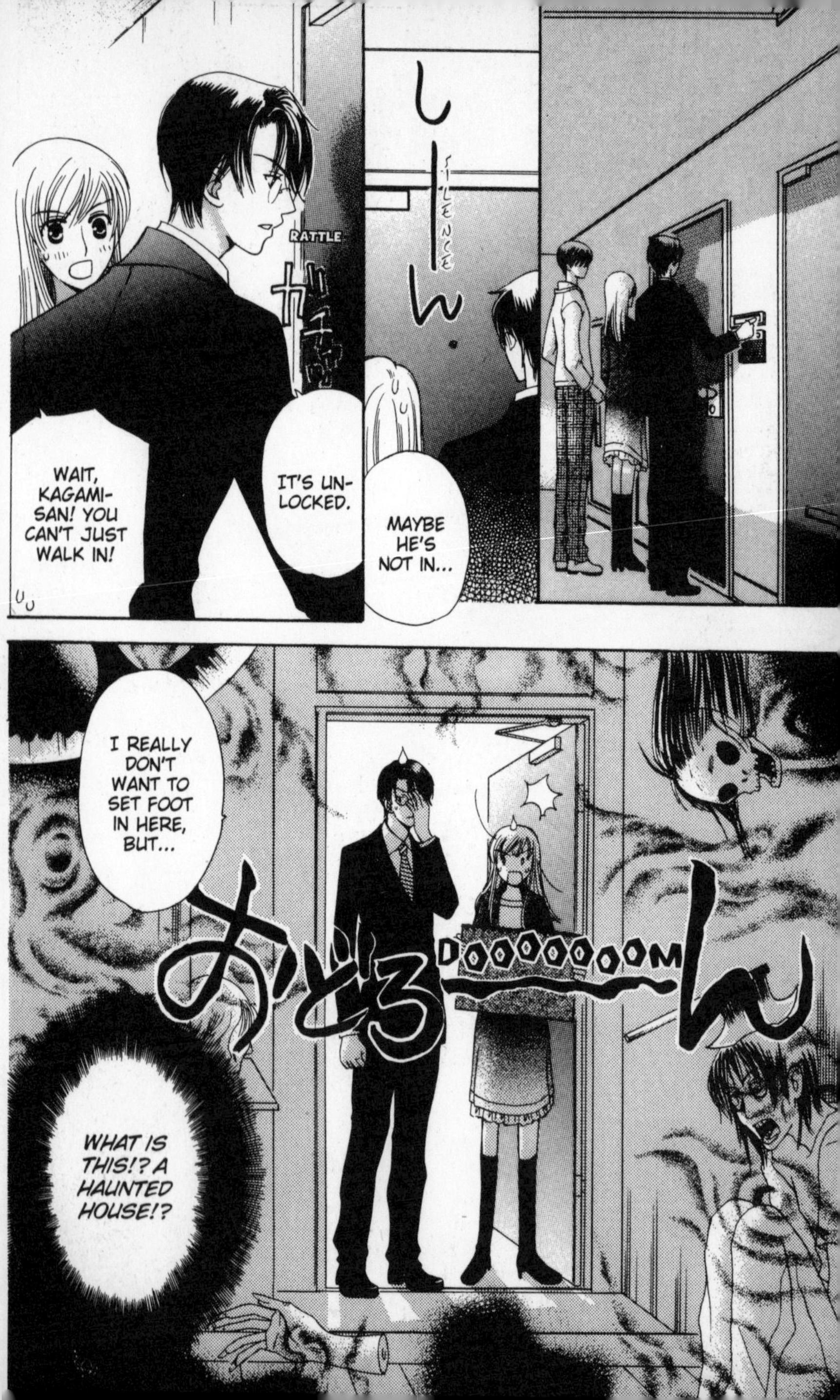
しーん。
SILENCE
MAYBE HE'S NOT IN...
RATTLE
IT'S UN-LOCKED.
WAIT, KAGAMI-SAN! YOU CAN'T JUST WALK IN!
I REALLY DON'T WANT TO SET FOOT IN HERE, BUT...
おどろーん
DOOOOOOOM
WHAT IS THIS!? A HAUNTED HOUSE!?

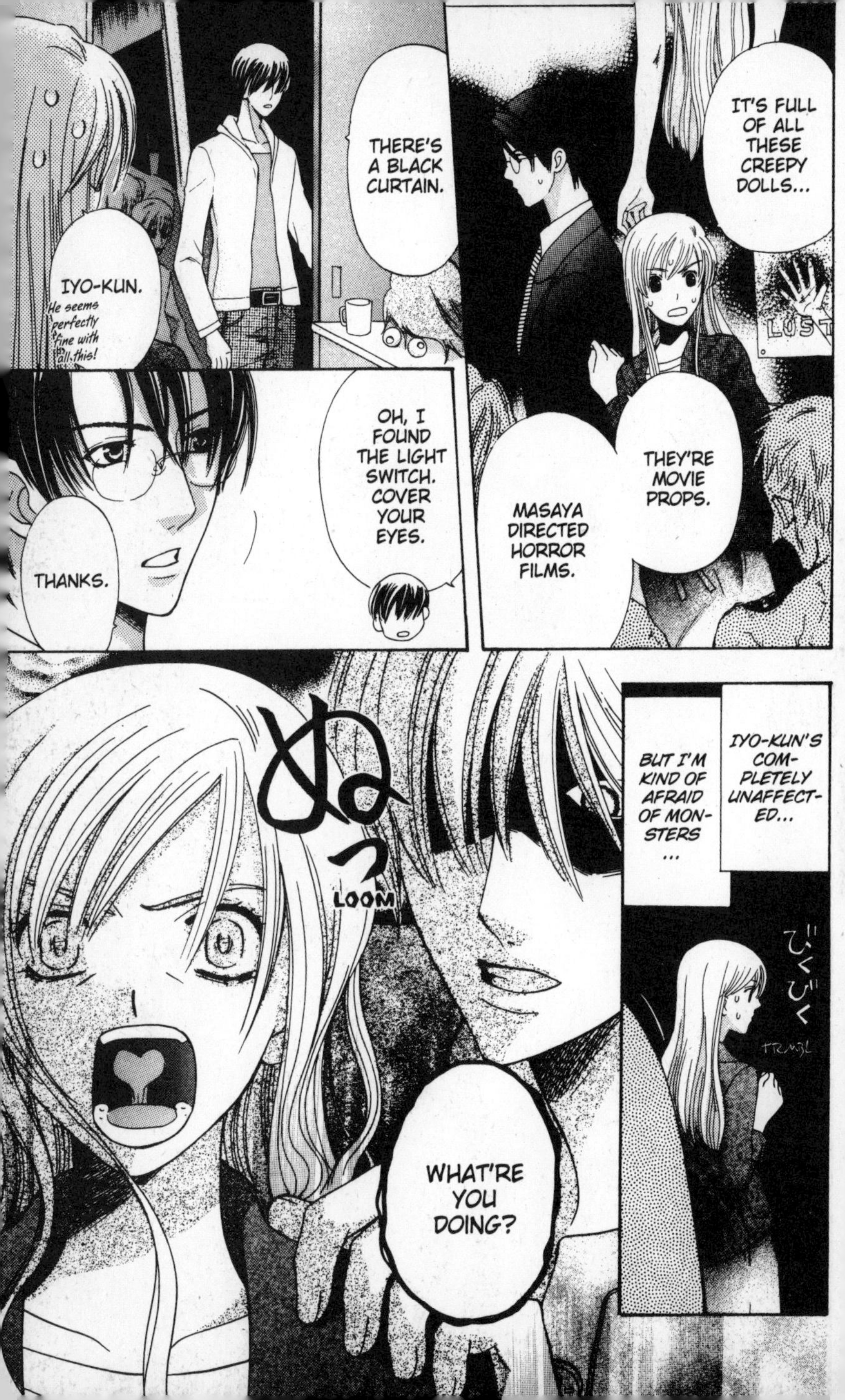

IT'S FULL OF ALL THESE CREEPY DOLLS...
THERE'S A BLACK CURTAIN.
IYO-KUN.
He seems perfectly fine with all this!
THEY'RE MOVIE PROPS.
MASAYA DIRECTED HORROR FILMS.
OH, I FOUND THE LIGHT SWITCH. COVER YOUR EYES.
THANKS.
IYO-KUN'S COM-PLETELY UNAFFECT-ED...
BUT I'M KIND OF AFRAID OF MON-STERS...
TRMBL
ぬっ
LOOM
WHAT'RE YOU DOING?

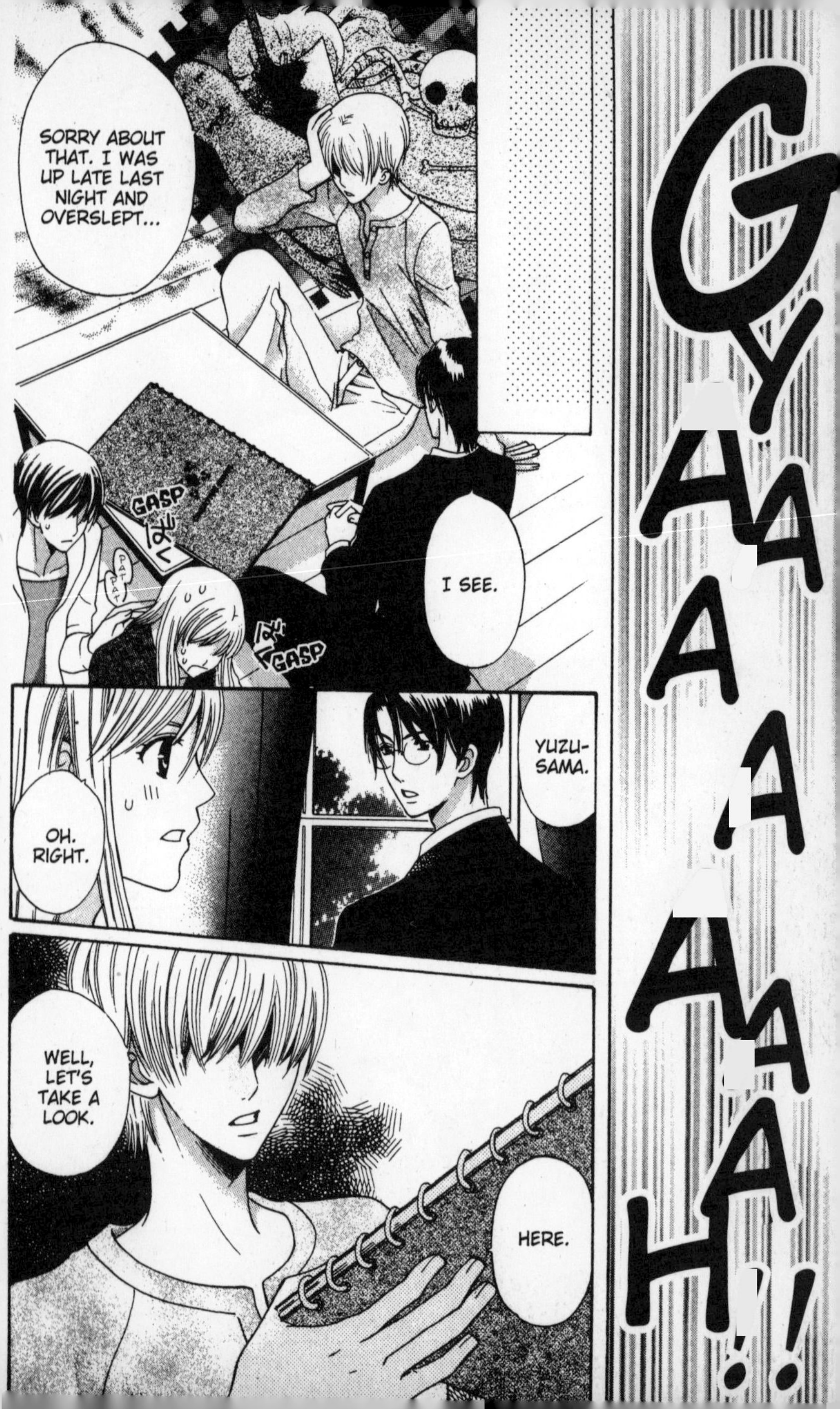
GYAAAAAAAH!!
SORRY ABOUT THAT. I WAS UP LATE LAST NIGHT AND OVERSLEPT...
I SEE.
GASP
ぱく
PAT PAT
ぱく
GASP
YUZU-SAMA.
OH. RIGHT.
HERE.
WELL, LET'S TAKE A LOOK.

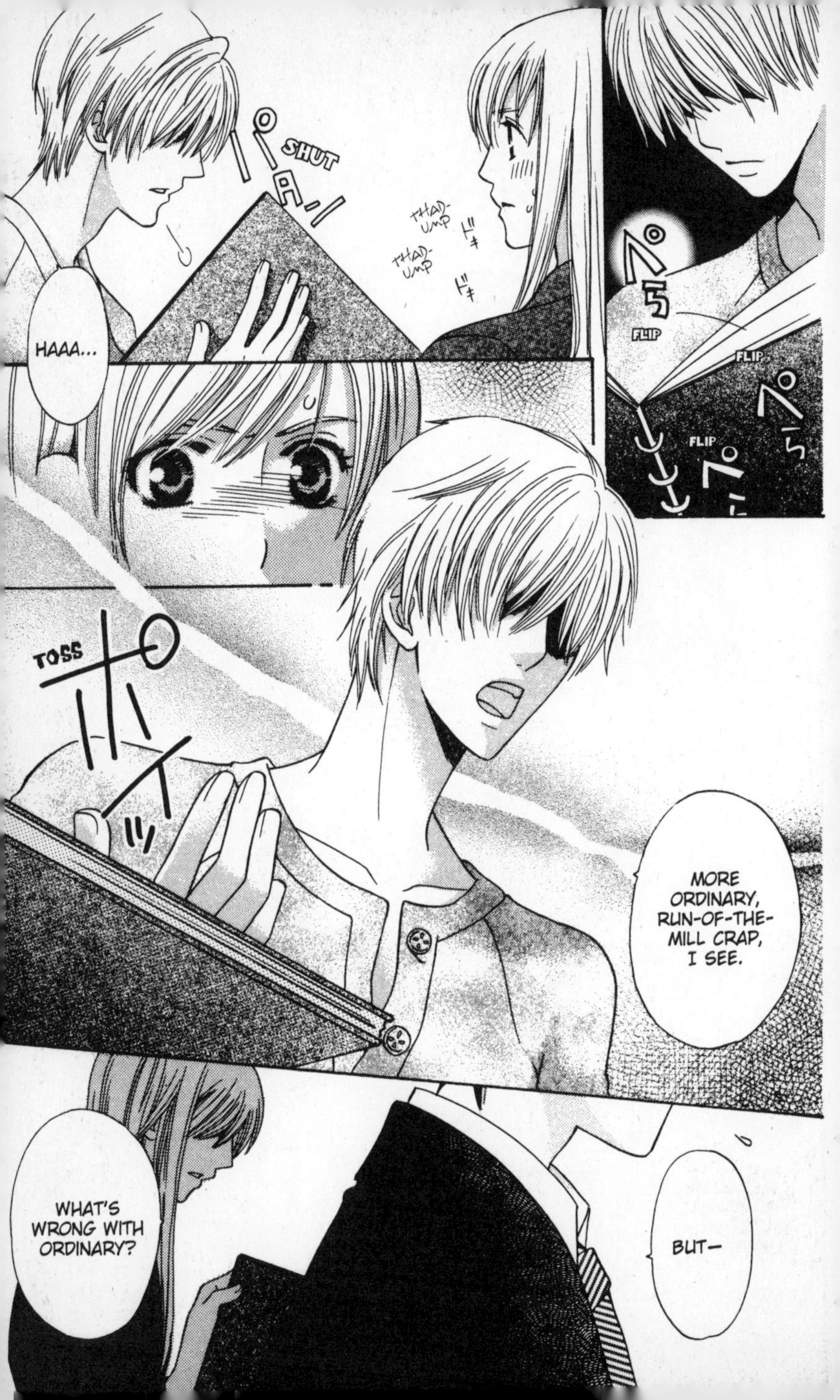
FLIP
FLIP
FLIP
THAD-UMP
THAD-UMP
SHUT
HAAA...
TOSS
MORE ORDINARY, RUN-OF-THE-MILL CRAP, I SEE.
BUT—
WHAT'S WRONG WITH ORDINARY?

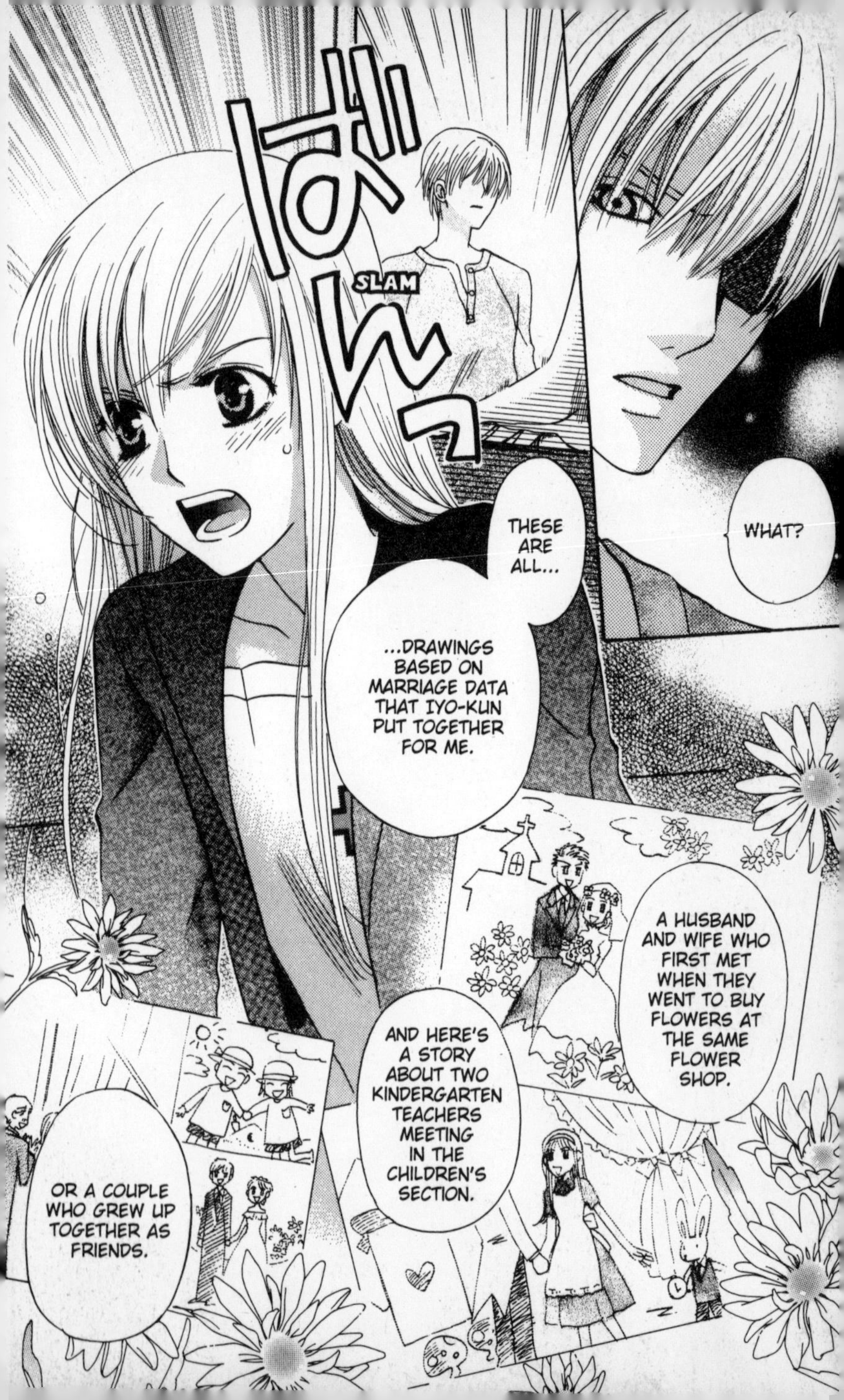
WHAT?
ばんっ
SLAM
THESE ARE ALL...
...DRAWINGS BASED ON MARRIAGE DATA THAT IYO-KUN PUT TOGETHER FOR ME.
A HUSBAND AND WIFE WHO FIRST MET WHEN THEY WENT TO BUY FLOWERS AT THE SAME FLOWER SHOP.
AND HERE'S A STORY ABOUT TWO KINDERGARTEN TEACHERS MEETING IN THE CHILDREN'S SECTION.
OR A COUPLE WHO GREW UP TOGETHER AS FRIENDS.

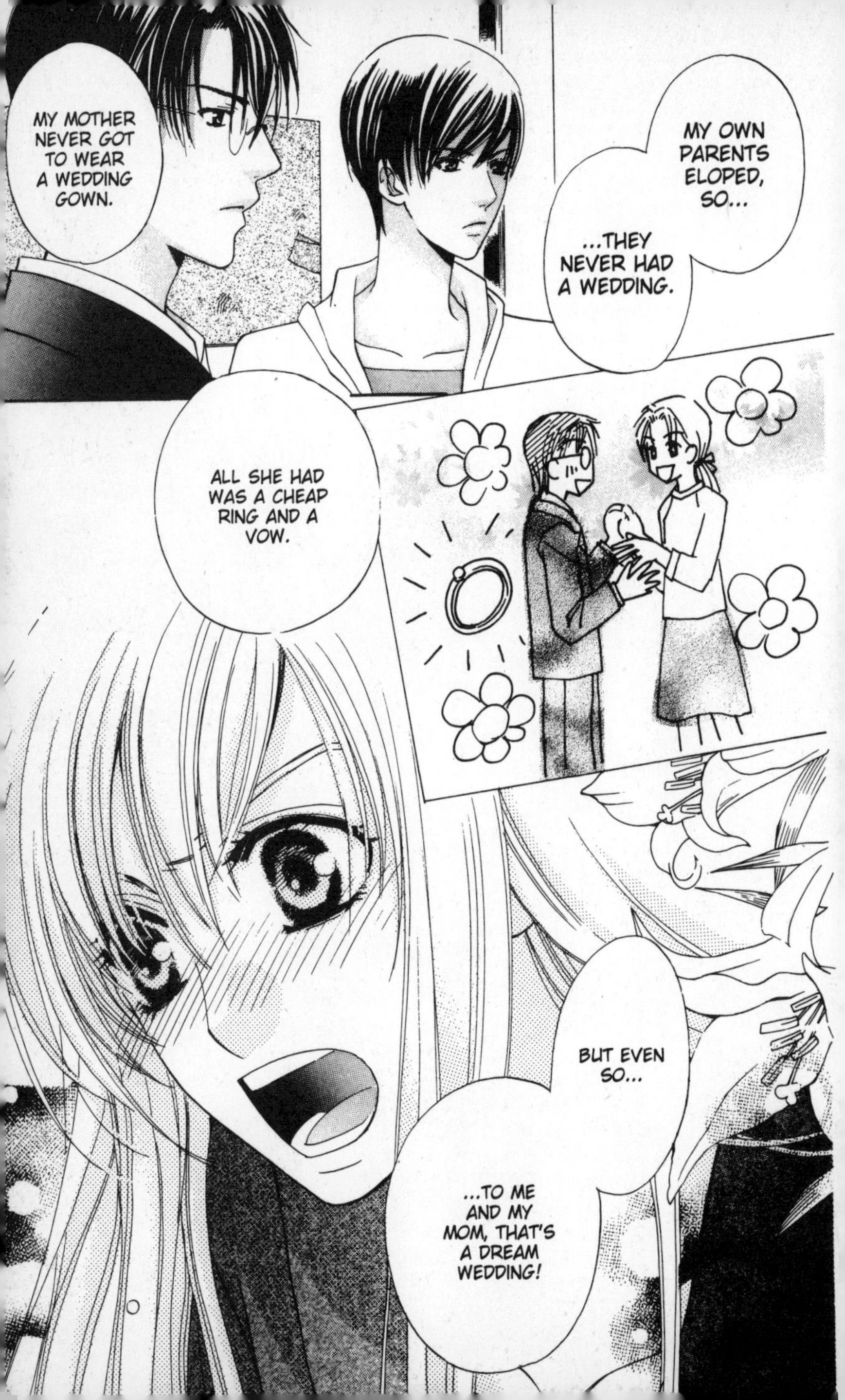
MY OWN PARENTS ELOPED, SO...
...THEY NEVER HAD A WEDDING.
MY MOTHER NEVER GOT TO WEAR A WEDDING GOWN.
ALL SHE HAD WAS A CHEAP RING AND A VOW.
BUT EVEN SO...
...TO ME AND MY MOM, THAT'S A DREAM WEDDING!

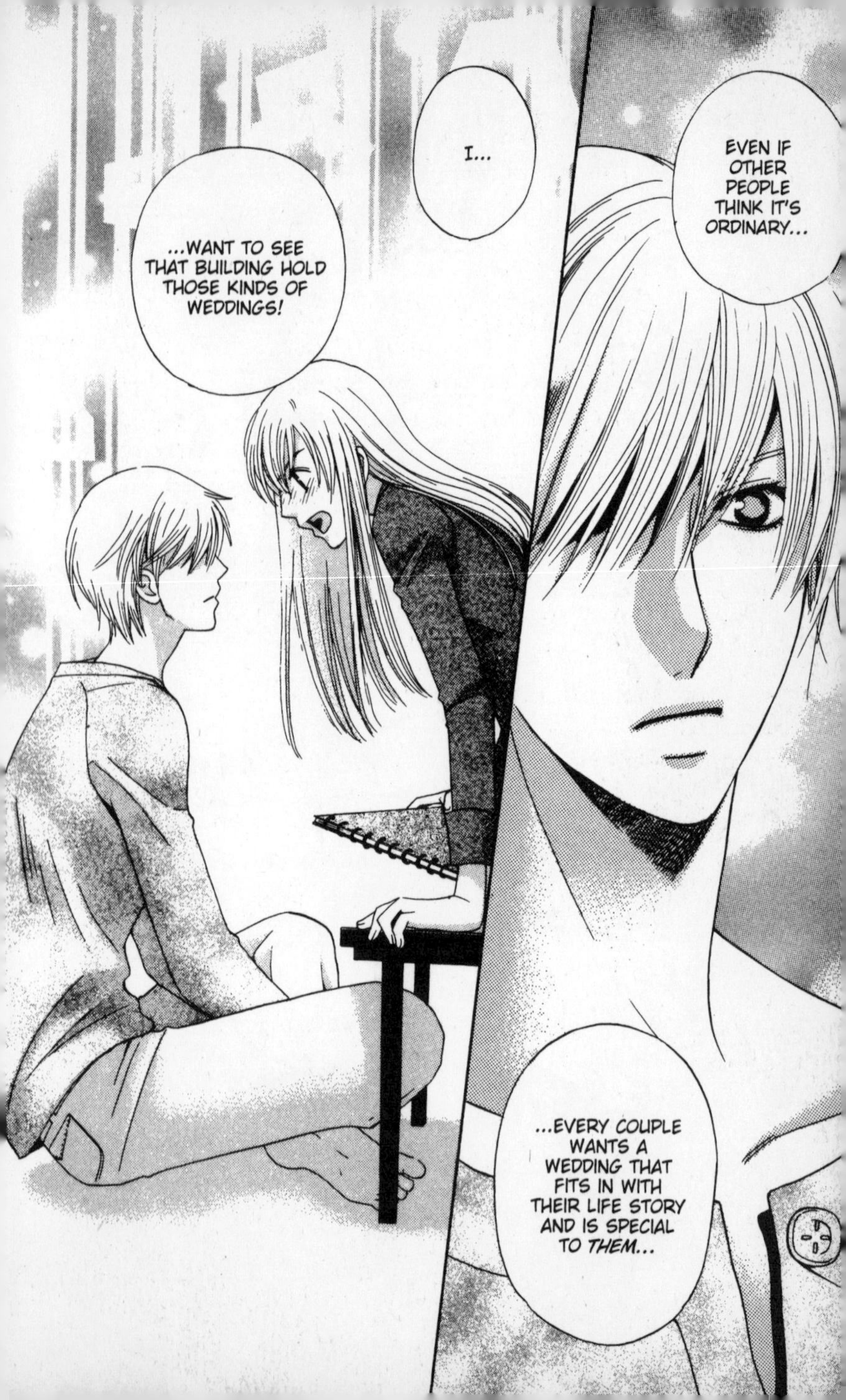
EVEN IF OTHER PEOPLE THINK IT'S ORDINARY...
...EVERY COUPLE WANTS A WEDDING THAT FITS IN WITH THEIR LIFE STORY AND IS SPECIAL TO *THEM*...
I...
...WANT TO SEE THAT BUILDING HOLD THOSE KINDS OF WEDDINGS!

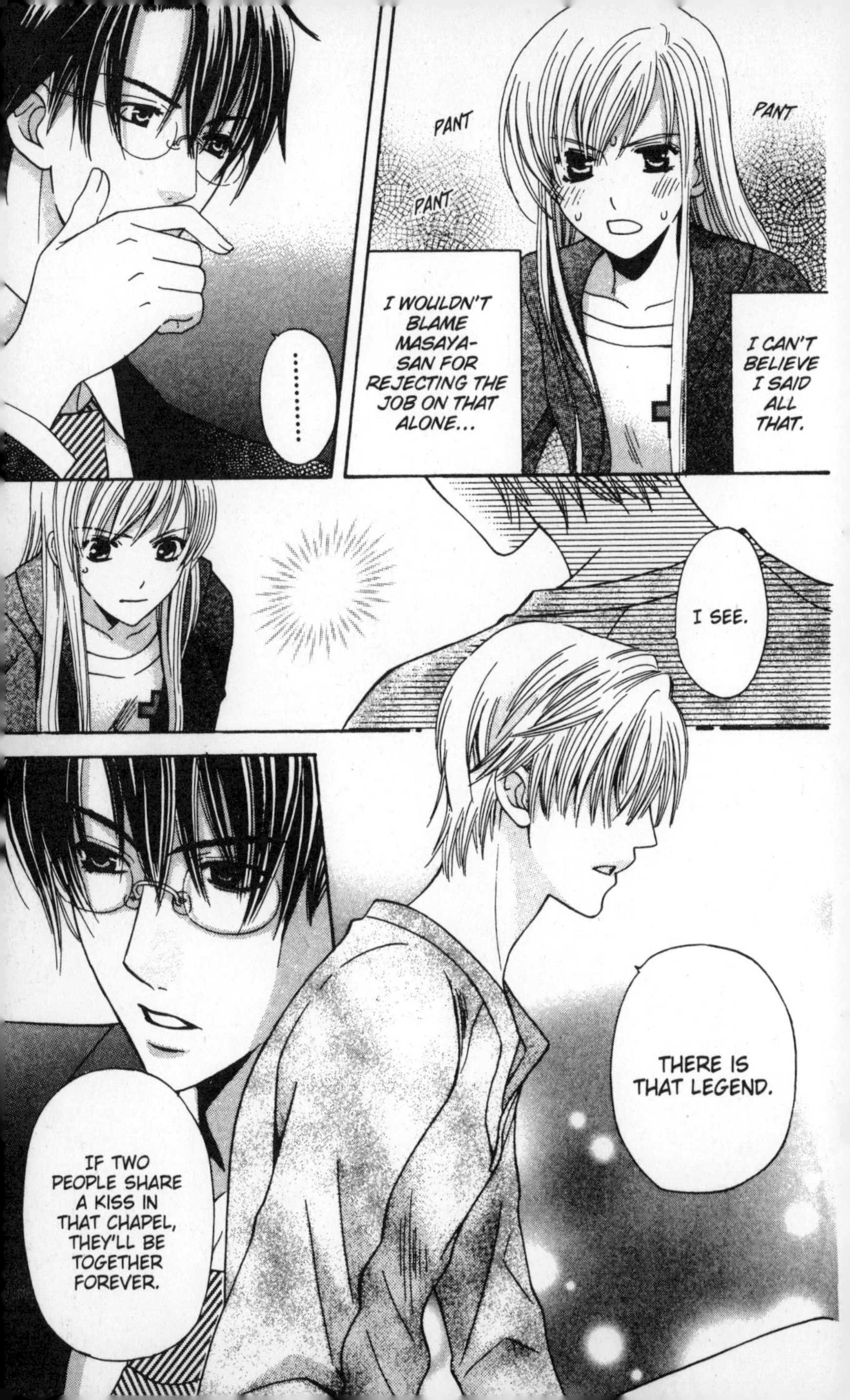
PANT
PANT
PANT
I CAN'T BELIEVE I SAID ALL THAT.
I WOULDN'T BLAME MASAYA-SAN FOR REJECTING THE JOB ON THAT ALONE...
......
I SEE.
THERE IS THAT LEGEND.
IF TWO PEOPLE SHARE A KISS IN THAT CHAPEL, THEY'LL BE TOGETHER FOREVER.

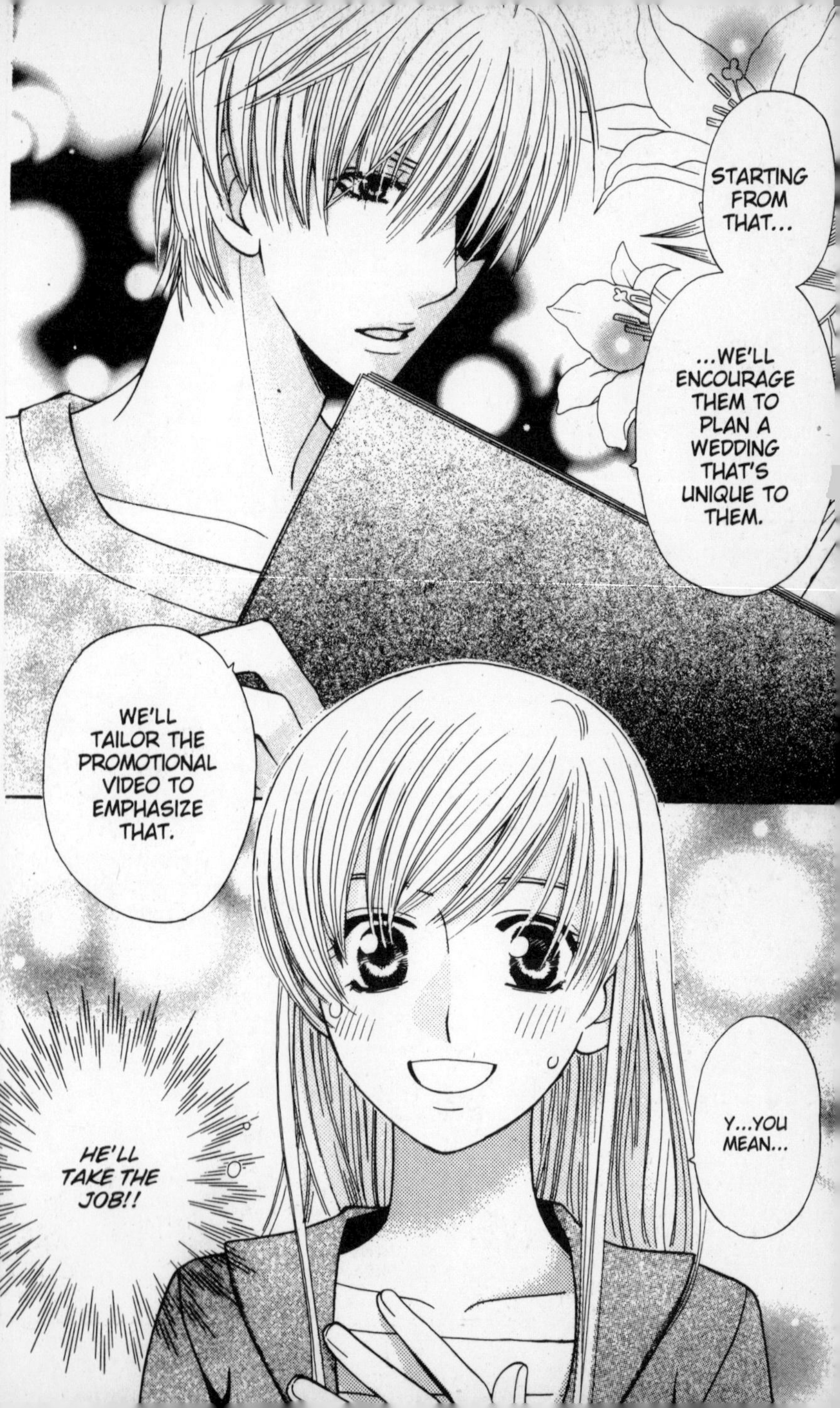
STARTING FROM THAT...
...WE'LL ENCOURAGE THEM TO PLAN A WEDDING THAT'S UNIQUE TO THEM.
WE'LL TAILOR THE PROMOTIONAL VIDEO TO EMPHASIZE THAT.
Y...YOU MEAN...
HE'LL TAKE THE JOB!!

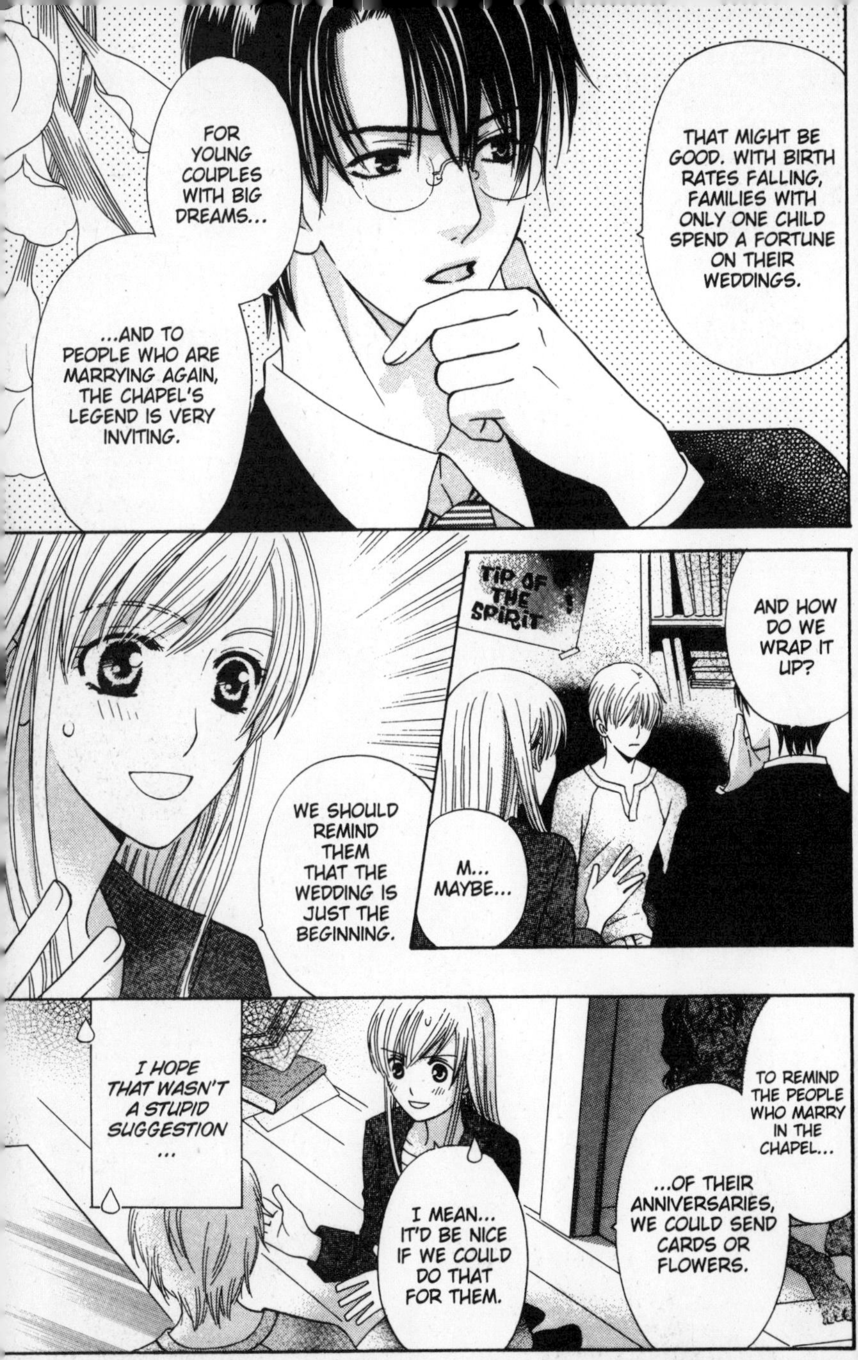
THAT MIGHT BE GOOD. WITH BIRTH RATES FALLING, FAMILIES WITH ONLY ONE CHILD SPEND A FORTUNE ON THEIR WEDDINGS.
FOR YOUNG COUPLES WITH BIG DREAMS...
...AND TO PEOPLE WHO ARE MARRYING AGAIN, THE CHAPEL'S LEGEND IS VERY INVITING.
AND HOW DO WE WRAP IT UP?
TIP OF THE SPIRIT
M... MAYBE...
WE SHOULD REMIND THEM THAT THE WEDDING IS JUST THE BEGINNING.
TO REMIND THE PEOPLE WHO MARRY IN THE CHAPEL...
...OF THEIR ANNIVERSARIES, WE COULD SEND CARDS OR FLOWERS.
I MEAN... IT'D BE NICE IF WE COULD DO THAT FOR THEM.
I HOPE THAT WASN'T A STUPID SUGGESTION...

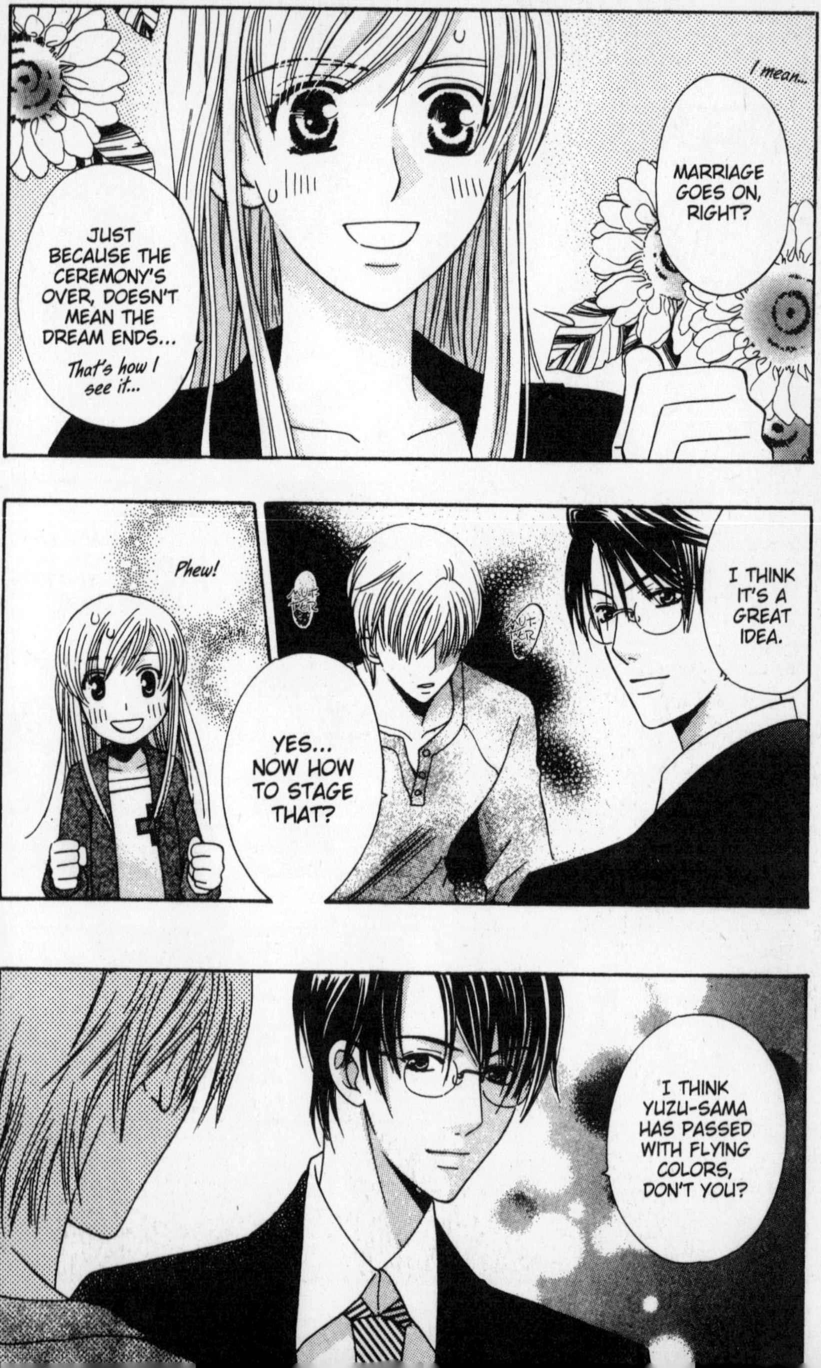
I mean...
MARRIAGE GOES ON, RIGHT?
JUST BECAUSE THE CEREMONY'S OVER, DOESN'T MEAN THE DREAM ENDS...
That's how I see it...
I THINK IT'S A GREAT IDEA.
MUTTER
MUTTER
YES... NOW HOW TO STAGE THAT?
Phew!
I THINK YUZU-SAMA HAS PASSED WITH FLYING COLORS, DON'T YOU?

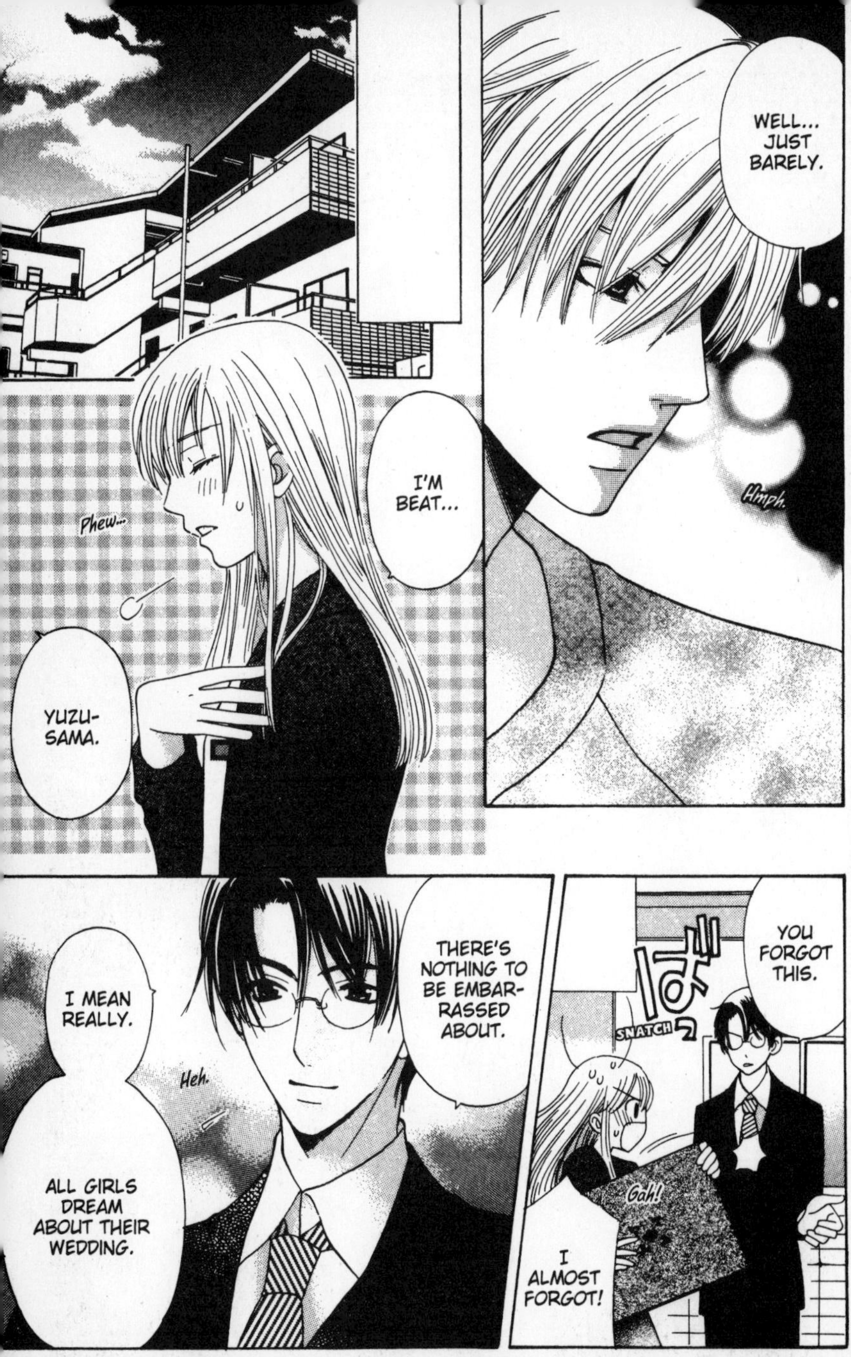
WELL... JUST BARELY.
Hmph.
I'M BEAT...
Phew...
YUZU-SAMA.
YOU FORGOT THIS.
SNATCH
Gah!
I ALMOST FORGOT!
THERE'S NOTHING TO BE EMBAR-RASSED ABOUT.
I MEAN REALLY.
Heh.
ALL GIRLS DREAM ABOUT THEIR WEDDING.

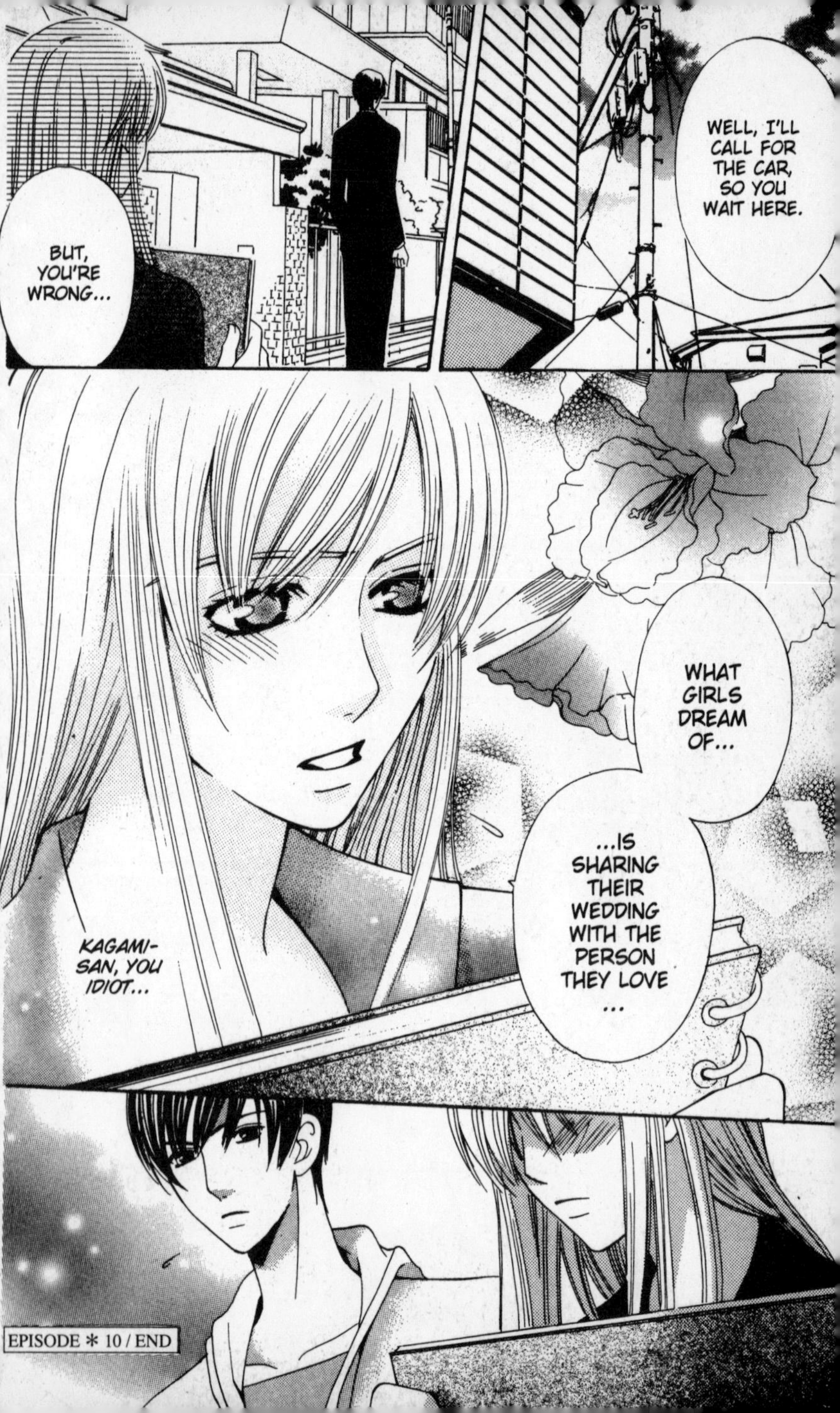
WELL, I'LL CALL FOR THE CAR, SO YOU WAIT HERE.
BUT, YOU'RE WRONG...
WHAT GIRLS DREAM OF...
...IS SHARING THEIR WEDDING WITH THE PERSON THEY LOVE ...
KAGAMI-SAN, YOU IDIOT...
EPISODE * 10 / END

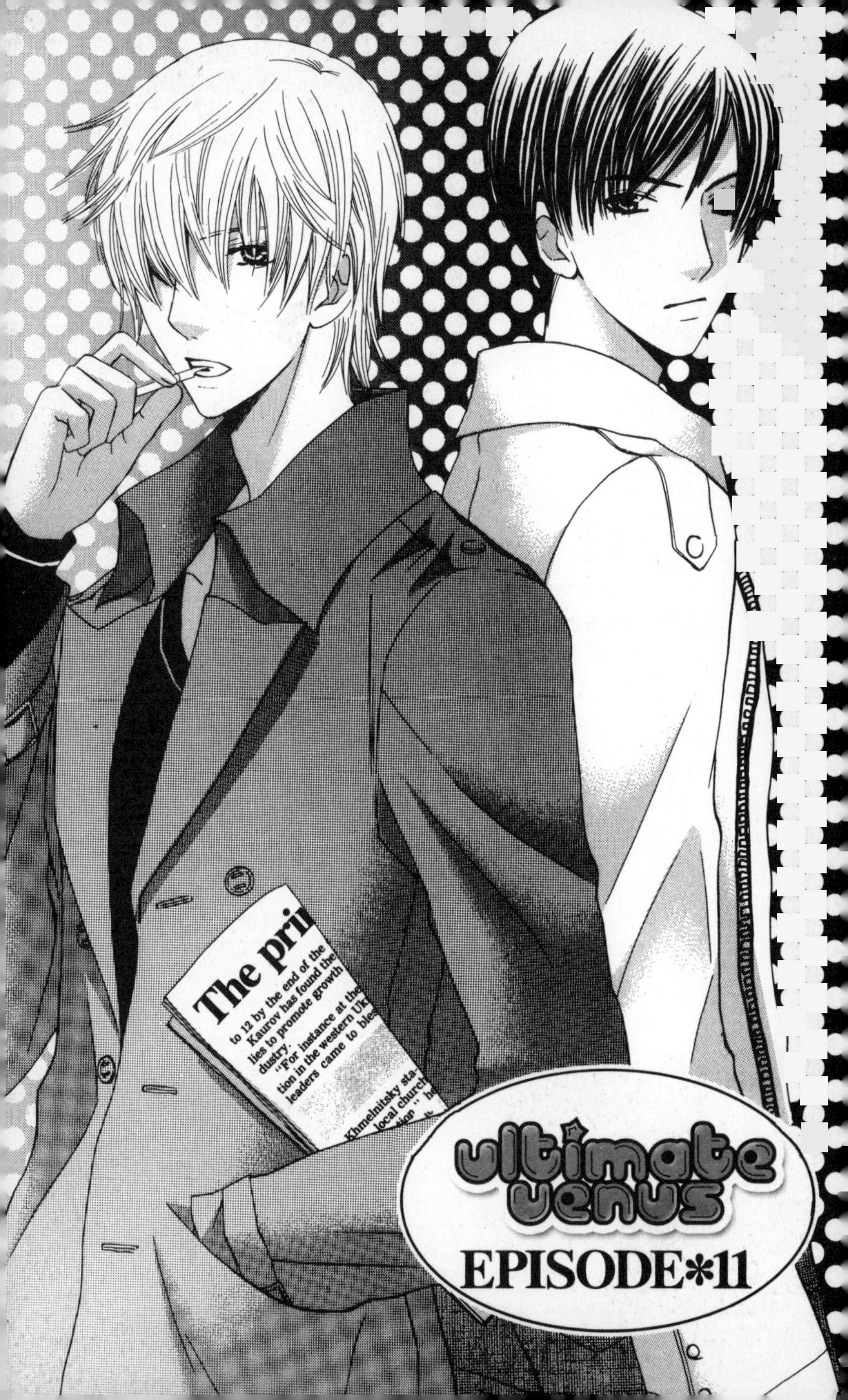
The pri
to 12 by the end of the
Kaurov has found the
lies to promote growth
dustry.
"For instance at the
tion in the western Uk
leaders came to bles
Khmelnitsky sta-
local church
ultimate venus
EPISODE*11

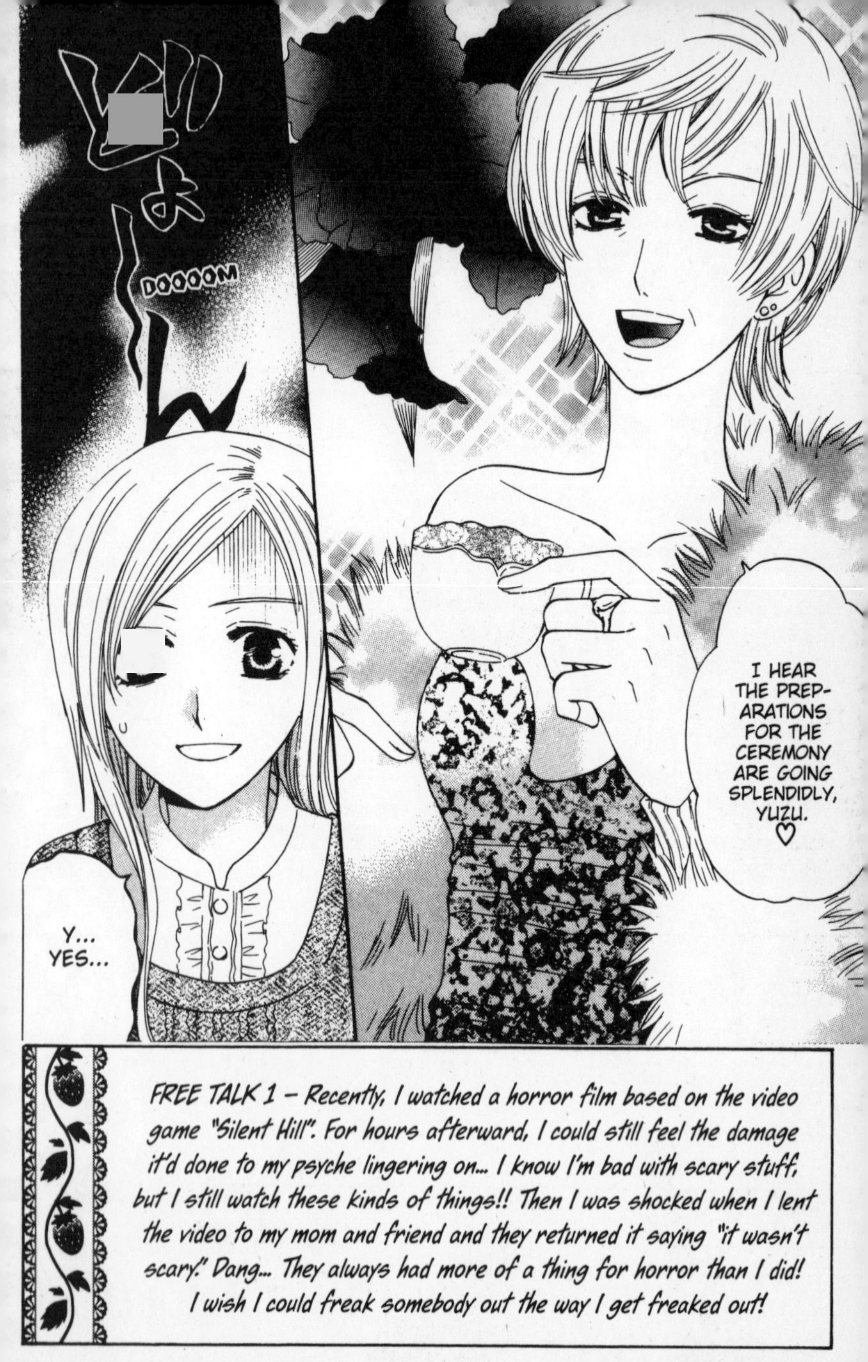
I HEAR THE PREP-ARATIONS FOR THE CEREMONY ARE GOING SPLENDIDLY, YUZU. ♡
DOOOOM
Y... YES...

FREE TALK 1 – Recently, I watched a horror film based on the video game "Silent Hill". For hours afterward, I could still feel the damage it'd done to my psyche lingering on... I know I'm bad with scary stuff, but I still watch these kinds of things!! Then I was shocked when I lent the video to my mom and friend and they returned it saying "it wasn't scary." Dang... They always had more of a thing for horror than I did! I wish I could freak somebody out the way I get freaked out!

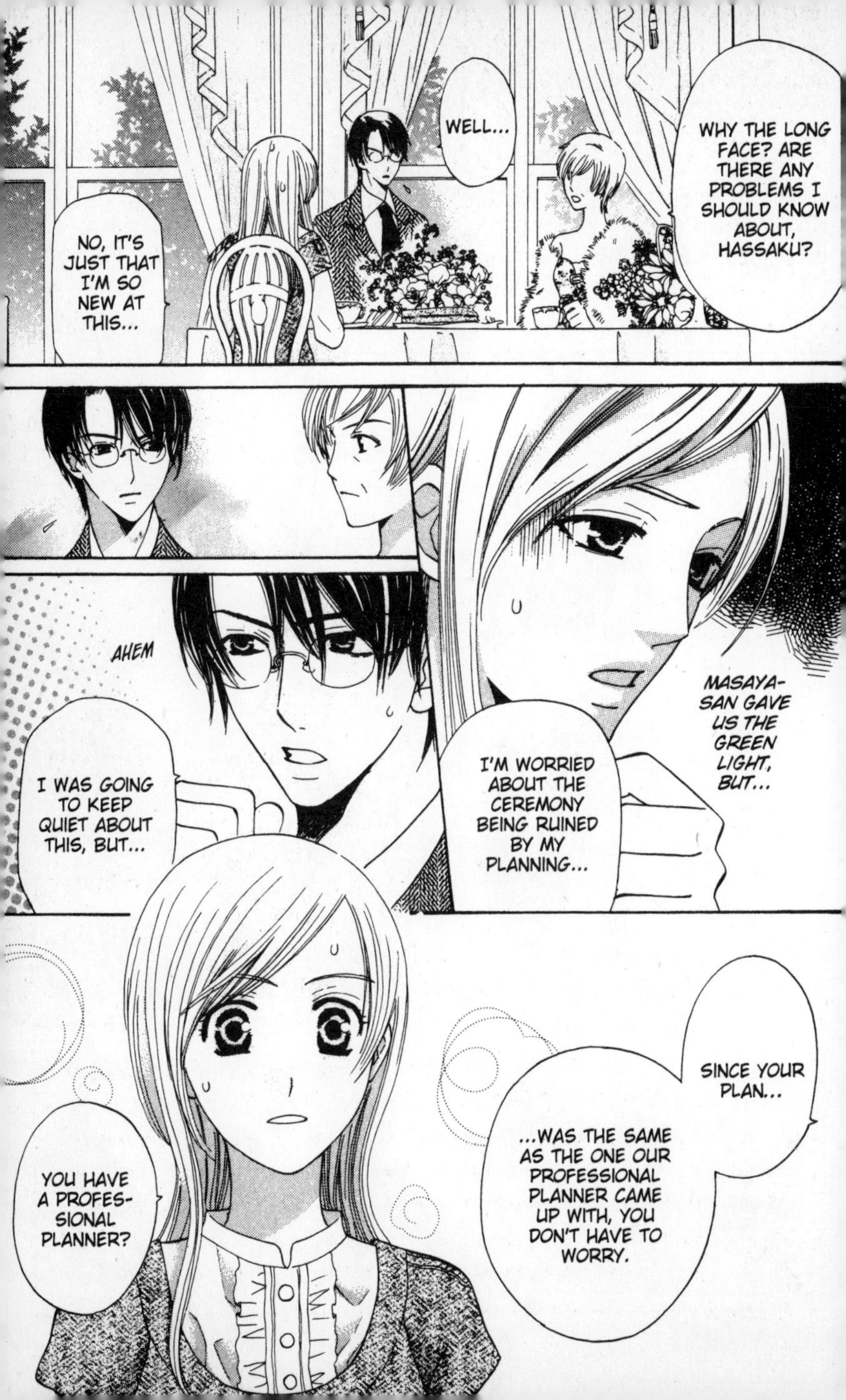
WHY THE LONG FACE? ARE THERE ANY PROBLEMS I SHOULD KNOW ABOUT, HASSAKU?
WELL...
NO, IT'S JUST THAT I'M SO NEW AT THIS...
MASAYA-SAN GAVE US THE GREEN LIGHT, BUT...
I'M WORRIED ABOUT THE CEREMONY BEING RUINED BY MY PLANNING...
AHEM
I WAS GOING TO KEEP QUIET ABOUT THIS, BUT...
SINCE YOUR PLAN...
...WAS THE SAME AS THE ONE OUR PROFESSIONAL PLANNER CAME UP WITH, YOU DON'T HAVE TO WORRY.
YOU HAVE A PROFES-SIONAL PLANNER?

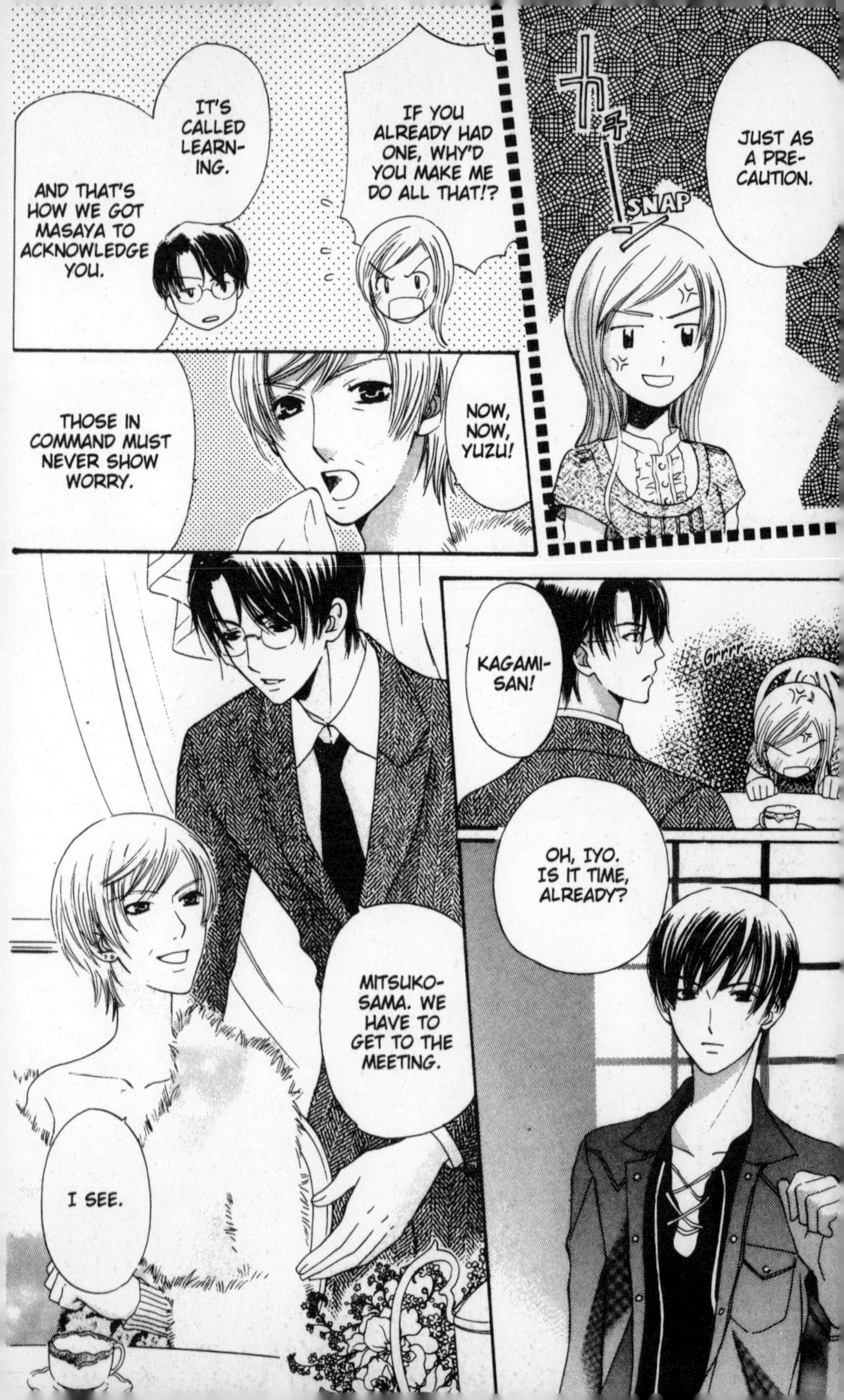
JUST AS A PRE-CAUTION.
SNAP
IF YOU ALREADY HAD ONE, WHY'D YOU MAKE ME DO ALL THAT!?
IT'S CALLED LEARN-ING.
AND THAT'S HOW WE GOT MASAYA TO ACKNOWLEDGE YOU.
NOW, NOW, YUZU!
THOSE IN COMMAND MUST NEVER SHOW WORRY.
KAGAMI-SAN!
Grrrr...
OH, IYO. IS IT TIME, ALREADY?
MITSUKO-SAMA. WE HAVE TO GET TO THE MEETING.
I SEE.

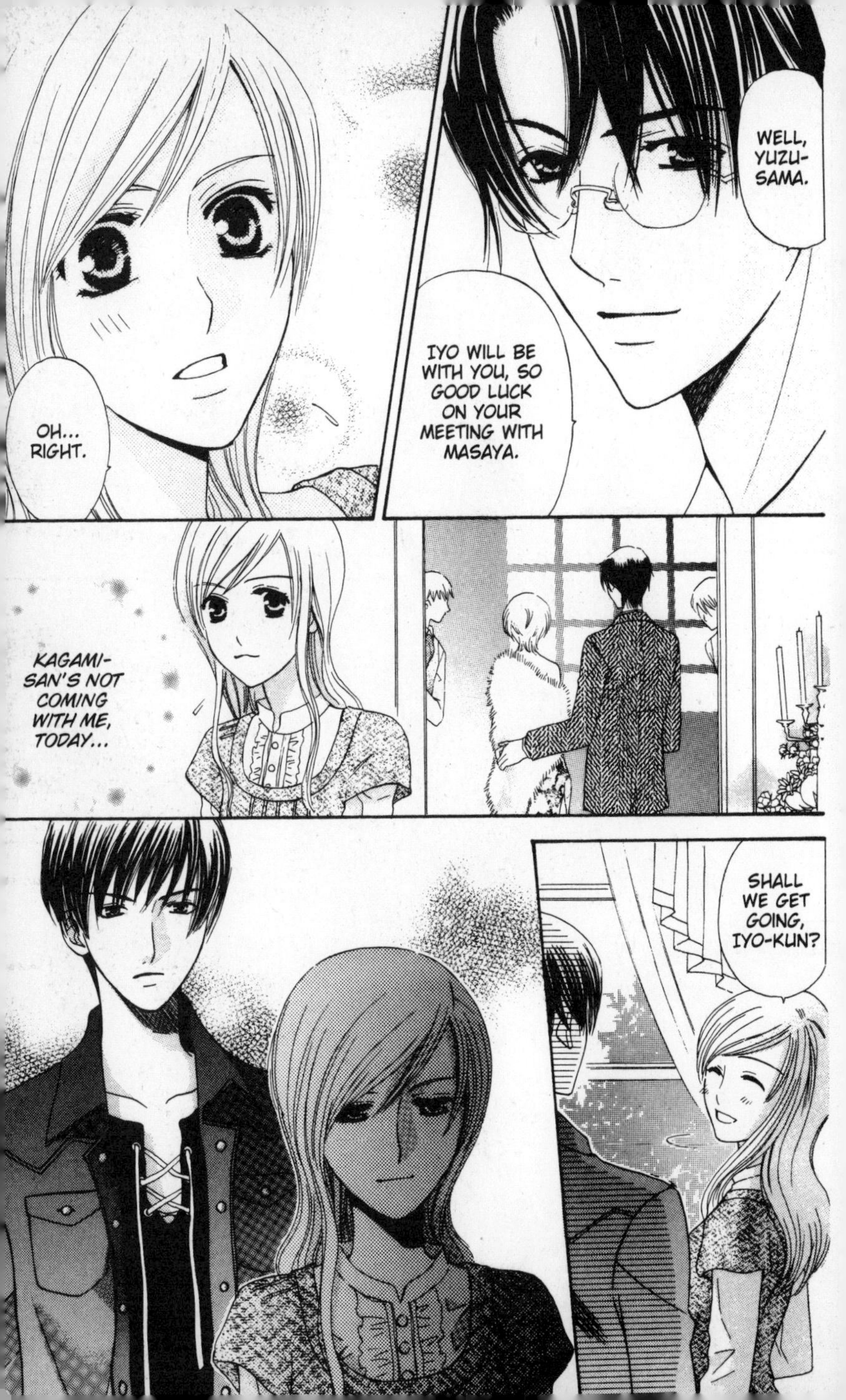
WELL, YUZU-SAMA.
IYO WILL BE WITH YOU, SO GOOD LUCK ON YOUR MEETING WITH MASAYA.
OH... RIGHT.
KAGAMI-SAN'S NOT COMING WITH ME, TODAY...
SHALL WE GET GOING, IYO-KUN?

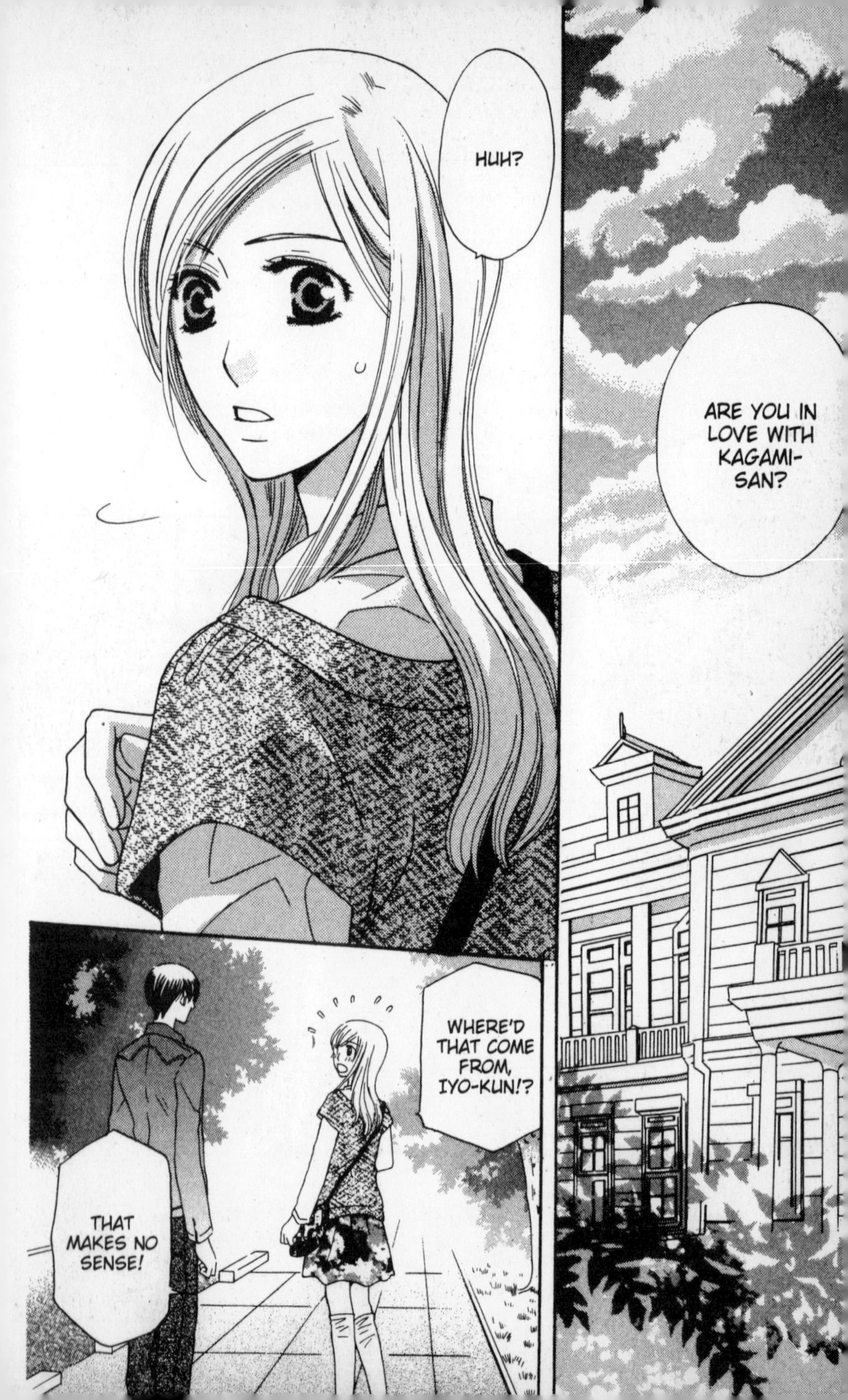
ARE YOU IN LOVE WITH KAGAMI-SAN?
HUH?
WHERE'D THAT COME FROM, IYO-KUN!?
THAT MAKES NO SENSE!

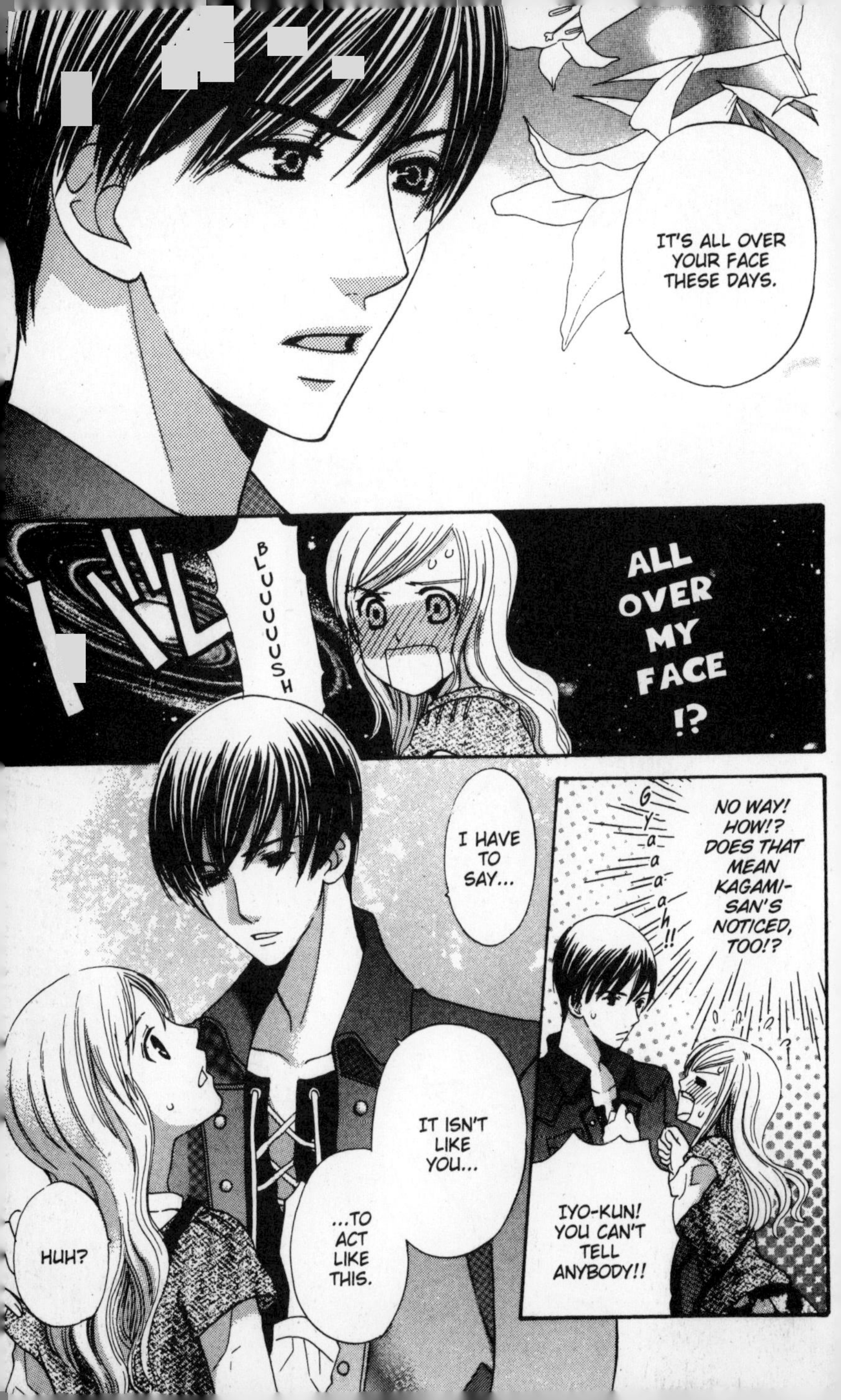
IT'S ALL OVER YOUR FACE THESE DAYS.
ALL OVER MY FACE !?
BLUUUUUSH
NO WAY! HOW!? DOES THAT MEAN KAGAMI-SAN'S NOTICED, TOO!?
Gyaaaaah!!
IYO-KUN! YOU CAN'T TELL ANYBODY!!
I HAVE TO SAY...
IT ISN'T LIKE YOU...
...TO ACT LIKE THIS.
HUH?

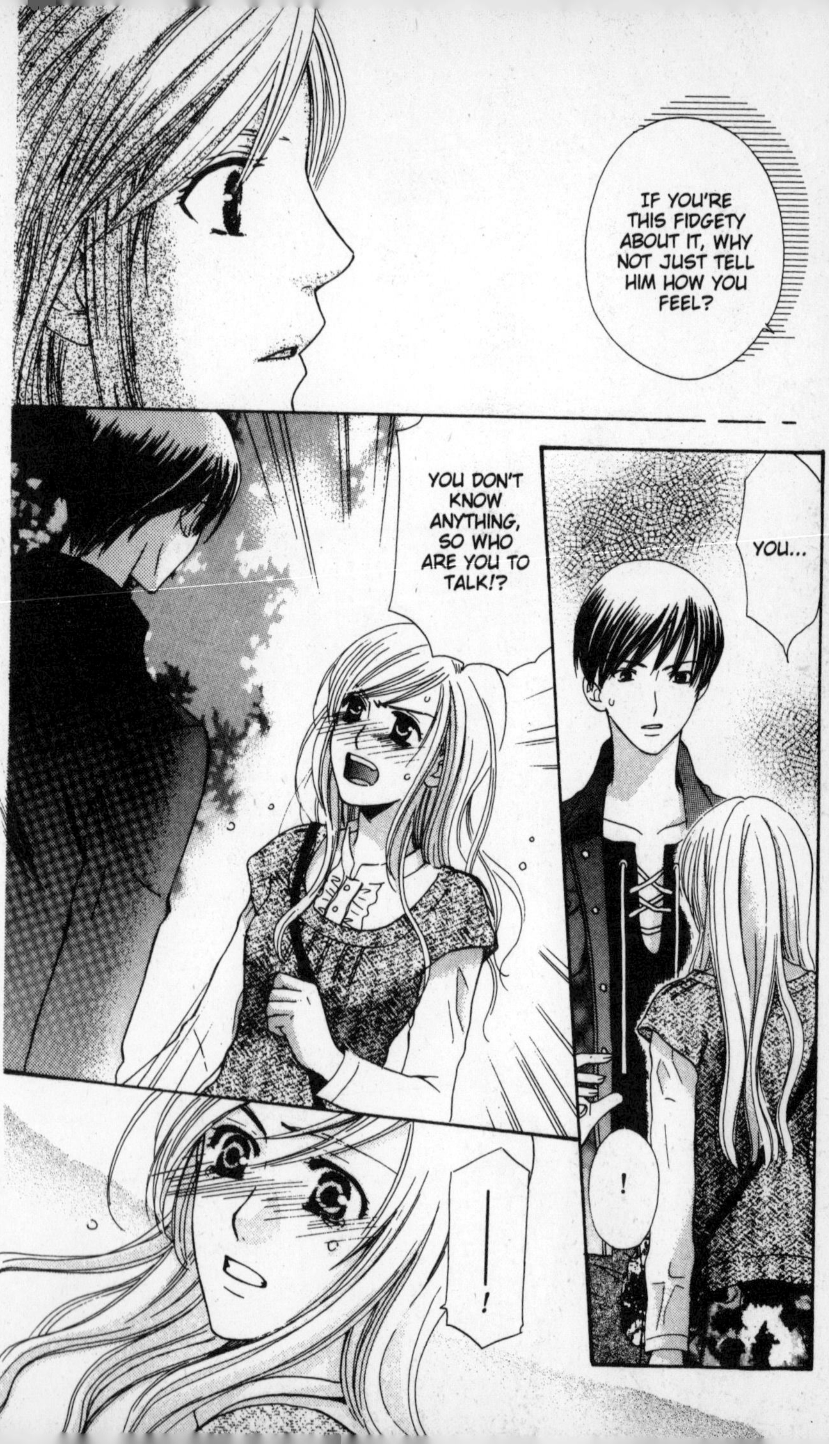
IF YOU'RE THIS FIDGETY ABOUT IT, WHY NOT JUST TELL HIM HOW YOU FEEL?
YOU...
!
YOU DON'T KNOW ANYTHING, SO WHO ARE YOU TO TALK!?
!

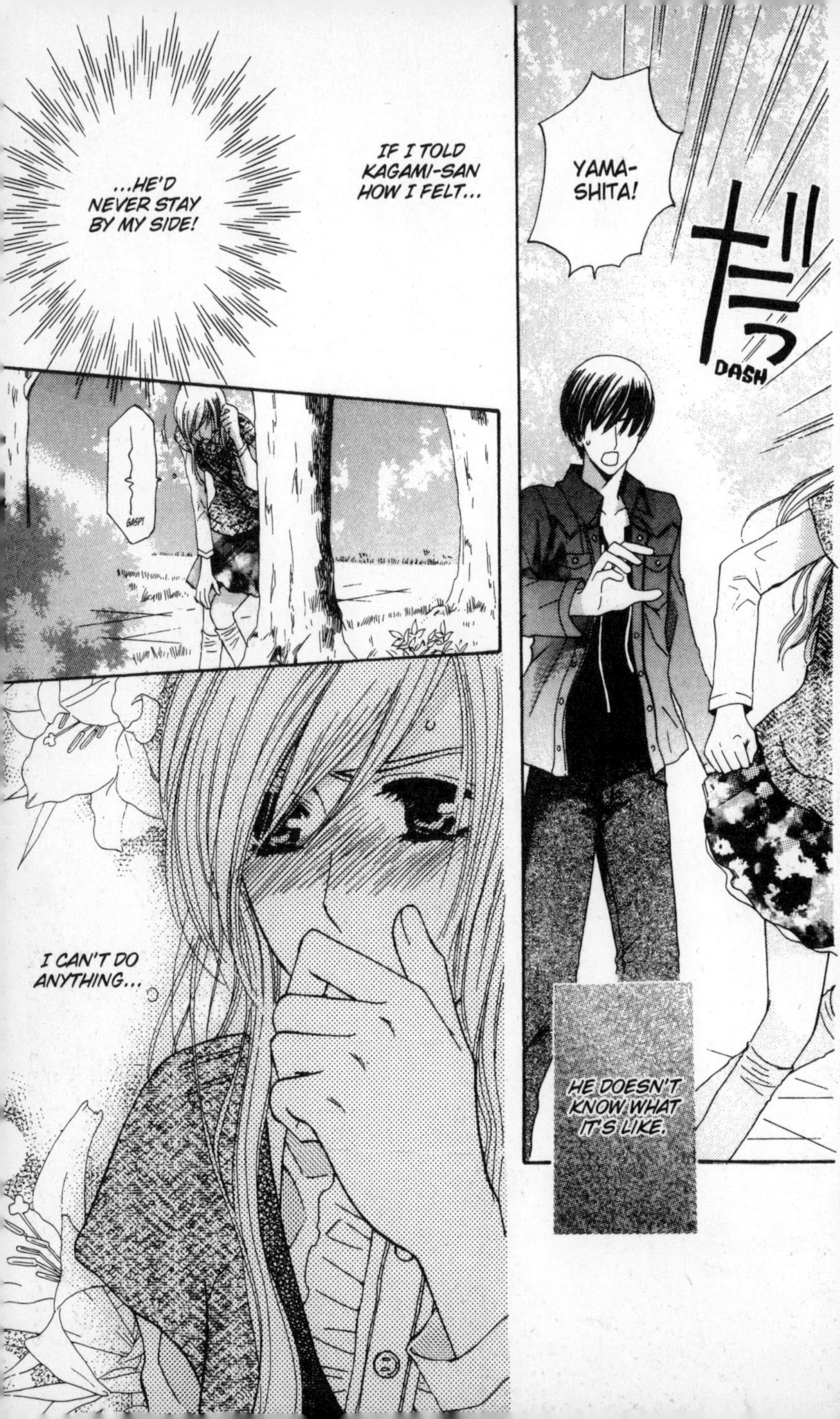
YAMA-SHITA!
ダッ
DASH
HE DOESN'T KNOW WHAT IT'S LIKE.
IF I TOLD KAGAMI-SAN HOW I FELT...
...HE'D NEVER STAY BY MY SIDE!
GASP!
I CAN'T DO ANYTHING...

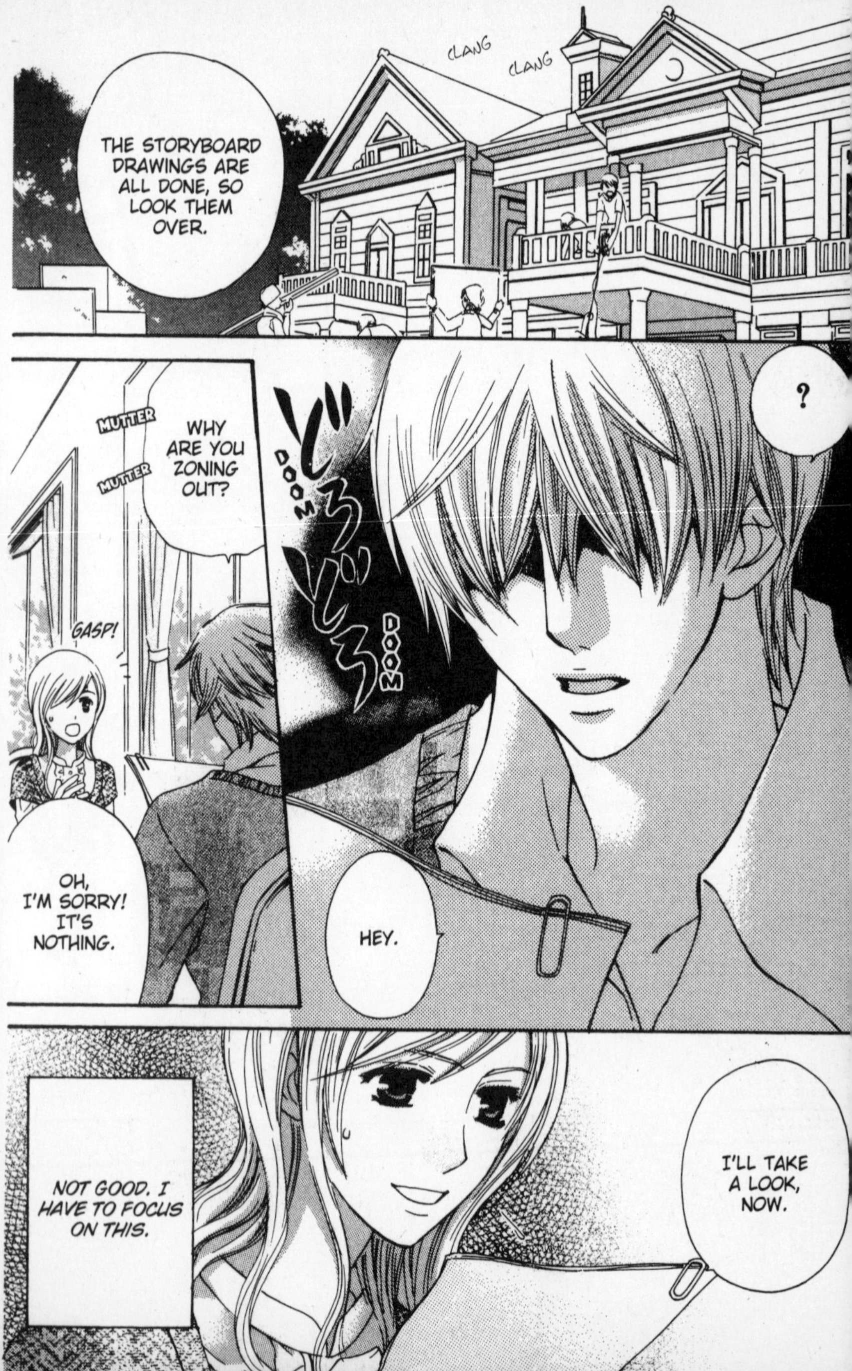
CLANG
CLANG
THE STORYBOARD DRAWINGS ARE ALL DONE, SO LOOK THEM OVER.
?
DOOM
DOOM
HEY.
MUTTER
MUTTER
WHY ARE YOU ZONING OUT?
GASP!
OH, I'M SORRY! IT'S NOTHING.
I'LL TAKE A LOOK, NOW.
NOT GOOD. I HAVE TO FOCUS ON THIS.

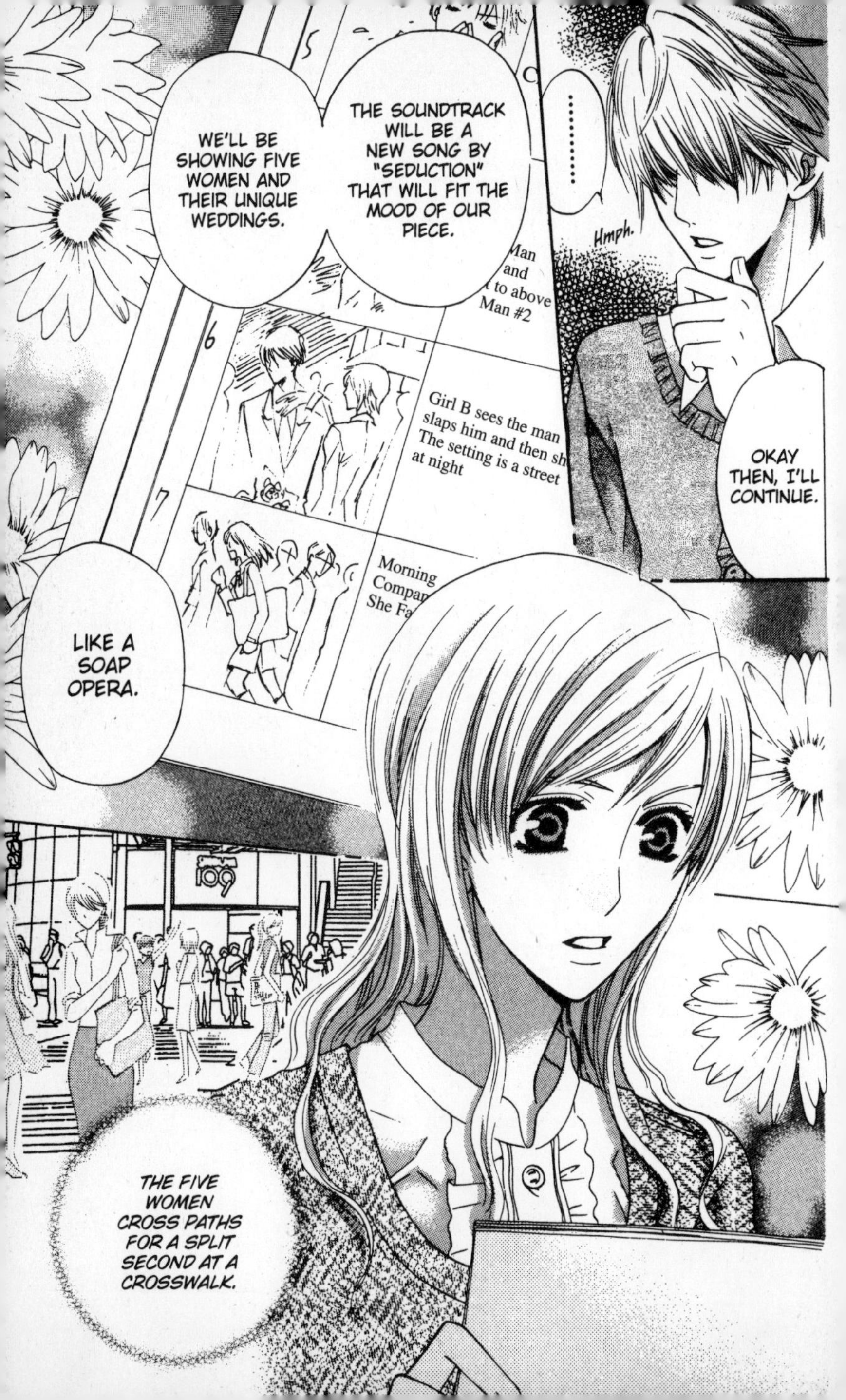

......
Hmph.
OKAY THEN, I'LL CONTINUE.
THE SOUNDTRACK WILL BE A NEW SONG BY "SEDUCTION" THAT WILL FIT THE MOOD OF OUR PIECE.
WE'LL BE SHOWING FIVE WOMEN AND THEIR UNIQUE WEDDINGS.
Man
and
t to above
Man #2
Girl B sees the man
slaps him and then sh
The setting is a street
at night
Morning
Compan
She Fa
LIKE A SOAP OPERA.
109
THE FIVE WOMEN CROSS PATHS FOR A SPLIT SECOND AT A CROSSWALK.

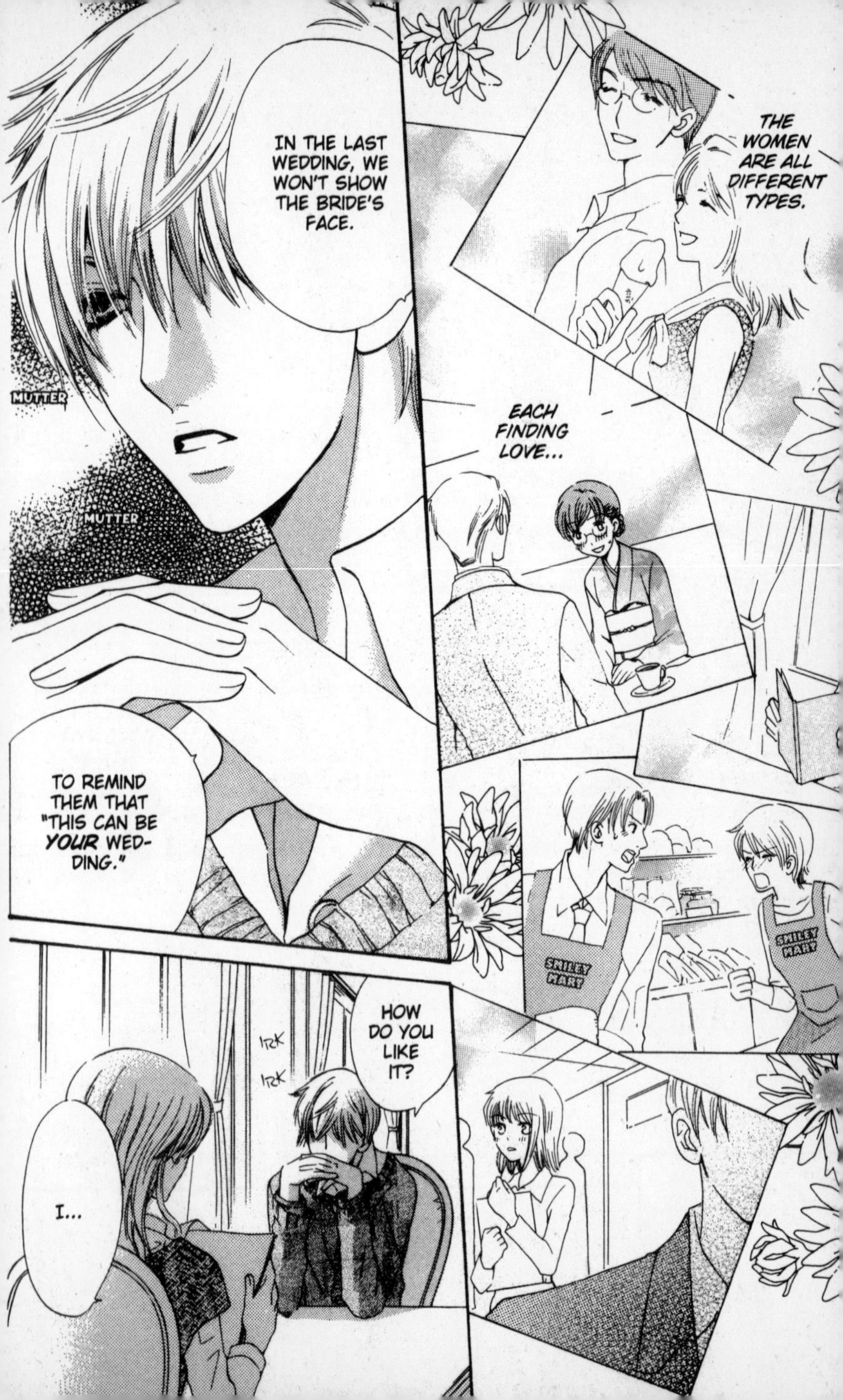
THE WOMEN ARE ALL DIFFERENT TYPES.
EACH FINDING LOVE...
IN THE LAST WEDDING, WE WON'T SHOW THE BRIDE'S FACE.
MUTTER
MUTTER
TO REMIND THEM THAT "THIS CAN BE *YOUR* WEDDING."
SMILEY MART
SMILEY MART
HOW DO YOU LIKE IT?
IRK
IRK
I...

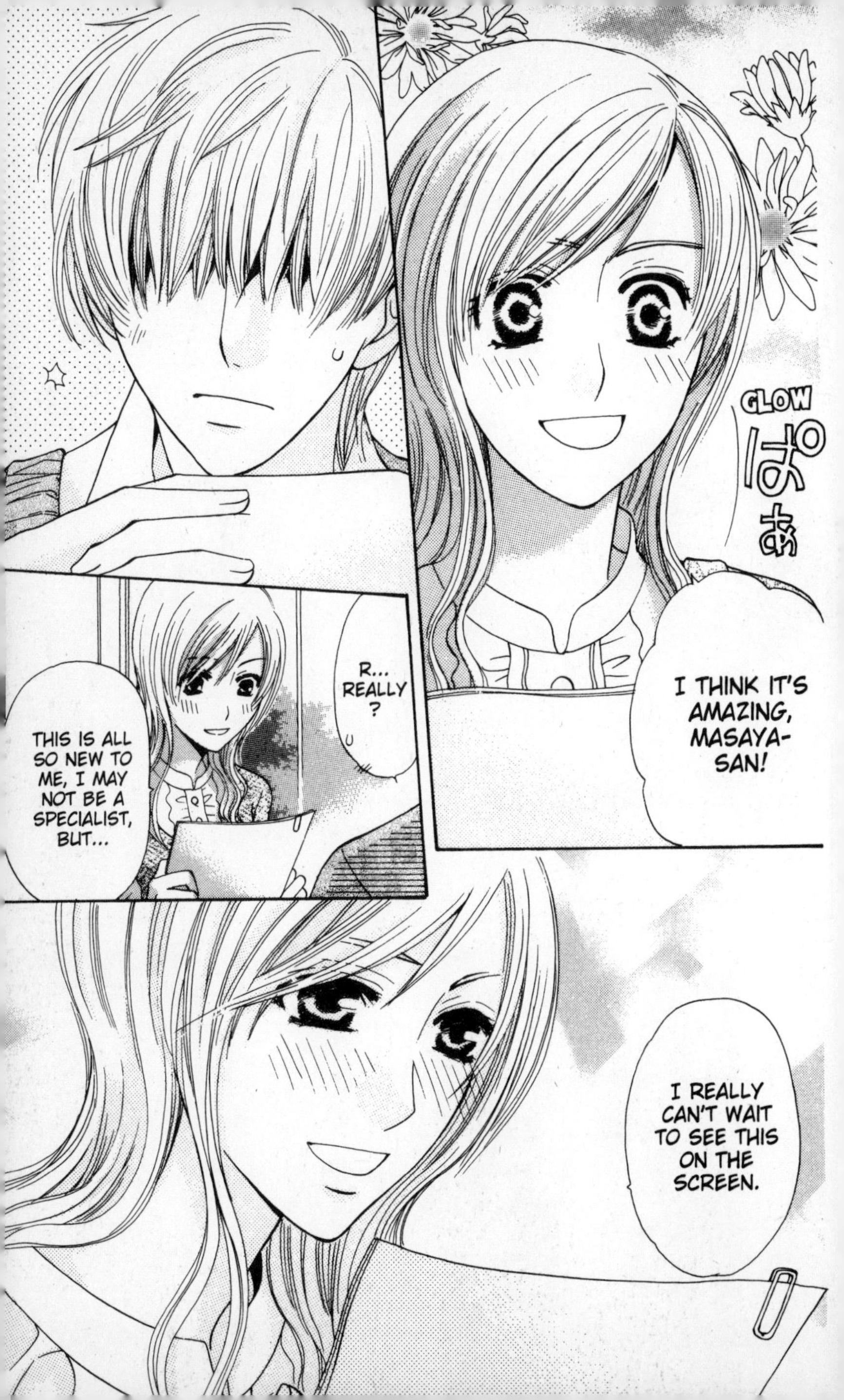
GLOW
ぱぁ
I THINK IT'S AMAZING, MASAYA-SAN!
R... REALLY?
THIS IS ALL SO NEW TO ME, I MAY NOT BE A SPECIALIST, BUT...
I REALLY CAN'T WAIT TO SEE THIS ON THE SCREEN.

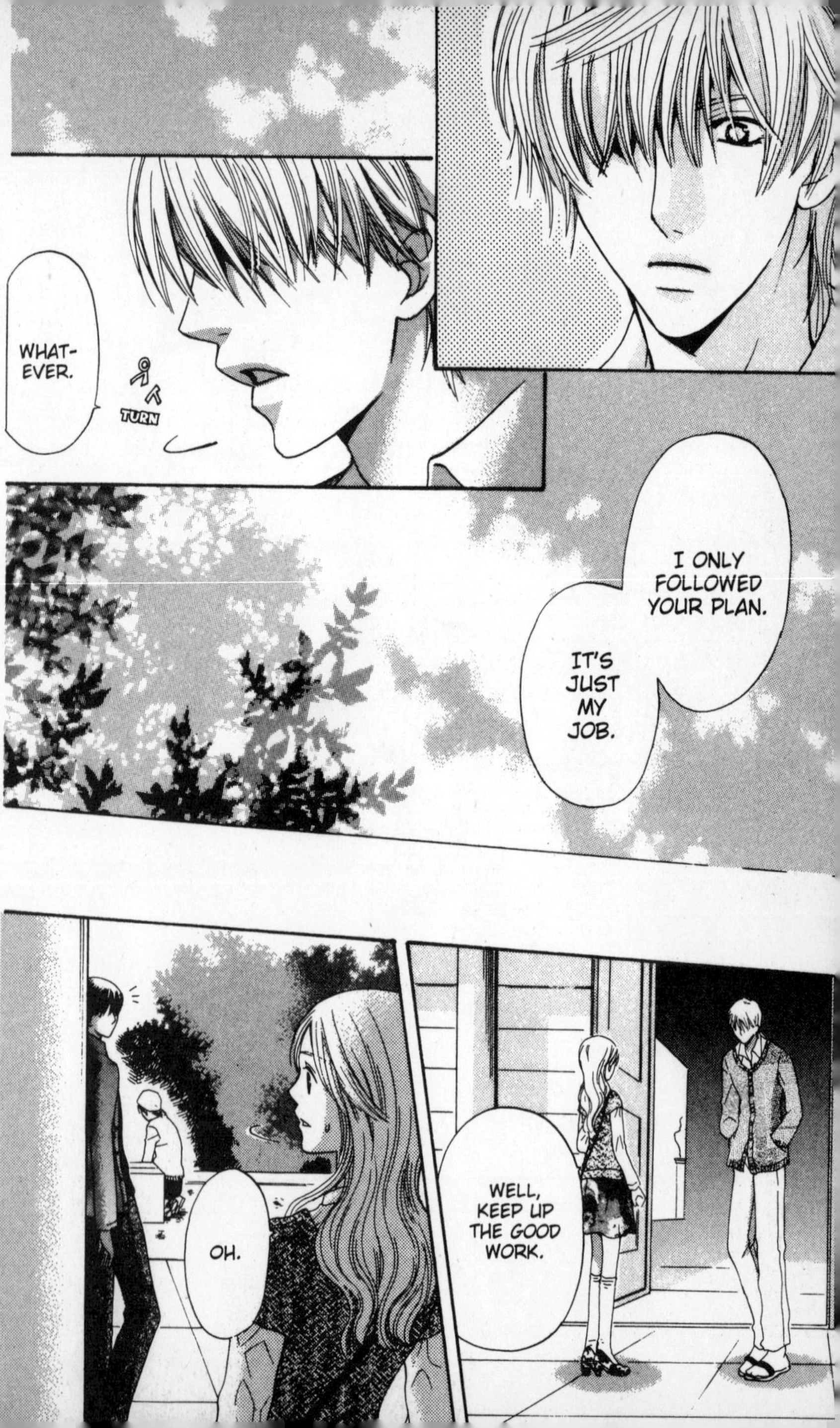
WHAT-EVER.
TURN
I ONLY FOLLOWED YOUR PLAN.
IT'S JUST MY JOB.
WELL, KEEP UP THE GOOD WORK.
OH.

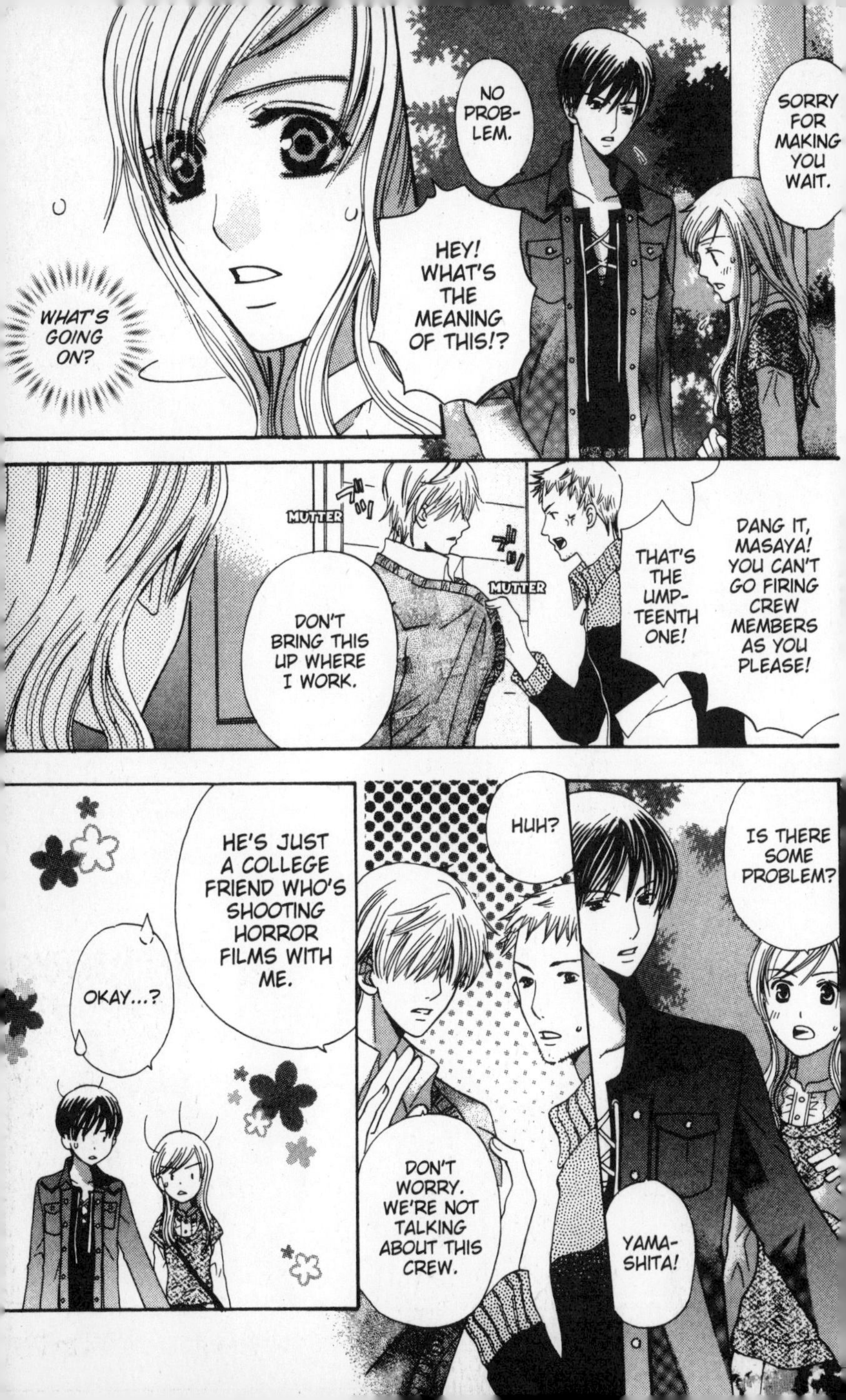
SORRY FOR MAKING YOU WAIT.
NO PROB-LEM.
HEY! WHAT'S THE MEANING OF THIS!?
WHAT'S GOING ON?
DANG IT, MASAYA! YOU CAN'T GO FIRING CREW MEMBERS AS YOU PLEASE!
THAT'S THE UMP-TEENTH ONE!
MUTTER
MUTTER
DON'T BRING THIS UP WHERE I WORK.
IS THERE SOME PROBLEM?
HUH?
YAMA-SHITA!
DON'T WORRY. WE'RE NOT TALKING ABOUT THIS CREW.
HE'S JUST A COLLEGE FRIEND WHO'S SHOOTING HORROR FILMS WITH ME.
OKAY...?

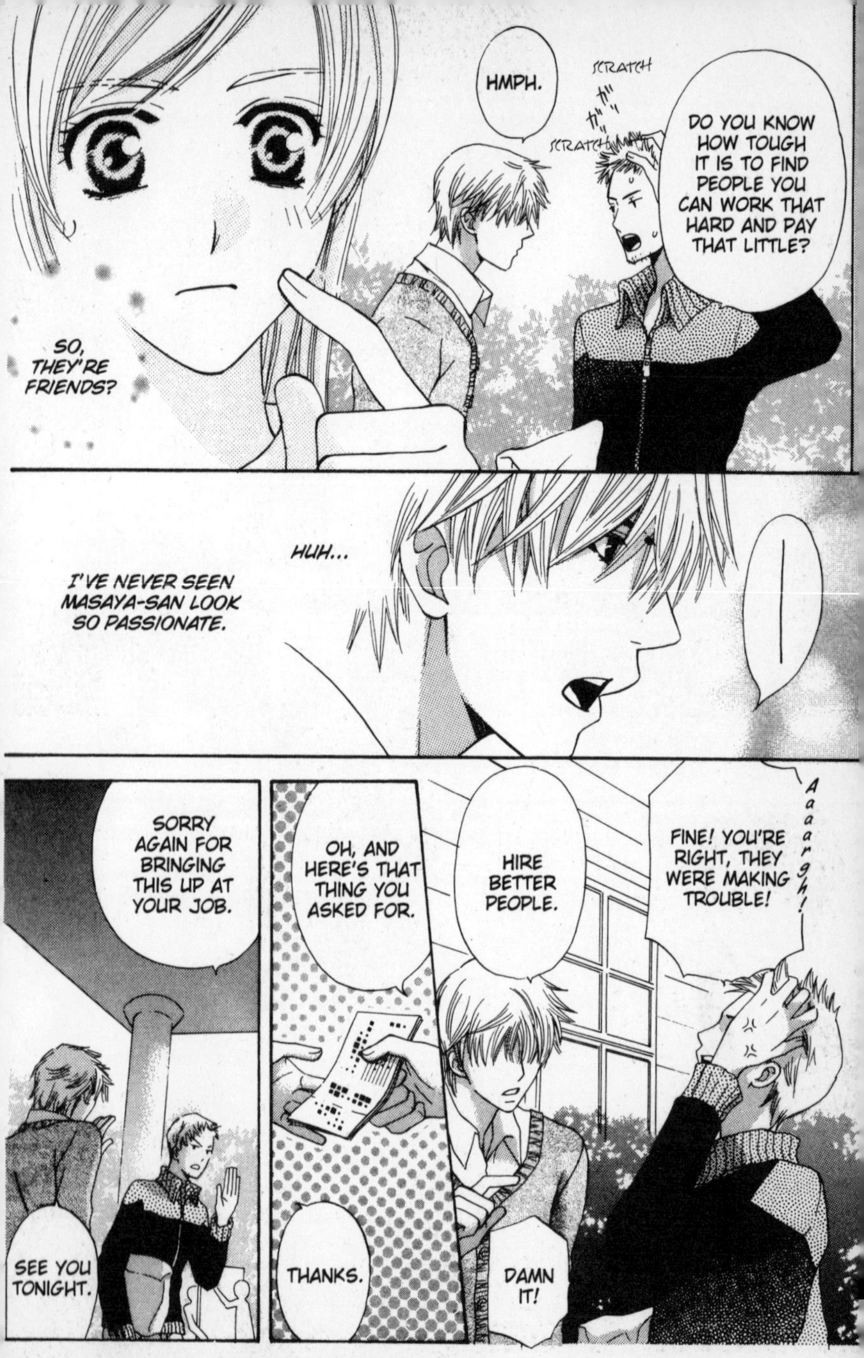
DO YOU KNOW HOW TOUGH IT IS TO FIND PEOPLE YOU CAN WORK THAT HARD AND PAY THAT LITTLE?
SCRATCH
ガ ガ
SCRATCH
HMPH.
SO, THEY'RE FRIENDS?
—
HUH...
I'VE NEVER SEEN MASAYA-SAN LOOK SO PASSIONATE.
Aaaargh!
FINE! YOU'RE RIGHT, THEY WERE MAKING TROUBLE!
HIRE BETTER PEOPLE.
DAMN IT!
OH, AND HERE'S THAT THING YOU ASKED FOR.
THANKS.
SORRY AGAIN FOR BRINGING THIS UP AT YOUR JOB.
SEE YOU TONIGHT.

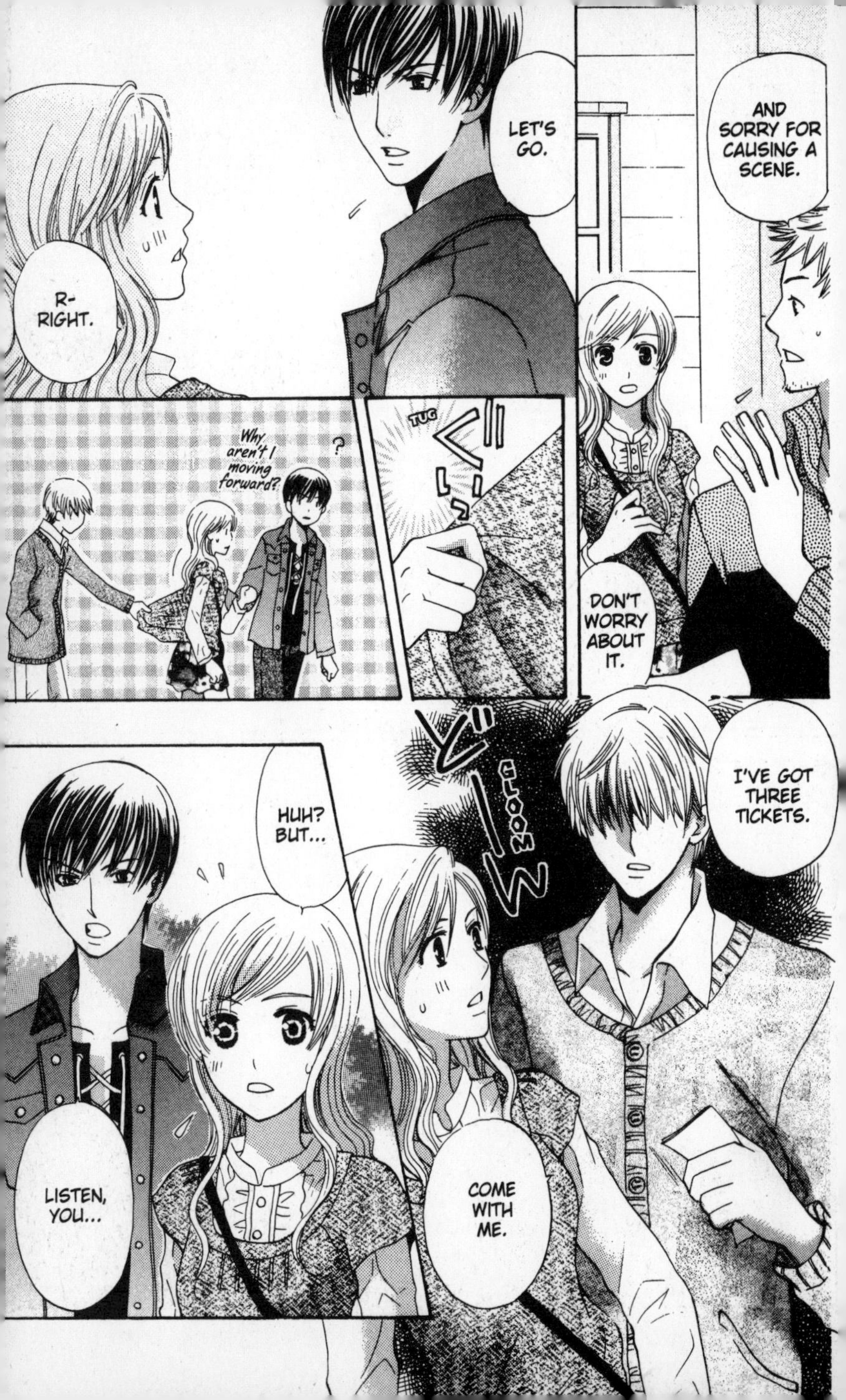
AND SORRY FOR CAUSING A SCENE.
DON'T WORRY ABOUT IT.
LET'S GO.
R-RIGHT.
TUG
Why aren't I moving forward?
GLOOM
I'VE GOT THREE TICKETS.
COME WITH ME.
HUH? BUT...
LISTEN, YOU...

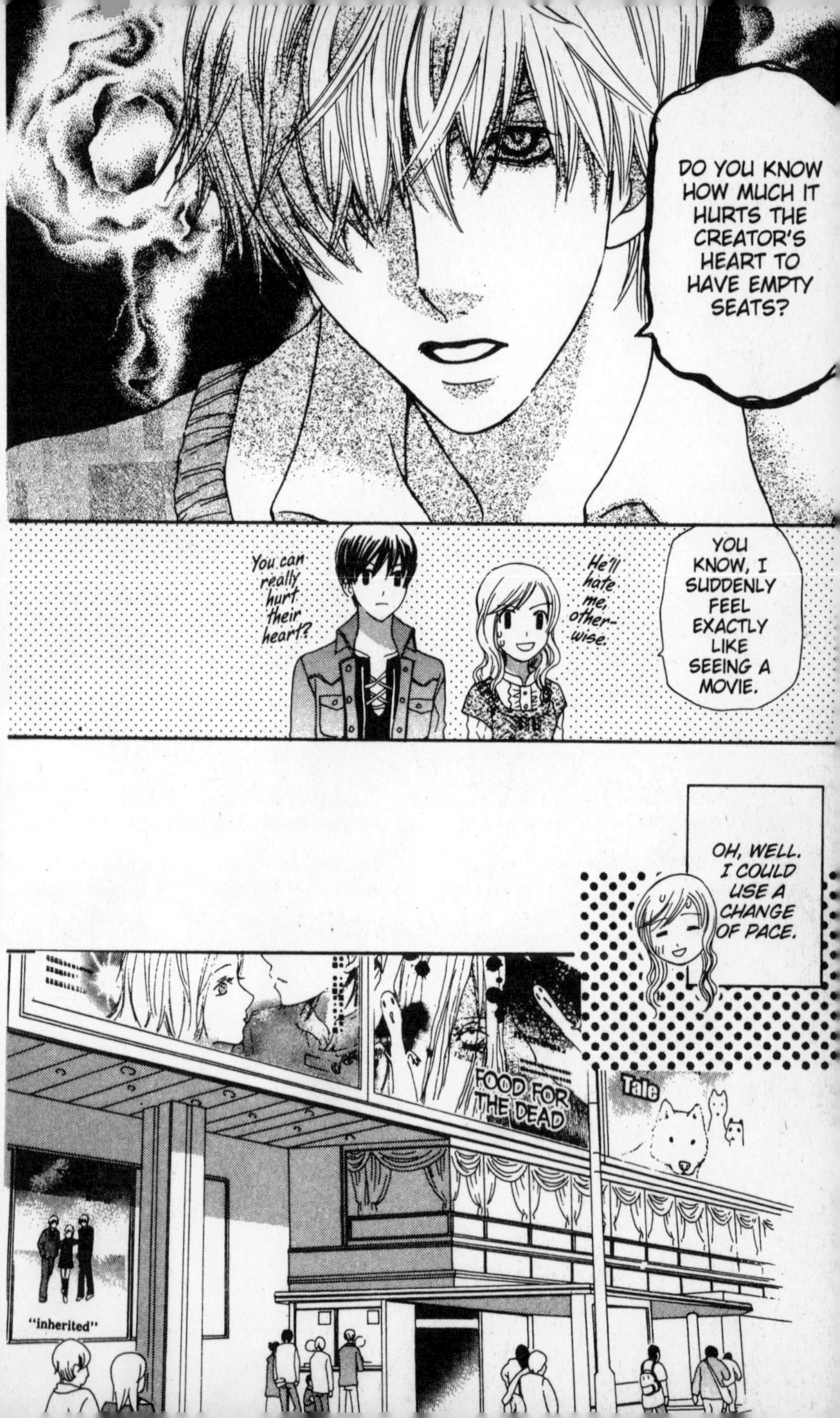
DO YOU KNOW HOW MUCH IT HURTS THE CREATOR'S HEART TO HAVE EMPTY SEATS?
YOU KNOW, I SUDDENLY FEEL EXACTLY LIKE SEEING A MOVIE.
He'll hate me, otherwise.
You can really hurt their heart?
OH, WELL. I COULD USE A CHANGE OF PACE.
Tale
FOOD FOR THE DEAD
"inherited"

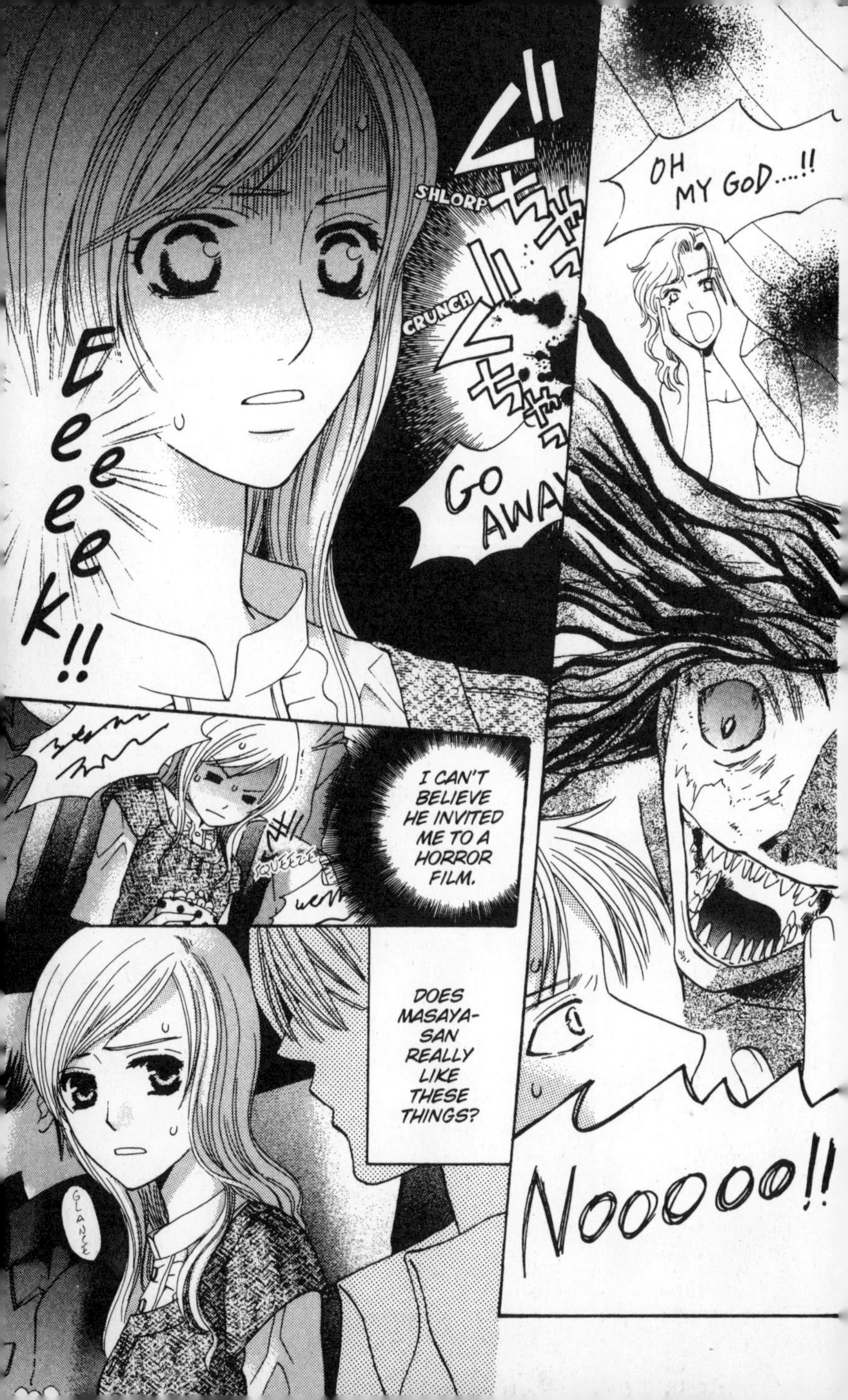

OH MY GOD....!!
NOOOOO!!
SHLORP
CRUNCH
GO AWAY
Eeeeek!!
SQUEEZE
I CAN'T BELIEVE HE INVITED ME TO A HORROR FILM.
DOES MASAYA-SAN REALLY LIKE THESE THINGS?
GLANCE

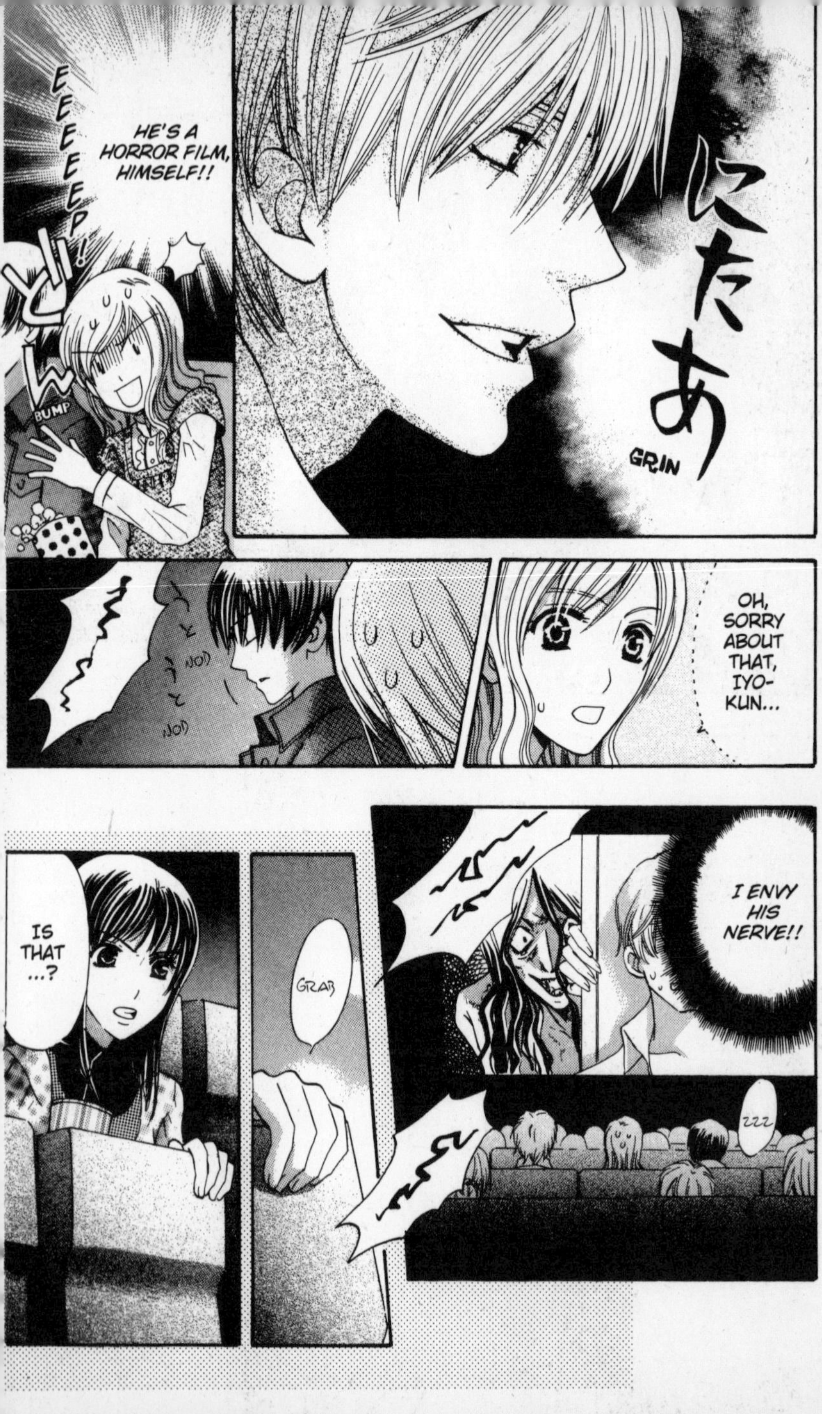
にたあ
GRIN
EEEEEEEP!
HE'S A HORROR FILM, HIMSELF!!
どん
BUMP
OH, SORRY ABOUT THAT, IYO-KUN...
NOD
NOD
I ENVY HIS NERVE!!
ZZZ
GRAB
IS THAT ...?

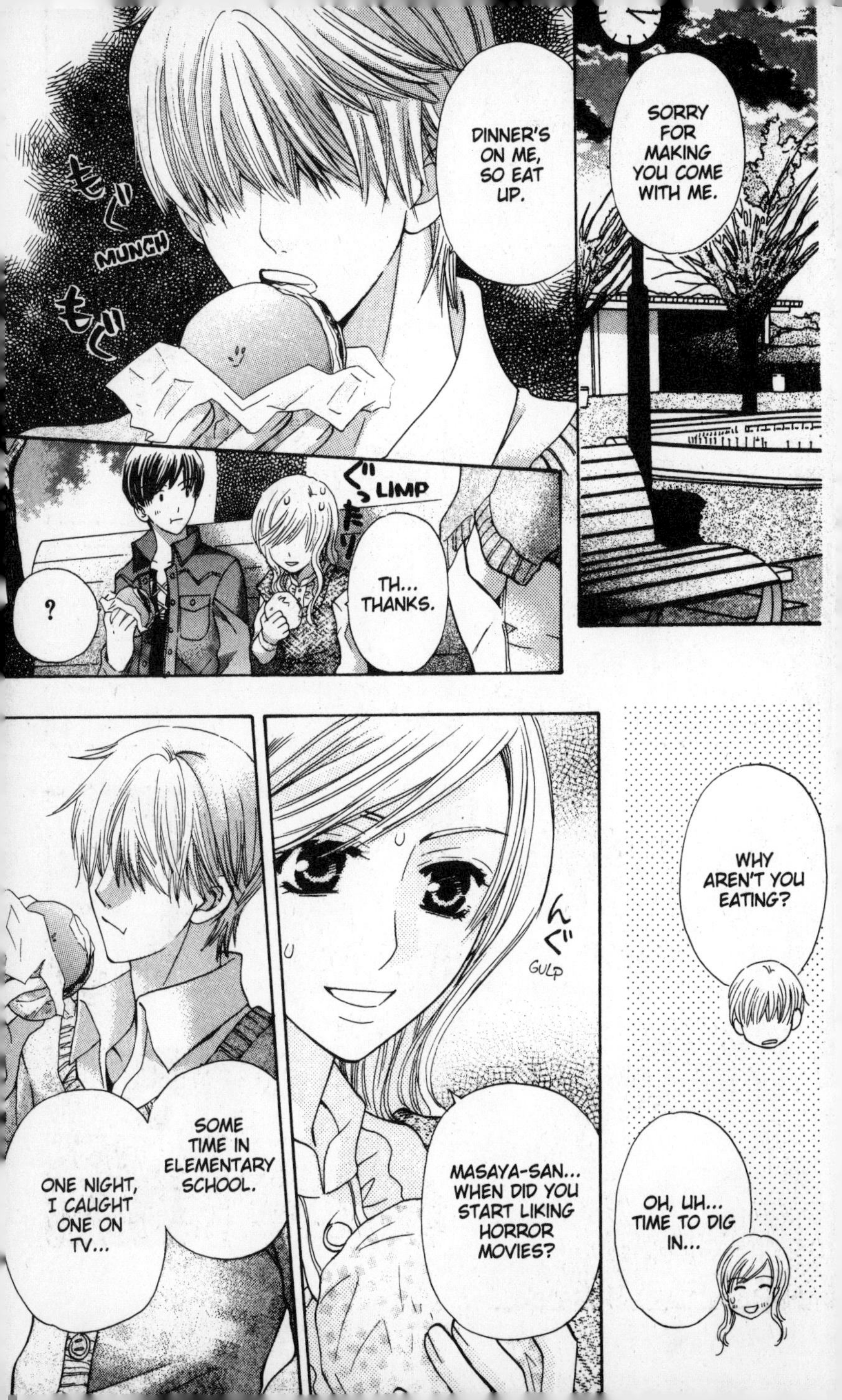
SORRY FOR MAKING YOU COME WITH ME.
DINNER'S ON ME, SO EAT UP.
もぐ
MUNCH
もぐ
LIMP
TH... THANKS.
?
WHY AREN'T YOU EATING?
OH, UH... TIME TO DIG IN...
んぐ
GULP
MASAYA-SAN... WHEN DID YOU START LIKING HORROR MOVIES?
SOME TIME IN ELEMENTARY SCHOOL.
ONE NIGHT, I CAUGHT ONE ON TV...

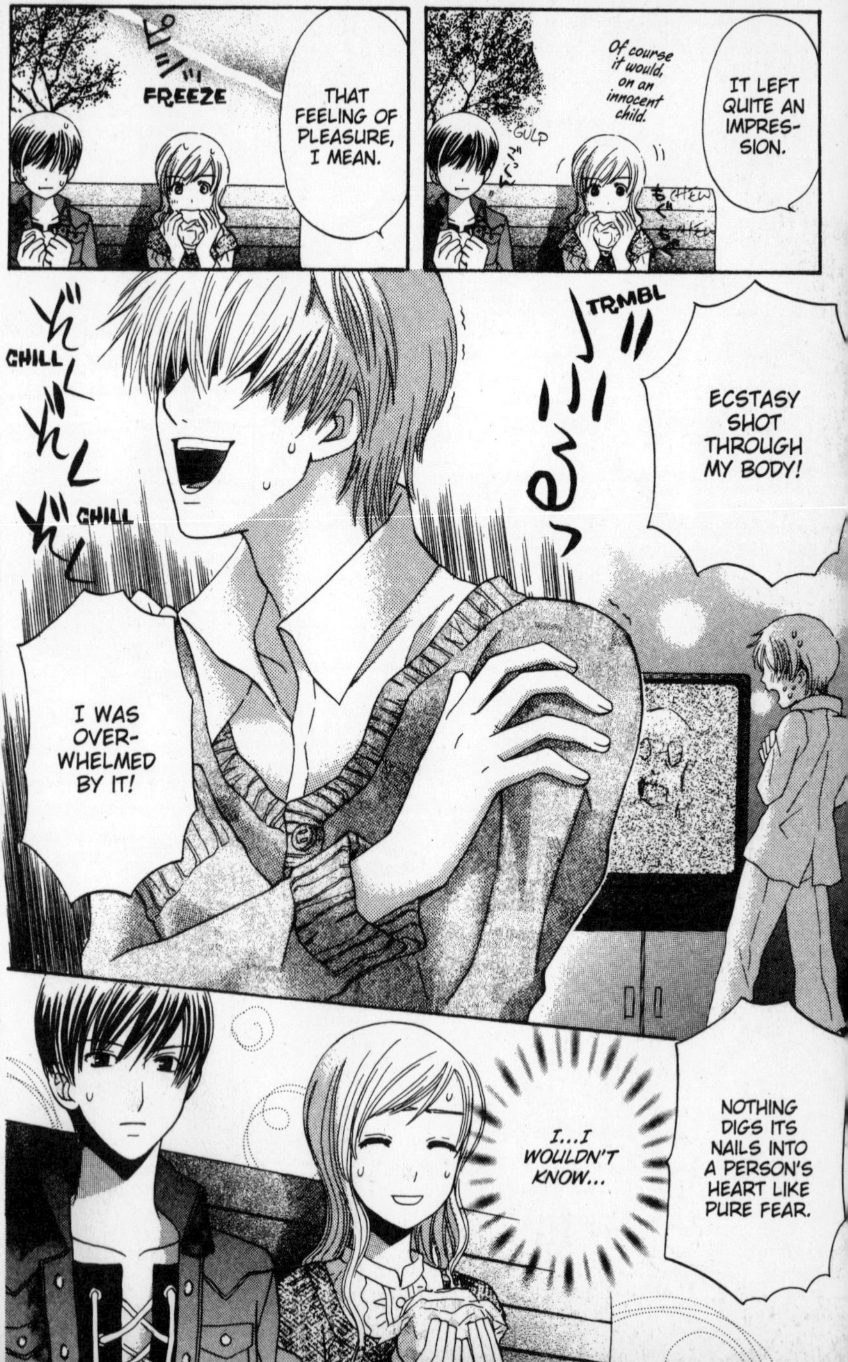
IT LEFT QUITE AN IMPRES-SION.
Of course it would, on an innocent child.
GULP
CHEW CHEW
THAT FEELING OF PLEASURE, I MEAN.
FREEZE
ECSTASY SHOT THROUGH MY BODY!
TRMBL
CHILL
CHILL
I WAS OVER-WHELMED BY IT!
NOTHING DIGS ITS NAILS INTO A PERSON'S HEART LIKE PURE FEAR.
I...I WOULDN'T KNOW...

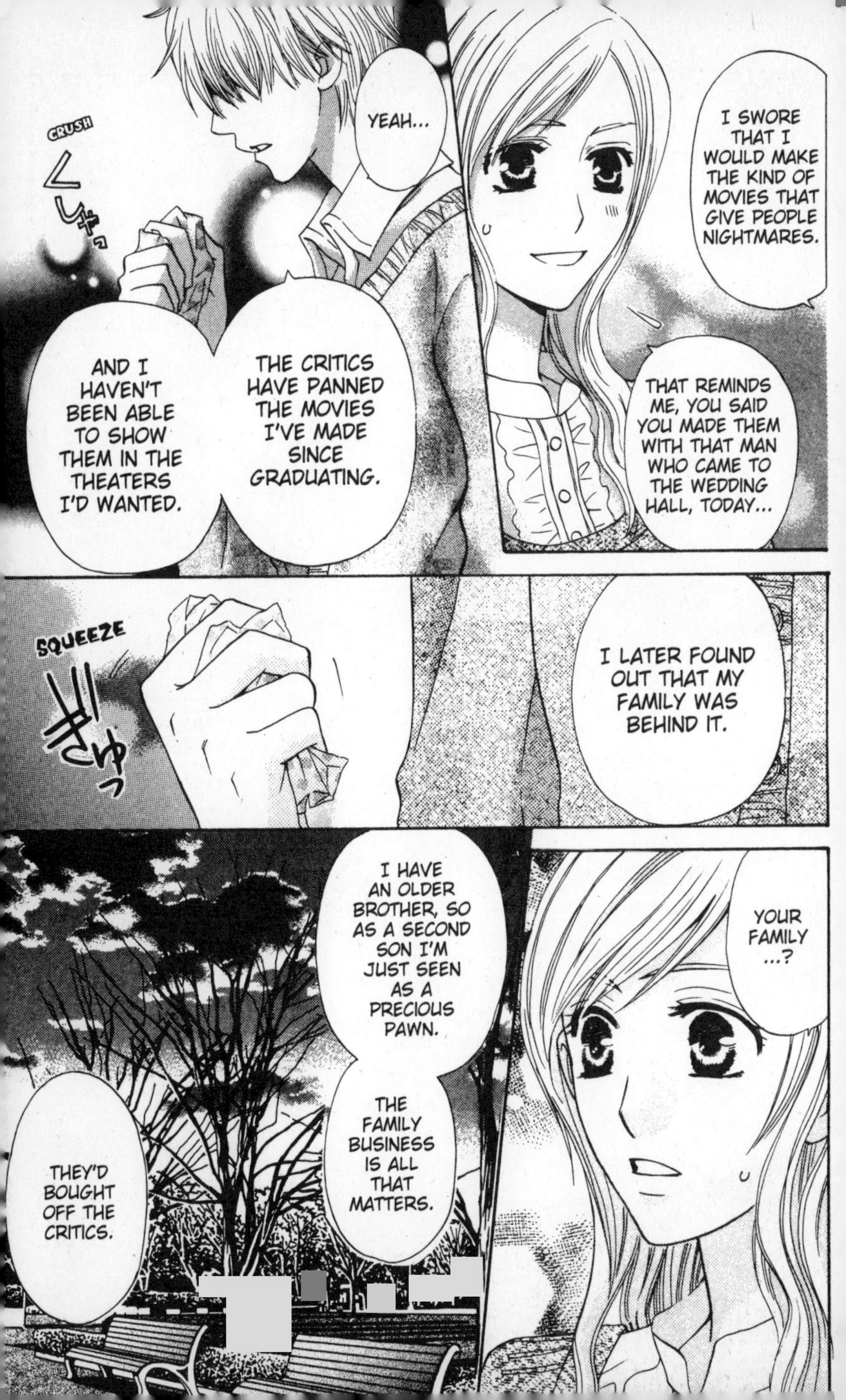
I SWORE THAT I WOULD MAKE THE KIND OF MOVIES THAT GIVE PEOPLE NIGHTMARES.
THAT REMINDS ME, YOU SAID YOU MADE THEM WITH THAT MAN WHO CAME TO THE WEDDING HALL, TODAY...
YEAH...
CRUSH
THE CRITICS HAVE PANNED THE MOVIES I'VE MADE SINCE GRADUATING.
AND I HAVEN'T BEEN ABLE TO SHOW THEM IN THE THEATERS I'D WANTED.
I LATER FOUND OUT THAT MY FAMILY WAS BEHIND IT.
SQUEEZE
YOUR FAMILY ...?
I HAVE AN OLDER BROTHER, SO AS A SECOND SON I'M JUST SEEN AS A PRECIOUS PAWN.
THE FAMILY BUSINESS IS ALL THAT MATTERS.
THEY'D BOUGHT OFF THE CRITICS.

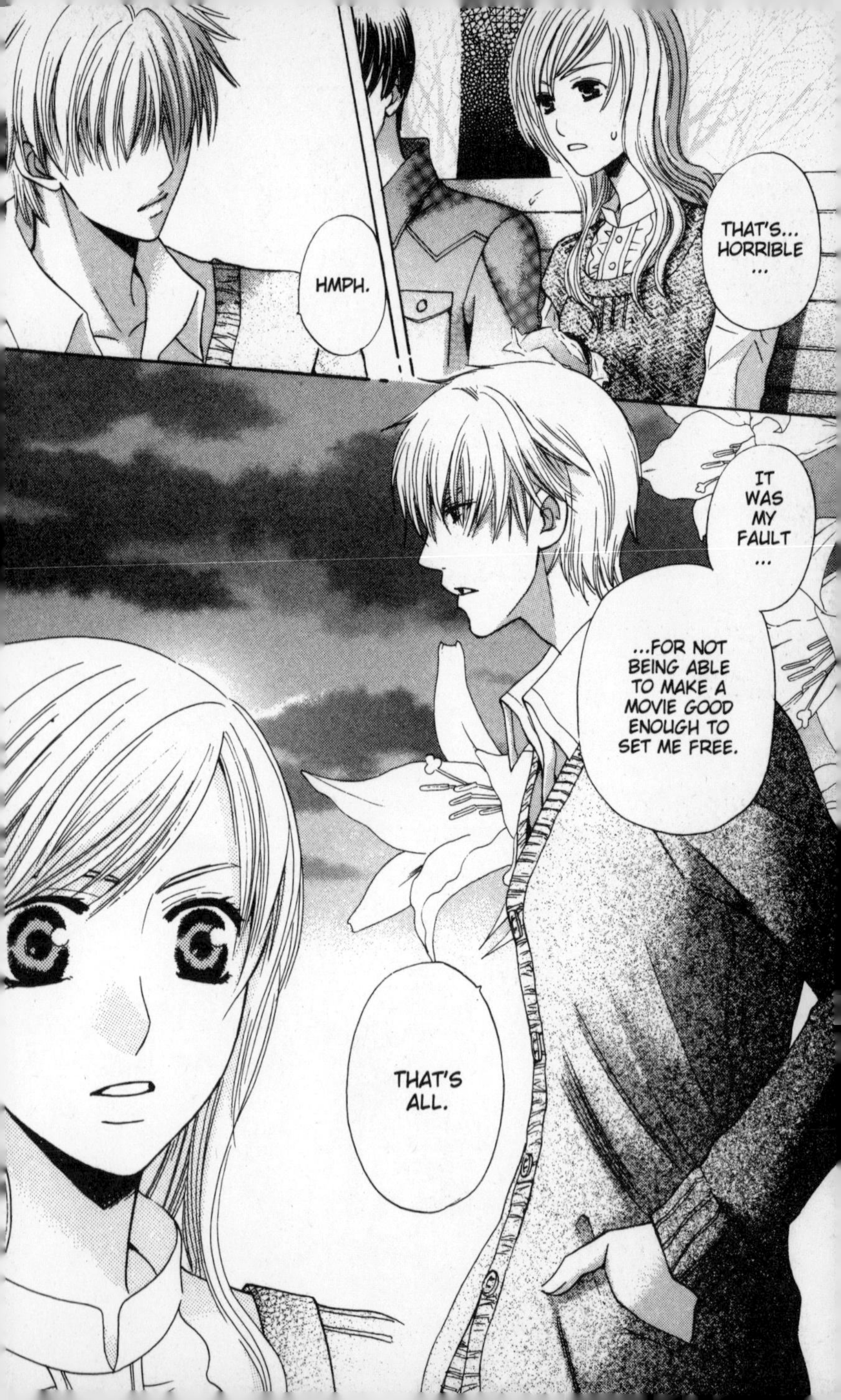
THAT'S... HORRIBLE ...
HMPH.
IT WAS MY FAULT ...
...FOR NOT BEING ABLE TO MAKE A MOVIE GOOD ENOUGH TO SET ME FREE.
THAT'S ALL.

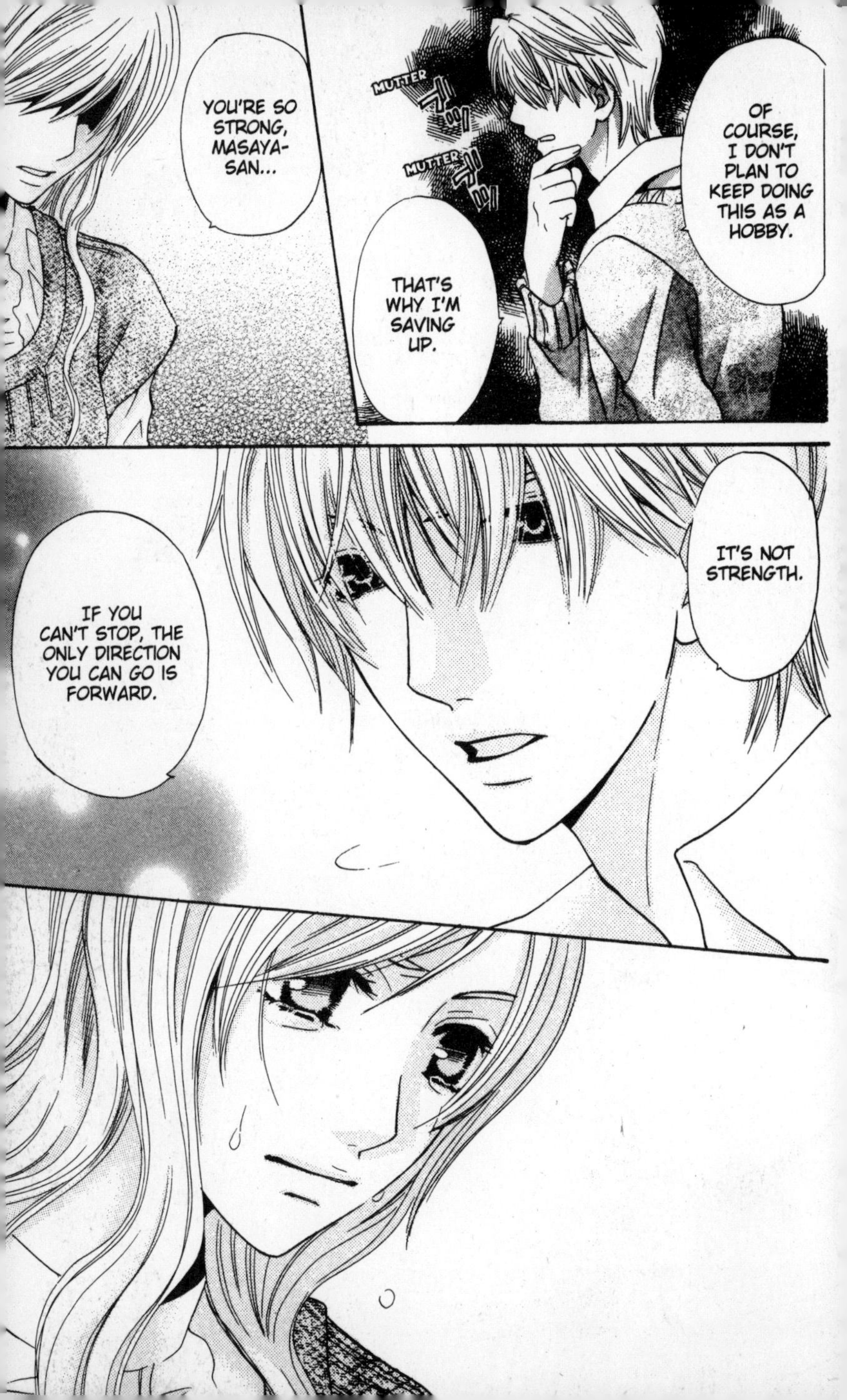
OF COURSE, I DON'T PLAN TO KEEP DOING THIS AS A HOBBY.
MUTTER
MUTTER
THAT'S WHY I'M SAVING UP.
YOU'RE SO STRONG, MASAYA-SAN...
IT'S NOT STRENGTH.
IF YOU CAN'T STOP, THE ONLY DIRECTION YOU CAN GO IS FORWARD.

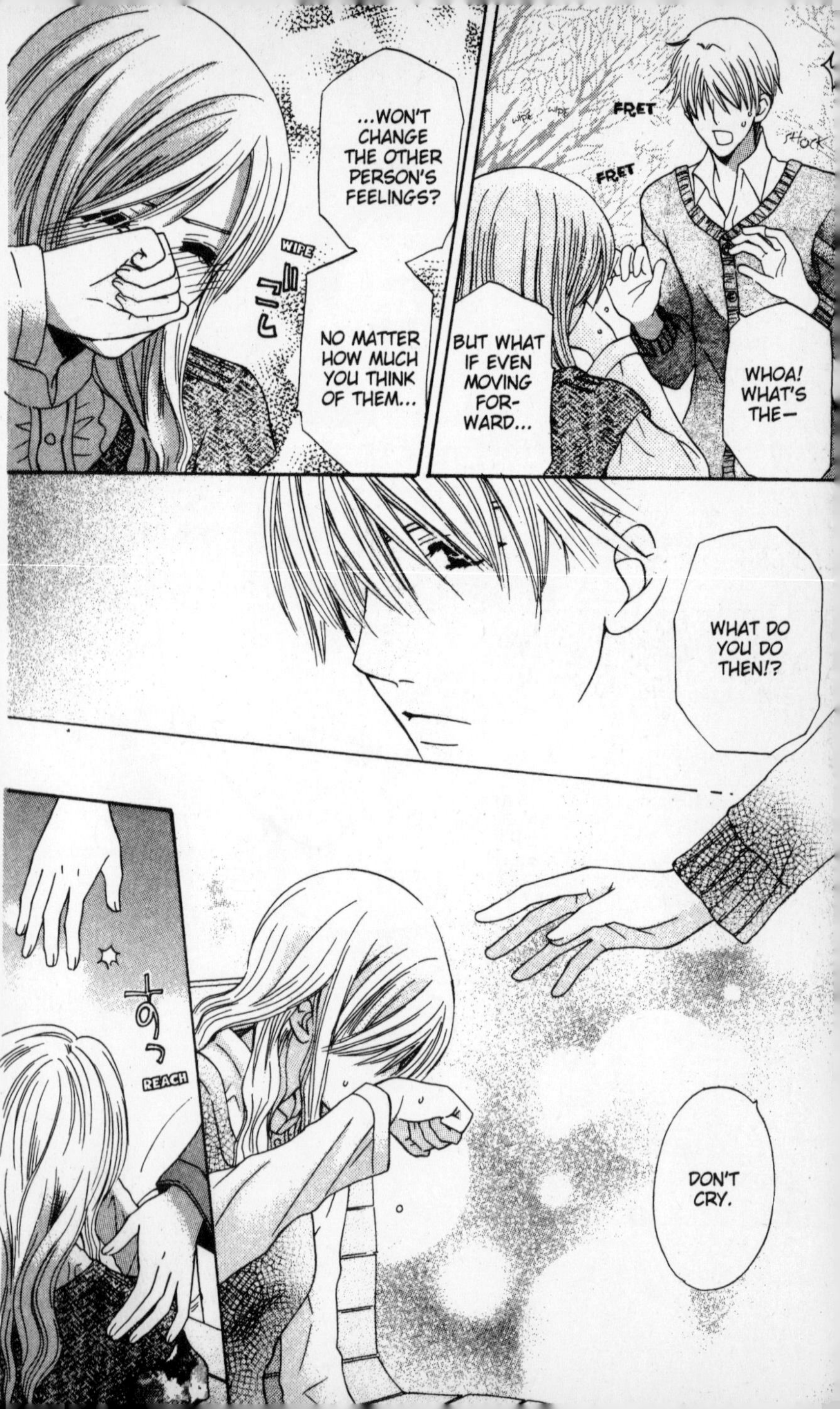
SHOCK
FRET
FRET
WIPE WIPE
WHOA! WHAT'S THE—
BUT WHAT IF EVEN MOVING FOR-WARD...
NO MATTER HOW MUCH YOU THINK OF THEM...
...WON'T CHANGE THE OTHER PERSON'S FEELINGS?
WIPE
WHAT DO YOU DO THEN!?
REACH
DON'T CRY.

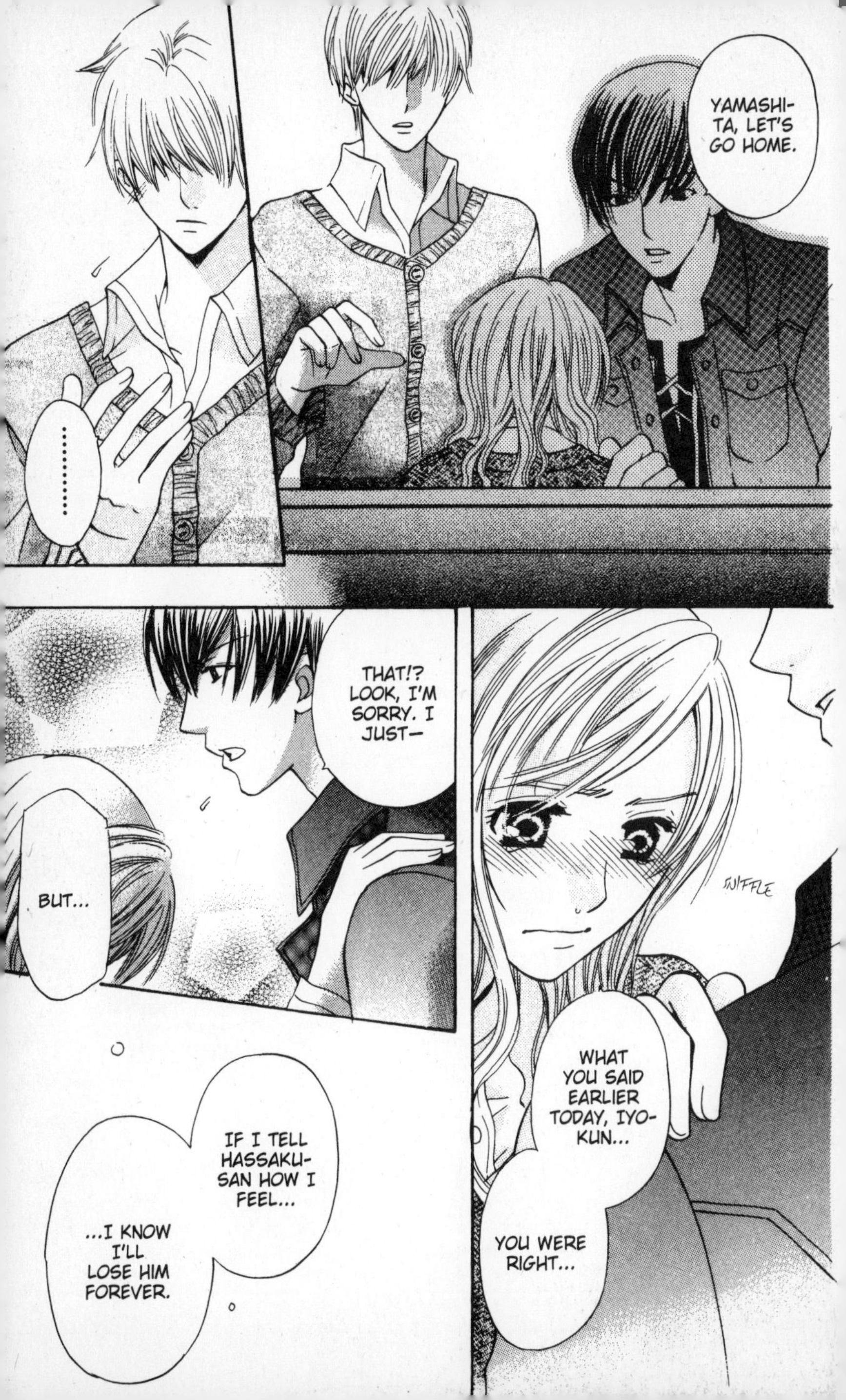
YAMASHITA, LET'S GO HOME.
......
SNIFFLE
WHAT YOU SAID EARLIER TODAY, IYO-KUN...
YOU WERE RIGHT...
THAT!? LOOK, I'M SORRY. I JUST—
BUT...
IF I TELL HASSAKU-SAN HOW I FEEL...
...I KNOW I'LL LOSE HIM FOREVER.

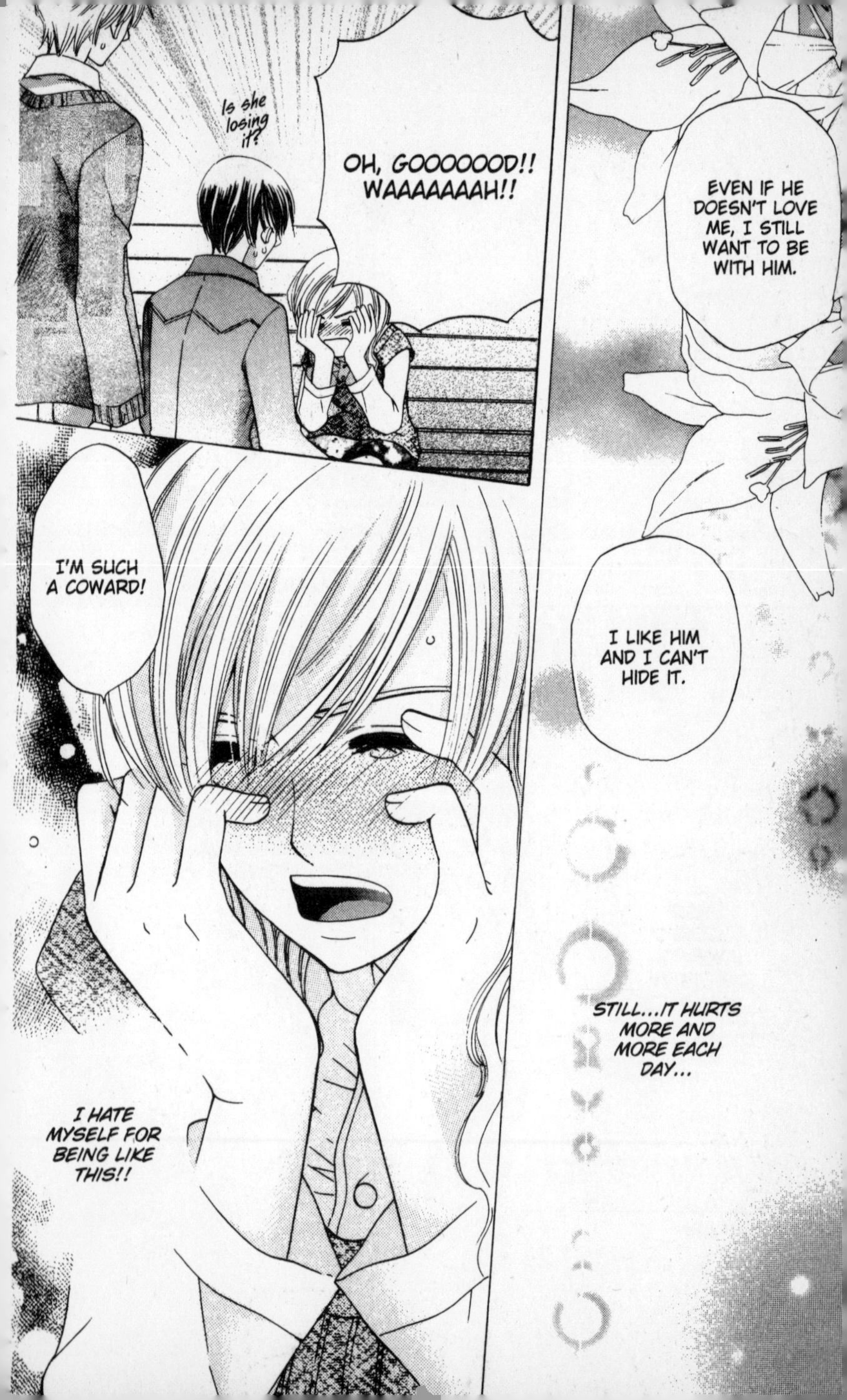
EVEN IF HE DOESN'T LOVE ME, I STILL WANT TO BE WITH HIM.
I LIKE HIM AND I CAN'T HIDE IT.
STILL...IT HURTS MORE AND MORE EACH DAY...
OH, GOOOOOOD!! WAAAAAAAH!!
Is she losing it?
I'M SUCH A COWARD!
I HATE MYSELF FOR BEING LIKE THIS!!

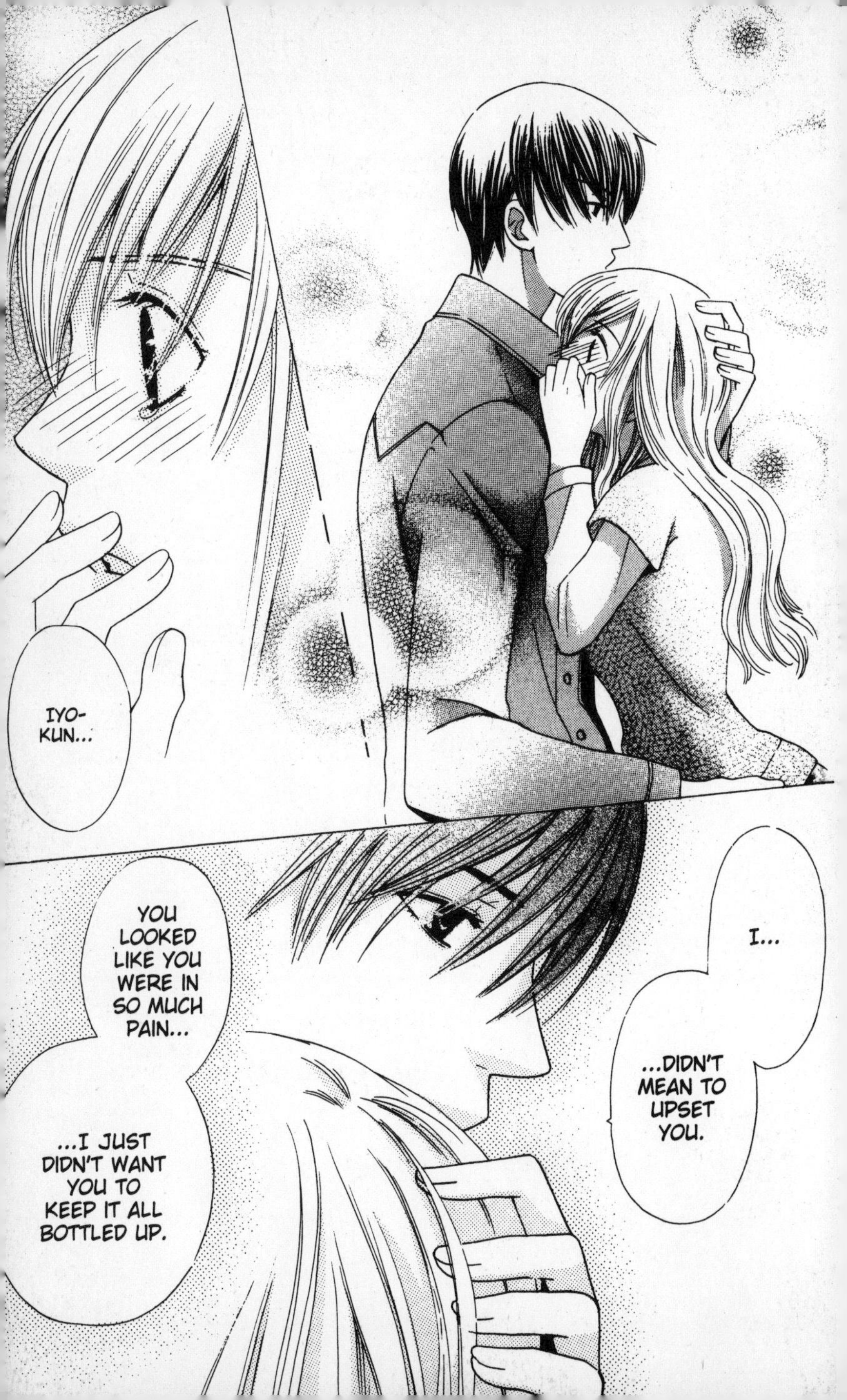
IYO-KUN...
I...
...DIDN'T MEAN TO UPSET YOU.
YOU LOOKED LIKE YOU WERE IN SO MUCH PAIN...
...I JUST DIDN'T WANT YOU TO KEEP IT ALL BOTTLED UP.

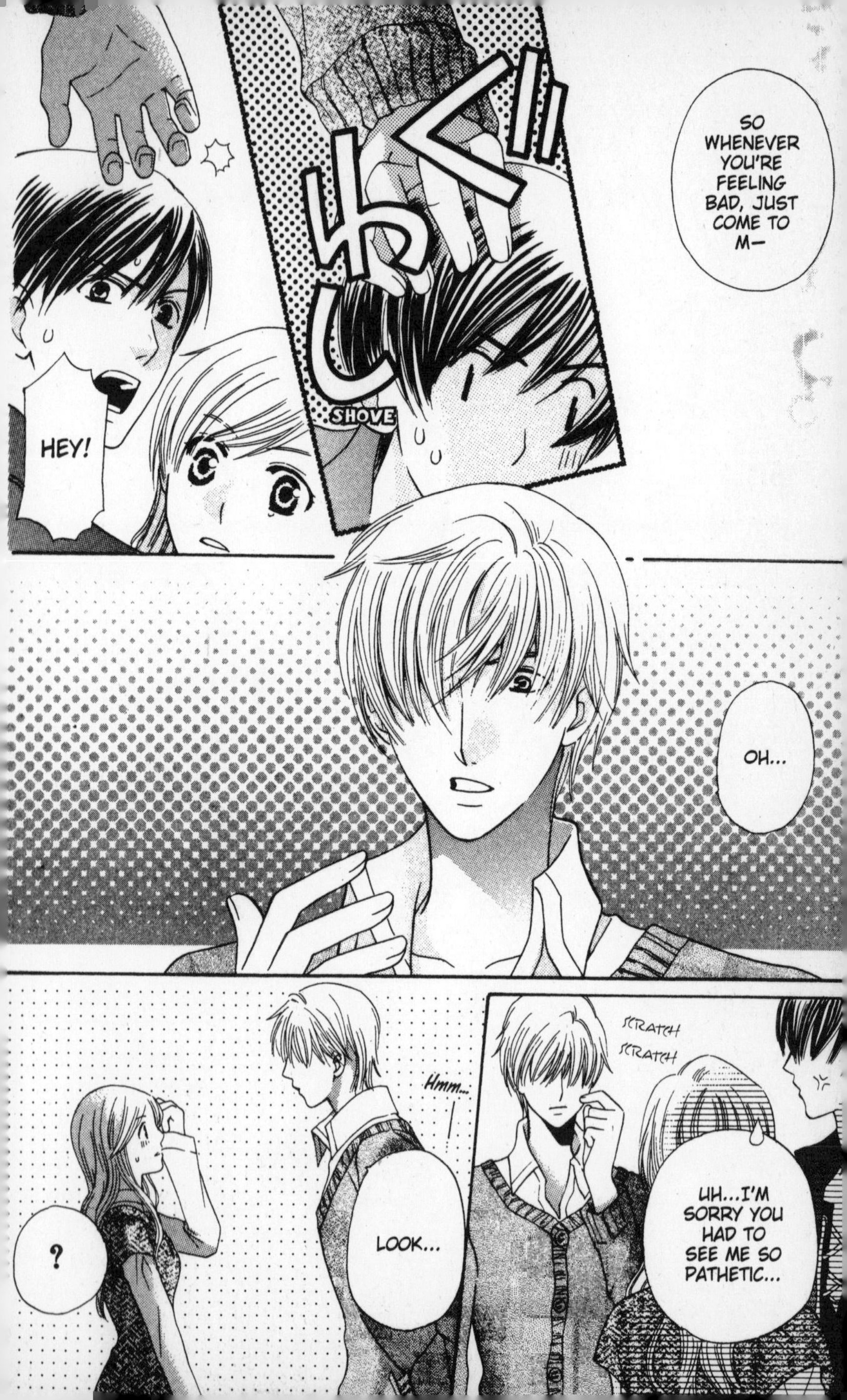
SO WHENEVER YOU'RE FEELING BAD, JUST COME TO M—
SHOVE
HEY!
OH...
SCRATCH
SCRATCH
UH...I'M SORRY YOU HAD TO SEE ME SO PATHETIC...
Hmm...
LOOK...
?

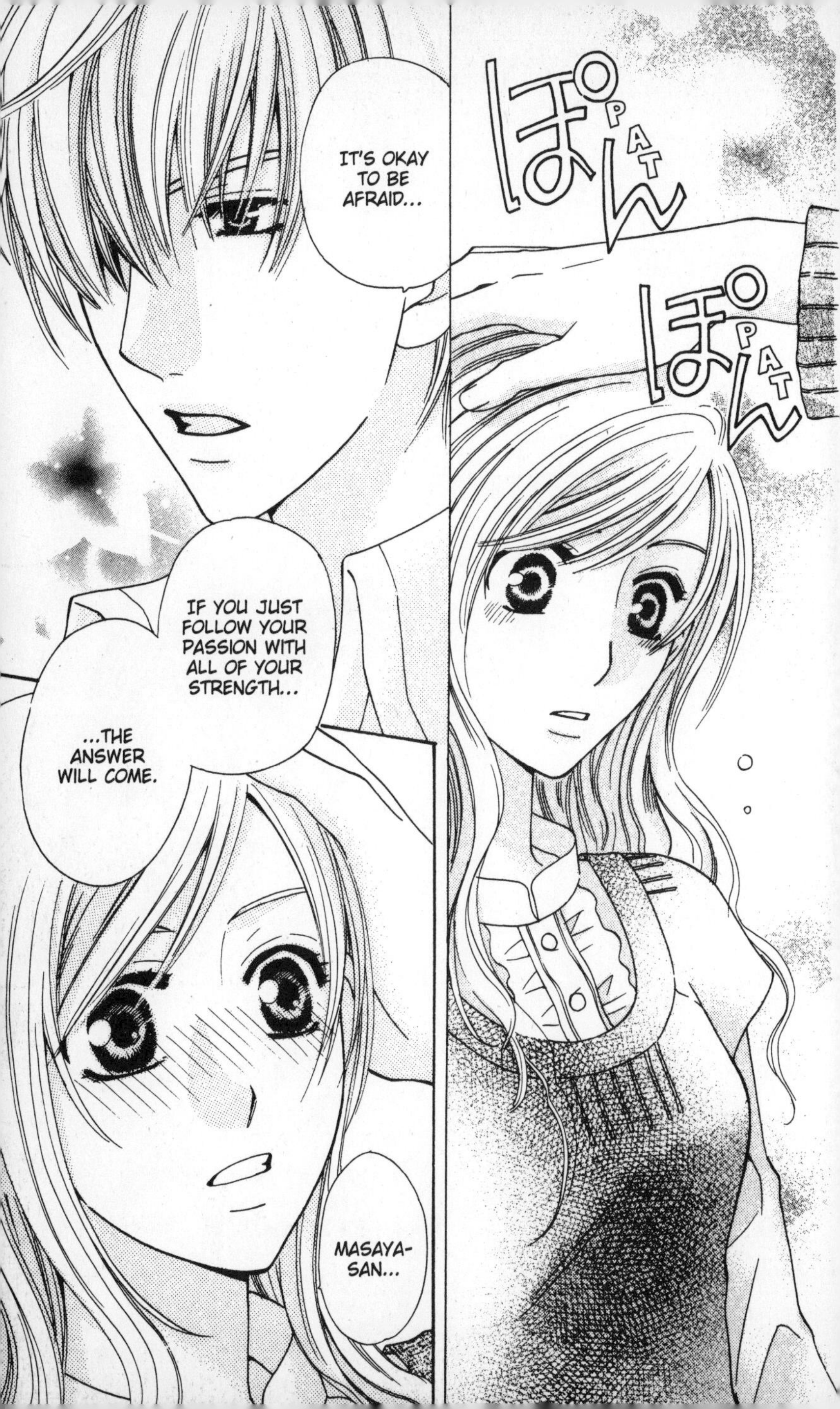
ぽん
PAT
ぽん
PAT
IT'S OKAY TO BE AFRAID...
IF YOU JUST FOLLOW YOUR PASSION WITH ALL OF YOUR STRENGTH...
...THE ANSWER WILL COME.
MASAYA-SAN...

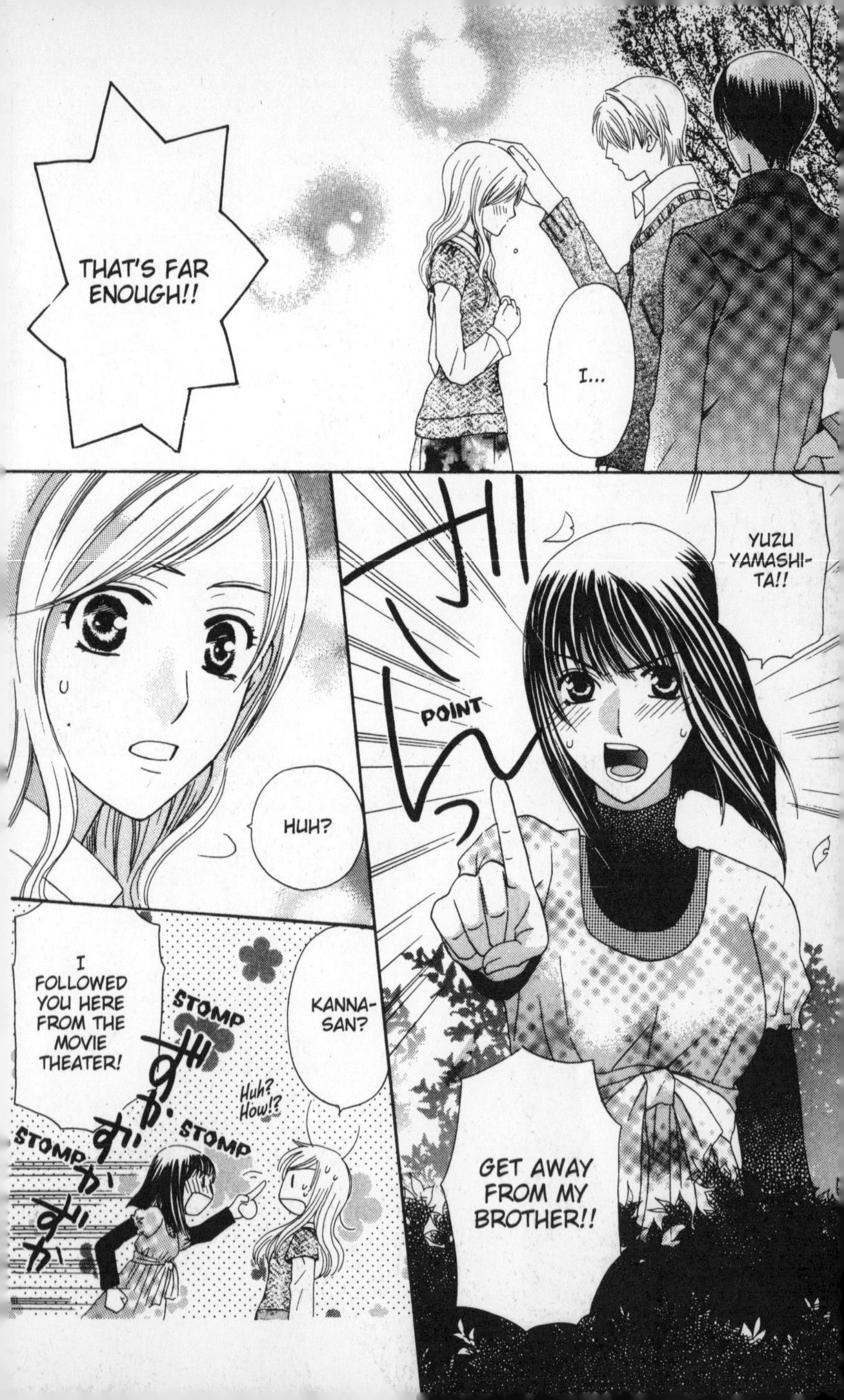
I...
THAT'S FAR ENOUGH!!
YUZU YAMASHITA!!
POINT
GET AWAY FROM MY BROTHER!!
HUH?
KANNA-SAN?
I FOLLOWED YOU HERE FROM THE MOVIE THEATER!
Huh? How!?
STOMP
STOMP
STOMP

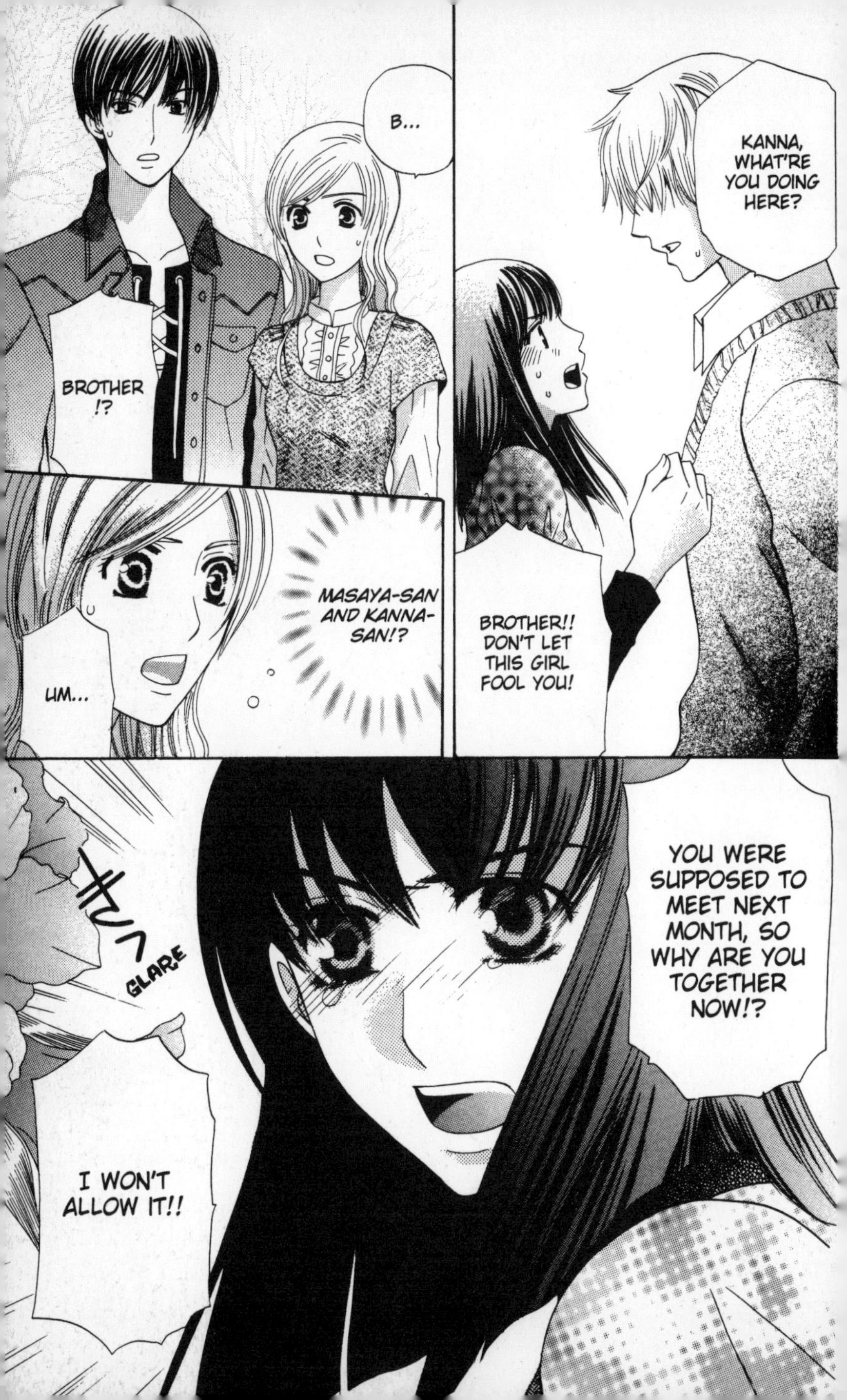
KANNA, WHAT'RE YOU DOING HERE?
BROTHER!! DON'T LET THIS GIRL FOOL YOU!
B...
BROTHER !?
MASAYA-SAN AND KANNA-SAN!?
UM...
YOU WERE SUPPOSED TO MEET NEXT MONTH, SO WHY ARE YOU TOGETHER NOW!?
GLARE
I WON'T ALLOW IT!!

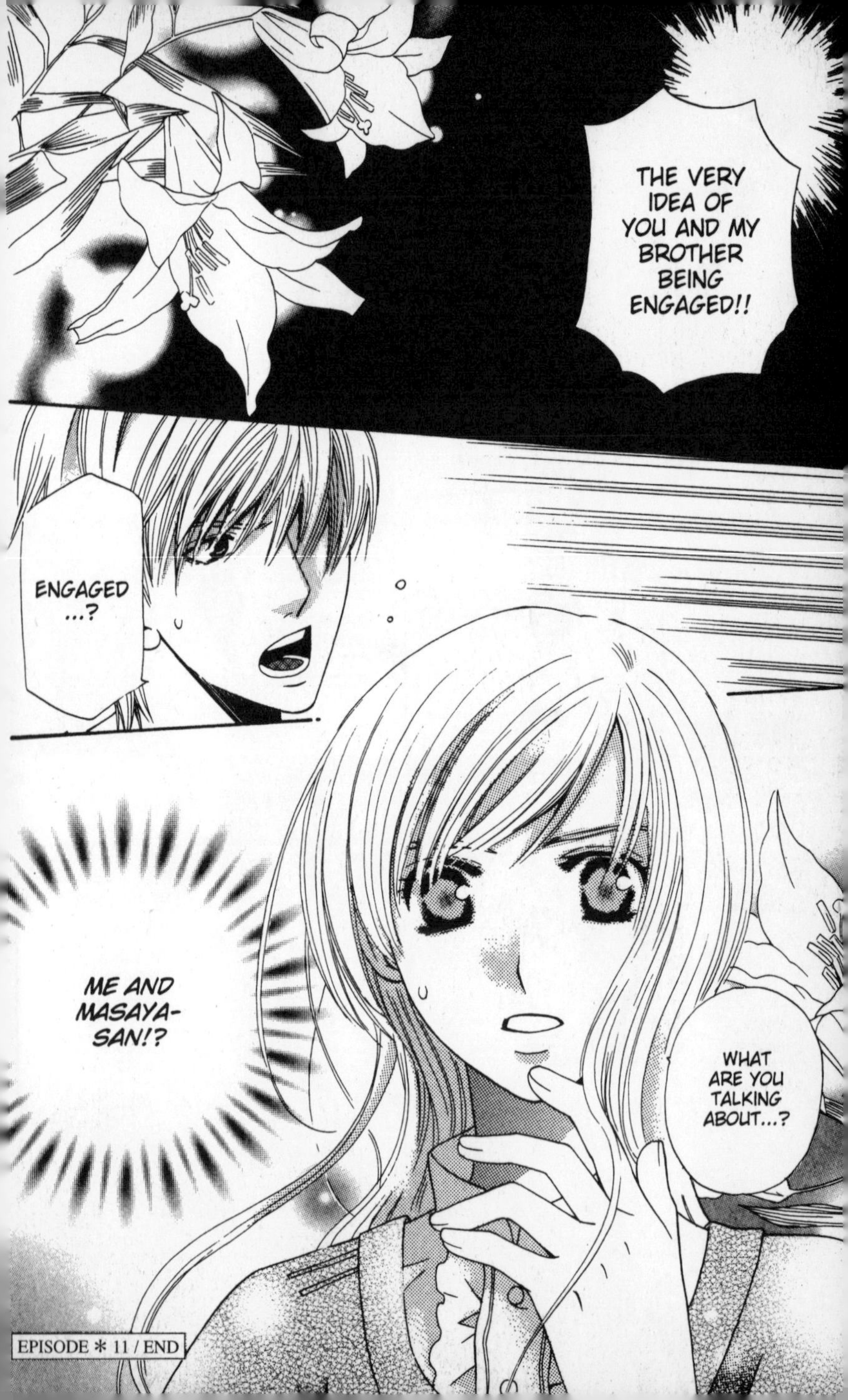
THE VERY IDEA OF YOU AND MY BROTHER BEING ENGAGED!!
ENGAGED ...?
ME AND MASAYA-SAN!?
WHAT ARE YOU TALKING ABOUT...?

EPISODE * 11 / END

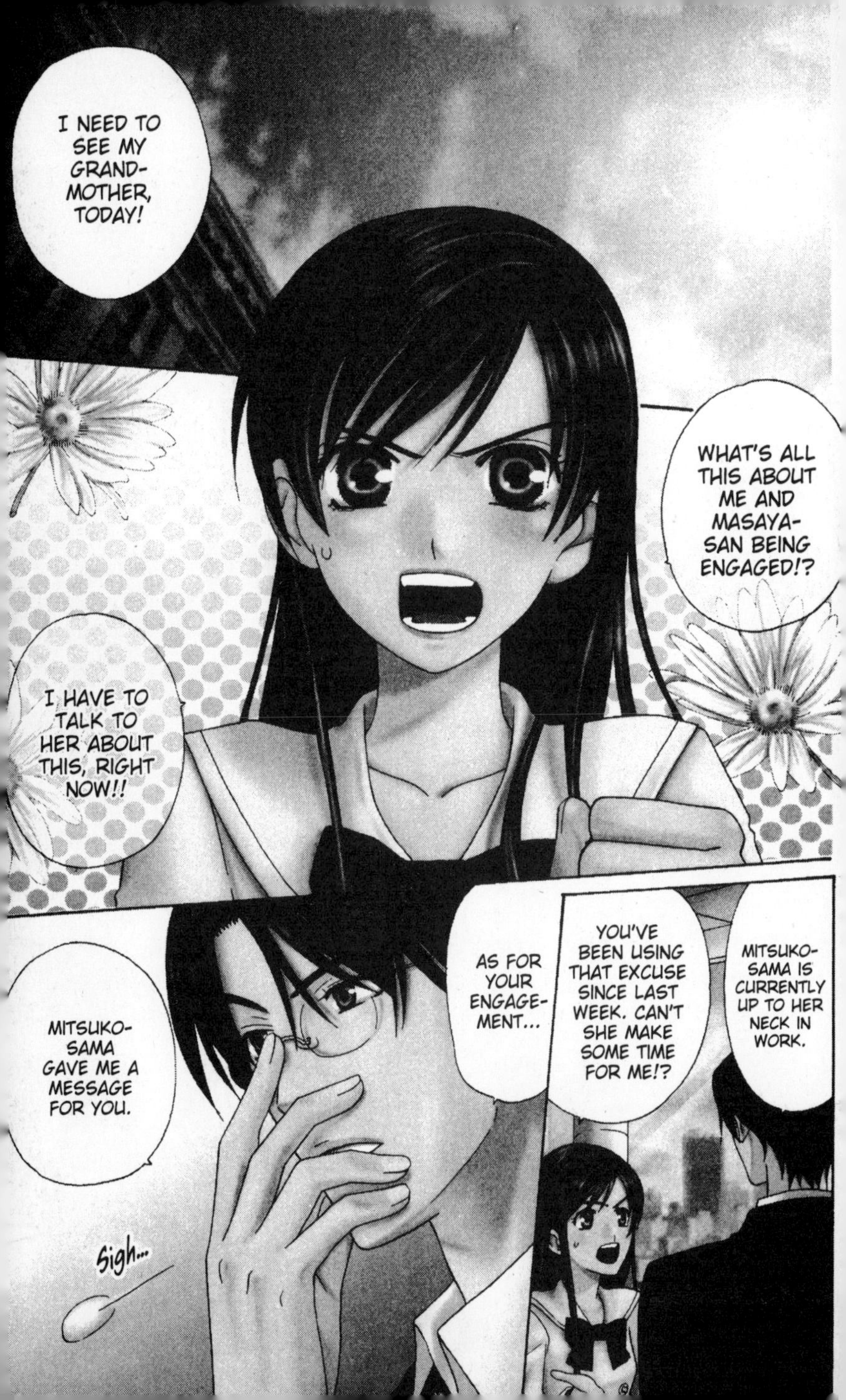
WHAT'S ALL THIS ABOUT ME AND MASAYA-SAN BEING ENGAGED!?
I NEED TO SEE MY GRAND-MOTHER, TODAY!
I HAVE TO TALK TO HER ABOUT THIS, RIGHT NOW!!
MITSUKO-SAMA IS CURRENTLY UP TO HER NECK IN WORK.
YOU'VE BEEN USING THAT EXCUSE SINCE LAST WEEK. CAN'T SHE MAKE SOME TIME FOR ME!?
AS FOR YOUR ENGAGE-MENT...
MITSUKO-SAMA GAVE ME A MESSAGE FOR YOU.
Sigh...

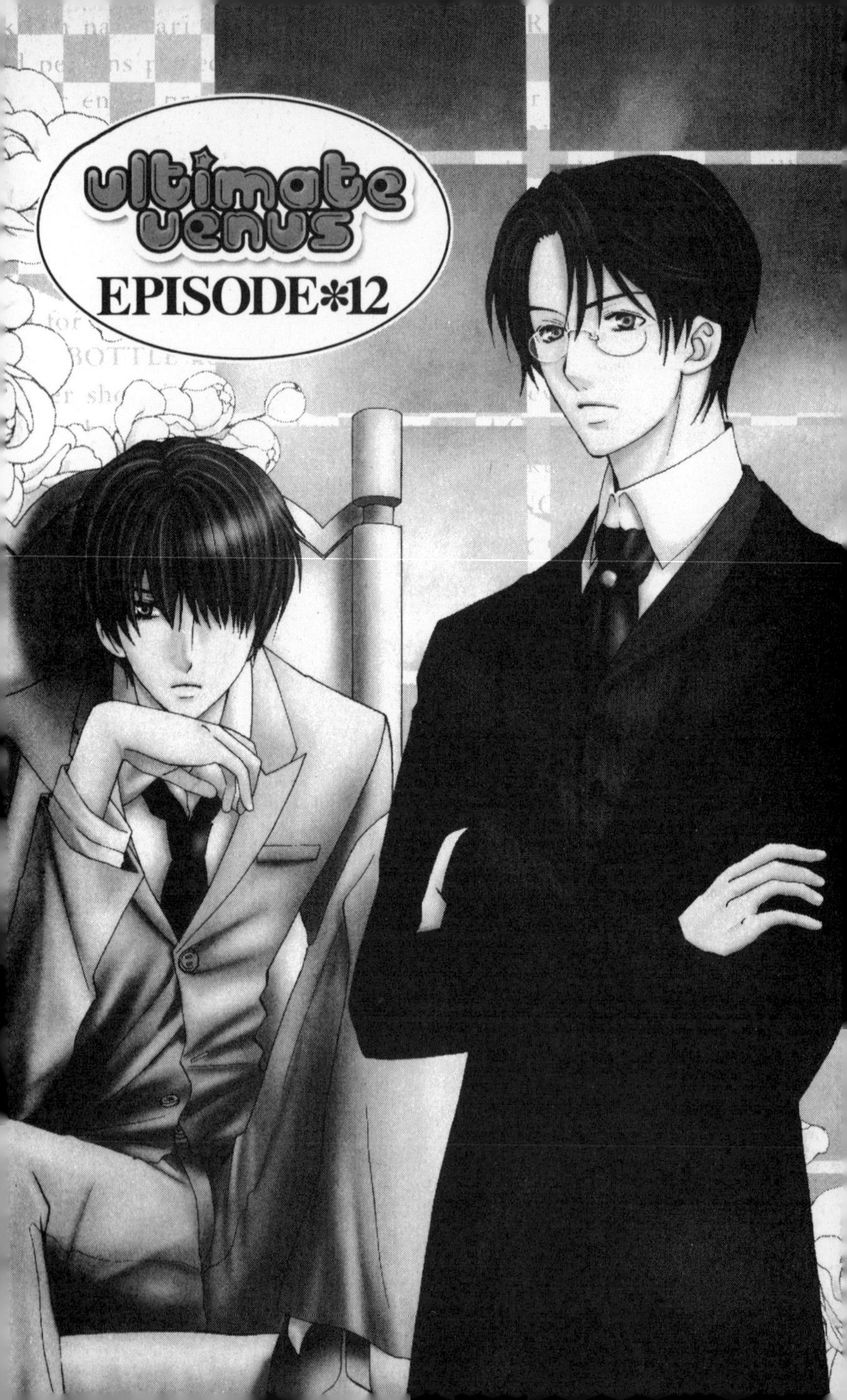
ultimate venus
EPISODE*12

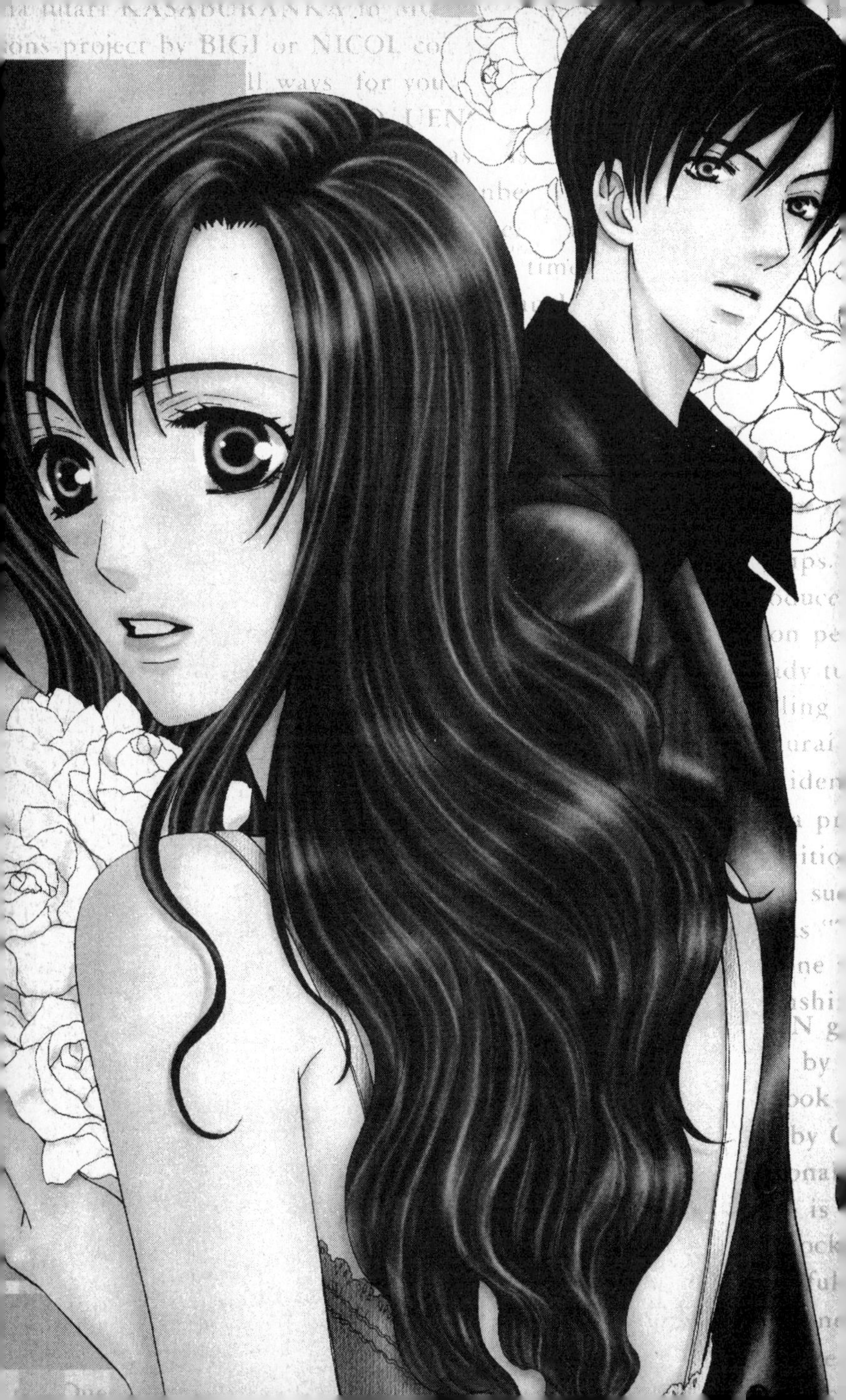
KASABURANKA
project by BIGI or NICOL
ways for you

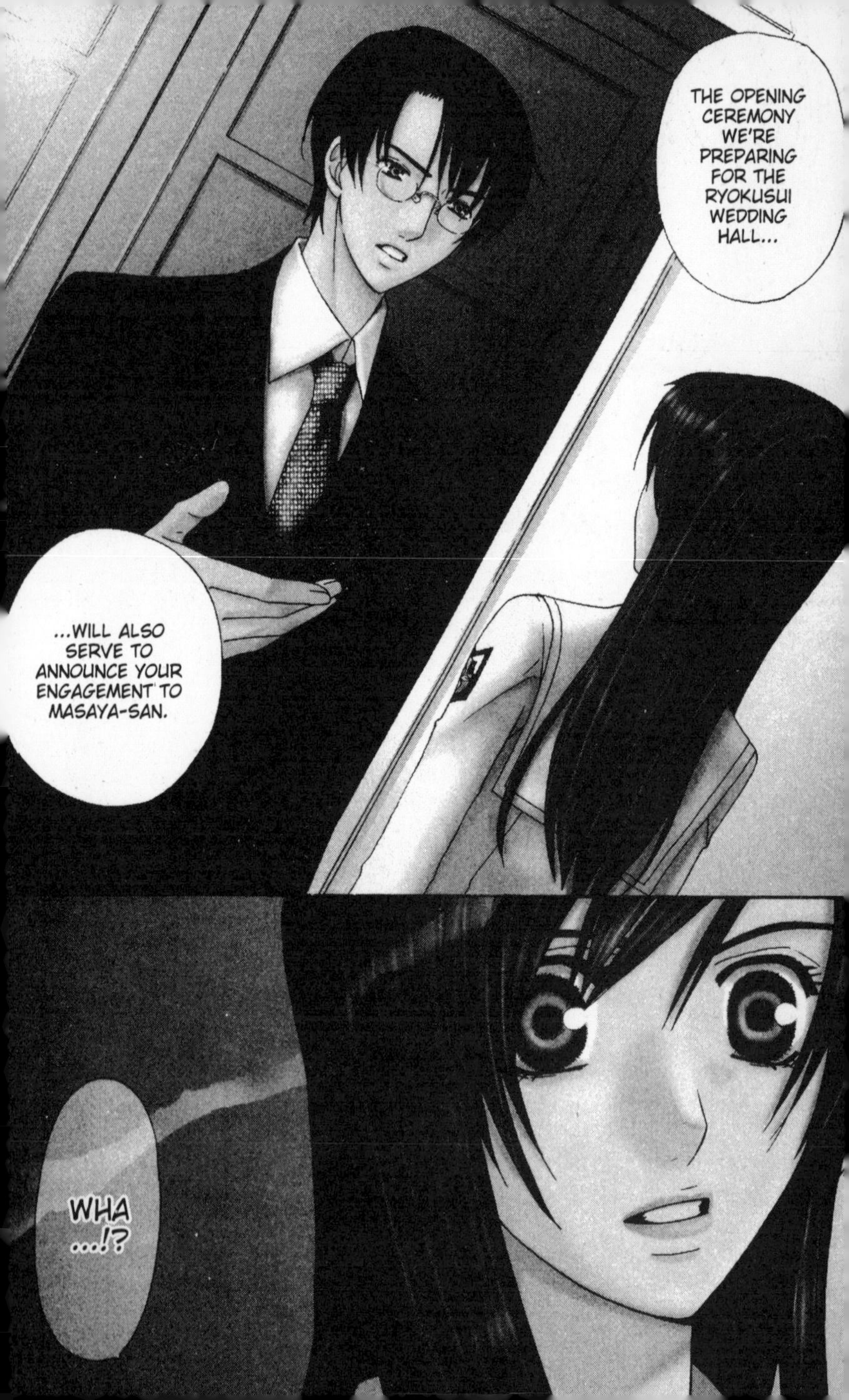
THE OPENING CEREMONY WE'RE PREPARING FOR THE RYOKUSUI WEDDING HALL...
...WILL ALSO SERVE TO ANNOUNCE YOUR ENGAGEMENT TO MASAYA-SAN.
WHA ...!?

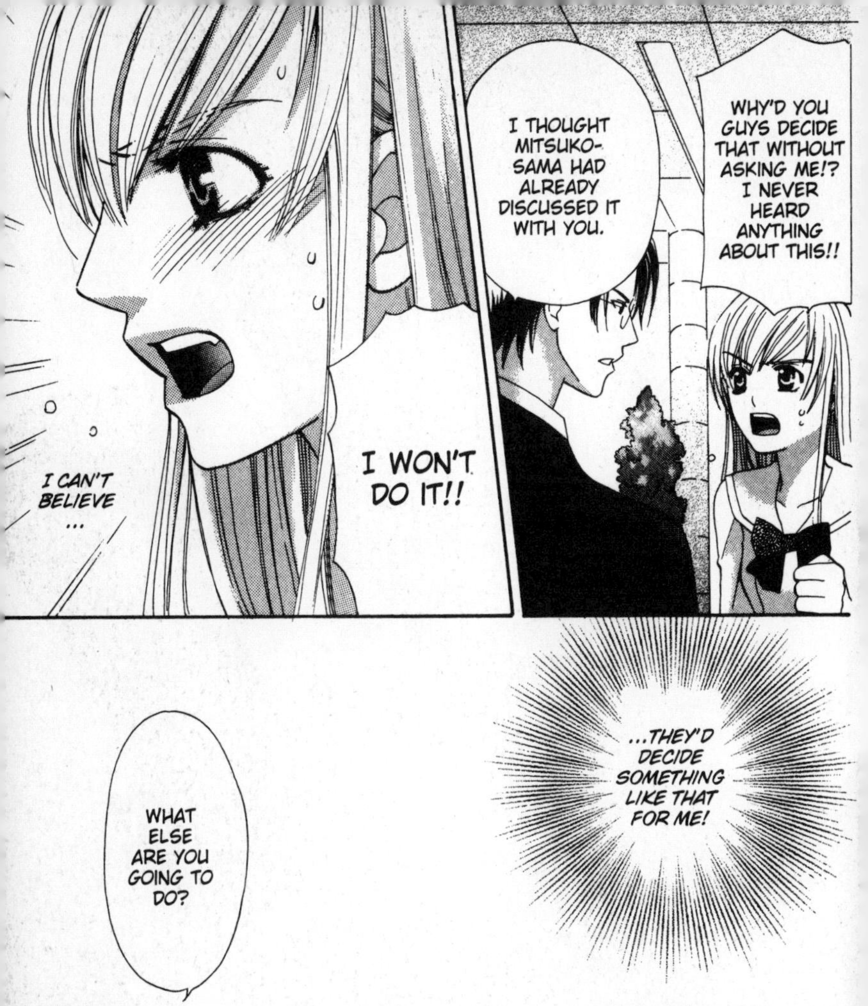
WHY'D YOU GUYS DECIDE THAT WITHOUT ASKING ME!? I NEVER HEARD ANYTHING ABOUT THIS!!
I THOUGHT MITSUKO-SAMA HAD ALREADY DISCUSSED IT WITH YOU.
I WON'T DO IT!!
I CAN'T BELIEVE ...
...THEY'D DECIDE SOMETHING LIKE THAT FOR ME!
WHAT ELSE ARE YOU GOING TO DO?

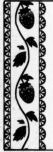

FREE TALK 2 – I'm making progress in being well-read. As of July, I've broken past 800,000 vocab words and it's only a matter of time before it's 1,000,000! The reading primer I bought for my vocab is filling up nicely. If not for this increase in my vocabulary, I just know that all those old books and English learning workbooks would have been wasted, so I'm glad I can read them now. My bookshelf's been full for a while, but adding all these Western books looks so impressive...

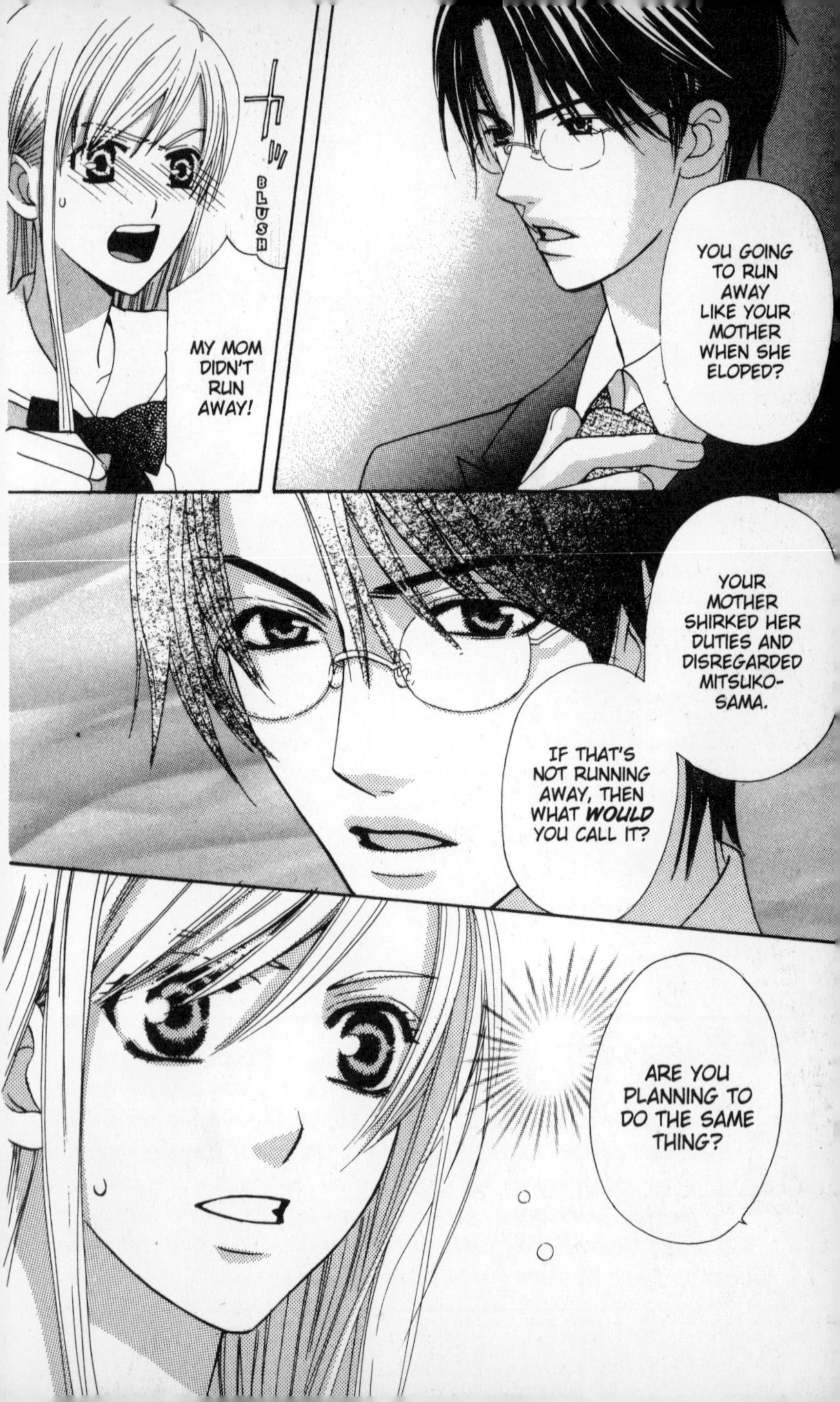
YOU GOING TO RUN AWAY LIKE YOUR MOTHER WHEN SHE ELOPED?
カッ
BLUSH
MY MOM DIDN'T RUN AWAY!
YOUR MOTHER SHIRKED HER DUTIES AND DISREGARDED MITSUKO-SAMA.
IF THAT'S NOT RUNNING AWAY, THEN WHAT ***WOULD*** YOU CALL IT?
ARE YOU PLANNING TO DO THE SAME THING?

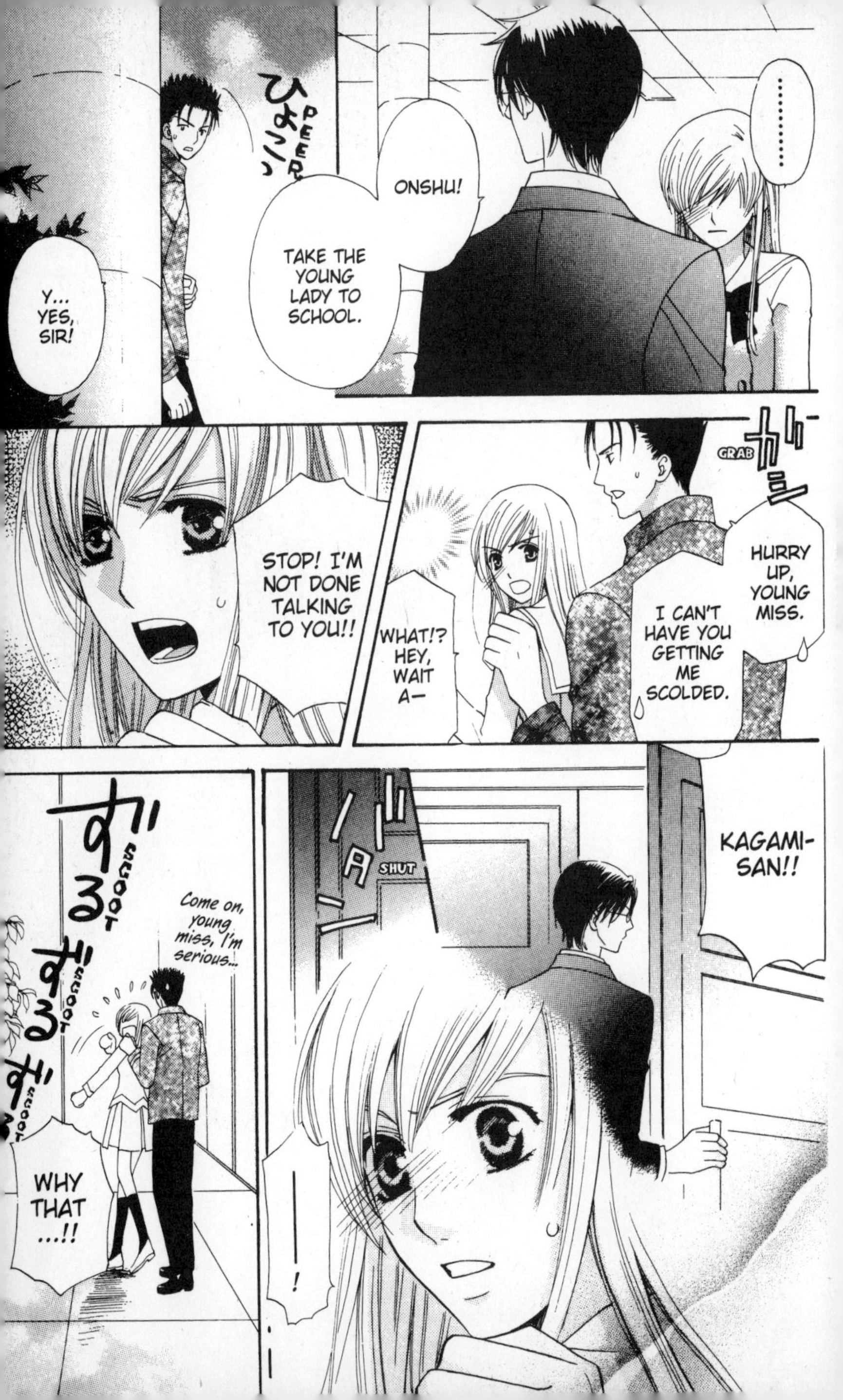
......
ONSHU!
TAKE THE YOUNG LADY TO SCHOOL.
PEER
Y... YES, SIR!
GRAB
HURRY UP, YOUNG MISS.
I CAN'T HAVE YOU GETTING ME SCOLDED.
WHAT!? HEY, WAIT A—
STOP! I'M NOT DONE TALKING TO YOU!!
KAGAMI-SAN!!
SHUT
—!
SCOOT SCOOT SCOOT
Come on, young miss, I'm serious...
WHY THAT ...!!

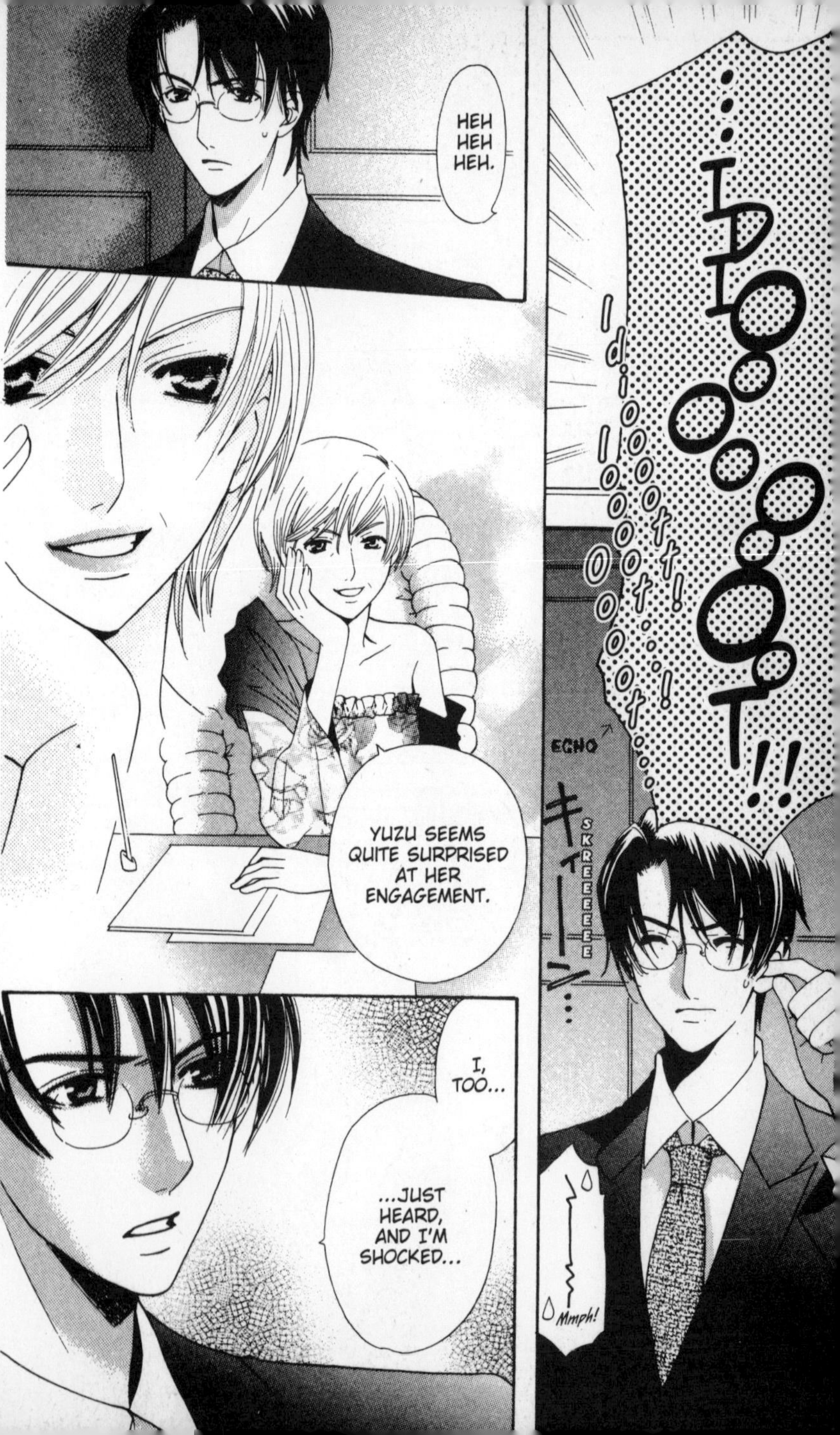
...IDIOOOOOOOOT!!
Idiooooot!
Ioooooot...!
Oooooot...
ECHO
SKREEEEEEE
Mmph!
HEH HEH HEH.
YUZU SEEMS QUITE SURPRISED AT HER ENGAGEMENT.
I, TOO...
...JUST HEARD, AND I'M SHOCKED...

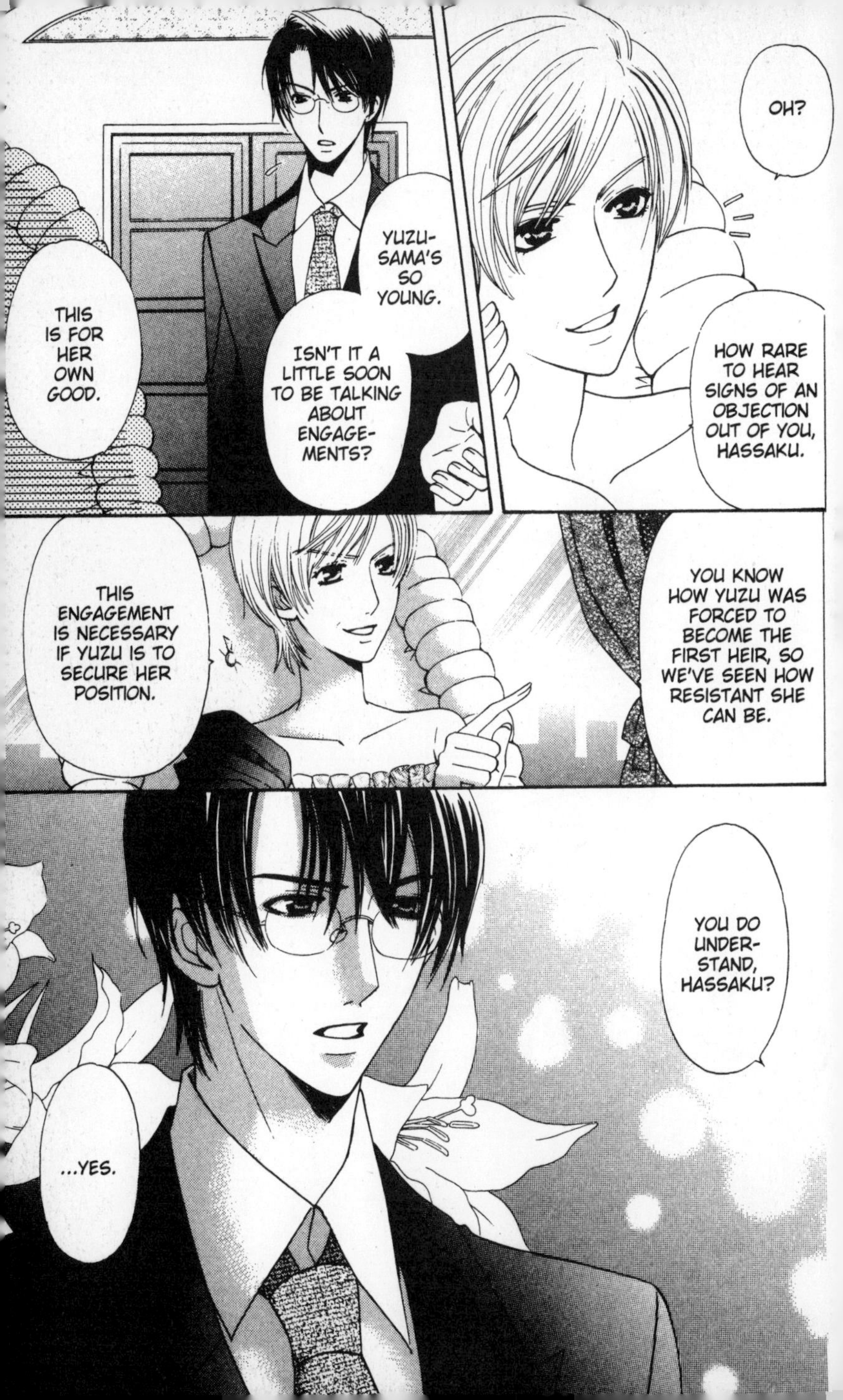
OH?
HOW RARE TO HEAR SIGNS OF AN OBJECTION OUT OF YOU, HASSAKU.
YUZU-SAMA'S SO YOUNG.
ISN'T IT A LITTLE SOON TO BE TALKING ABOUT ENGAGE-MENTS?
THIS IS FOR HER OWN GOOD.
YOU KNOW HOW YUZU WAS FORCED TO BECOME THE FIRST HEIR, SO WE'VE SEEN HOW RESISTANT SHE CAN BE.
THIS ENGAGEMENT IS NECESSARY IF YUZU IS TO SECURE HER POSITION.
YOU DO UNDER-STAND, HASSAKU?
...YES.

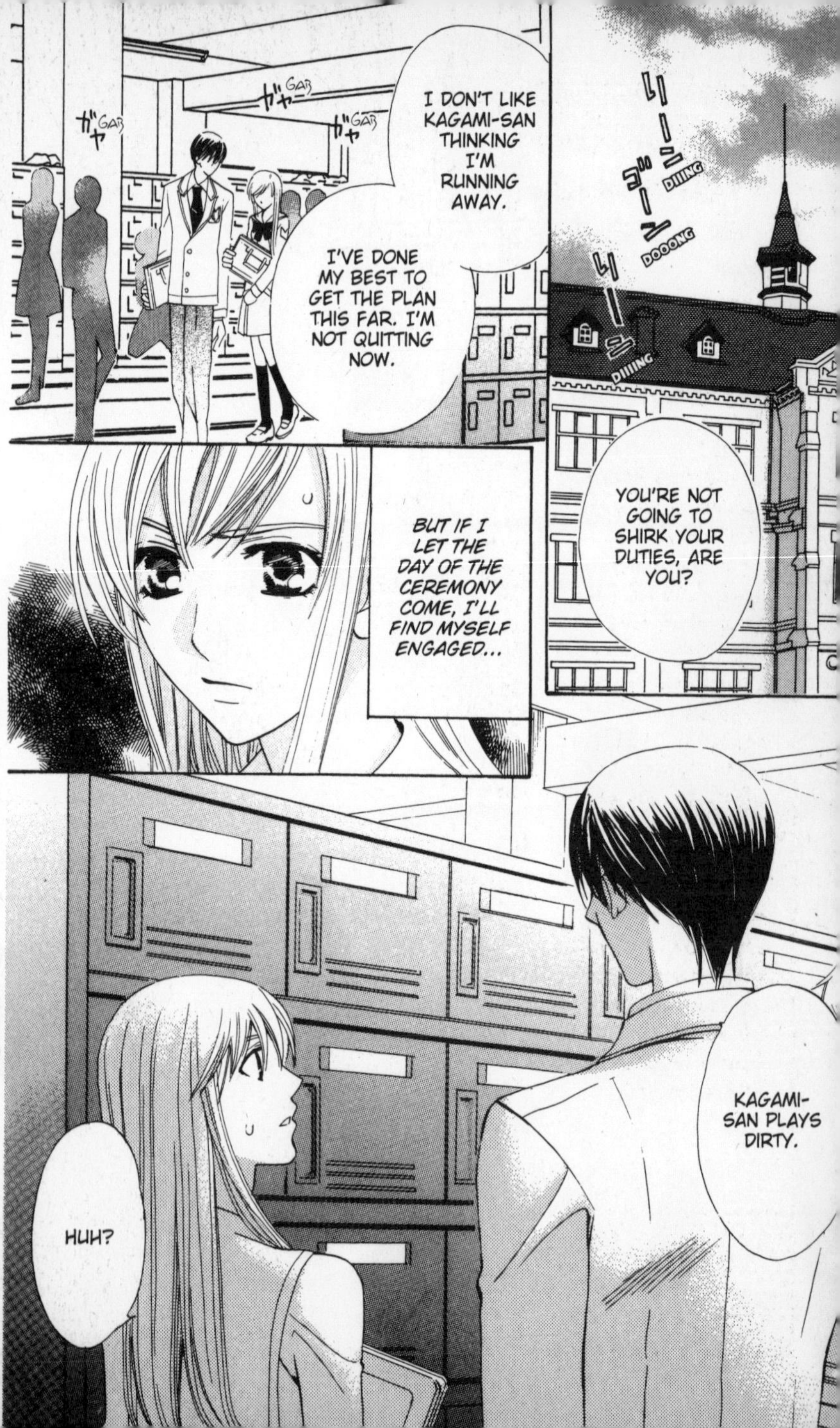
DIIING
DOOONG
DIIING
YOU'RE NOT GOING TO SHIRK YOUR DUTIES, ARE YOU?
GAB
GAB
GAB
I DON'T LIKE KAGAMI-SAN THINKING I'M RUNNING AWAY.
I'VE DONE MY BEST TO GET THE PLAN THIS FAR. I'M NOT QUITTING NOW.
BUT IF I LET THE DAY OF THE CEREMONY COME, I'LL FIND MYSELF ENGAGED...
KAGAMI-SAN PLAYS DIRTY.
HUH?

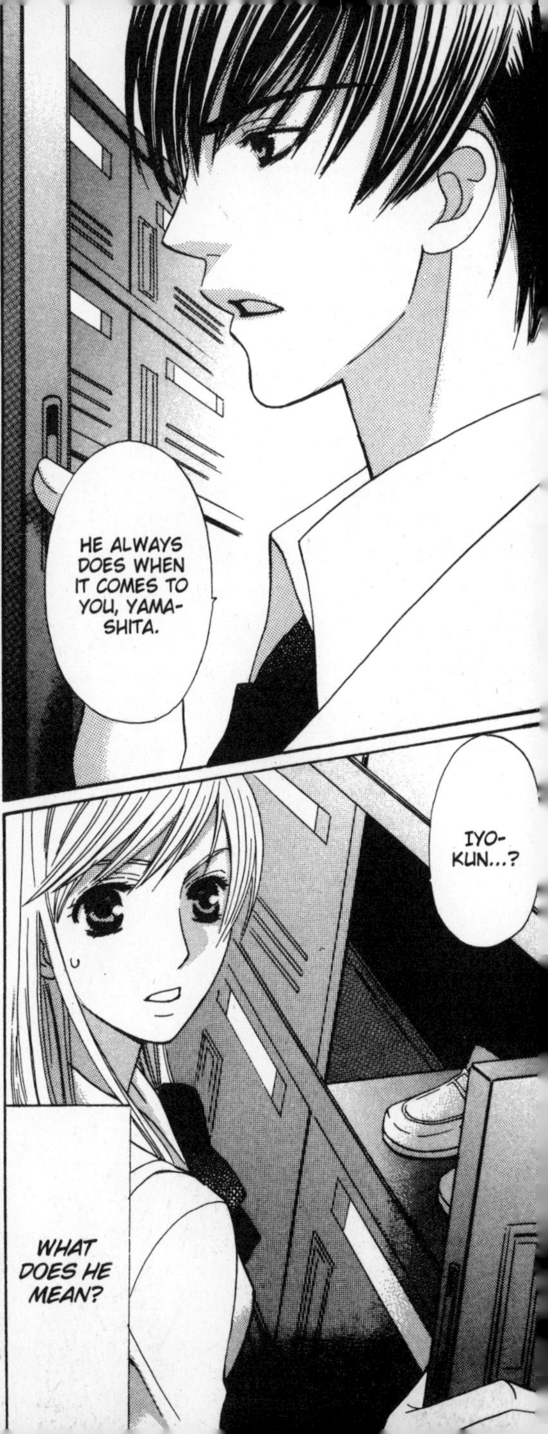
HE ALWAYS DOES WHEN IT COMES TO YOU, YAMA-SHITA.
IYO-KUN...?
WHAT DOES HE MEAN?

★ FREE TALK ★ ③

This is the first time a one-shot of mine has been printed in one of my comics! Yay!!
I really do have a lot of short one-shots, but this is the only book whose page length allowed for it to be featured, too.
"Naughty Honey♥"
This story was serialized in Puchi Princess magazine, so it's a weeeeee bit more adult-oriented than what is usually shown in Princess magazine. Still, my editor gave me the green light to feature it, saying it's still around the typical shojo manga level. Ha ha ha...haaaah...
It's not all that old, so I hope everybody can still enjoy it!!

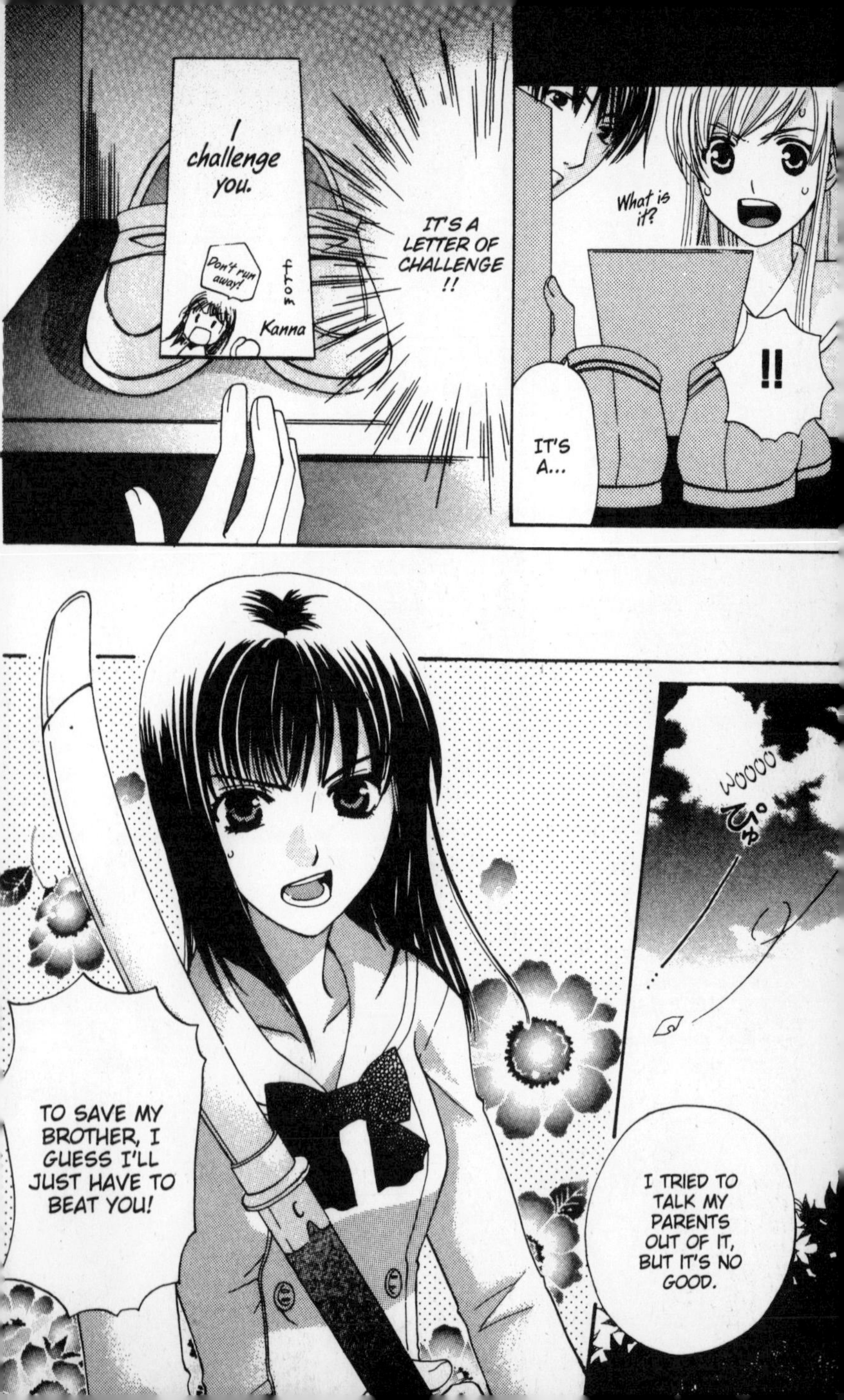
What is it?
!!
IT'S A...
I challenge you.
Don't run away!
from Kanna
IT'S A LETTER OF CHALLENGE!!
WOOOO
ぴゅ
...
I TRIED TO TALK MY PARENTS OUT OF IT, BUT IT'S NO GOOD.
TO SAVE MY BROTHER, I GUESS I'LL JUST HAVE TO BEAT YOU!

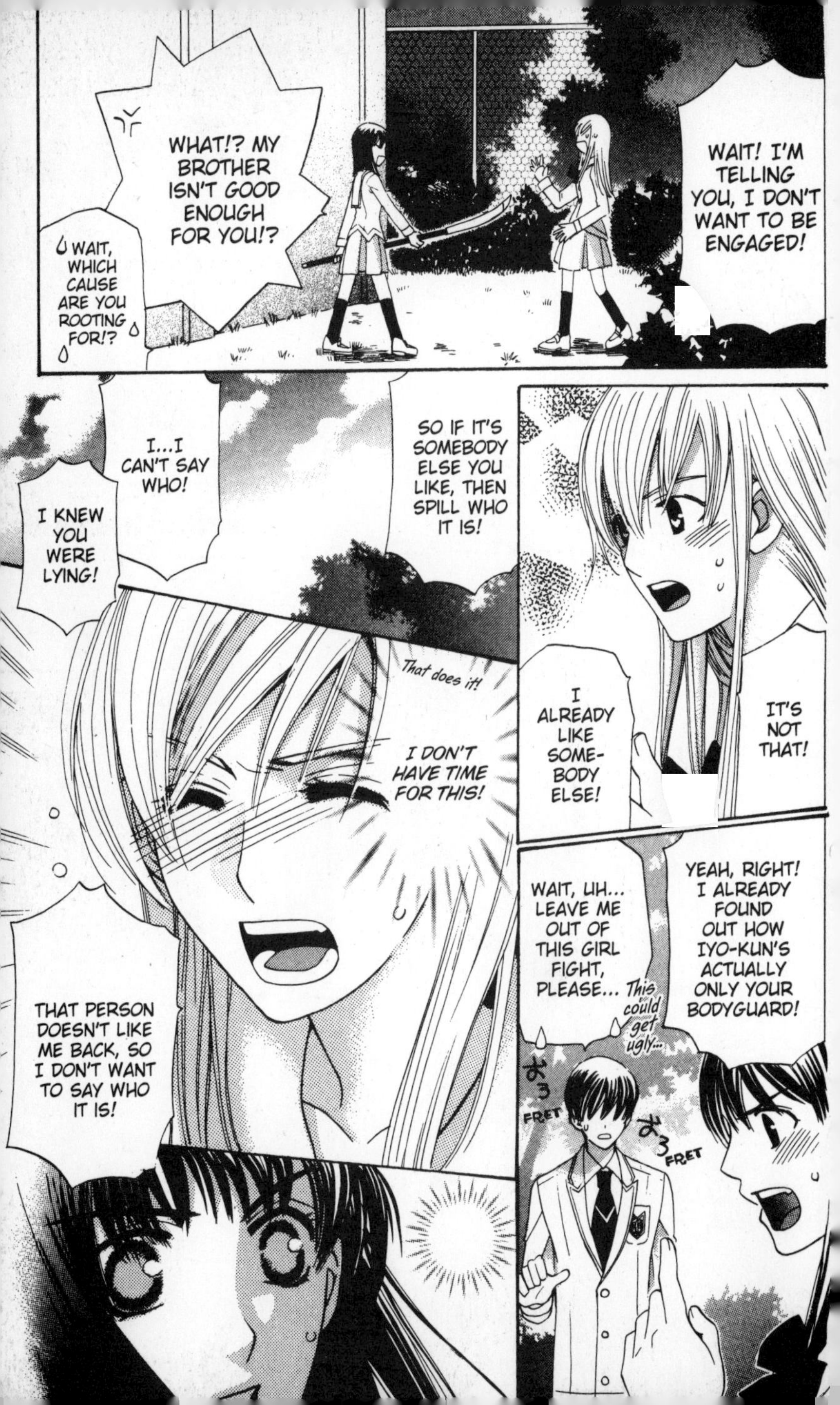

WAIT! I'M TELLING YOU, I DON'T WANT TO BE ENGAGED!
WHAT!? MY BROTHER ISN'T GOOD ENOUGH FOR YOU!?
WAIT, WHICH CAUSE ARE YOU ROOTING FOR!?
IT'S NOT THAT!
I ALREADY LIKE SOME-BODY ELSE!
SO IF IT'S SOMEBODY ELSE YOU LIKE, THEN SPILL WHO IT IS!
I...I CAN'T SAY WHO!
I KNEW YOU WERE LYING!
YEAH, RIGHT! I ALREADY FOUND OUT HOW IYO-KUN'S ACTUALLY ONLY YOUR BODYGUARD!
WAIT, UH... LEAVE ME OUT OF THIS GIRL FIGHT, PLEASE...
This could get ugly...
FRET
FRET
That does it!
I DON'T HAVE TIME FOR THIS!
THAT PERSON DOESN'T LIKE ME BACK, SO I DON'T WANT TO SAY WHO IT IS!

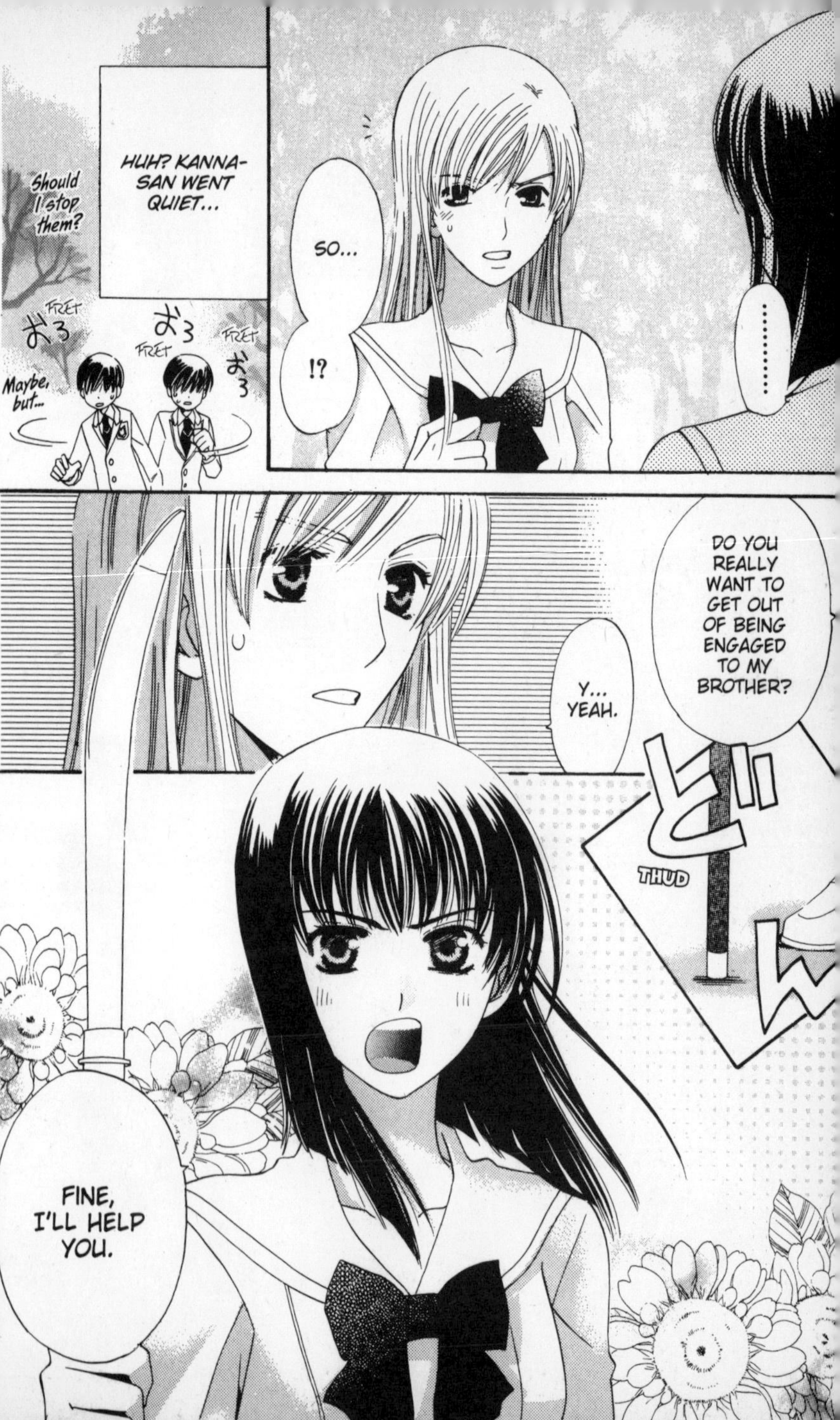
……
SO…
!?
HUH? KANNA-SAN WENT QUIET…
Should I stop them?
おろ FRET
おろ FRET
おろ FRET
Maybe, but…
DO YOU REALLY WANT TO GET OUT OF BEING ENGAGED TO MY BROTHER?
Y… YEAH.
どん
THUD
FINE, I'LL HELP YOU.

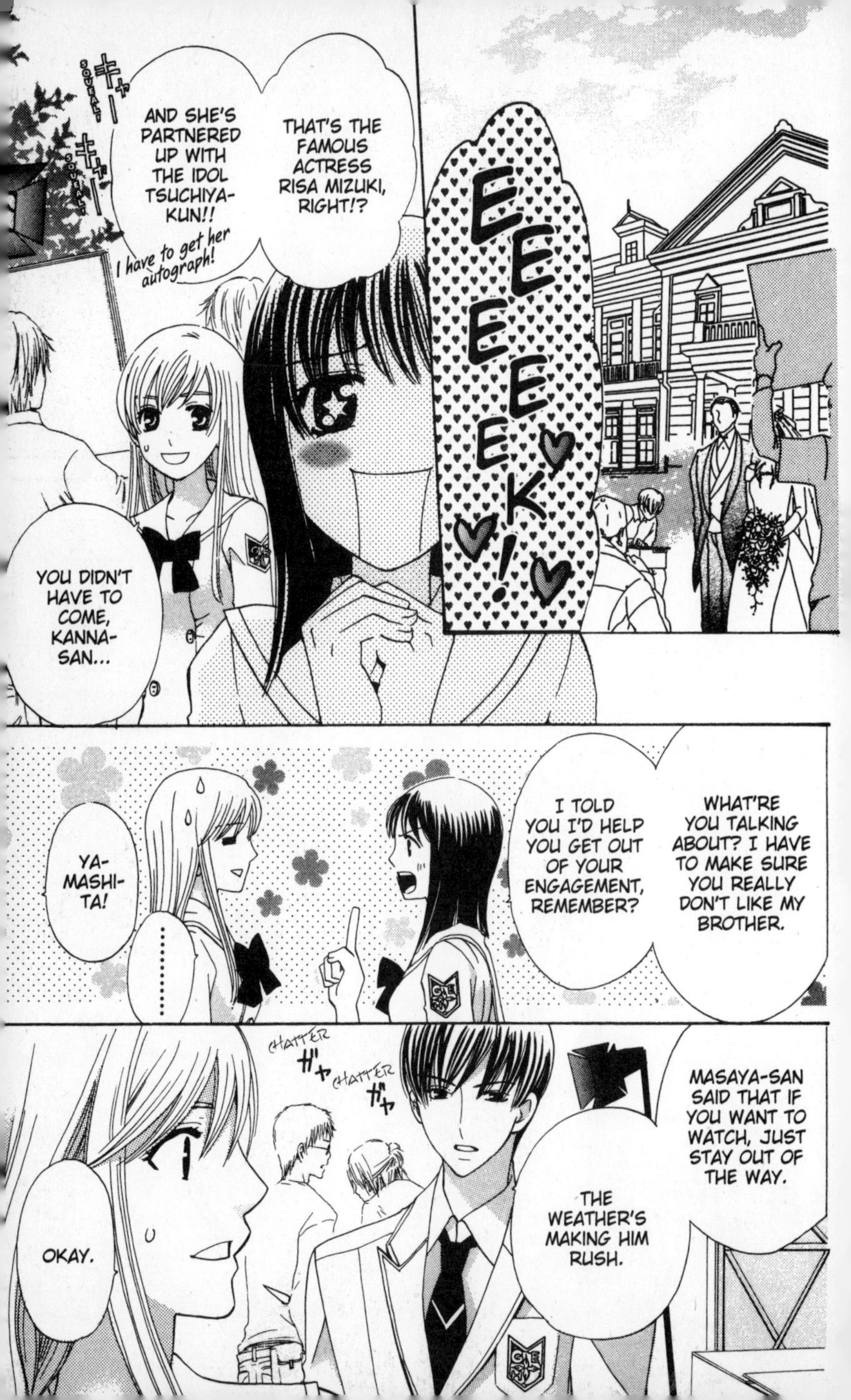
EEEEEK!
THAT'S THE FAMOUS ACTRESS RISA MIZUKI, RIGHT!?
AND SHE'S PARTNERED UP WITH THE IDOL TSUCHIYA-KUN!!
SQUEAL!
SQUEAL!
I have to get her autograph!
YOU DIDN'T HAVE TO COME, KANNA-SAN...
WHAT'RE YOU TALKING ABOUT? I HAVE TO MAKE SURE YOU REALLY DON'T LIKE MY BROTHER.
I TOLD YOU I'D HELP YOU GET OUT OF YOUR ENGAGEMENT, REMEMBER?
YA-MASHI-TA!
......
MASAYA-SAN SAID THAT IF YOU WANT TO WATCH, JUST STAY OUT OF THE WAY.
THE WEATHER'S MAKING HIM RUSH.
CHATTER
CHATTER
OKAY.

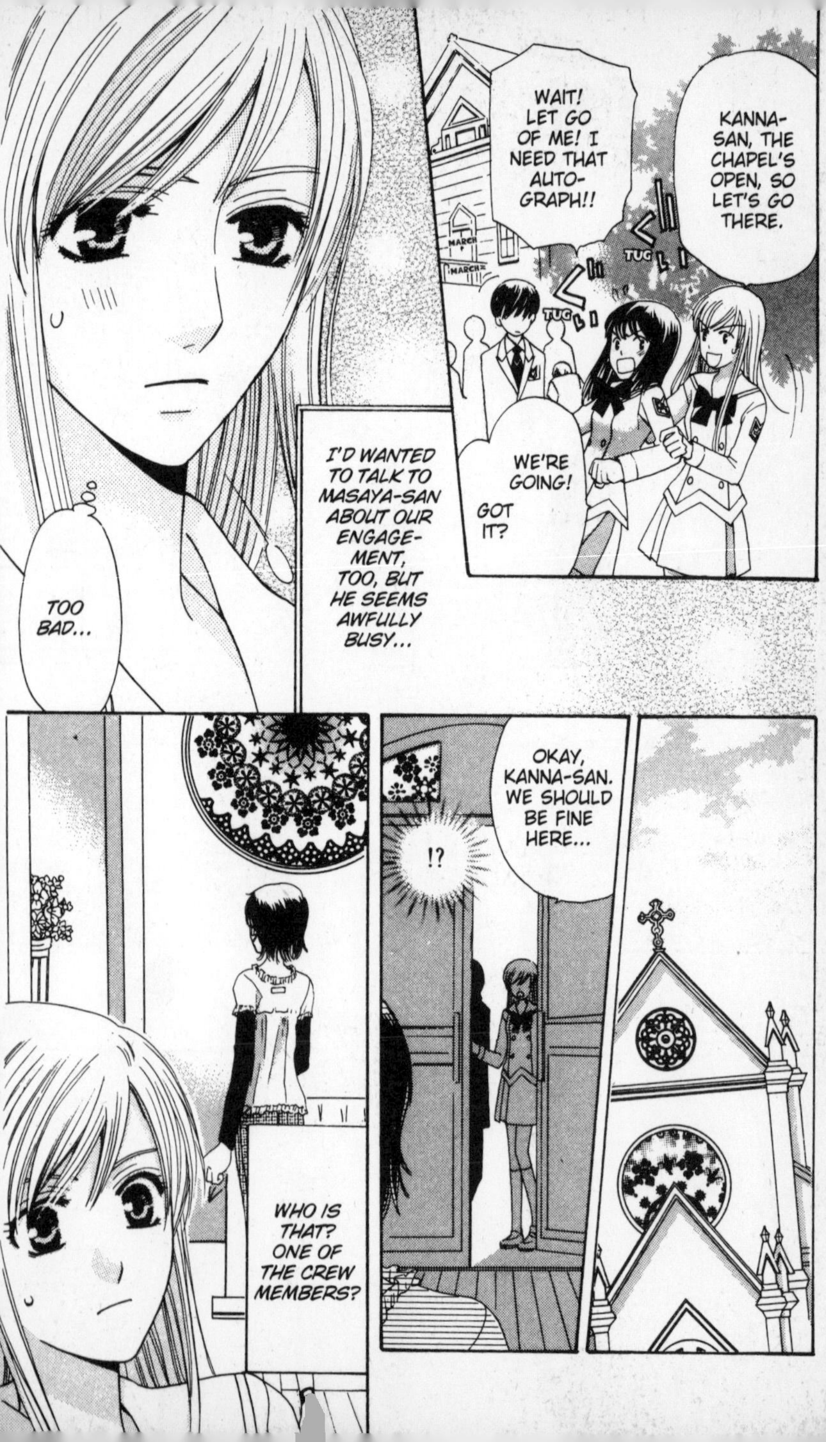
KANNA-SAN, THE CHAPEL'S OPEN, SO LET'S GO THERE.
WAIT! LET GO OF ME! I NEED THAT AUTOGRAPH!!
TUG
TUG
WE'RE GOING!
GOT IT?
I'D WANTED TO TALK TO MASAYA-SAN ABOUT OUR ENGAGEMENT, TOO, BUT HE SEEMS AWFULLY BUSY...
TOO BAD...
OKAY, KANNA-SAN. WE SHOULD BE FINE HERE...
!?
WHO IS THAT? ONE OF THE CREW MEMBERS?

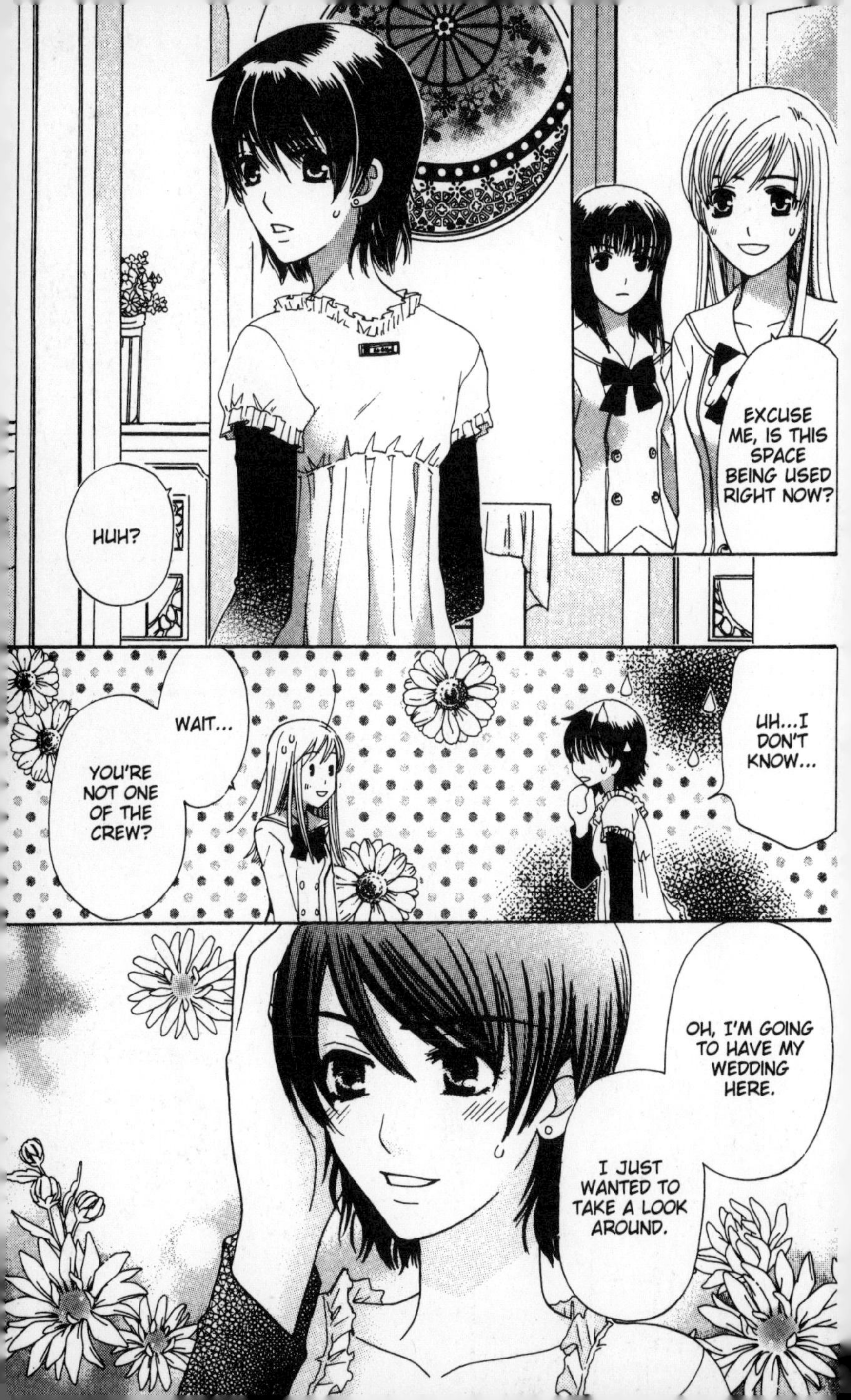
EXCUSE ME, IS THIS SPACE BEING USED RIGHT NOW?
HUH?
UH...I DON'T KNOW...
WAIT...
YOU'RE NOT ONE OF THE CREW?
OH, I'M GOING TO HAVE MY WEDDING HERE.
I JUST WANTED TO TAKE A LOOK AROUND.

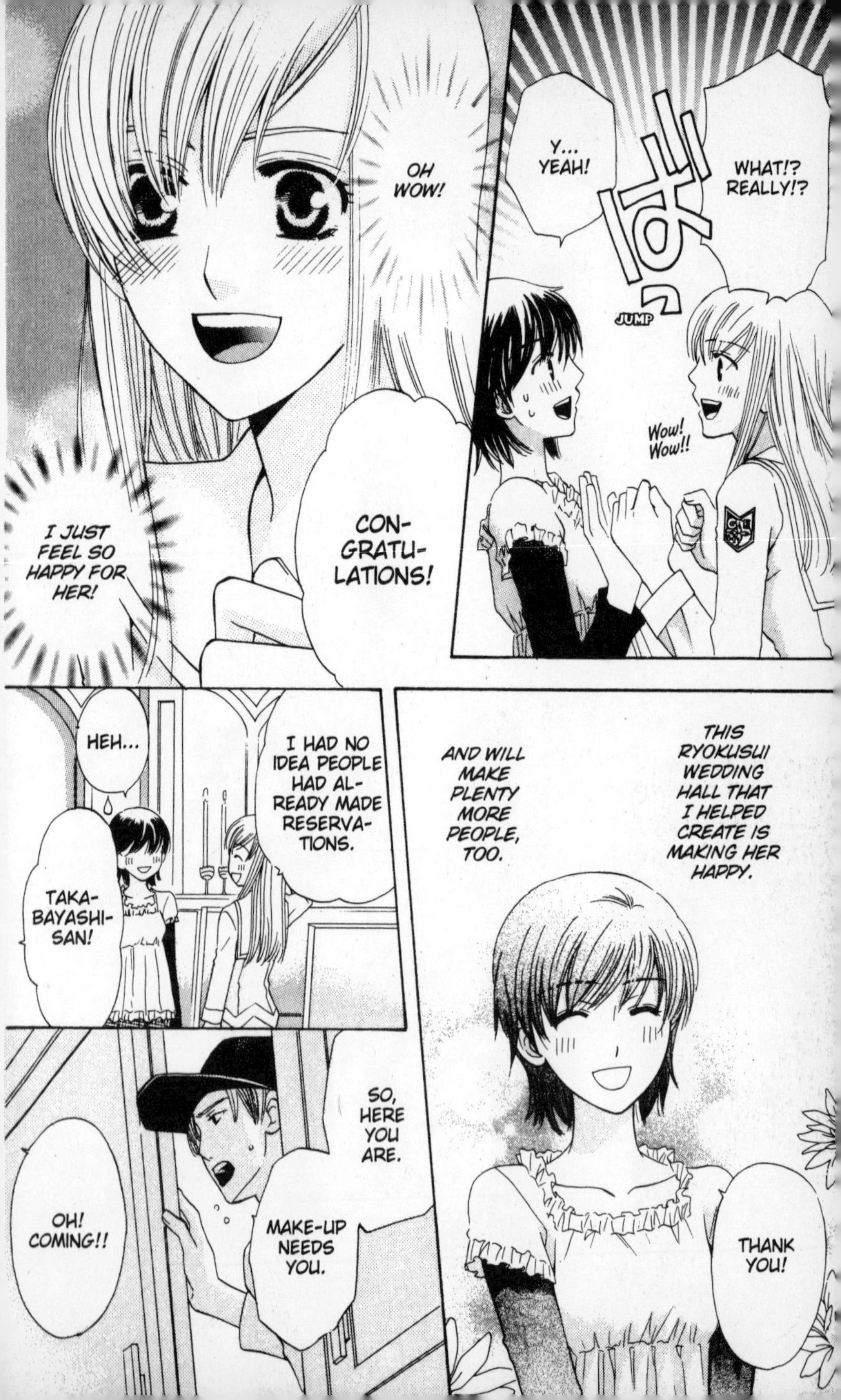
WHAT!? REALLY!?
Y... YEAH!
ぱっ
JUMP
Wow! Wow!!
OH WOW!
CON-GRATU-LATIONS!
I JUST FEEL SO HAPPY FOR HER!
THIS RYOKUSUI WEDDING HALL THAT I HELPED CREATE IS MAKING HER HAPPY.
AND WILL MAKE PLENTY MORE PEOPLE, TOO.
THANK YOU!
I HAD NO IDEA PEOPLE HAD AL-READY MADE RESERVA-TIONS.
HEH...
TAKA-BAYASHI-SAN!
SO, HERE YOU ARE.
MAKE-UP NEEDS YOU.
OH! COMING!!

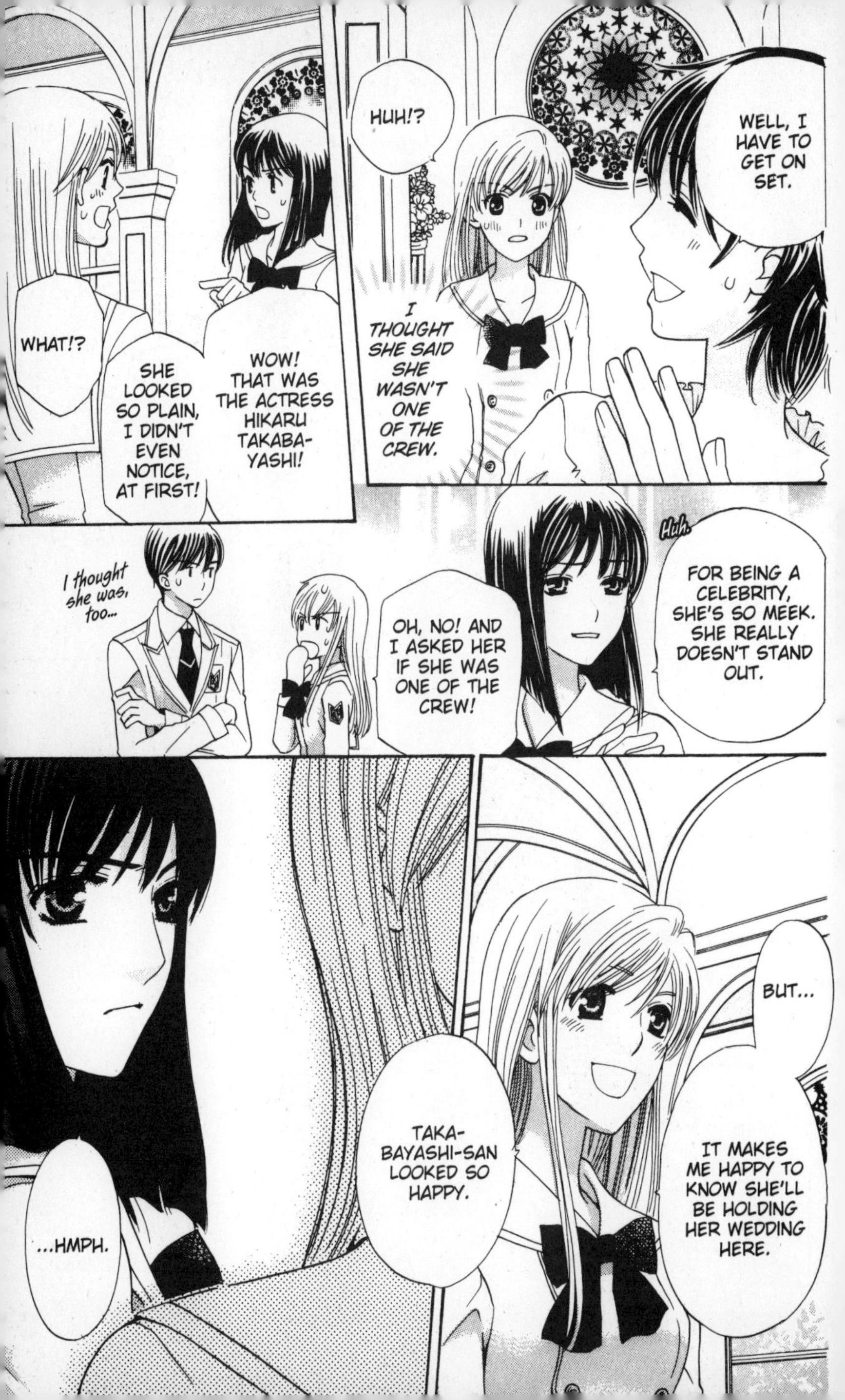

WELL, I HAVE TO GET ON SET.
HUH!?
I THOUGHT SHE SAID SHE WASN'T ONE OF THE CREW.
WOW! THAT WAS THE ACTRESS HIKARU TAKABA-YASHI!
SHE LOOKED SO PLAIN, I DIDN'T EVEN NOTICE, AT FIRST!
WHAT!?
Huh.
FOR BEING A CELEBRITY, SHE'S SO MEEK. SHE REALLY DOESN'T STAND OUT.
OH, NO! AND I ASKED HER IF SHE WAS ONE OF THE CREW!
I thought she was, too...
BUT...
IT MAKES ME HAPPY TO KNOW SHE'LL BE HOLDING HER WEDDING HERE.
TAKA-BAYASHI-SAN LOOKED SO HAPPY.
...HMPH.

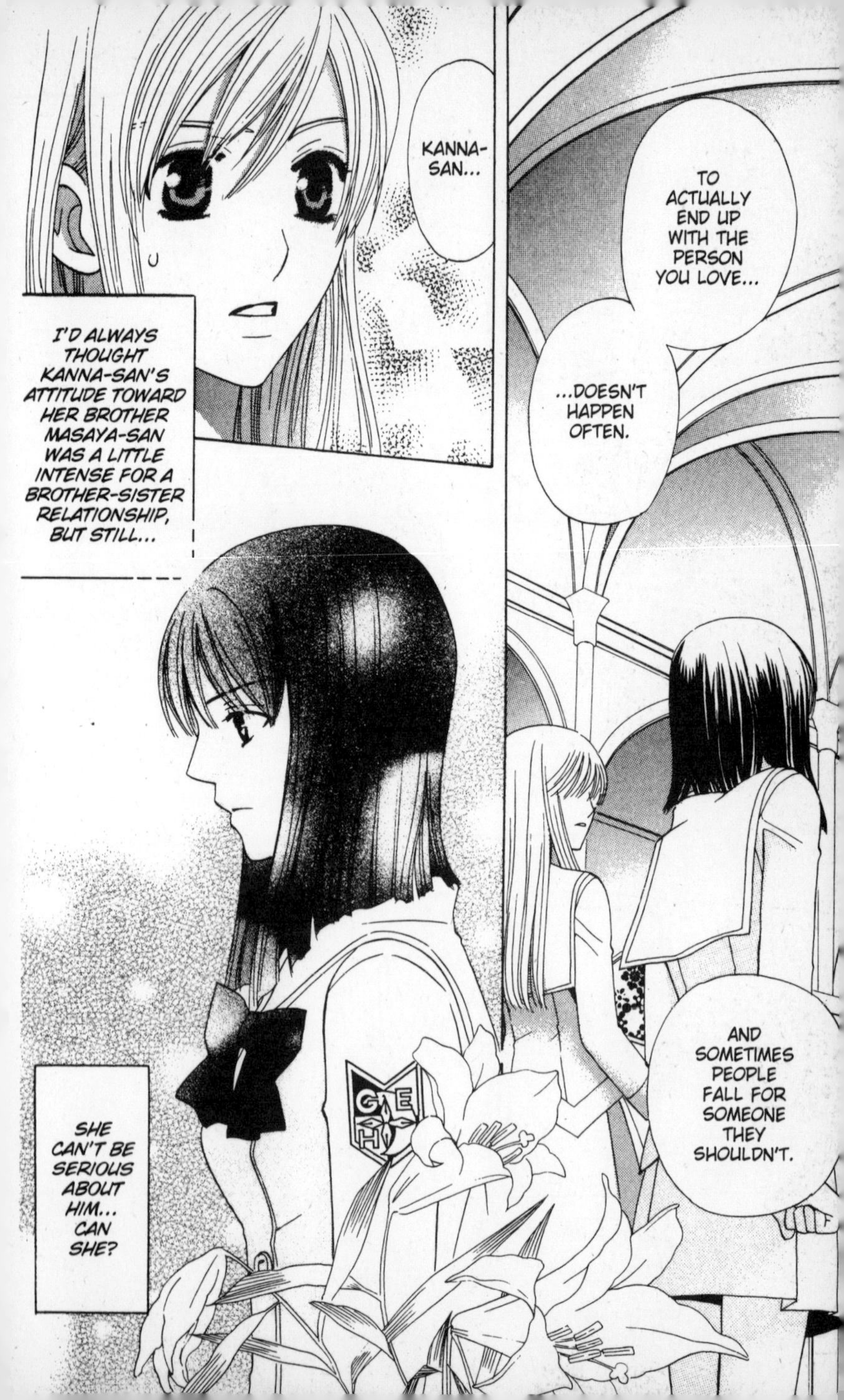
TO ACTUALLY END UP WITH THE PERSON YOU LOVE...
...DOESN'T HAPPEN OFTEN.
AND SOMETIMES PEOPLE FALL FOR SOMEONE THEY SHOULDN'T.
KANNA-SAN...
I'D ALWAYS THOUGHT KANNA-SAN'S ATTITUDE TOWARD HER BROTHER MASAYA-SAN WAS A LITTLE INTENSE FOR A BROTHER-SISTER RELATIONSHIP, BUT STILL...
SHE CAN'T BE SERIOUS ABOUT HIM... CAN SHE?

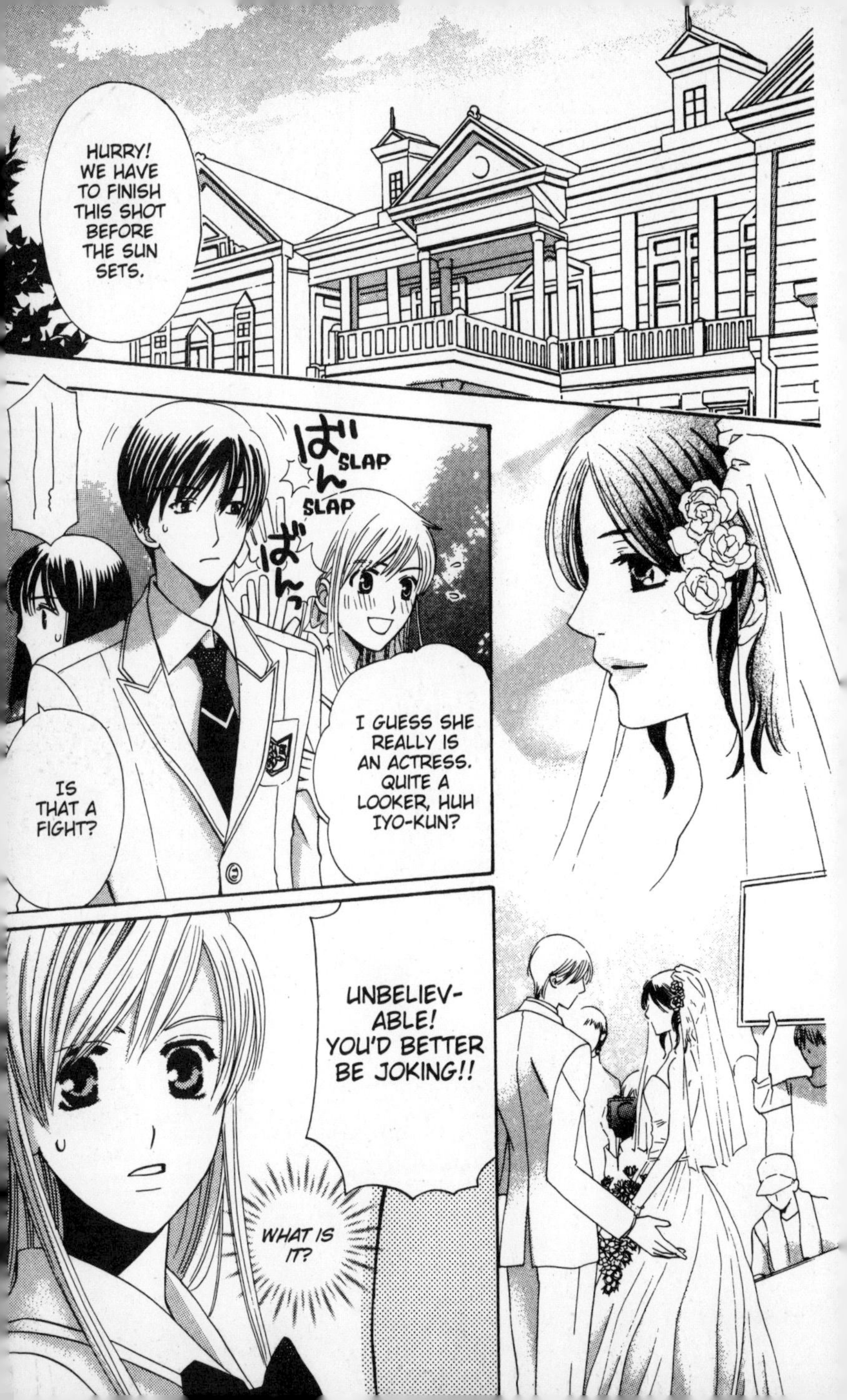
HURRY! WE HAVE TO FINISH THIS SHOT BEFORE THE SUN SETS.
ばん SLAP
ばんっ SLAP
I GUESS SHE REALLY IS AN ACTRESS. QUITE A LOOKER, HUH IYO-KUN?
IS THAT A FIGHT?
UNBELIEV-ABLE! YOU'D BETTER BE JOKING!!
WHAT IS IT?

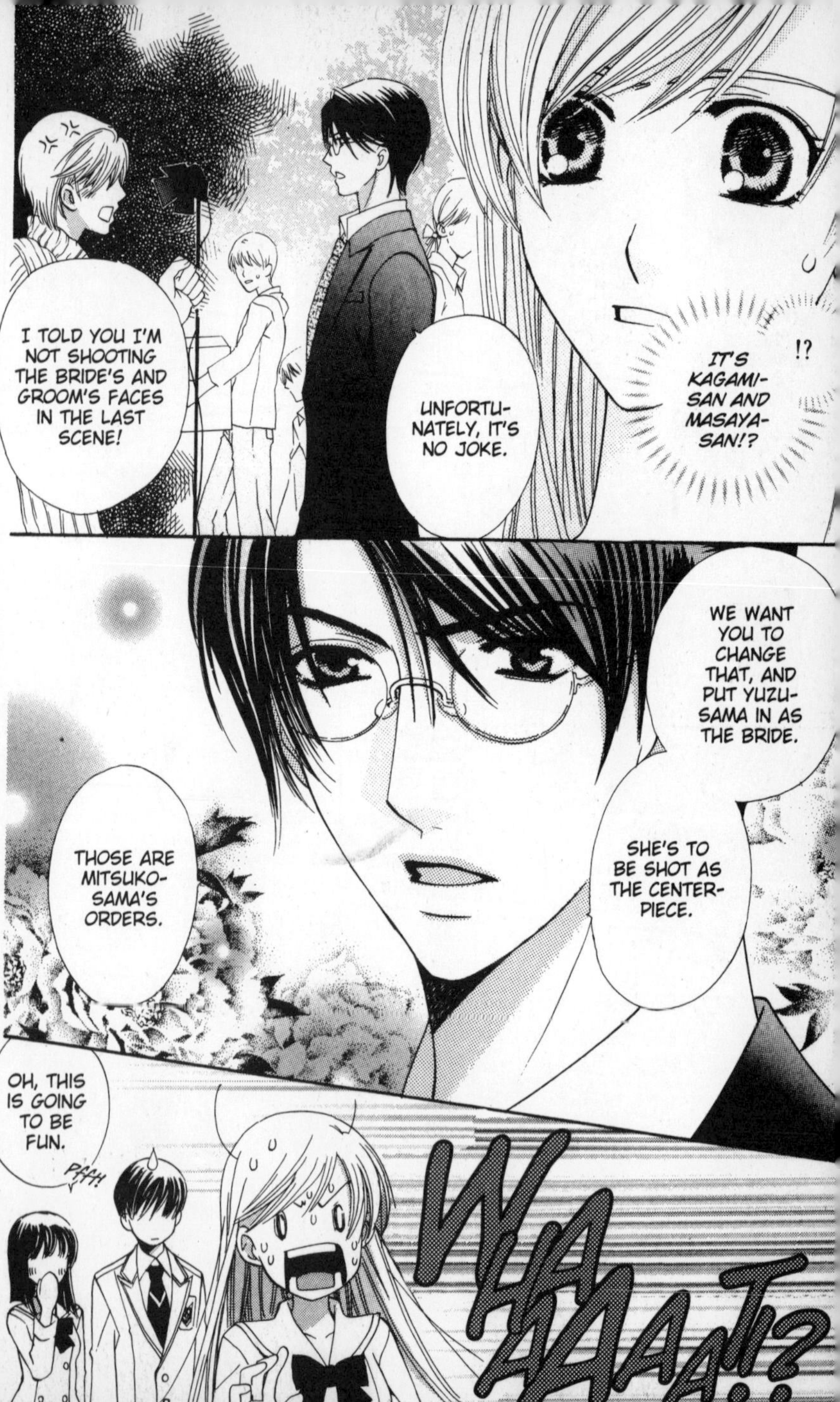

!?
IT'S KAGAMI-SAN AND MASAYA-SAN!?
UNFORTUNATELY, IT'S NO JOKE.
I TOLD YOU I'M NOT SHOOTING THE BRIDE'S AND GROOM'S FACES IN THE LAST SCENE!
WE WANT YOU TO CHANGE THAT, AND PUT YUZU-SAMA IN AS THE BRIDE.
SHE'S TO BE SHOT AS THE CENTER-PIECE.
THOSE ARE MITSUKO-SAMA'S ORDERS.
WHAAAAAT!?
PFFH!
OH, THIS IS GOING TO BE FUN.

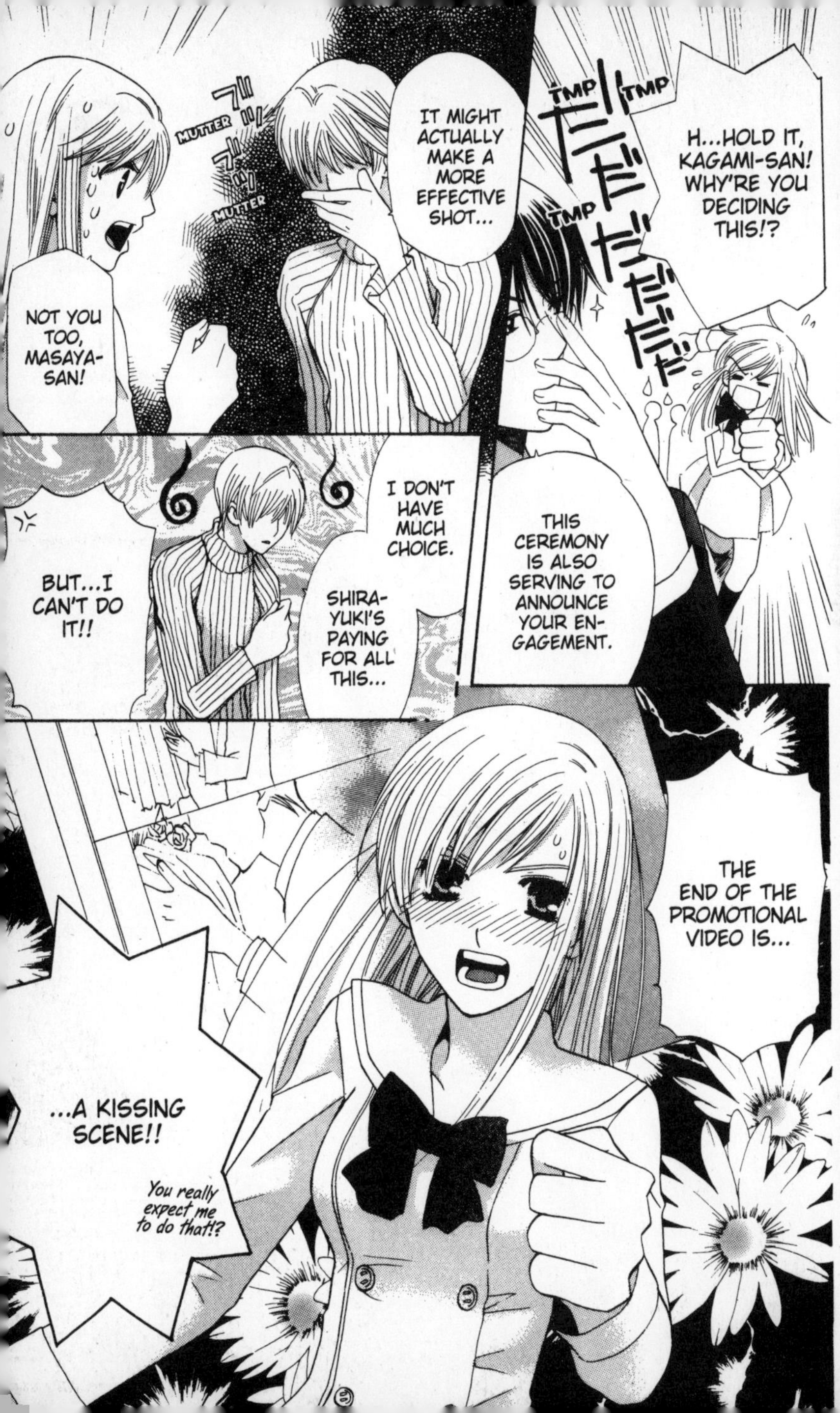
TMP TMP TMP
H...HOLD IT, KAGAMI-SAN! WHY'RE YOU DECIDING THIS!?
THIS CEREMONY IS ALSO SERVING TO ANNOUNCE YOUR EN-GAGEMENT.
IT MIGHT ACTUALLY MAKE A MORE EFFECTIVE SHOT...
MUTTER MUTTER
NOT YOU TOO, MASAYA-SAN!
I DON'T HAVE MUCH CHOICE.
SHIRA-YUKI'S PAYING FOR ALL THIS...
BUT...I CAN'T DO IT!!
THE END OF THE PROMOTIONAL VIDEO IS...
...A KISSING SCENE!!
You really expect me to do that!?

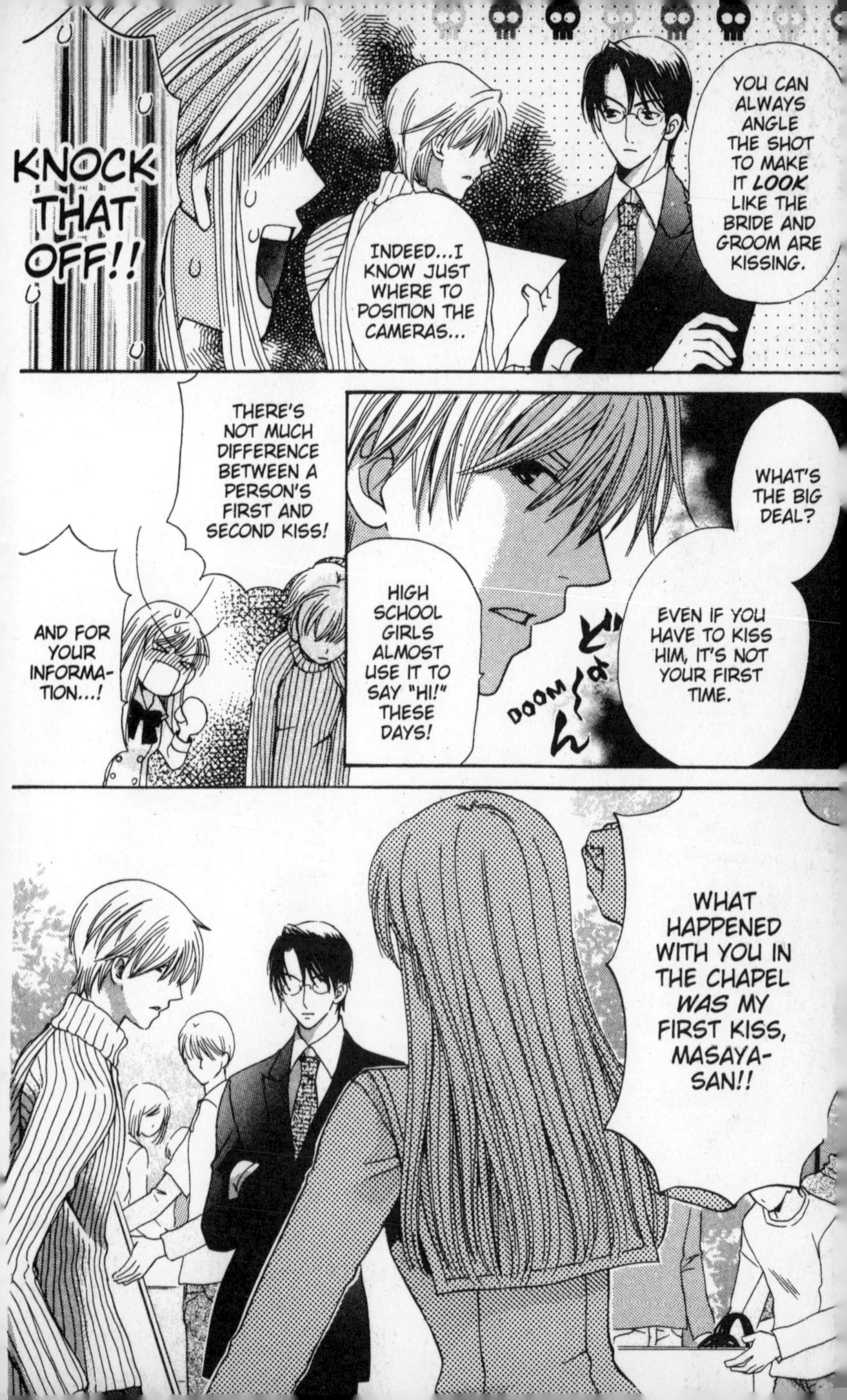
YOU CAN ALWAYS ANGLE THE SHOT TO MAKE IT *LOOK* LIKE THE BRIDE AND GROOM ARE KISSING.
INDEED...I KNOW JUST WHERE TO POSITION THE CAMERAS...
KNOCK THAT OFF!!
WHAT'S THE BIG DEAL?
EVEN IF YOU HAVE TO KISS HIM, IT'S NOT YOUR FIRST TIME.
DOOM
HIGH SCHOOL GIRLS ALMOST USE IT TO SAY "HI!" THESE DAYS!
THERE'S NOT MUCH DIFFERENCE BETWEEN A PERSON'S FIRST AND SECOND KISS!
AND FOR YOUR INFORMATION...!
WHAT HAPPENED WITH YOU IN THE CHAPEL *WAS* MY FIRST KISS, MASAYA-SAN!!

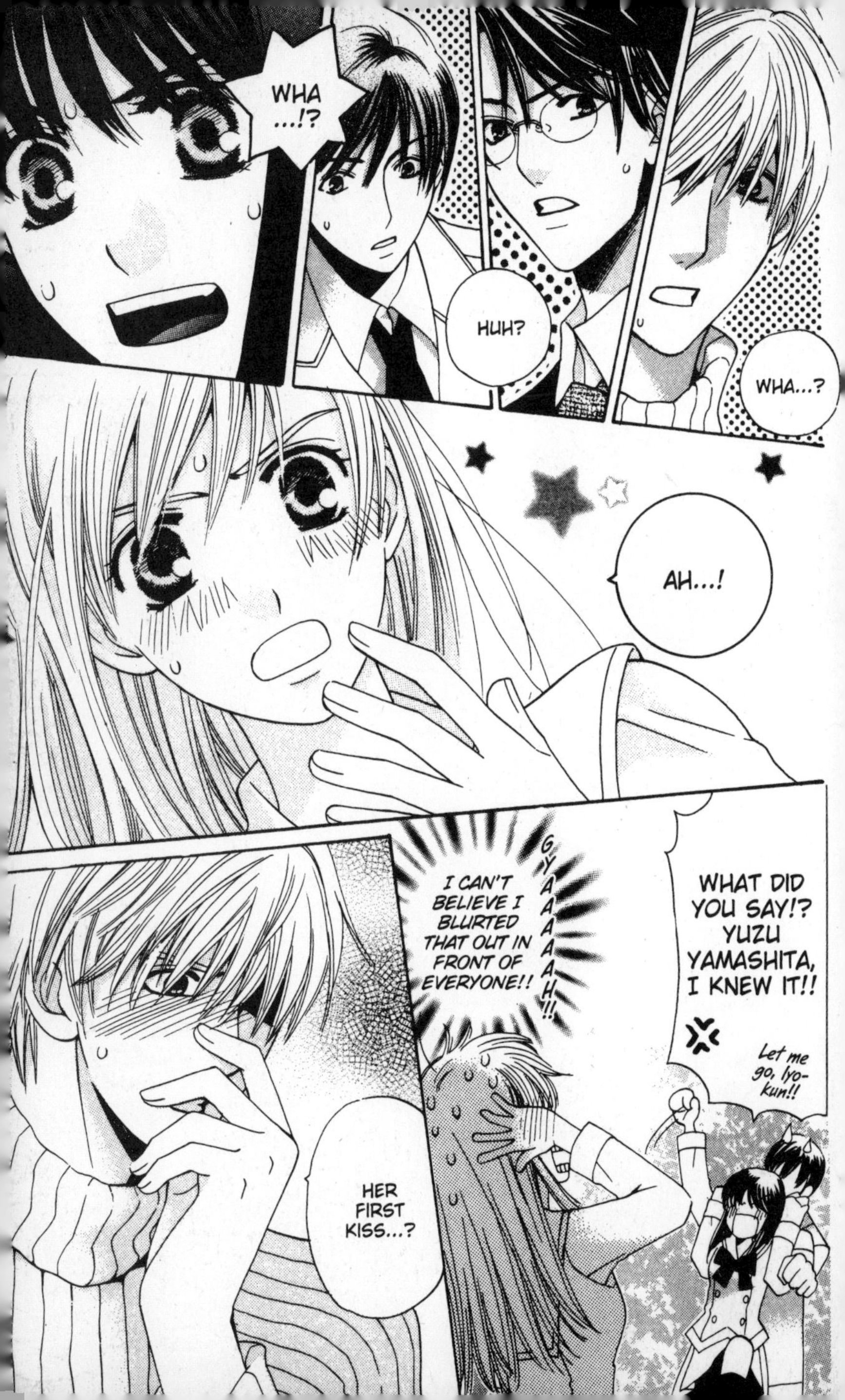
WHA...?
HUH?
WHA ...!?
AH...!
WHAT DID YOU SAY!? YUZU YAMASHITA, I KNEW IT!!
Let me go, Iyo-kun!!
GYAAAAAAAH!!
I CAN'T BELIEVE I BLURTED THAT OUT IN FRONT OF EVERYONE!!
HER FIRST KISS...?

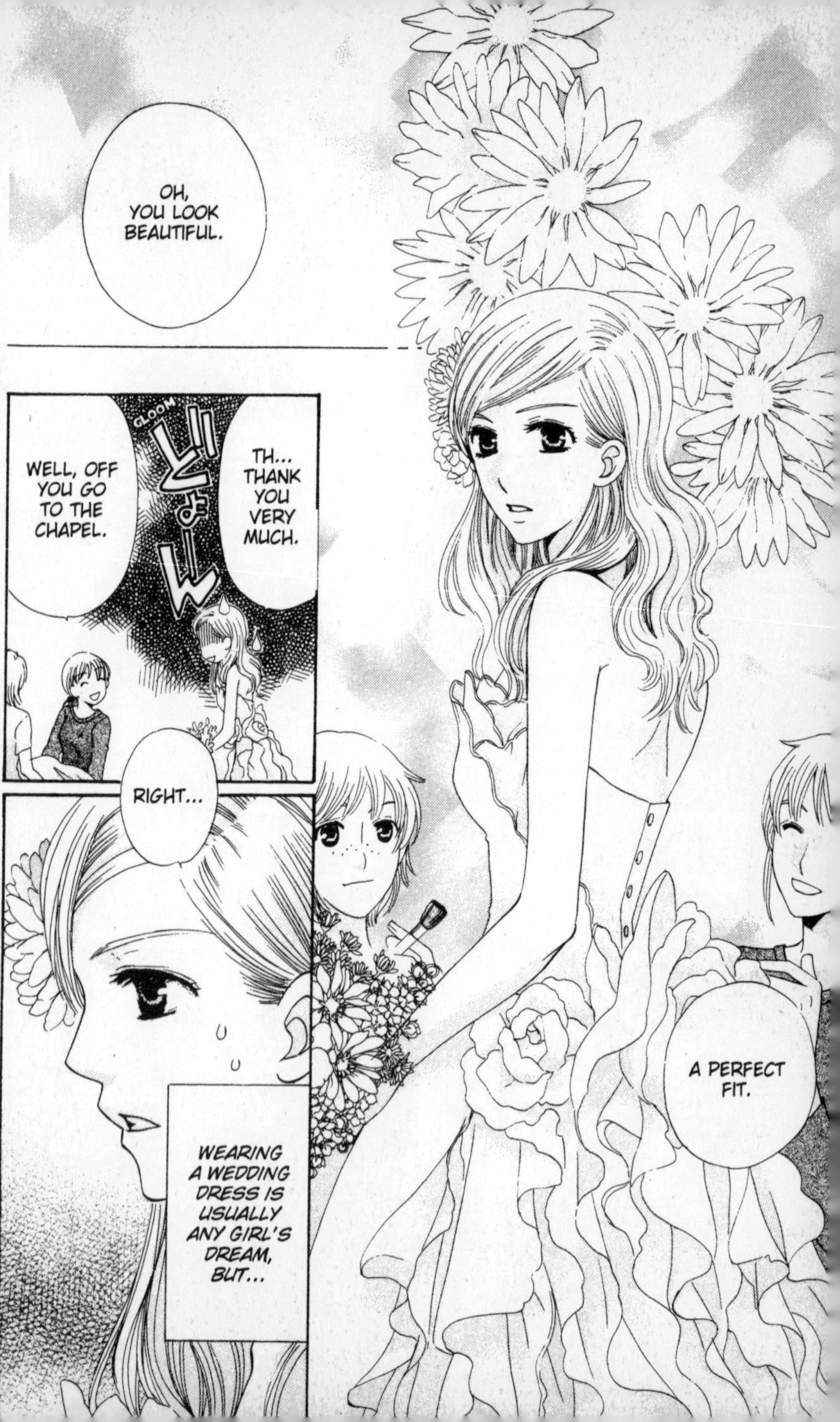

OH, YOU LOOK BEAUTIFUL.
A PERFECT FIT.
TH... THANK YOU VERY MUCH.
GLOOM
WELL, OFF YOU GO TO THE CHAPEL.
RIGHT...
WEARING A WEDDING DRESS IS USUALLY ANY GIRL'S DREAM, BUT...

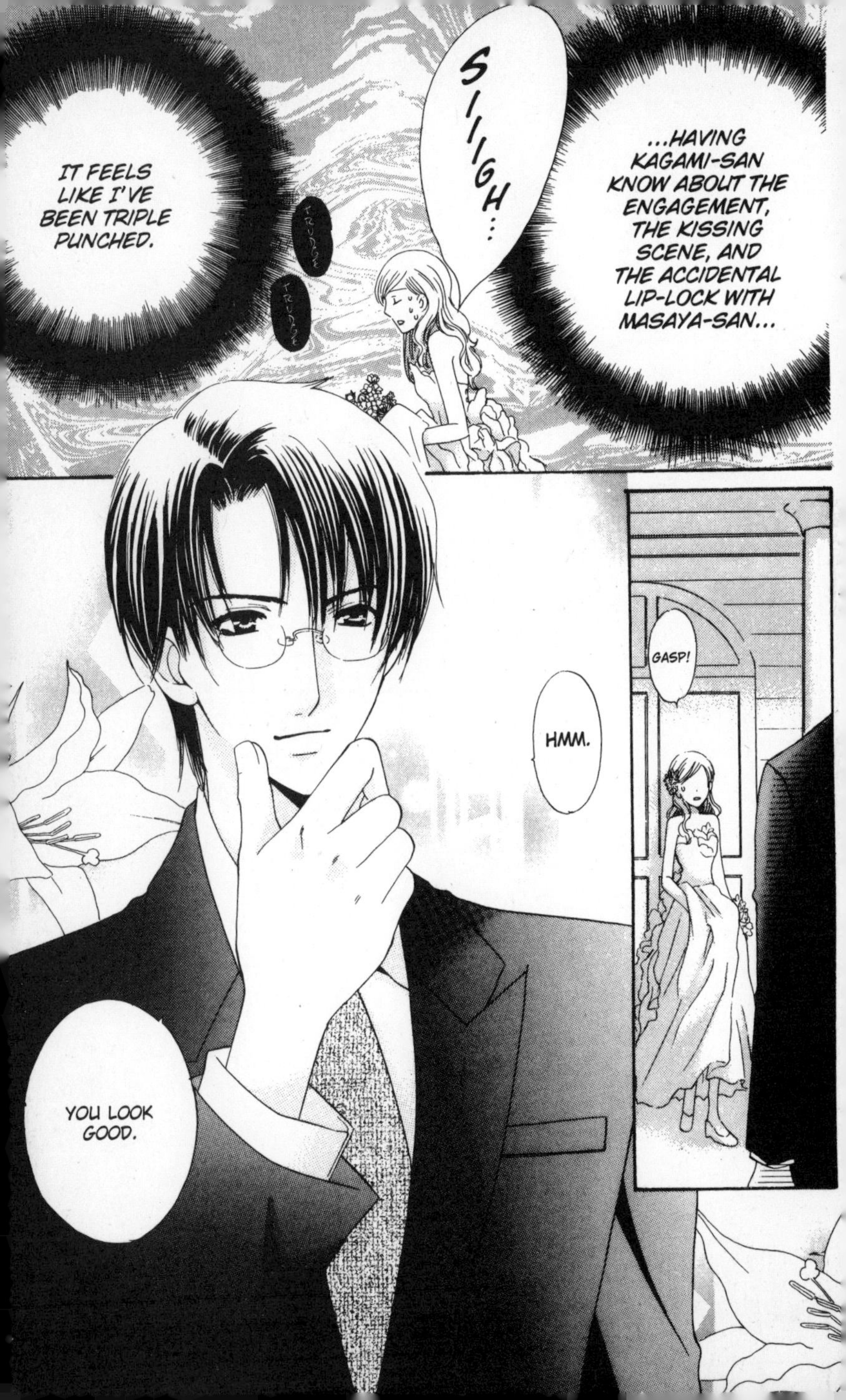
...HAVING KAGAMI-SAN KNOW ABOUT THE ENGAGEMENT, THE KISSING SCENE, AND THE ACCIDENTAL LIP-LOCK WITH MASAYA-SAN...
SIIIGH...
TRUDGE
TRUDGE
IT FEELS LIKE I'VE BEEN TRIPLE PUNCHED.
GASP!
HMM.
YOU LOOK GOOD.

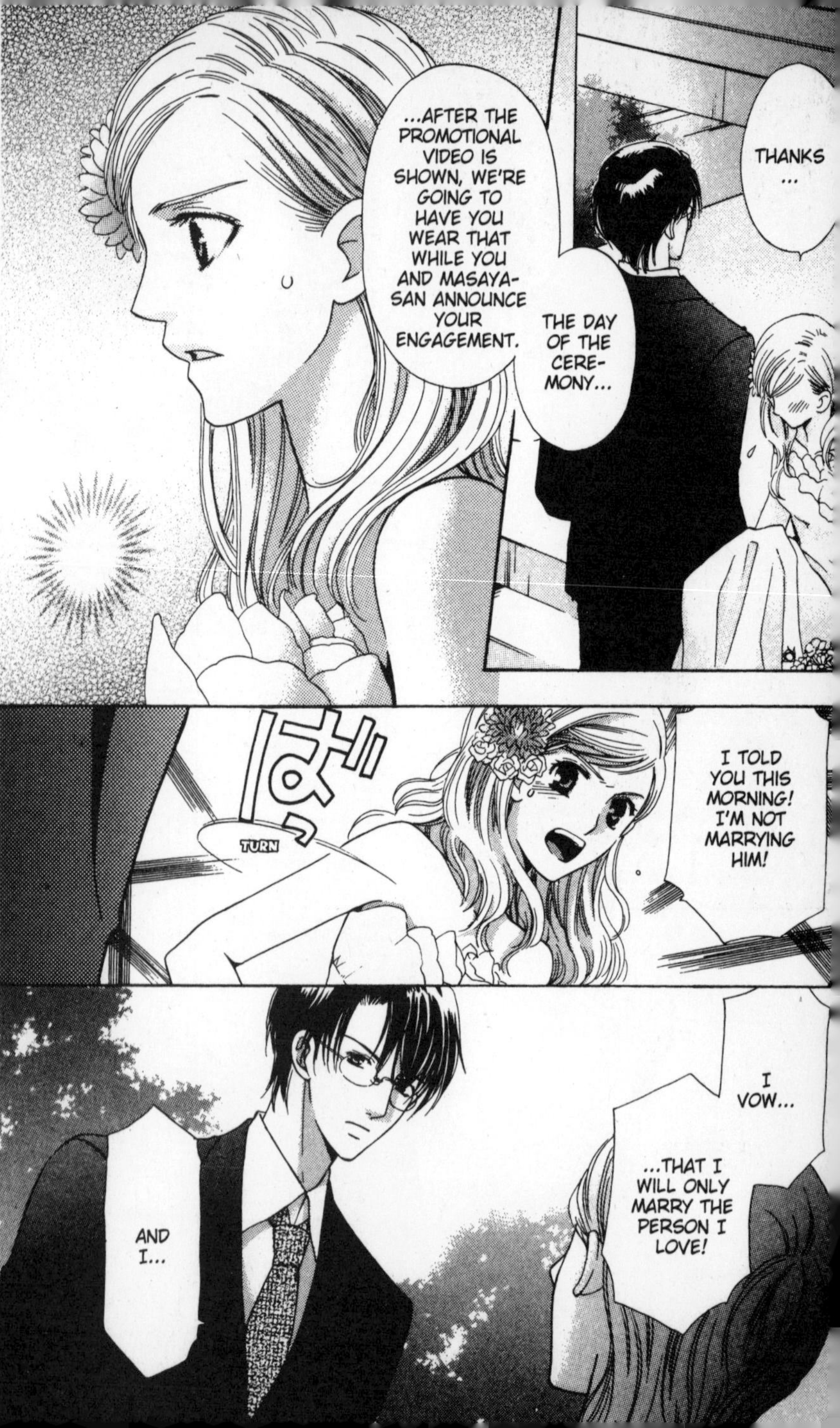
THANKS...
THE DAY OF THE CEREMONY...
...AFTER THE PROMOTIONAL VIDEO IS SHOWN, WE'RE GOING TO HAVE YOU WEAR THAT WHILE YOU AND MASAYA-SAN ANNOUNCE YOUR ENGAGEMENT.
I TOLD YOU THIS MORNING! I'M NOT MARRYING HIM!
ぱっ
TURN
I VOW...
...THAT I WILL ONLY MARRY THE PERSON I LOVE!
AND I...

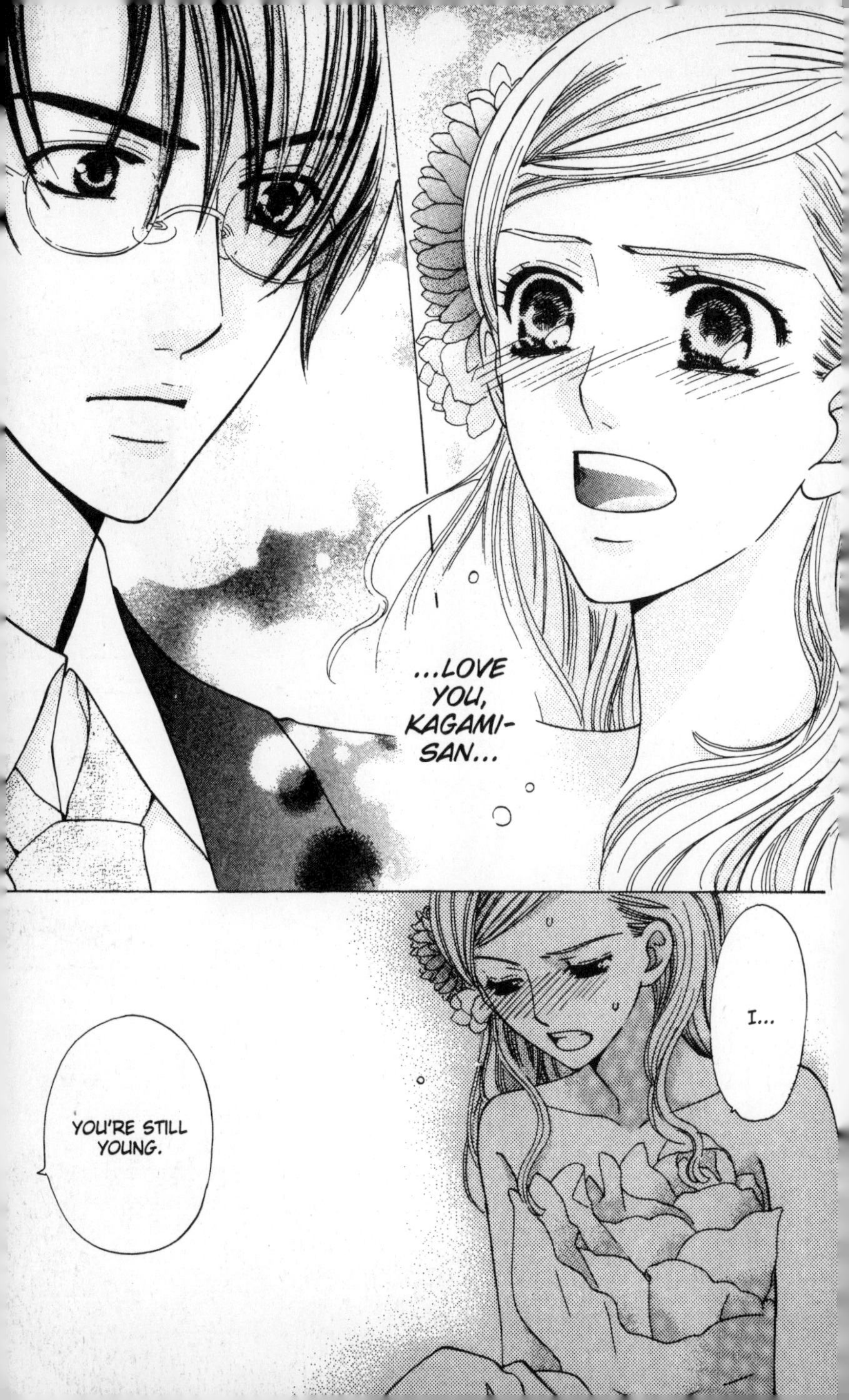
...LOVE YOU, KAGAMI-SAN...
I...
YOU'RE STILL YOUNG.

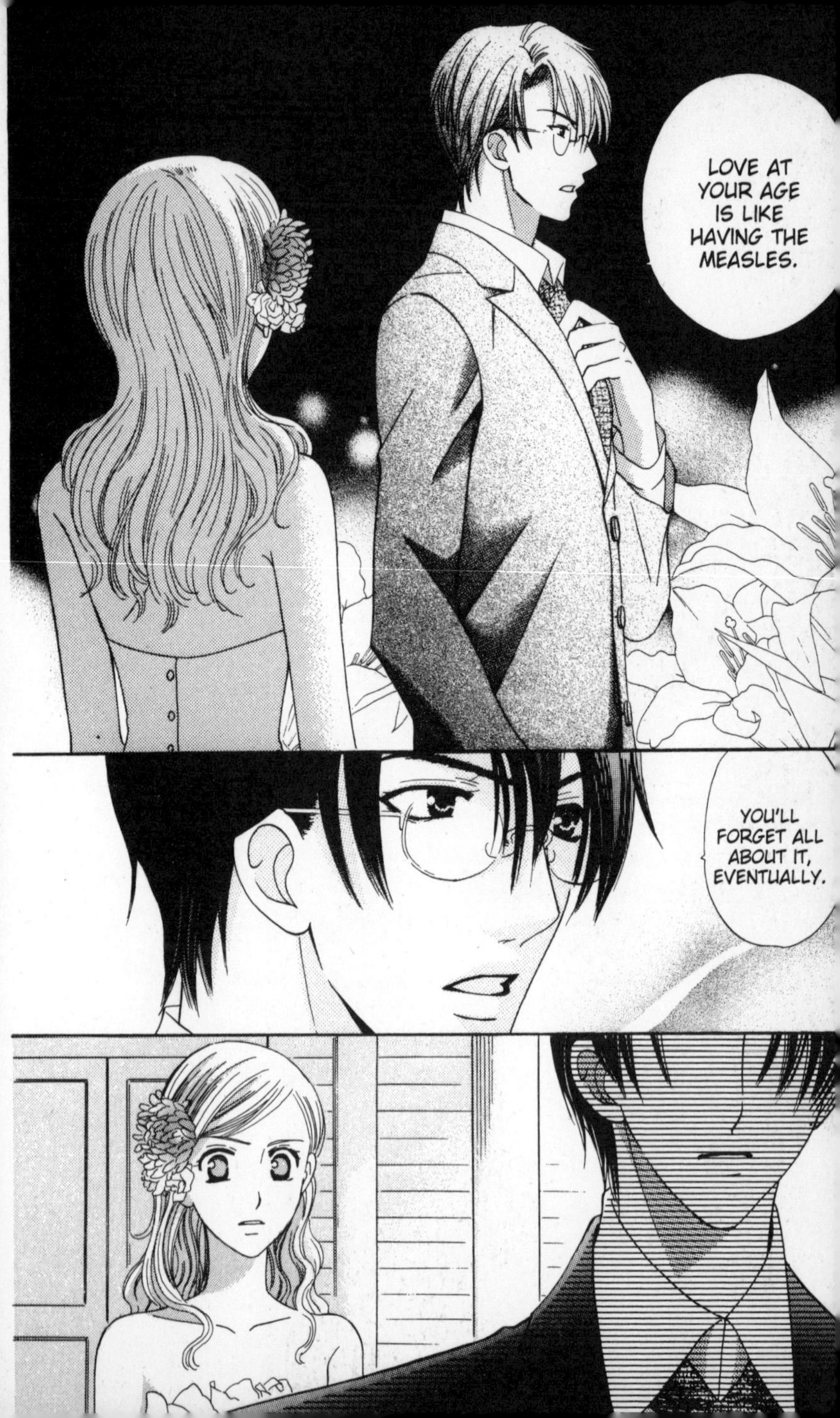
LOVE AT YOUR AGE IS LIKE HAVING THE MEASLES.
YOU'LL FORGET ALL ABOUT IT, EVENTUALLY.

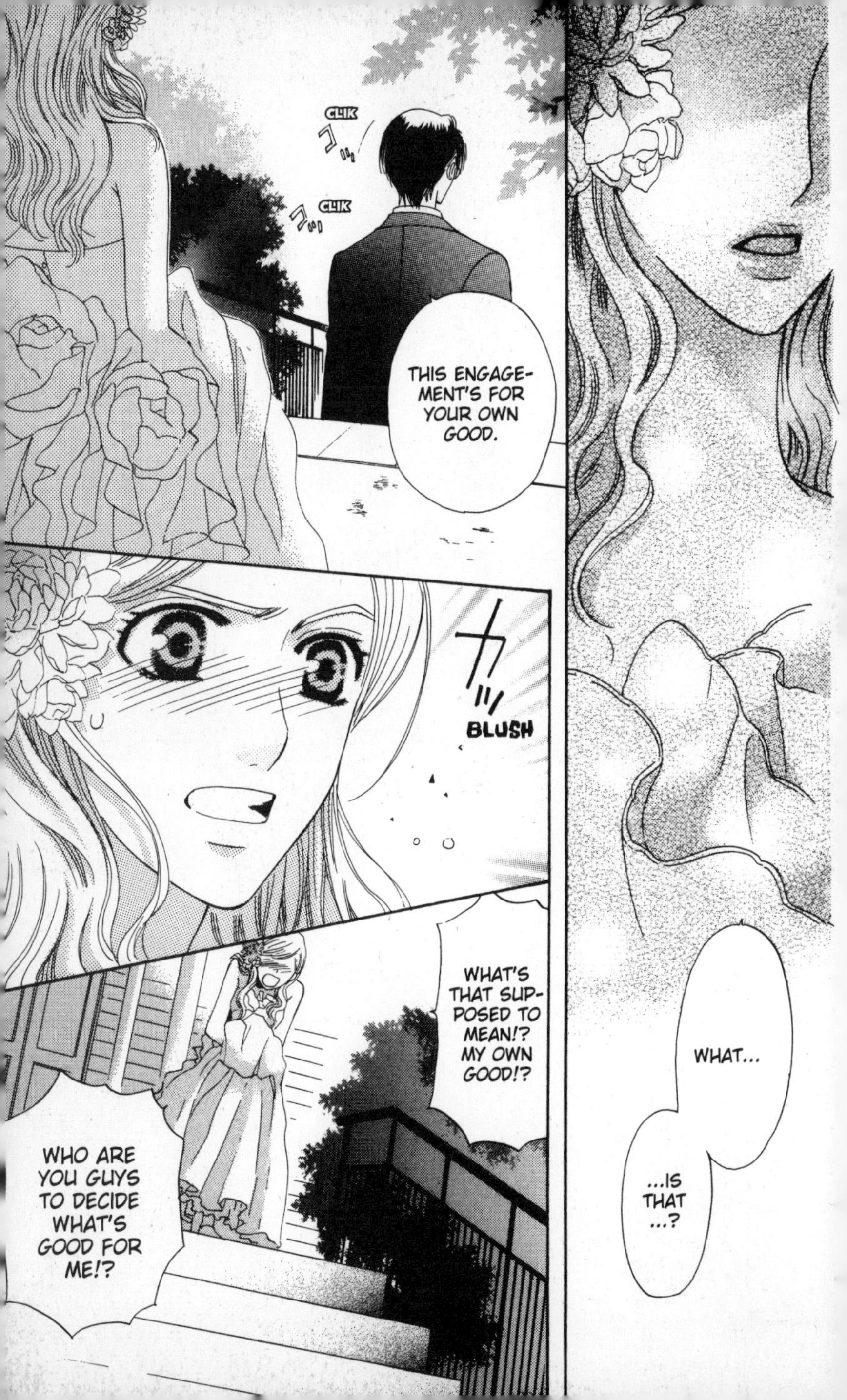
WHAT...
...IS THAT ...?
CLIK
CLIK
THIS ENGAGE-MENT'S FOR YOUR OWN GOOD.
BLUSH
WHAT'S THAT SUP-POSED TO MEAN!? MY OWN GOOD!?
WHO ARE YOU GUYS TO DECIDE WHAT'S GOOD FOR ME!?

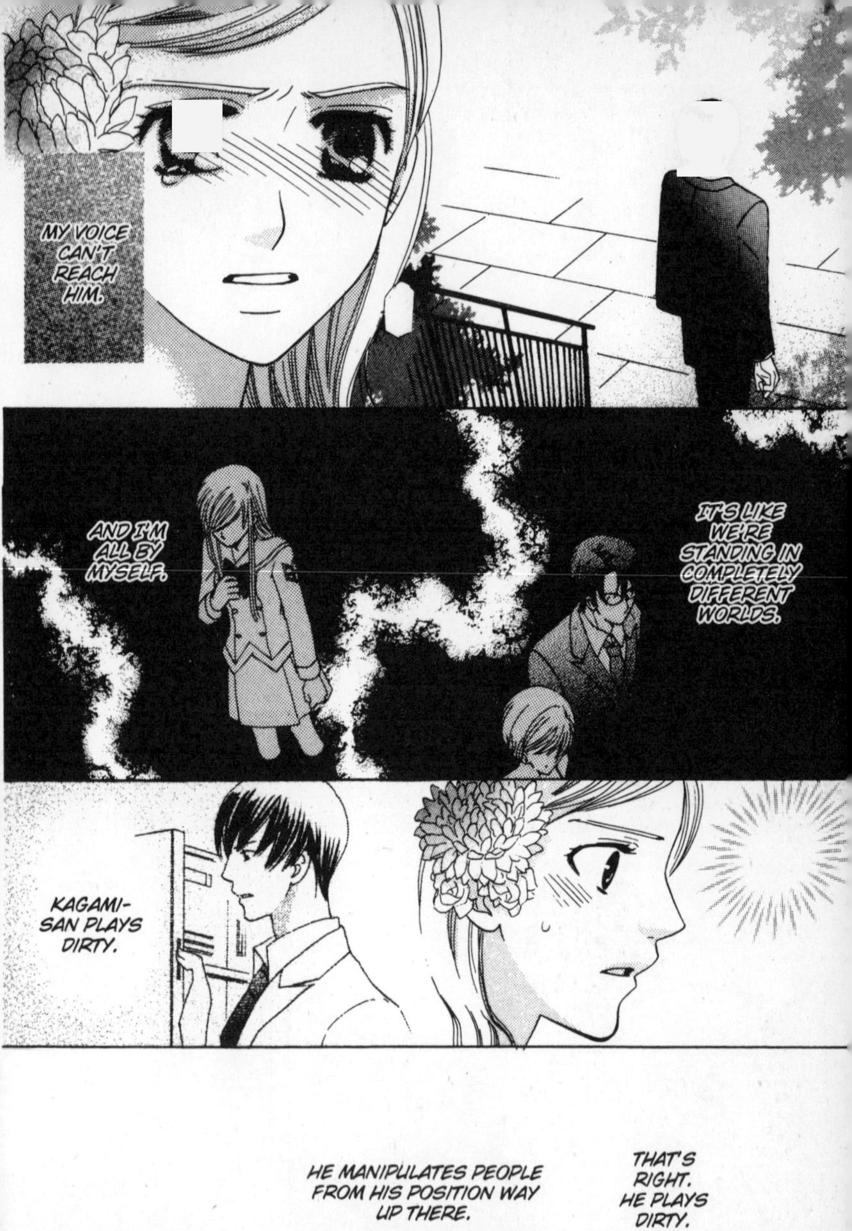
MY VOICE CAN'T REACH HIM.
IT'S LIKE WE'RE STANDING IN COMPLETELY DIFFERENT WORLDS.
AND I'M ALL BY MYSELF.
KAGAMI-SAN PLAYS DIRTY.
THAT'S RIGHT. HE PLAYS DIRTY.
HE MANIPULATES PEOPLE FROM HIS POSITION WAY UP THERE.

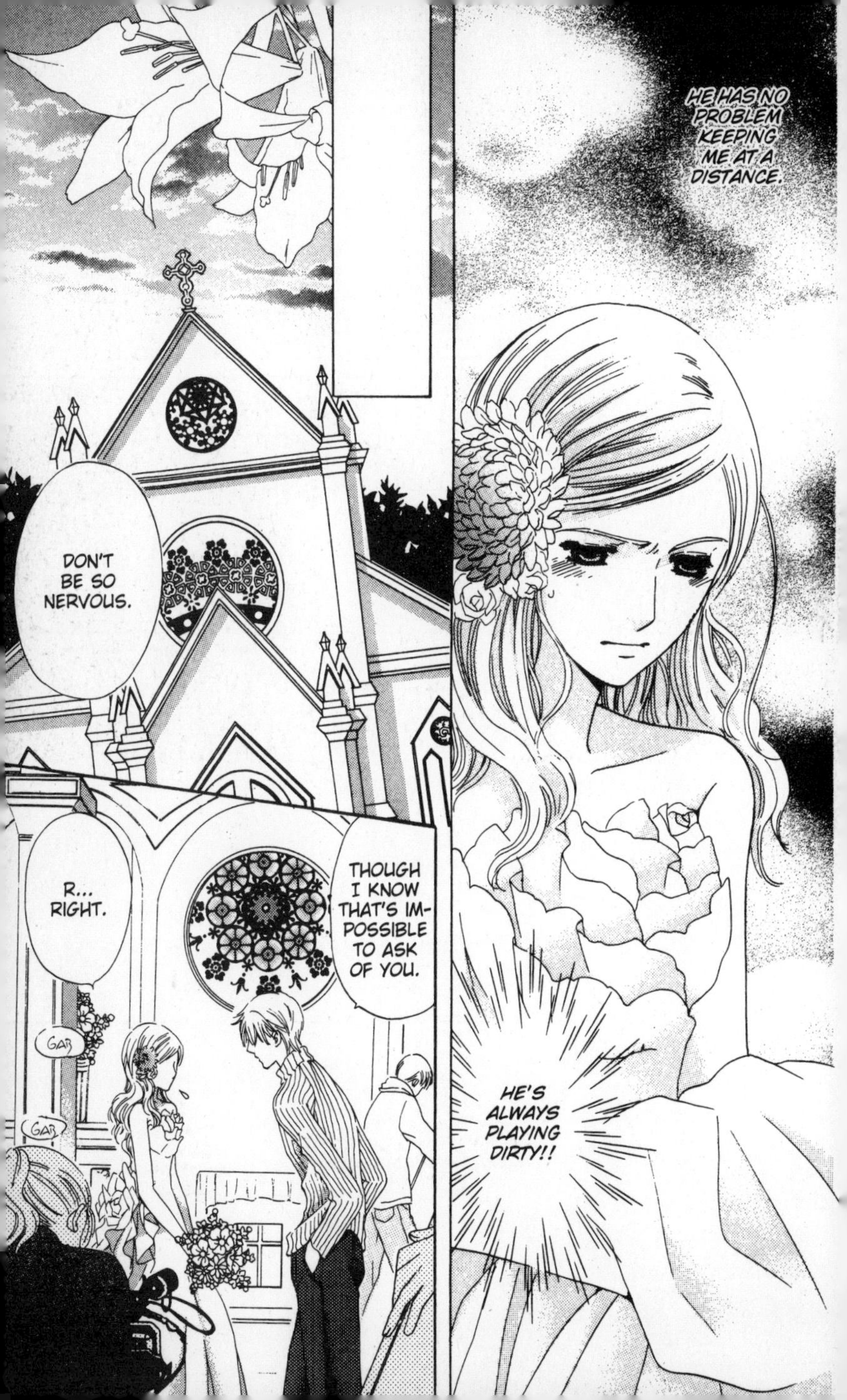
HE HAS NO PROBLEM KEEPING ME AT A DISTANCE.
HE'S ALWAYS PLAYING DIRTY!!
DON'T BE SO NERVOUS.
THOUGH I KNOW THAT'S IM-POSSIBLE TO ASK OF YOU.
R... RIGHT.
GAR
GAR

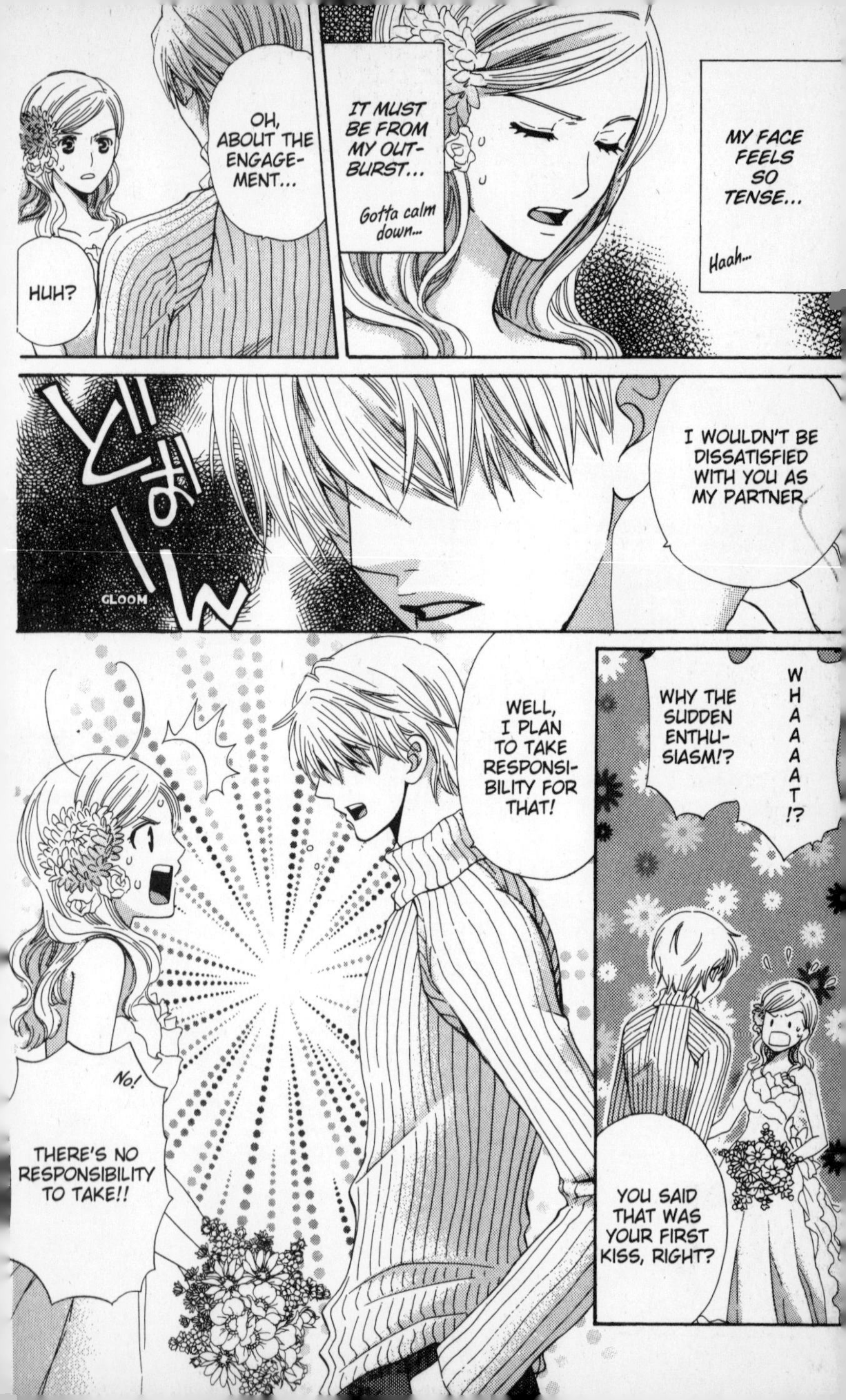
MY FACE FEELS SO TENSE...
Haah...
IT MUST BE FROM MY OUT-BURST...
Gotta calm down...
OH, ABOUT THE ENGAGE-MENT...
HUH?
I WOULDN'T BE DISSATISFIED WITH YOU AS MY PARTNER.
GLOOM
WHAAAAAT!?
WHY THE SUDDEN ENTHU-SIASM!?
YOU SAID THAT WAS YOUR FIRST KISS, RIGHT?
WELL, I PLAN TO TAKE RESPONSI-BILITY FOR THAT!
No!
THERE'S NO RESPONSIBILITY TO TAKE!!

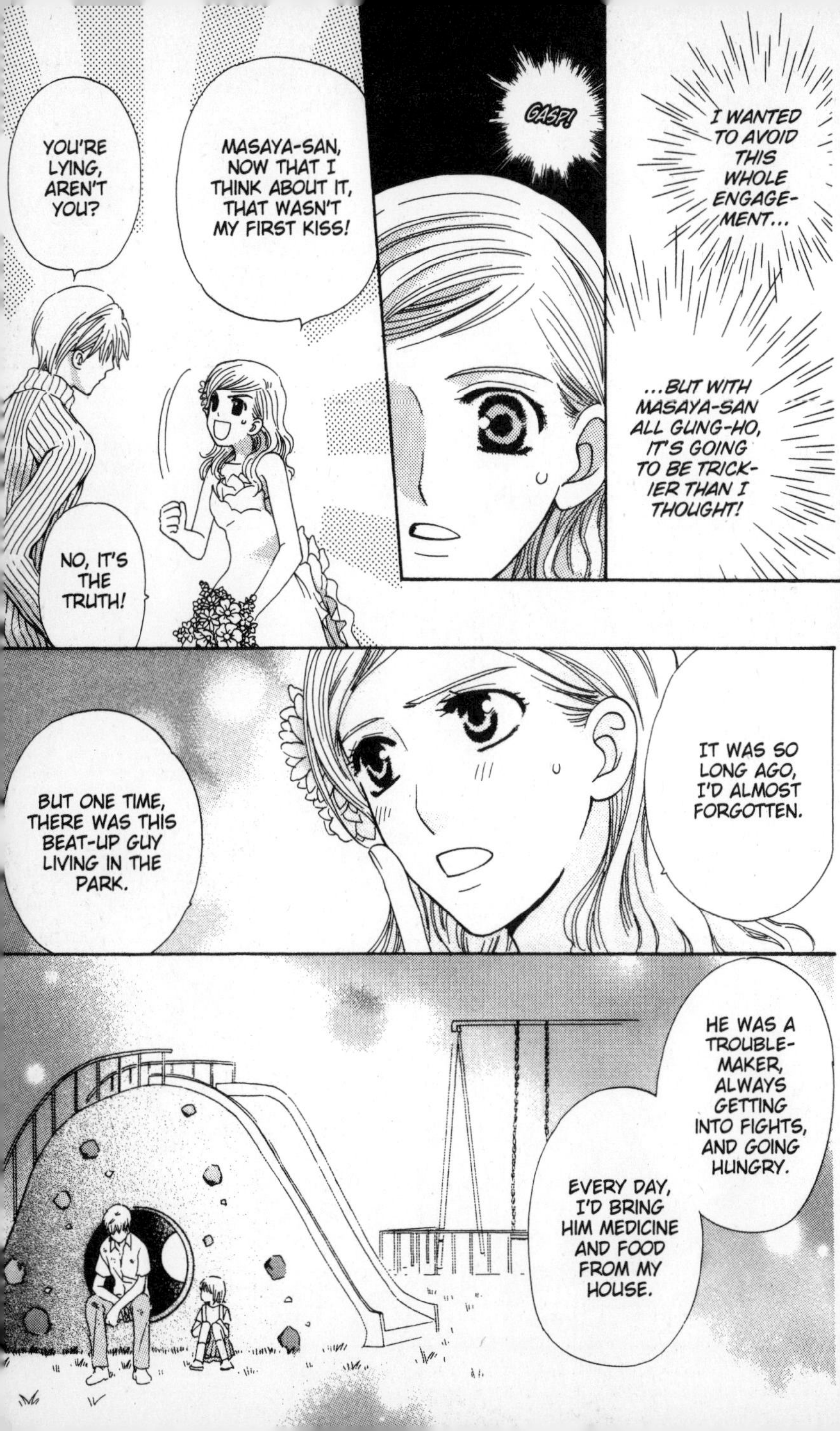
GASP!
I WANTED TO AVOID THIS WHOLE ENGAGE-MENT...
...BUT WITH MASAYA-SAN ALL GUNG-HO, IT'S GOING TO BE TRICK-IER THAN I THOUGHT!
MASAYA-SAN, NOW THAT I THINK ABOUT IT, THAT WASN'T MY FIRST KISS!
YOU'RE LYING, AREN'T YOU?
NO, IT'S THE TRUTH!
IT WAS SO LONG AGO, I'D ALMOST FORGOTTEN.
BUT ONE TIME, THERE WAS THIS BEAT-UP GUY LIVING IN THE PARK.
HE WAS A TROUBLE-MAKER, ALWAYS GETTING INTO FIGHTS, AND GOING HUNGRY.
EVERY DAY, I'D BRING HIM MEDICINE AND FOOD FROM MY HOUSE.

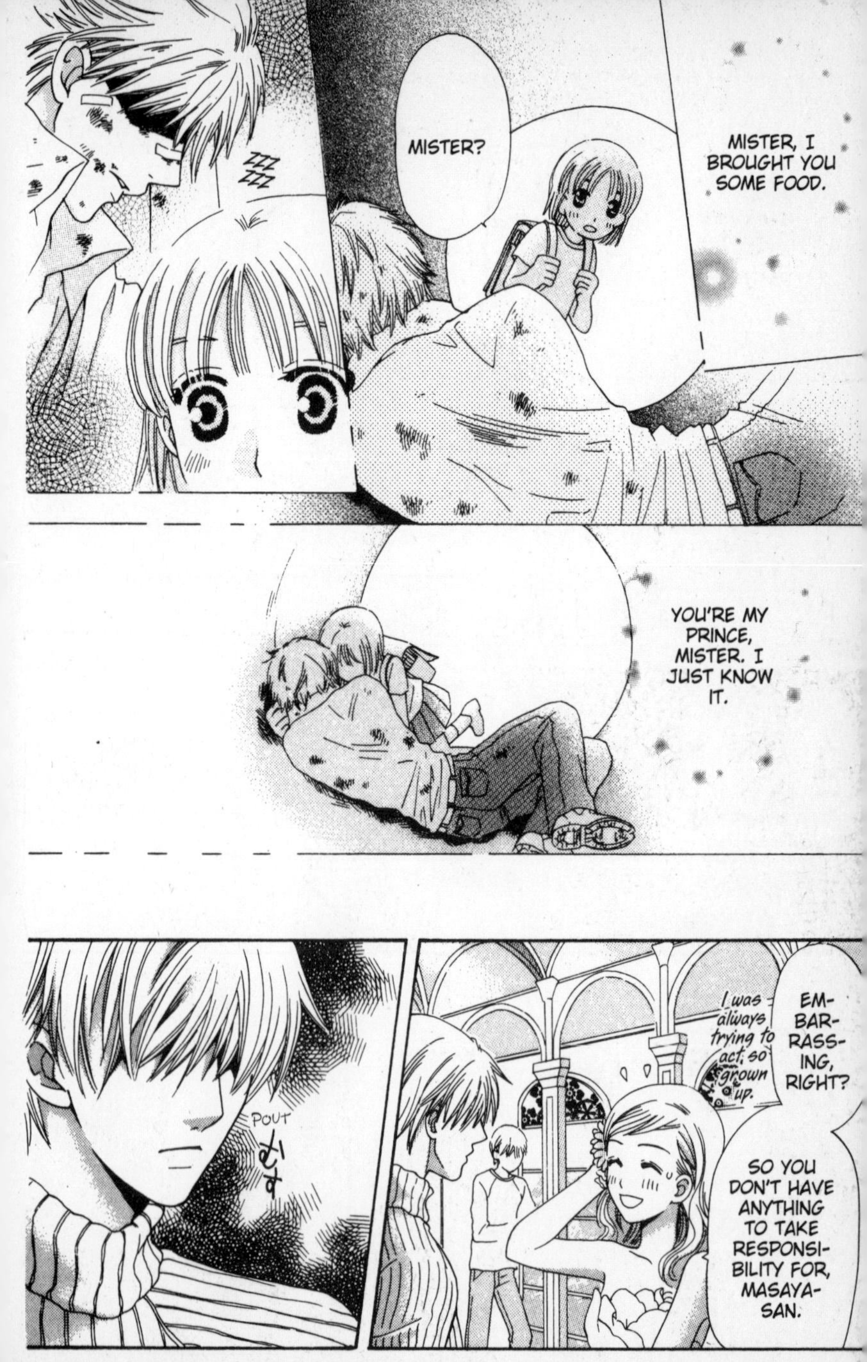
MISTER, I BROUGHT YOU SOME FOOD.
MISTER?
ZZZ ZZZ
YOU'RE MY PRINCE, MISTER. I JUST KNOW IT.
EM-BAR-RASS-ING, RIGHT?
I was always trying to act so grown up.
SO YOU DON'T HAVE ANYTHING TO TAKE RESPONSI-BILITY FOR, MASAYA-SAN.
POUT
むす

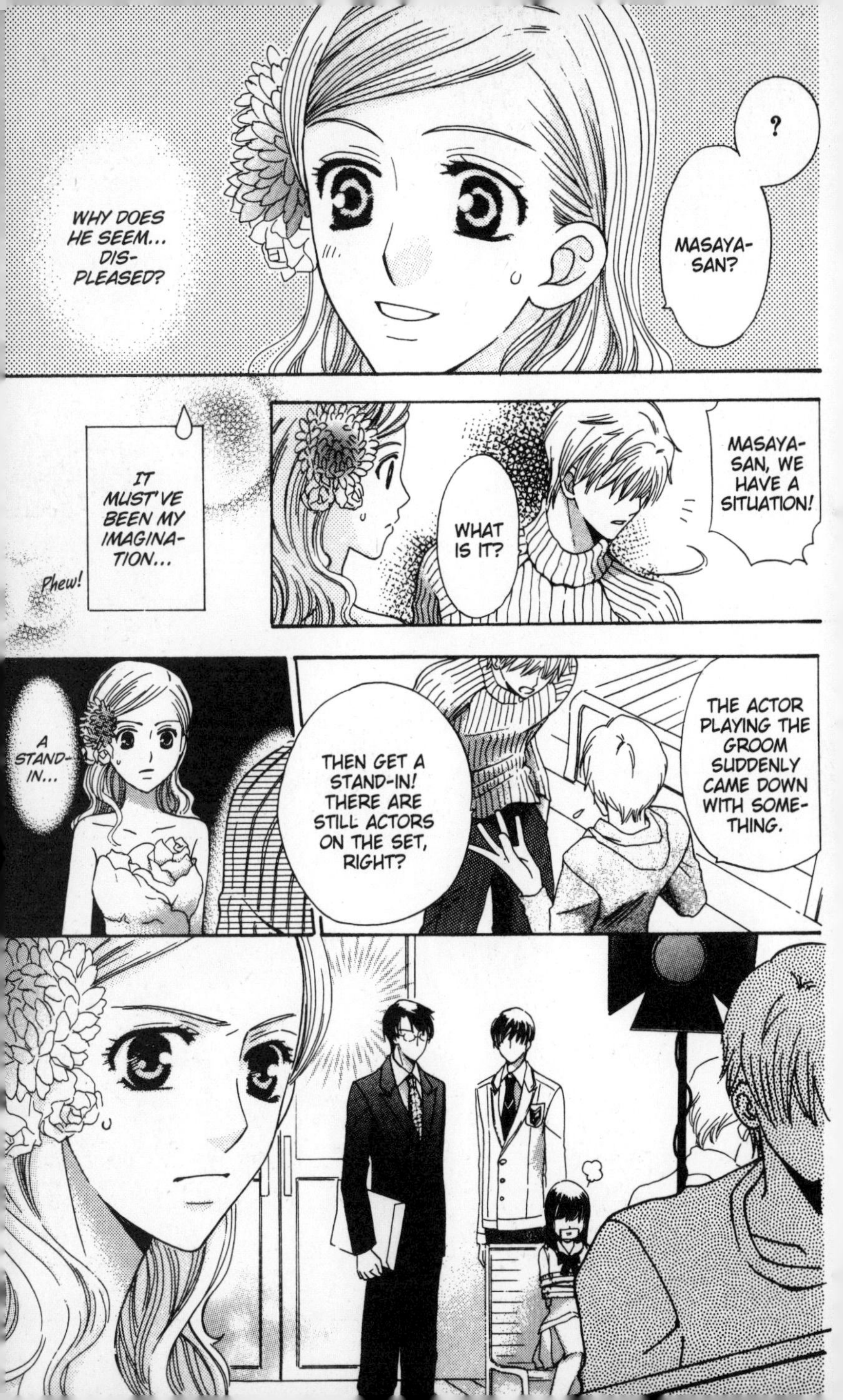
?
MASAYA-SAN?
WHY DOES HE SEEM... DIS-PLEASED?
MASAYA-SAN, WE HAVE A SITUATION!
WHAT IS IT?
IT MUST'VE BEEN MY IMAGINATION...
Phew!
THE ACTOR PLAYING THE GROOM SUDDENLY CAME DOWN WITH SOME-THING.
THEN GET A STAND-IN! THERE ARE STILL ACTORS ON THE SET, RIGHT?
A STAND-IN...

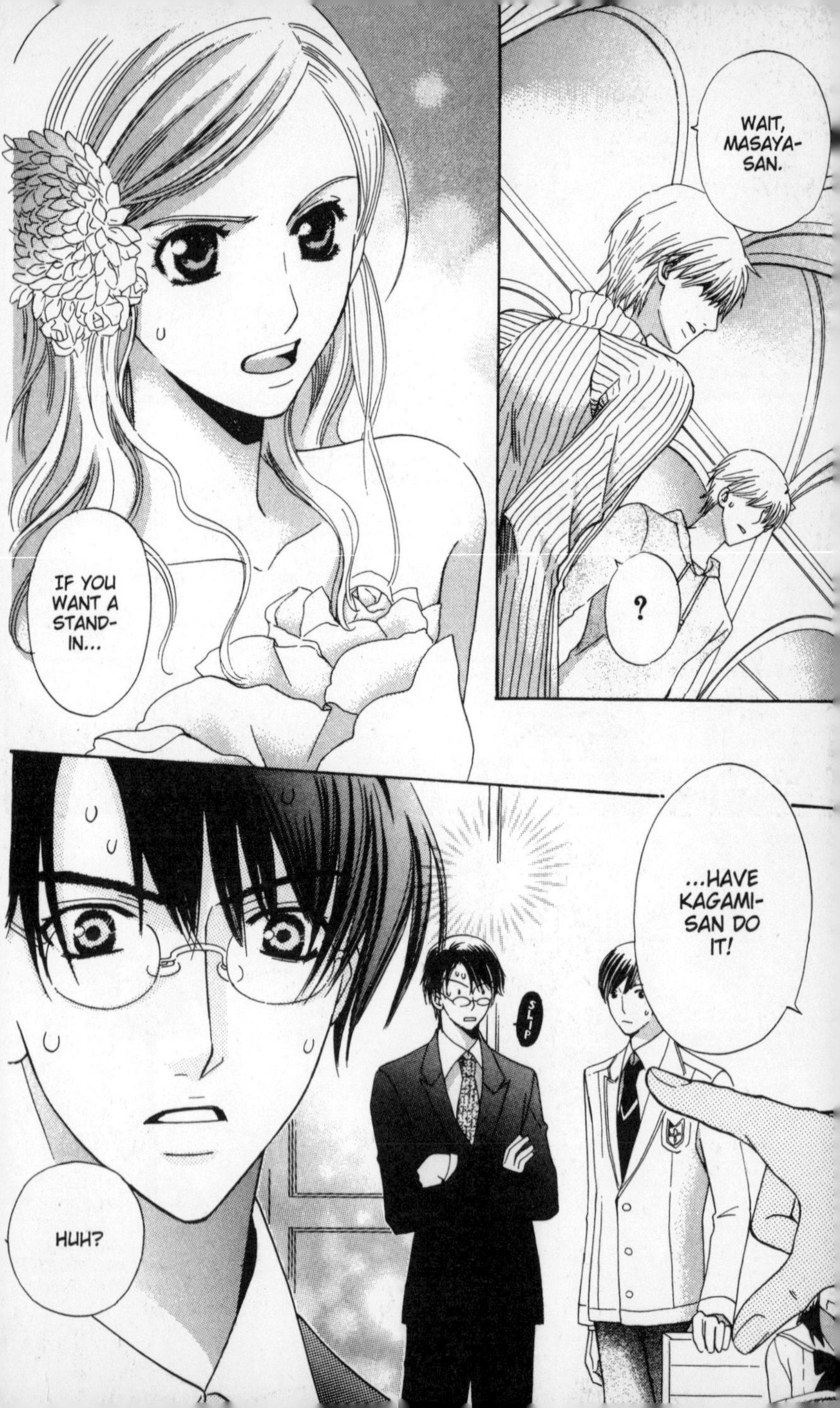
WAIT, MASAYA-SAN.
?
IF YOU WANT A STAND-IN...
...HAVE KAGAMI-SAN DO IT!
SLIP
HUH?

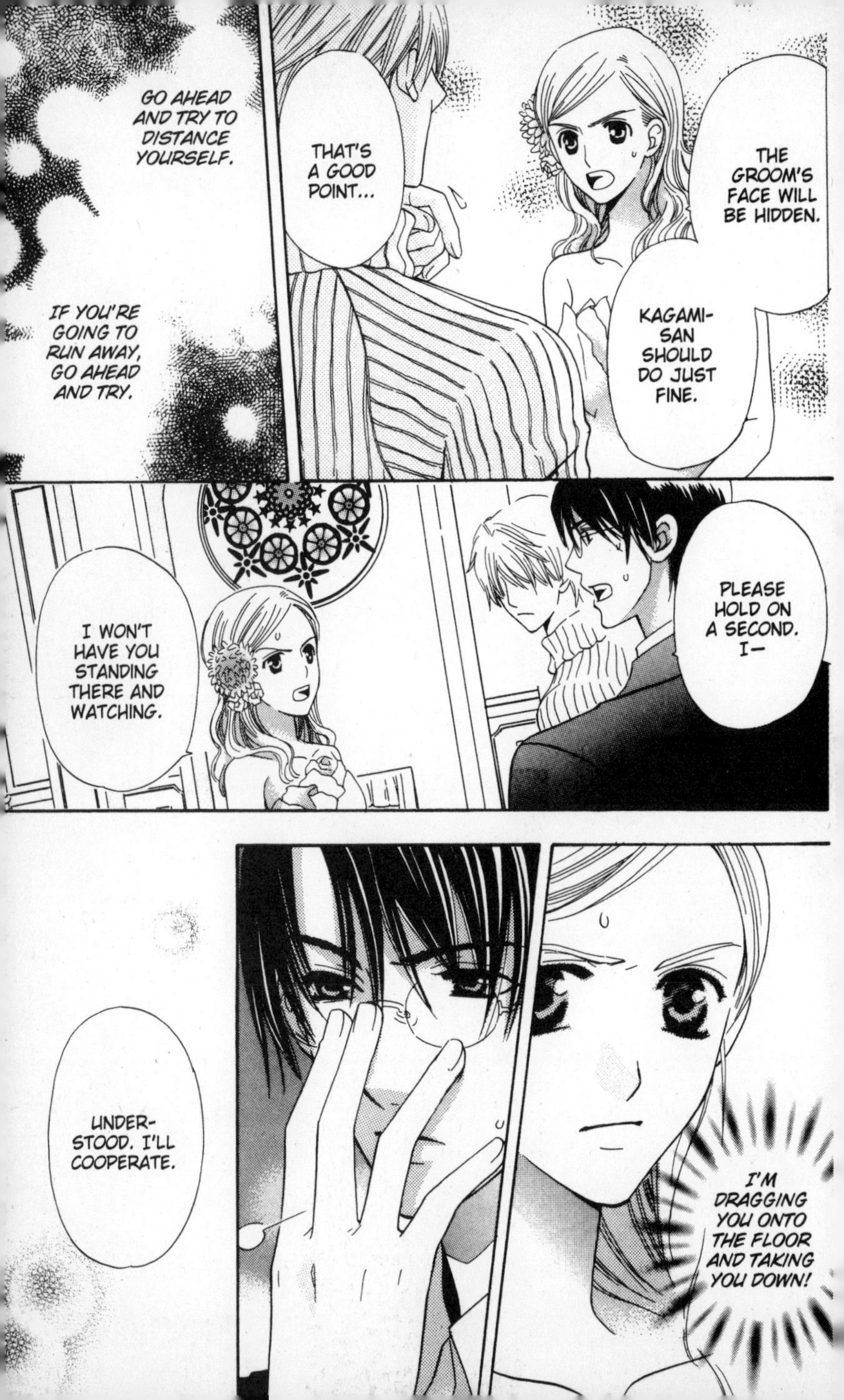
THE GROOM'S FACE WILL BE HIDDEN.
KAGAMI-SAN SHOULD DO JUST FINE.
THAT'S A GOOD POINT...
GO AHEAD AND TRY TO DISTANCE YOURSELF.
IF YOU'RE GOING TO RUN AWAY, GO AHEAD AND TRY.
PLEASE HOLD ON A SECOND. I—
I WON'T HAVE YOU STANDING THERE AND WATCHING.
I'M DRAGGING YOU ONTO THE FLOOR AND TAKING YOU DOWN!
UNDER-STOOD. I'LL COOPERATE.

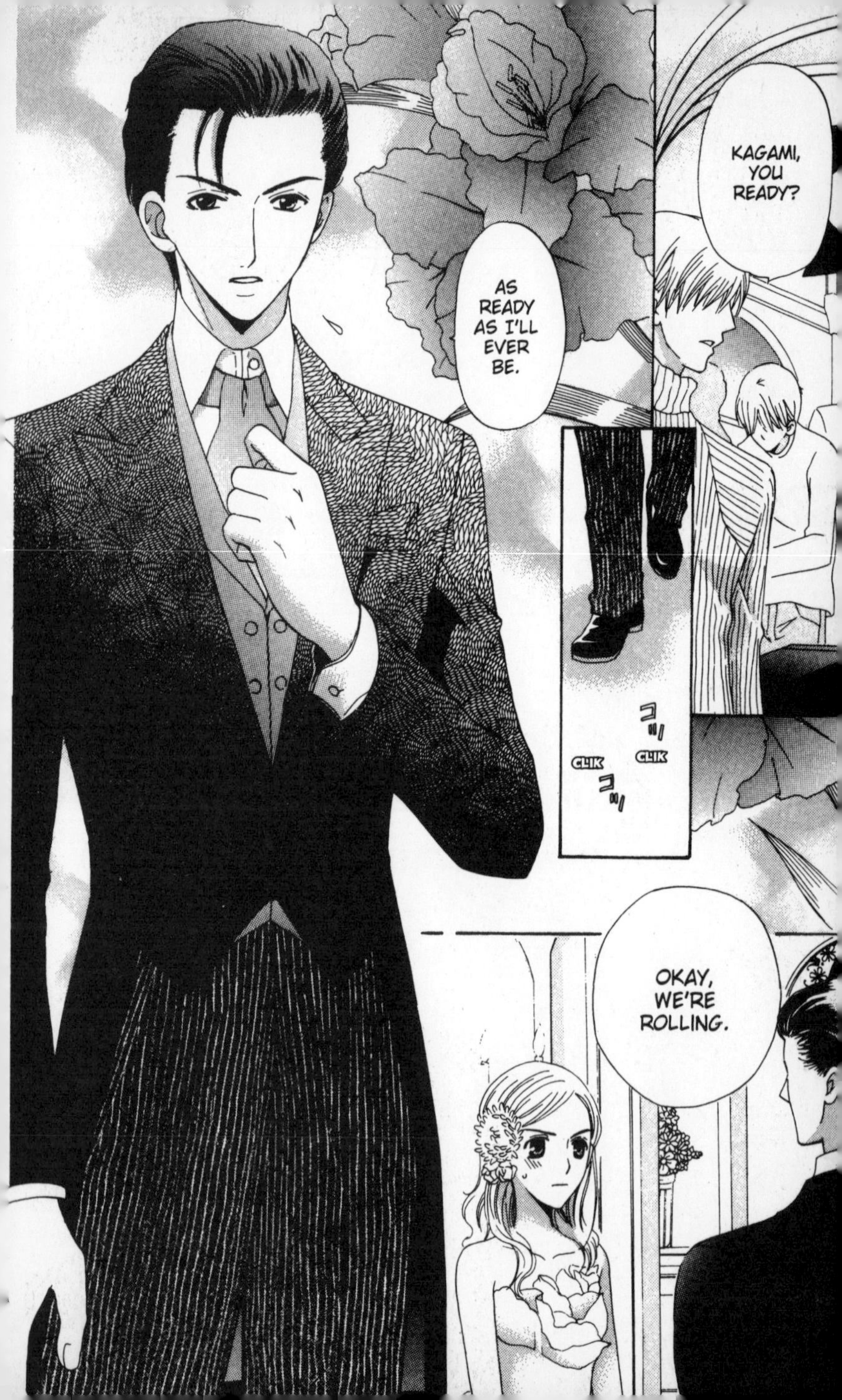

KAGAMI, YOU READY?
AS READY AS I'LL EVER BE.
CLIK
CLIK
OKAY, WE'RE ROLLING.

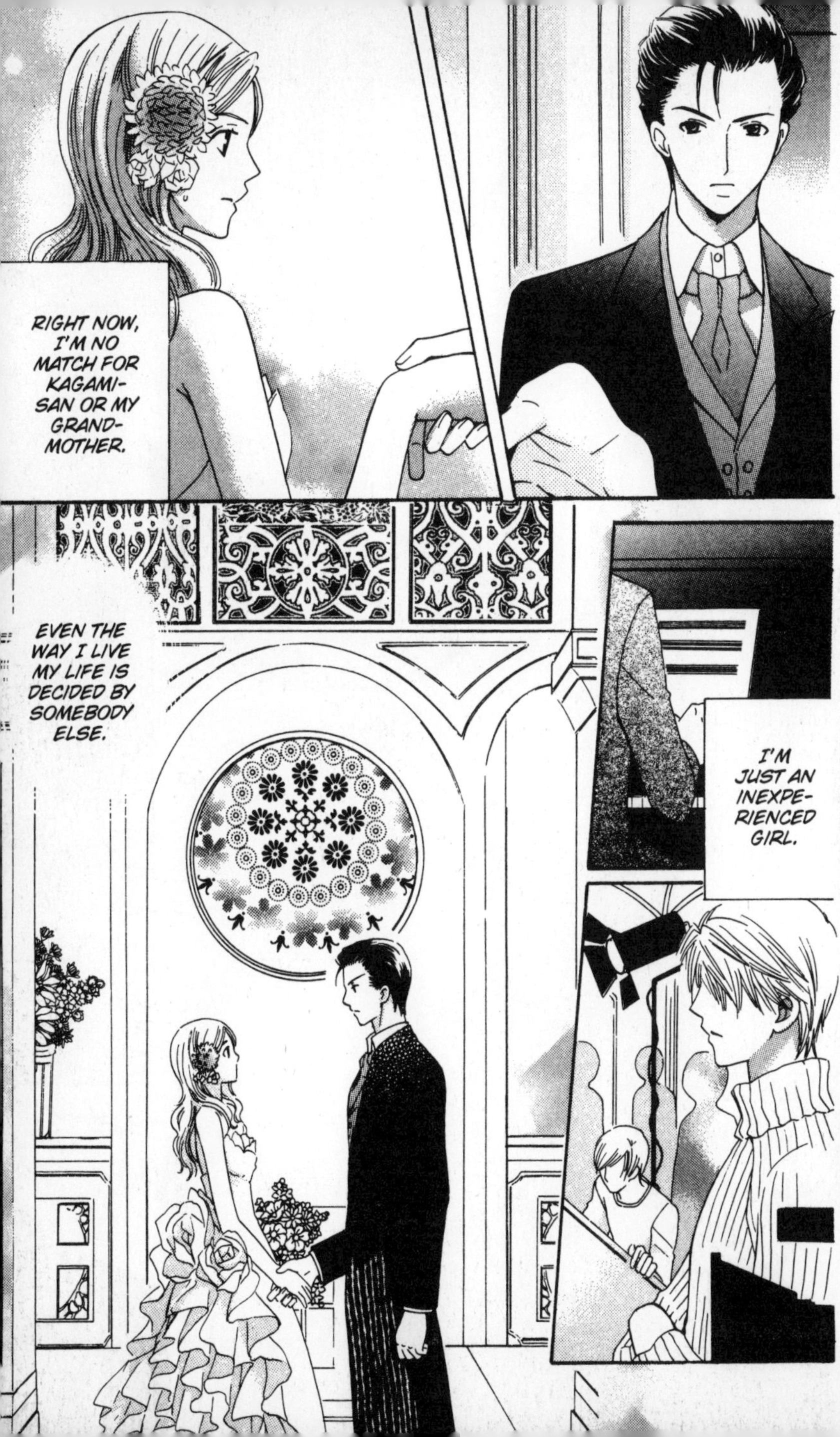
RIGHT NOW, I'M NO MATCH FOR KAGAMI-SAN OR MY GRAND-MOTHER.
I'M JUST AN INEXPE-RIENCED GIRL.
EVEN THE WAY I LIVE MY LIFE IS DECIDED BY SOMEBODY ELSE.

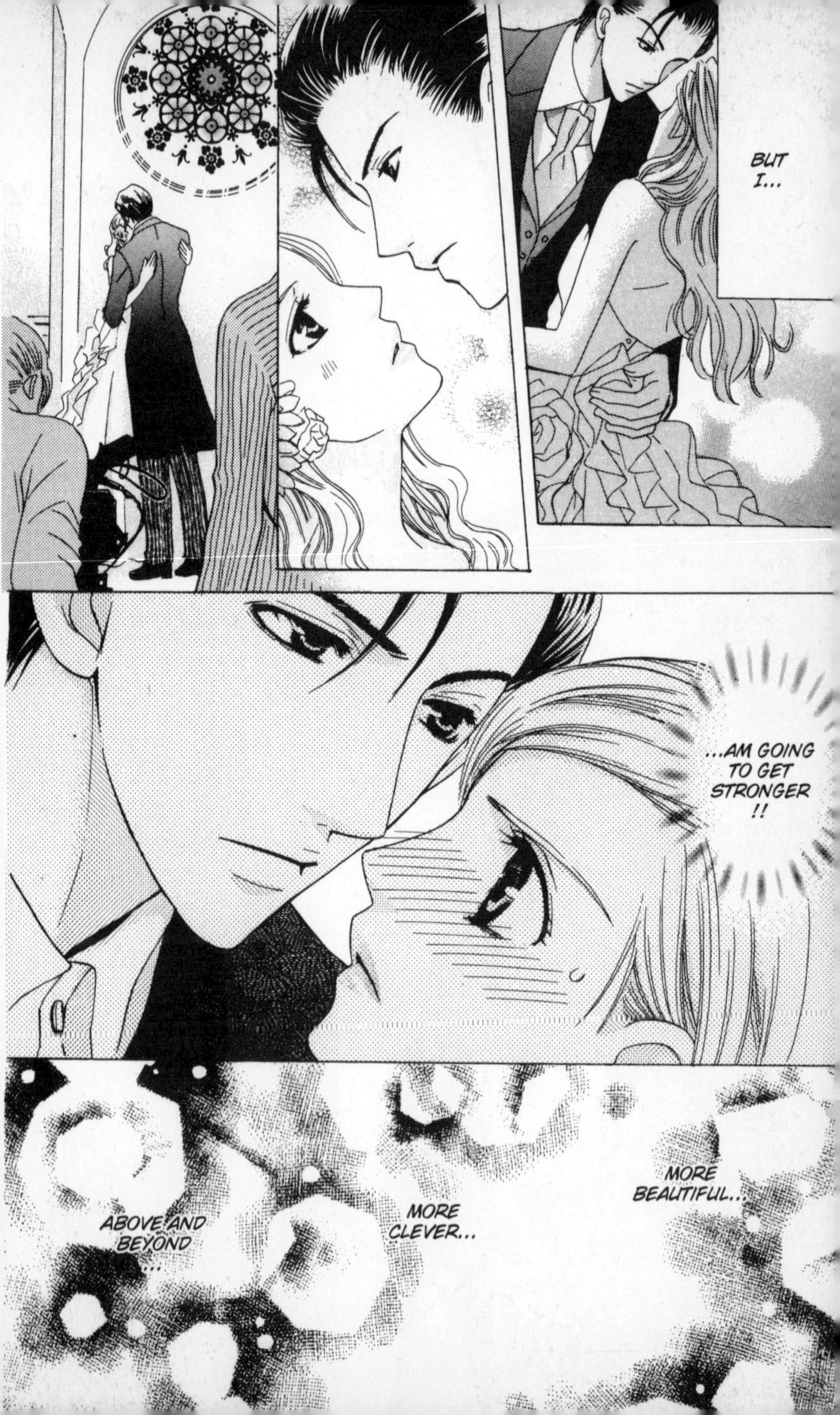
BUT I...
...AM GOING TO GET STRONGER !!
MORE BEAUTIFUL...
MORE CLEVER...
ABOVE AND BEYOND ...

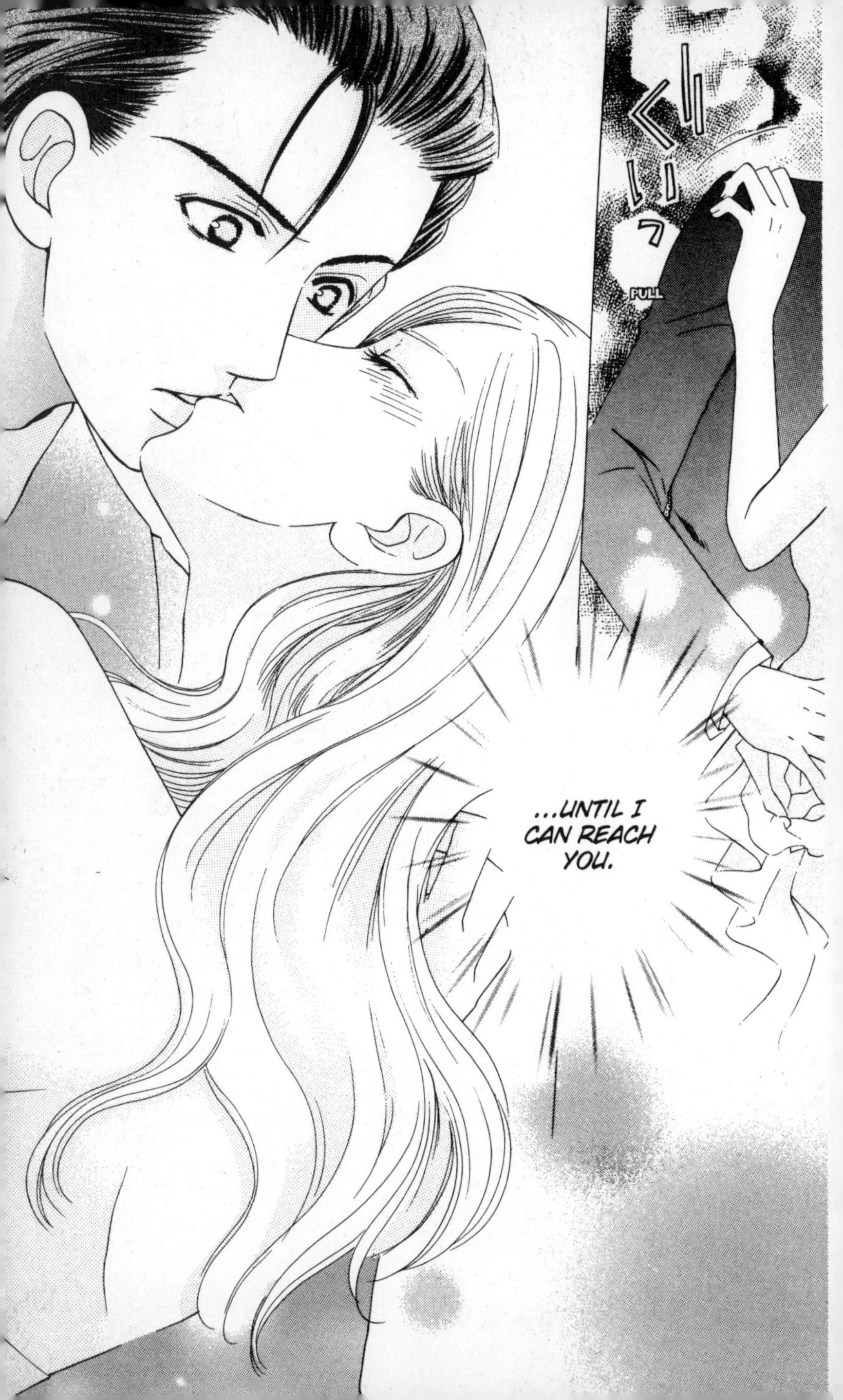
PULL
...UNTIL I
CAN REACH
YOU.

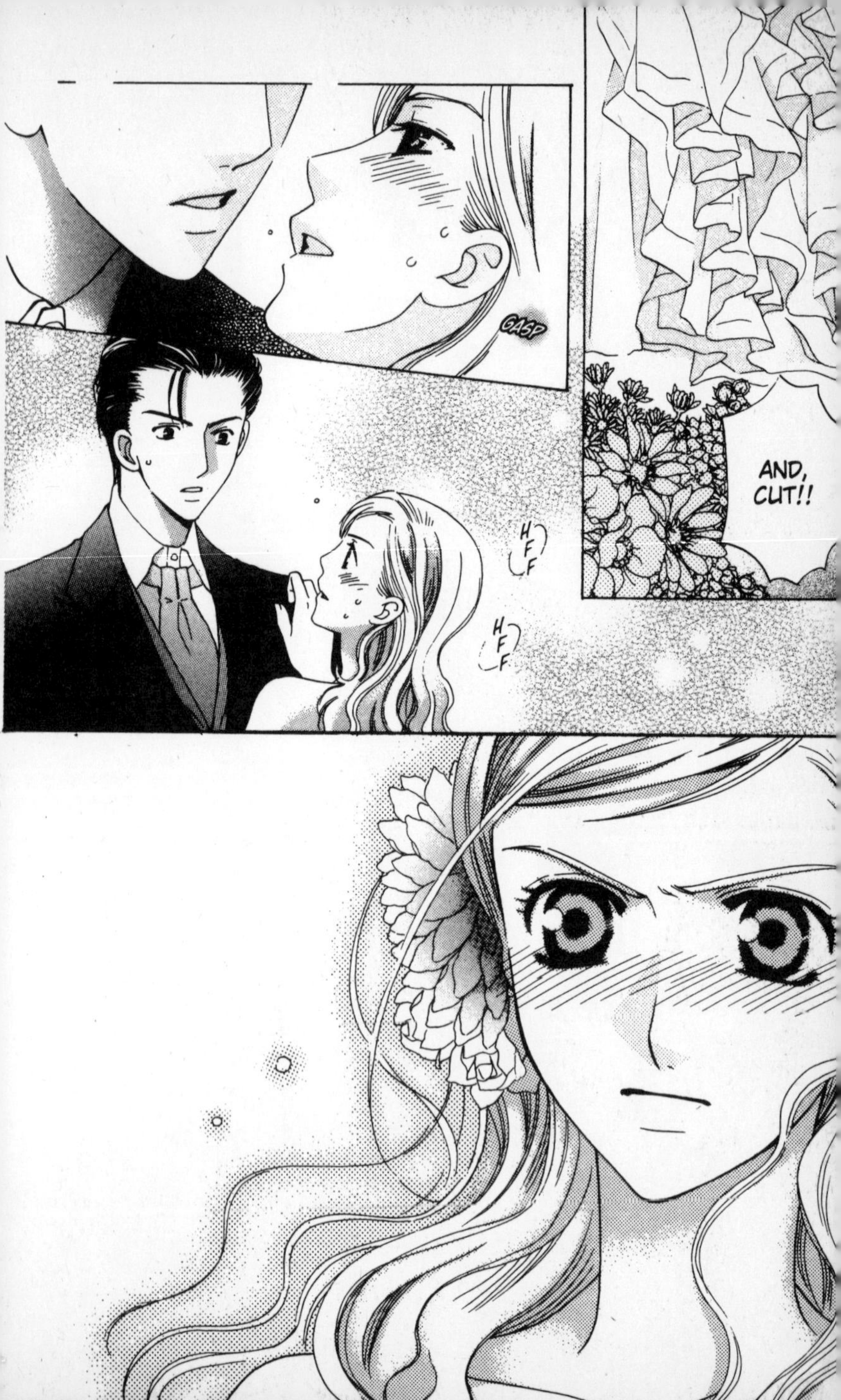
AND, CUT!!
GASP
HFF
HFF

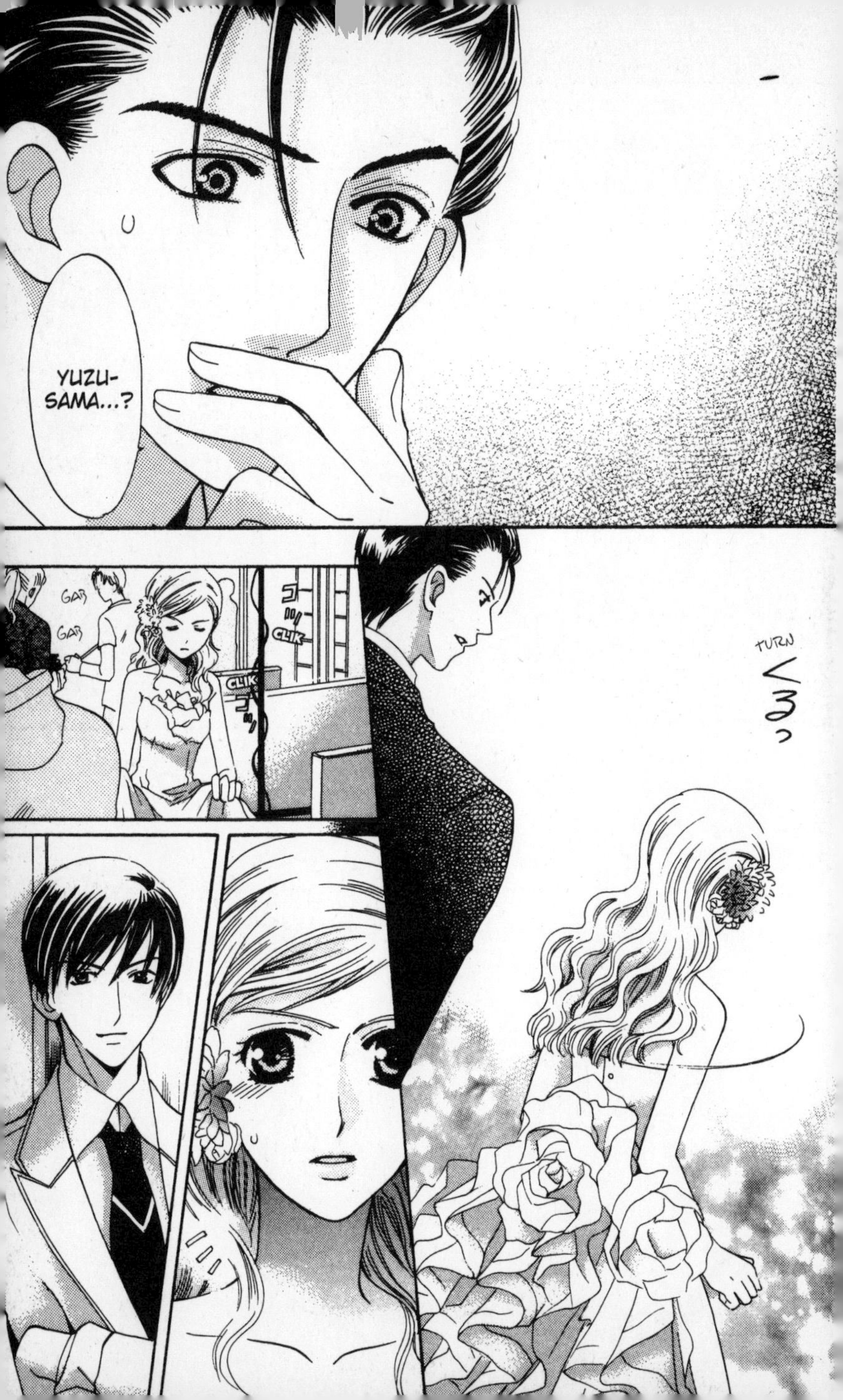
YUZU-
SAMA...?
TURN
くるっ
GAB
GAB
CLIK
CLIK

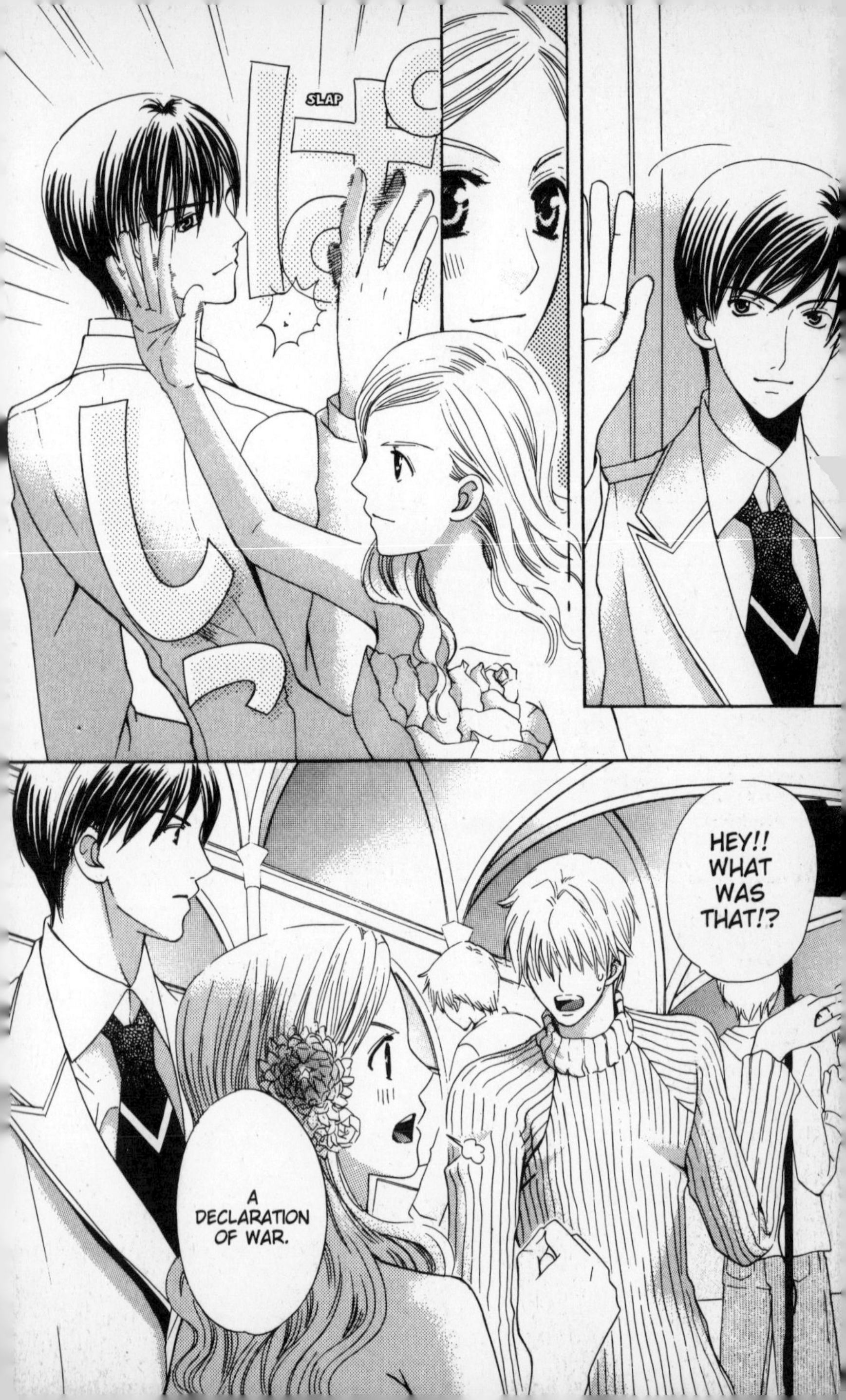
SLAP
HEY!! WHAT WAS THAT!?
A DECLARATION OF WAR.

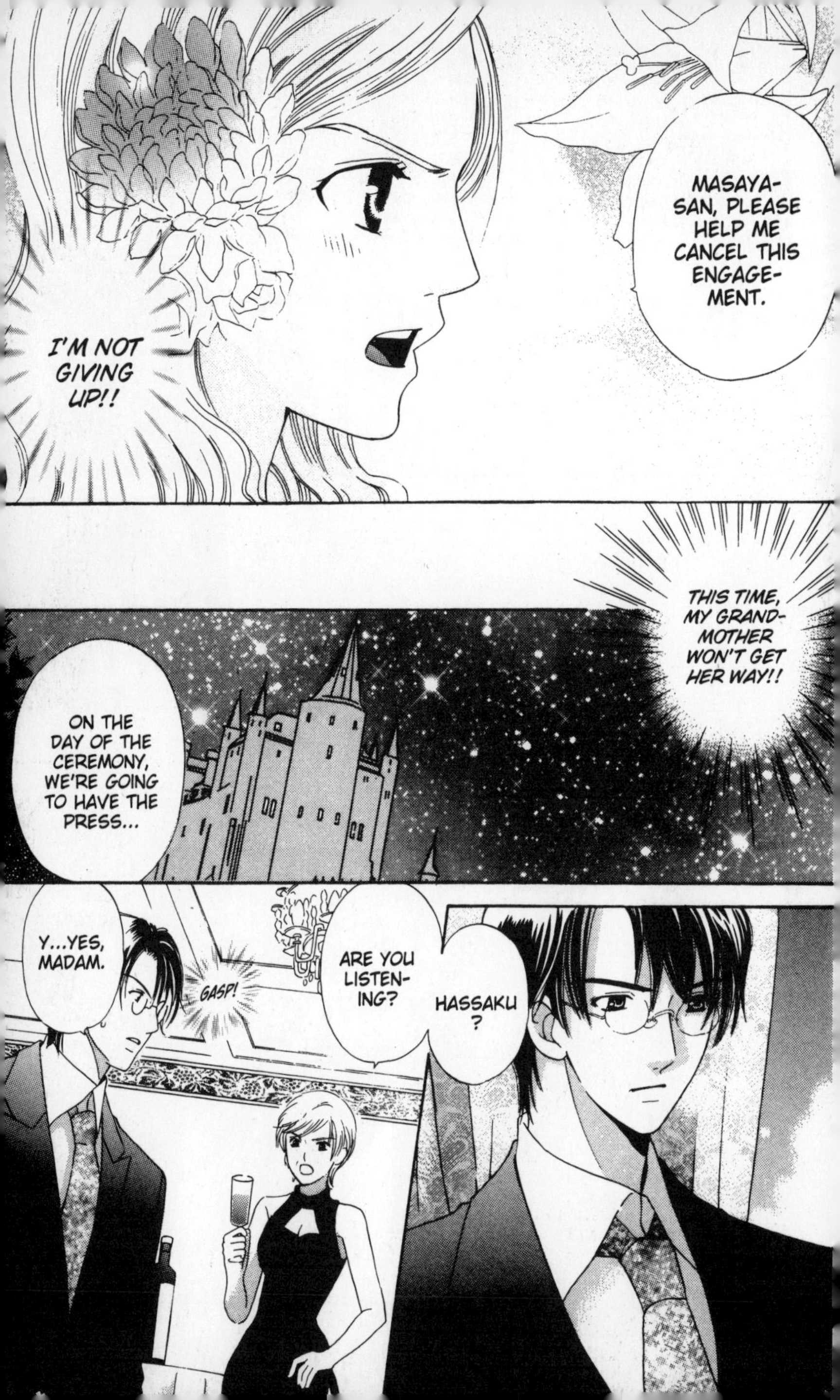
MASAYA-SAN, PLEASE HELP ME CANCEL THIS ENGAGEMENT.
I'M NOT GIVING UP!!
THIS TIME, MY GRANDMOTHER WON'T GET HER WAY!!
ON THE DAY OF THE CEREMONY, WE'RE GOING TO HAVE THE PRESS...
ARE YOU LISTENING?
HASSAKU?
GASP!
Y...YES, MADAM.

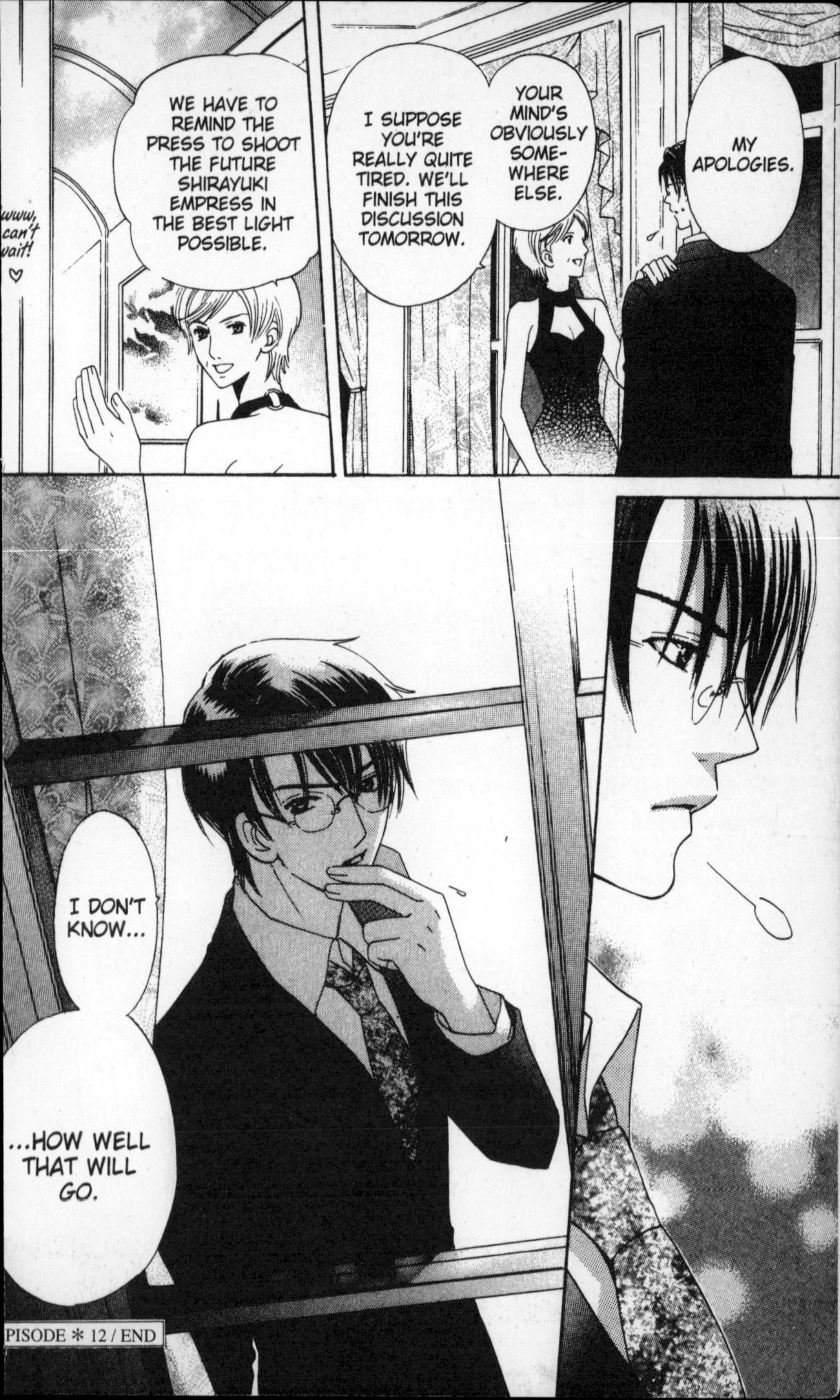
YOUR MIND'S OBVIOUSLY SOME-WHERE ELSE.
MY APOLOGIES.
I SUPPOSE YOU'RE REALLY QUITE TIRED. WE'LL FINISH THIS DISCUSSION TOMORROW.
WE HAVE TO REMIND THE PRESS TO SHOOT THE FUTURE SHIRAYUKI EMPRESS IN THE BEST LIGHT POSSIBLE.
www, can't wait! ♡
I DON'T KNOW...
...HOW WELL THAT WILL GO.
PISODE ✻ 12 / END

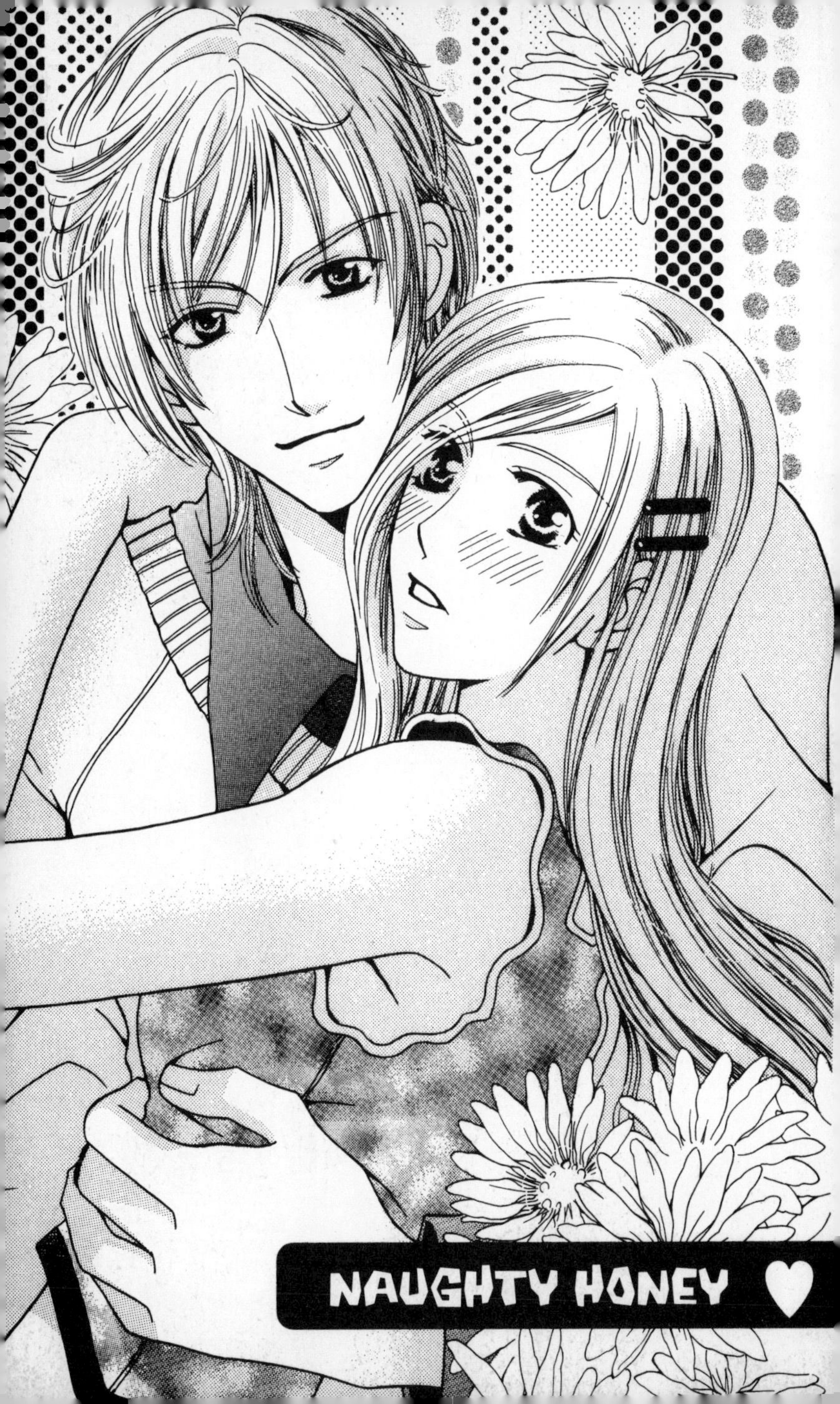
NAUGHTY HONEY ♥

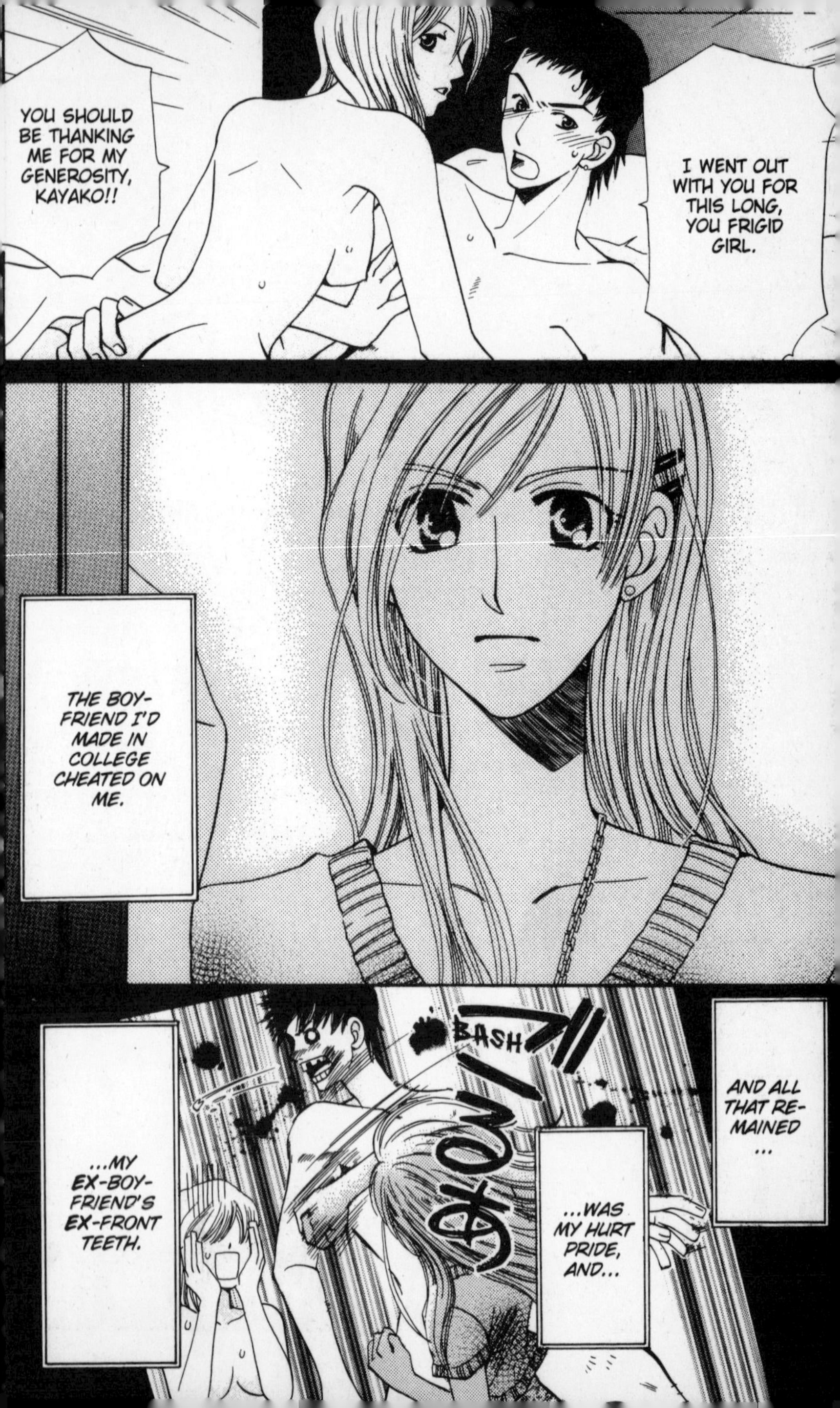
I WENT OUT WITH YOU FOR THIS LONG, YOU FRIGID GIRL.
YOU SHOULD BE THANKING ME FOR MY GENEROSITY, KAYAKO!!
THE BOY-FRIEND I'D MADE IN COLLEGE CHEATED ON ME.
AND ALL THAT RE-MAINED...
BASH
...WAS MY HURT PRIDE, AND...
...MY EX-BOY-FRIEND'S EX-FRONT TEETH.

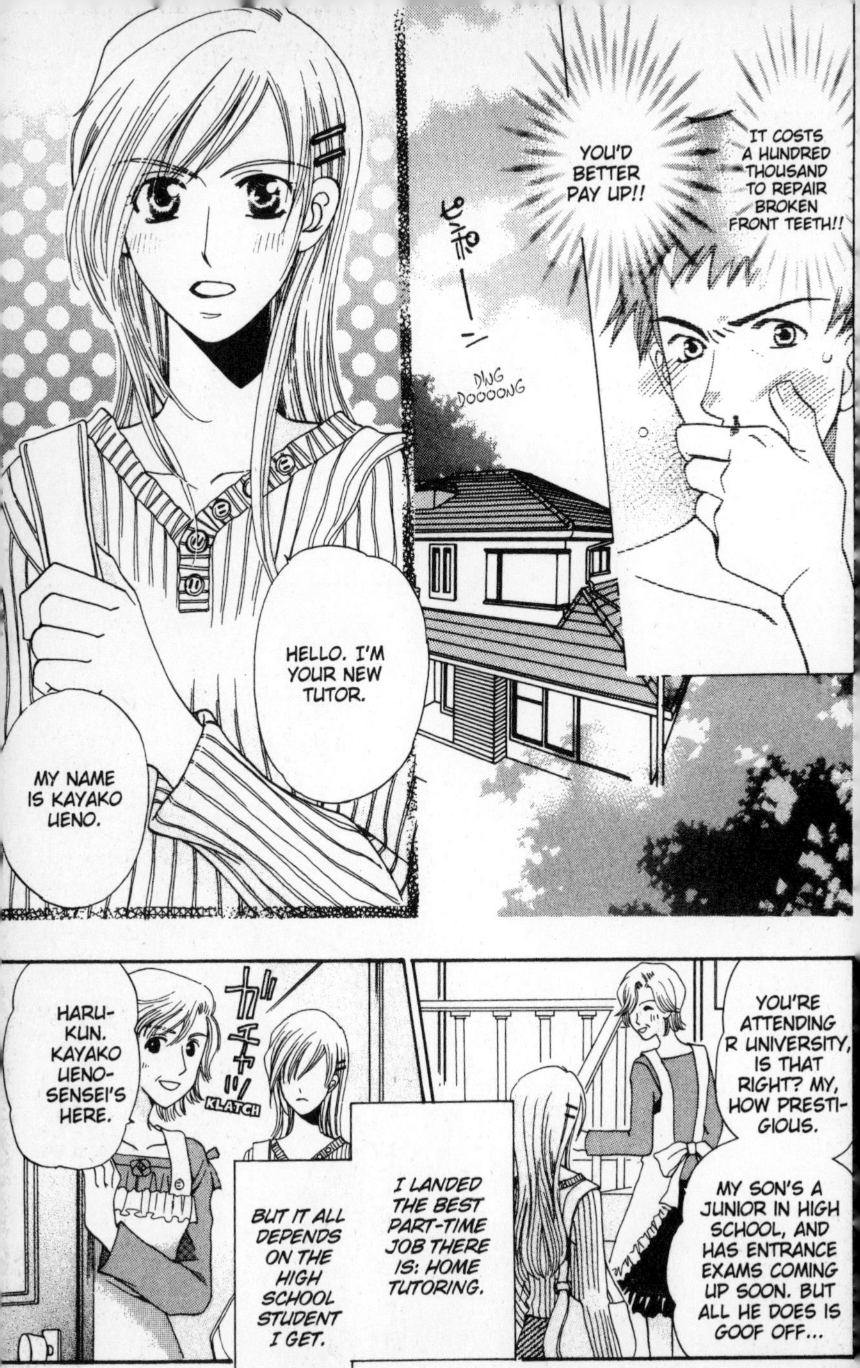
IT COSTS A HUNDRED THOUSAND TO REPAIR BROKEN FRONT TEETH!!
YOU'D BETTER PAY UP!!
ピンポーン
DING DOOOONG
HELLO. I'M YOUR NEW TUTOR.
MY NAME IS KAYAKO UENO.
YOU'RE ATTENDING R UNIVERSITY, IS THAT RIGHT? MY, HOW PRESTIGIOUS.
MY SON'S A JUNIOR IN HIGH SCHOOL, AND HAS ENTRANCE EXAMS COMING UP SOON. BUT ALL HE DOES IS GOOF OFF...
I LANDED THE BEST PART-TIME JOB THERE IS: HOME TUTORING.
BUT IT ALL DEPENDS ON THE HIGH SCHOOL STUDENT I GET.
ガチャッ
KLATCH
HARU-KUN. KAYAKO UENO-SENSEI'S HERE.

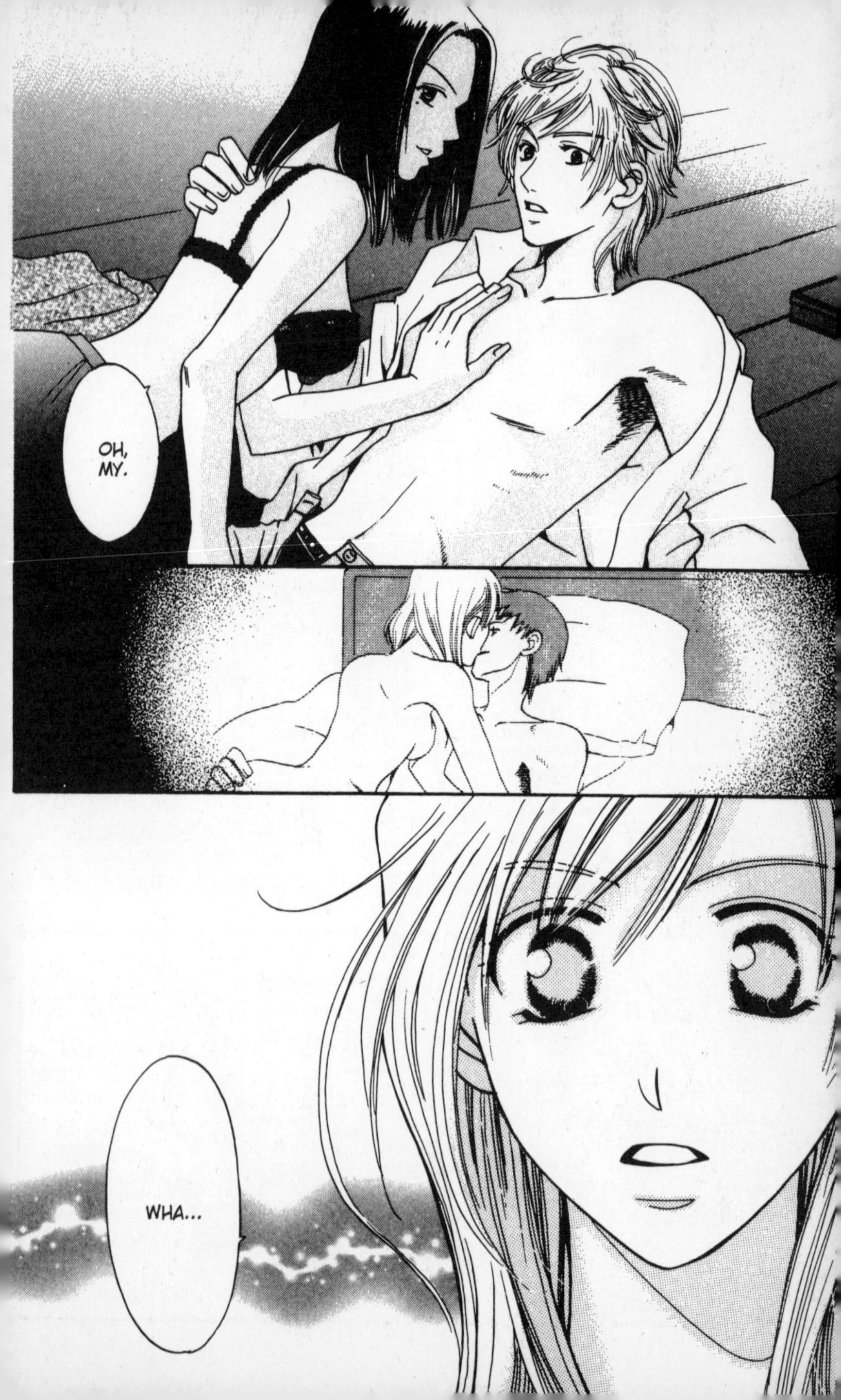
OH, MY.
WHA...

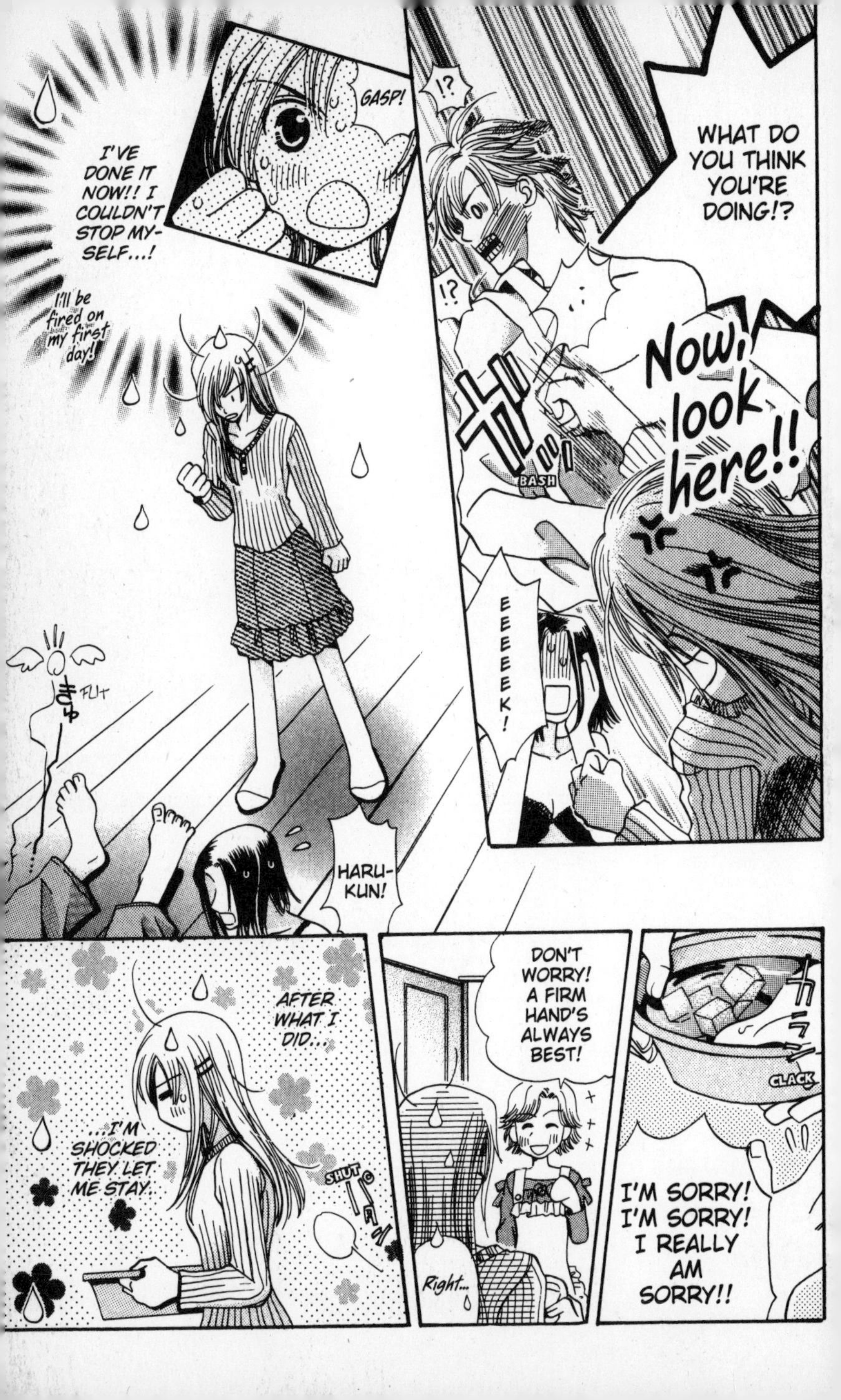
!?
WHAT DO YOU THINK YOU'RE DOING!?
!?
Now, look here!!
BASH
EEEEEEK!
GASP!
I'VE DONE IT NOW!! I COULDN'T STOP MY-SELF...!
I'll be fired on my first day!
FLIT
HARU-KUN!
CLACK
I'M SORRY! I'M SORRY! I REALLY AM SORRY!!
DON'T WORRY! A FIRM HAND'S ALWAYS BEST!
Right...
AFTER WHAT I DID...
...I'M SHOCKED THEY LET ME STAY.
SHUT

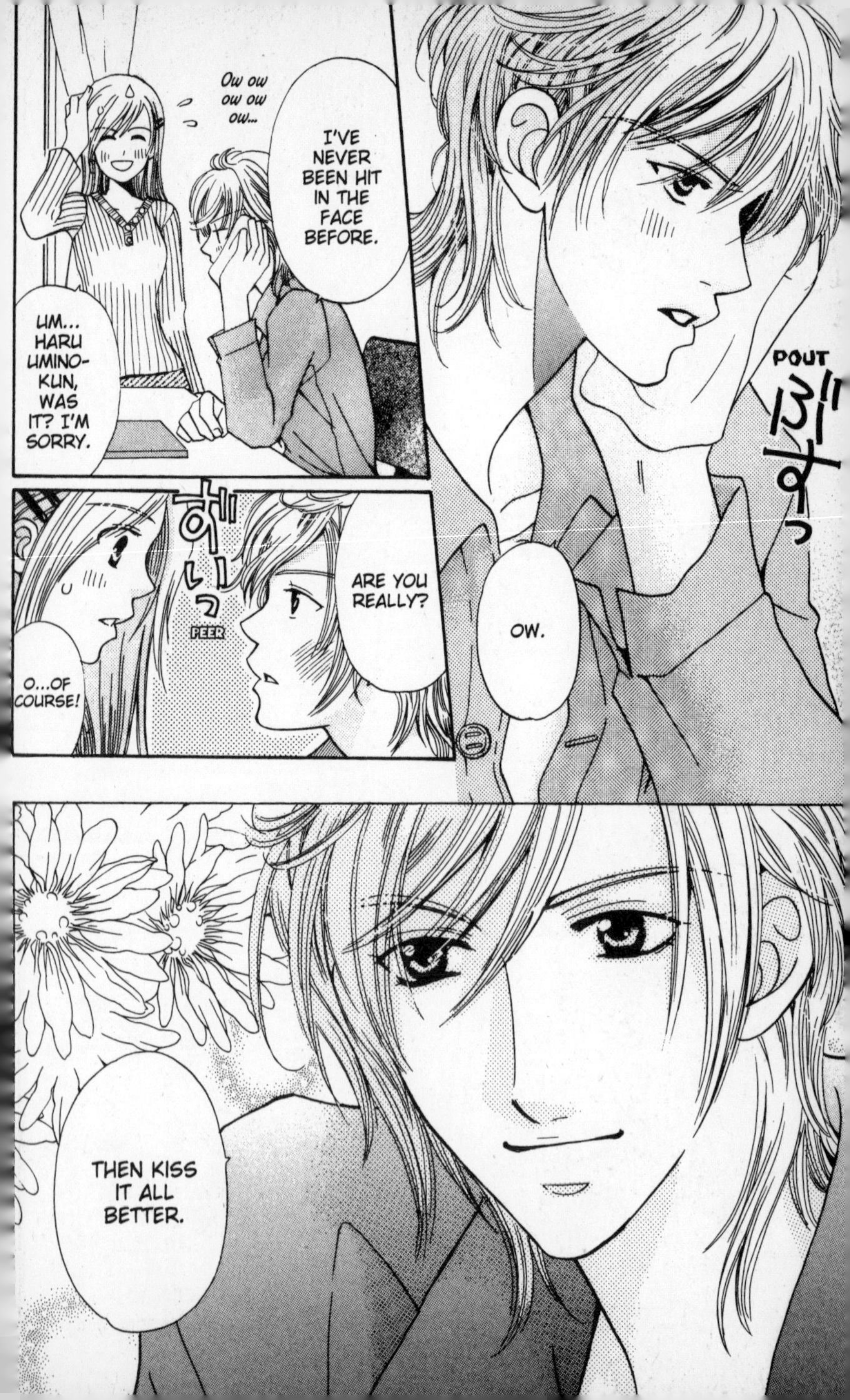
POUT
ぶすっ
OW.
I'VE NEVER BEEN HIT IN THE FACE BEFORE.
Ow ow ow ow ow...
UM... HARU UMINO-KUN, WAS IT? I'M SORRY.
ARE YOU REALLY?
PEER
O...OF COURSE!
THEN KISS IT ALL BETTER.

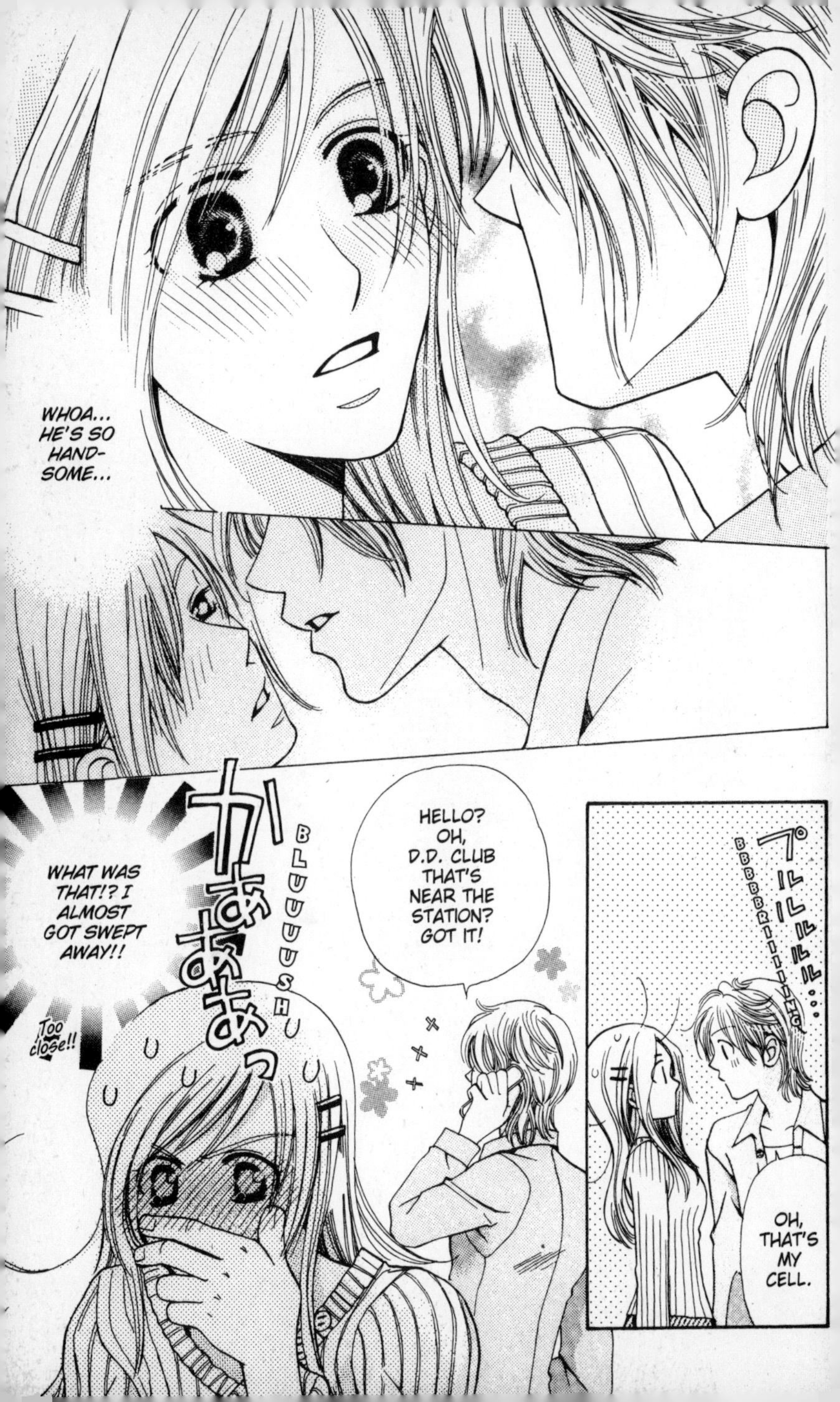
WHOA... HE'S SO HAND-SOME...
BBBBRIIIIING
OH, THAT'S MY CELL.
HELLO? OH, D.D. CLUB THAT'S NEAR THE STATION? GOT IT!
かあああっ
BLUUUUUSH
WHAT WAS THAT!? I ALMOST GOT SWEPT AWAY!!
Too close!!

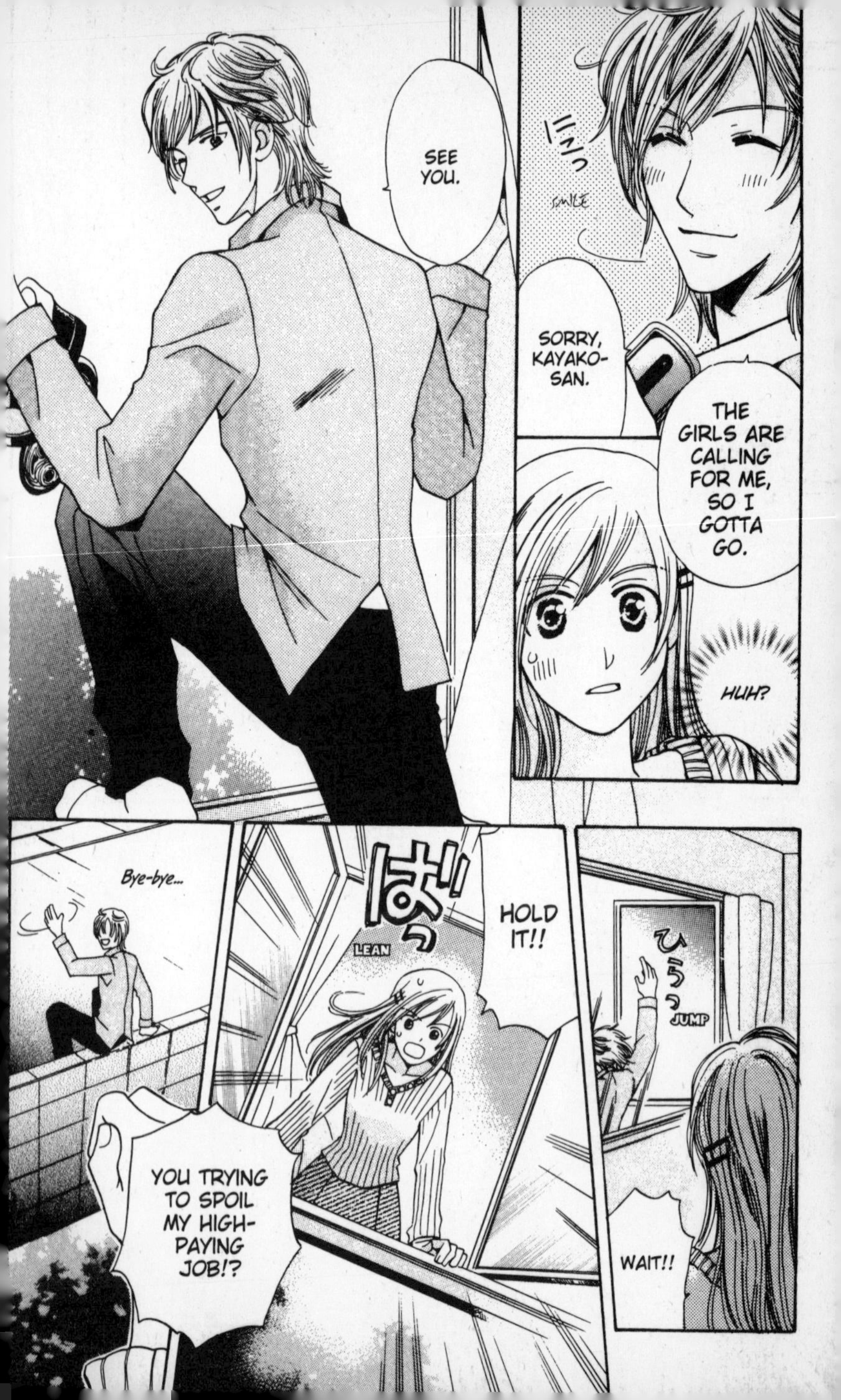

ニコっ
SMILE
SORRY, KAYAKO-SAN.
THE GIRLS ARE CALLING FOR ME, SO I GOTTA GO.
HUH?
SEE YOU.
ひらっ
JUMP
WAIT!!
ばっ
LEAN
HOLD IT!!
Bye-bye...
YOU TRYING TO SPOIL MY HIGH-PAYING JOB!?

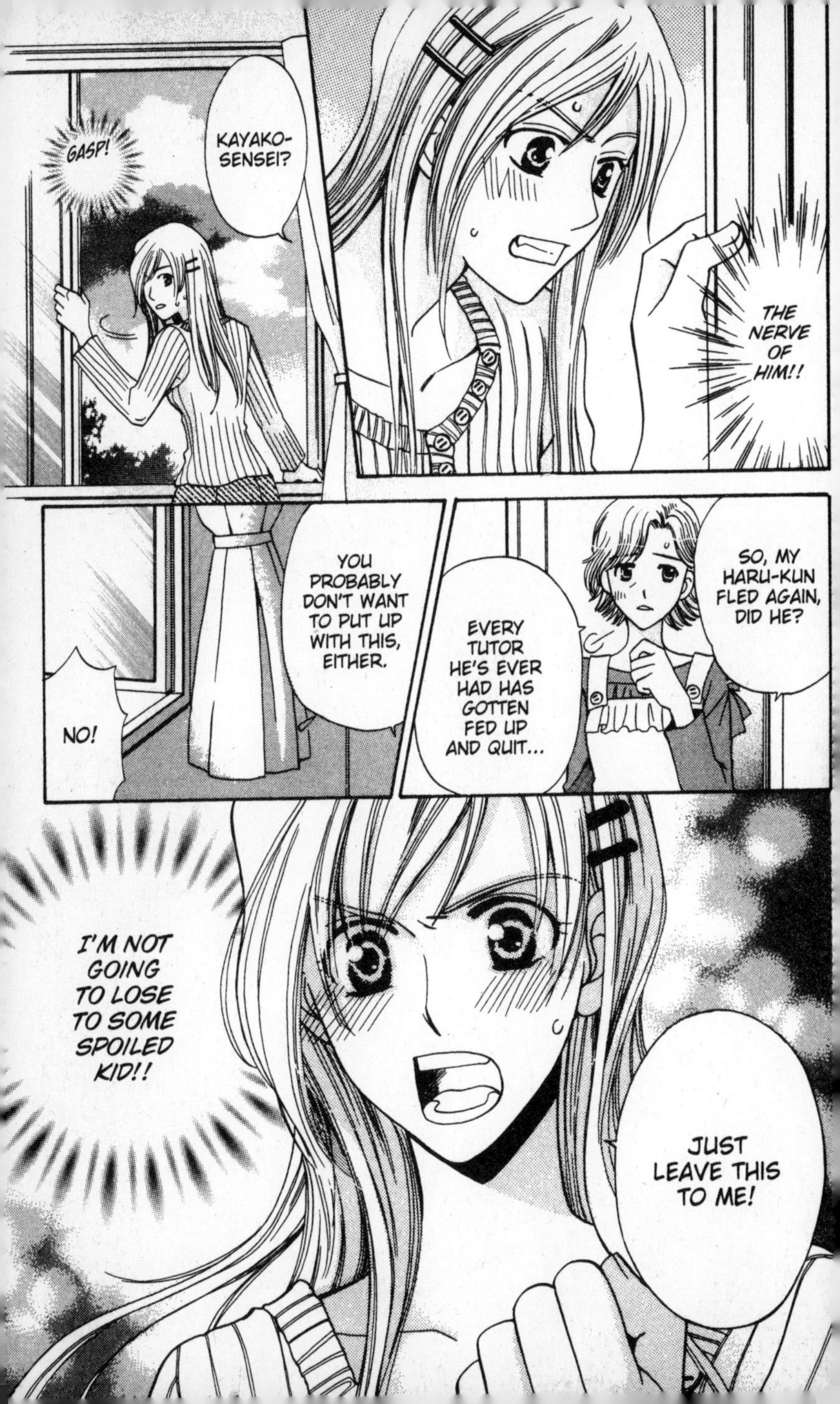
THE NERVE OF HIM!!
KAYAKO-SENSEI?
GASP!
SO, MY HARU-KUN FLED AGAIN, DID HE?
EVERY TUTOR HE'S EVER HAD HAS GOTTEN FED UP AND QUIT...
YOU PROBABLY DON'T WANT TO PUT UP WITH THIS, EITHER.
NO!
JUST LEAVE THIS TO ME!
I'M NOT GOING TO LOSE TO SOME SPOILED KID!!

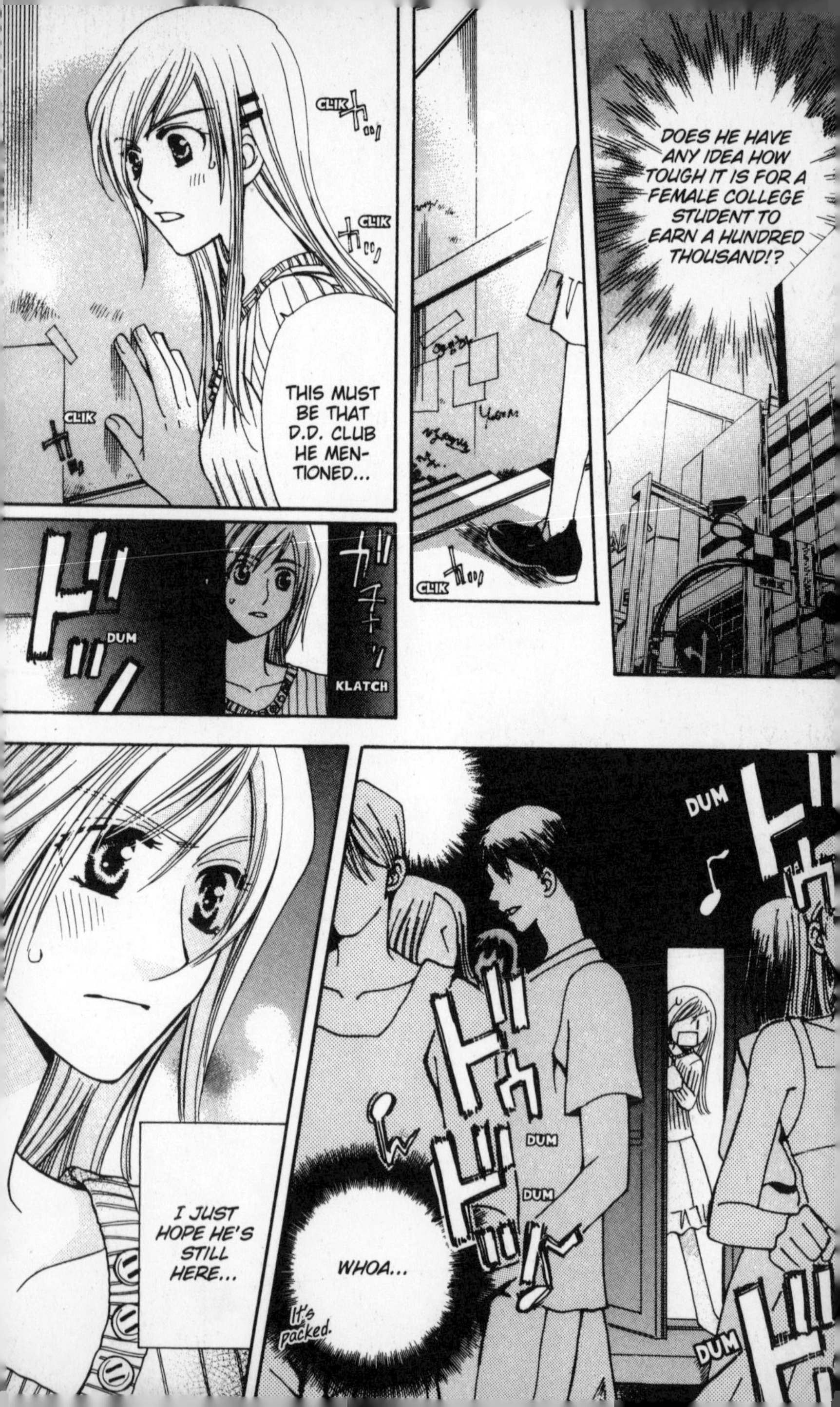

DOES HE HAVE ANY IDEA HOW TOUGH IT IS FOR A FEMALE COLLEGE STUDENT TO EARN A HUNDRED THOUSAND!?
CLIK
CLIK
CLIK
THIS MUST BE THAT D.D. CLUB HE MENTIONED...
CLIK
KLATCH
DUM
DUM
DUM
DUM
WHOA...
It's packed.
DUM
I JUST HOPE HE'S STILL HERE...

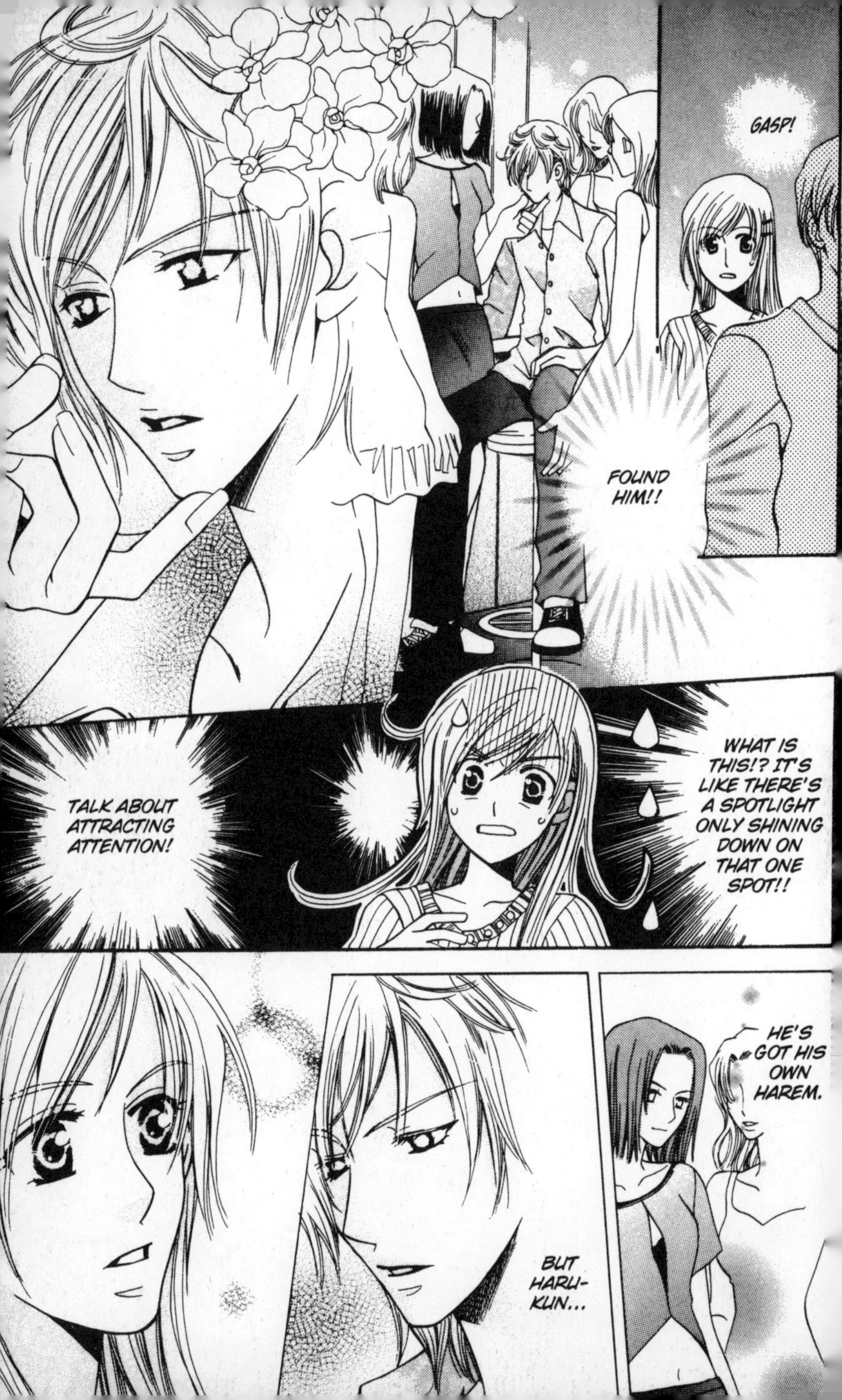
GASP!
FOUND HIM!!
WHAT IS THIS!? IT'S LIKE THERE'S A SPOTLIGHT ONLY SHINING DOWN ON THAT ONE SPOT!!
TALK ABOUT ATTRACTING ATTENTION!
HE'S GOT HIS OWN HAREM.
BUT HARU-KUN...

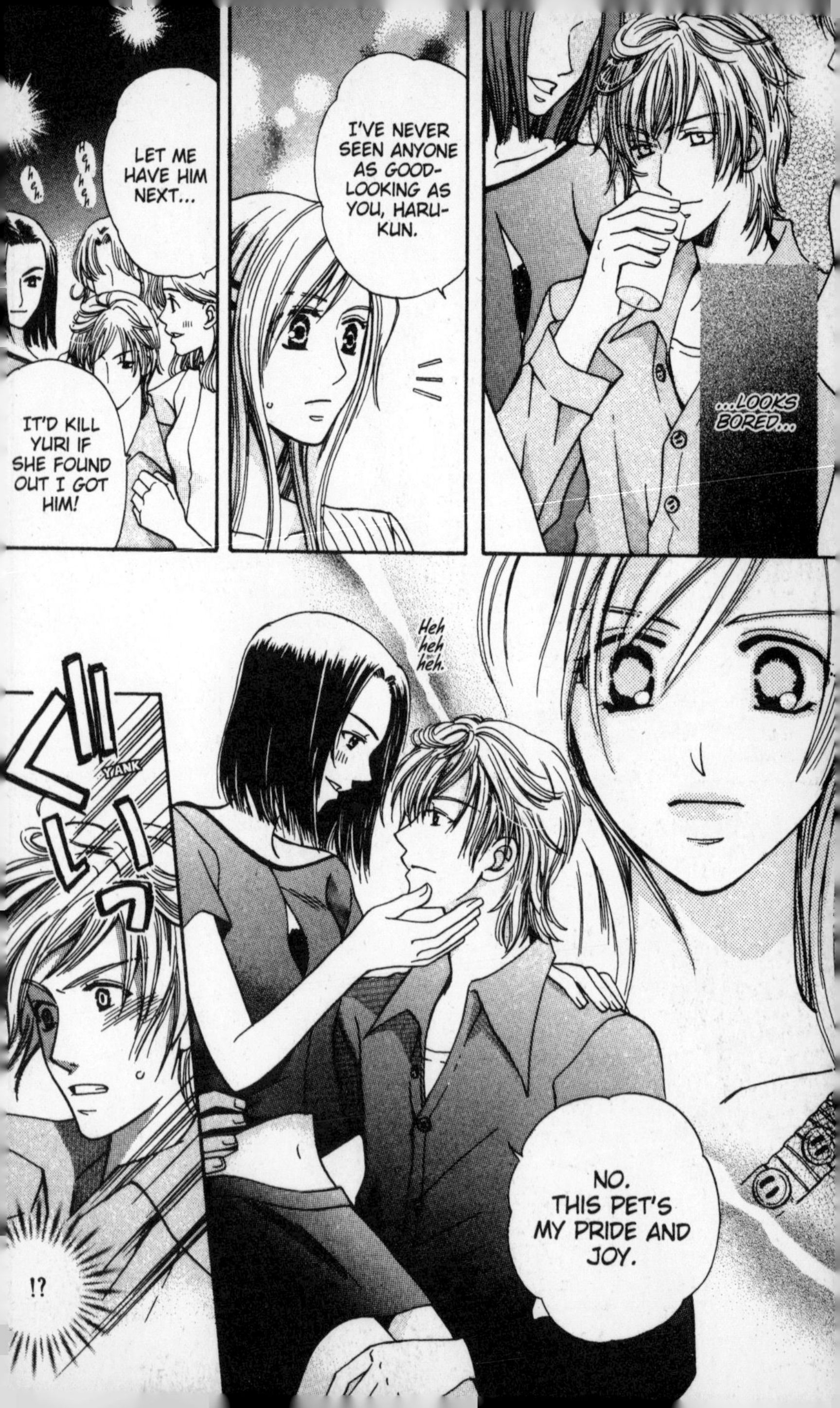
...LOOKS BORED...
I'VE NEVER SEEN ANYONE AS GOOD-LOOKING AS YOU, HARU-KUN.
LET ME HAVE HIM NEXT...
Heh heh
heh.
IT'D KILL YURI IF SHE FOUND OUT I GOT HIM!
Heh heh heh.
NO. THIS PET'S MY PRIDE AND JOY.
YANK
!?

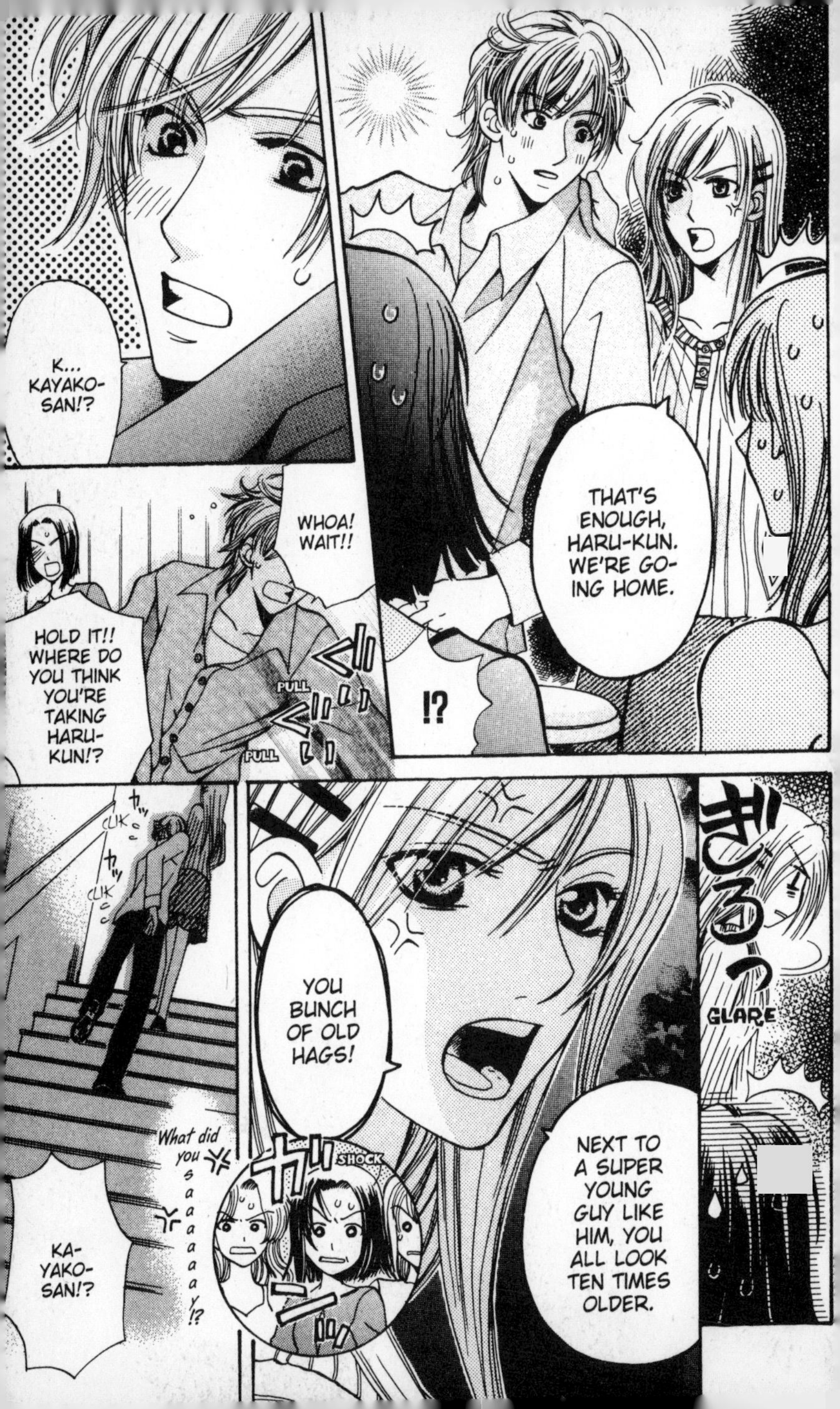

THAT'S ENOUGH, HARU-KUN. WE'RE GO-ING HOME.
!?
K... KAYAKO-SAN!?
WHOA! WAIT!!
HOLD IT!! WHERE DO YOU THINK YOU'RE TAKING HARU-KUN!?
PULL
PULL
ぎろっ
GLARE
YOU BUNCH OF OLD HAGS!
NEXT TO A SUPER YOUNG GUY LIKE HIM, YOU ALL LOOK TEN TIMES OLDER.
SHOCK
What did you saaaaaaay!?
CLIK
CLIK
KA-YAKO-SAN!?

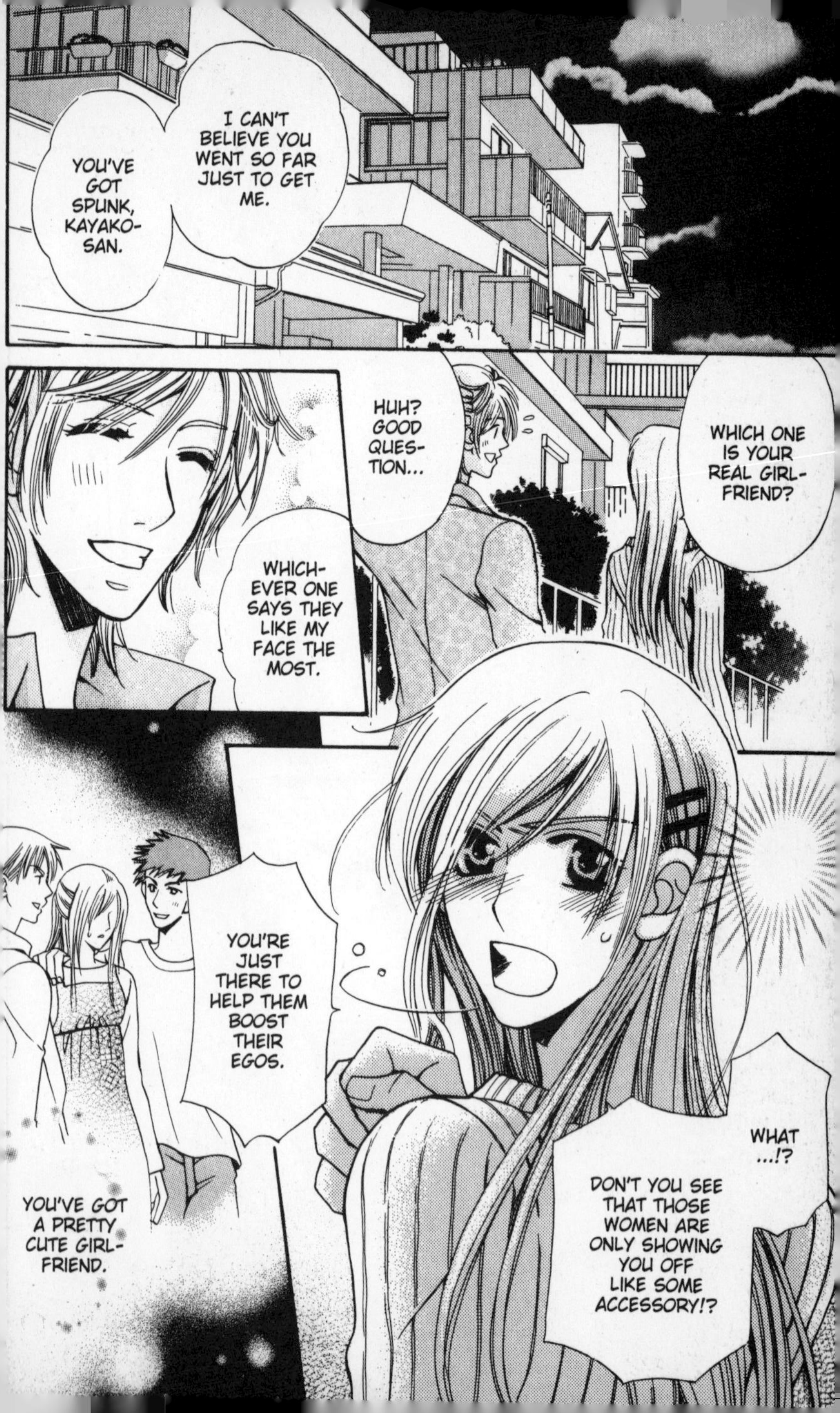
I CAN'T BELIEVE YOU WENT SO FAR JUST TO GET ME.
YOU'VE GOT SPUNK, KAYAKO-SAN.
WHICH ONE IS YOUR REAL GIRL-FRIEND?
HUH? GOOD QUES-TION...
WHICH-EVER ONE SAYS THEY LIKE MY FACE THE MOST.
WHAT ...!?
DON'T YOU SEE THAT THOSE WOMEN ARE ONLY SHOWING YOU OFF LIKE SOME ACCESSORY!?
YOU'RE JUST THERE TO HELP THEM BOOST THEIR EGOS.
YOU'VE GOT A PRETTY CUTE GIRL-FRIEND.

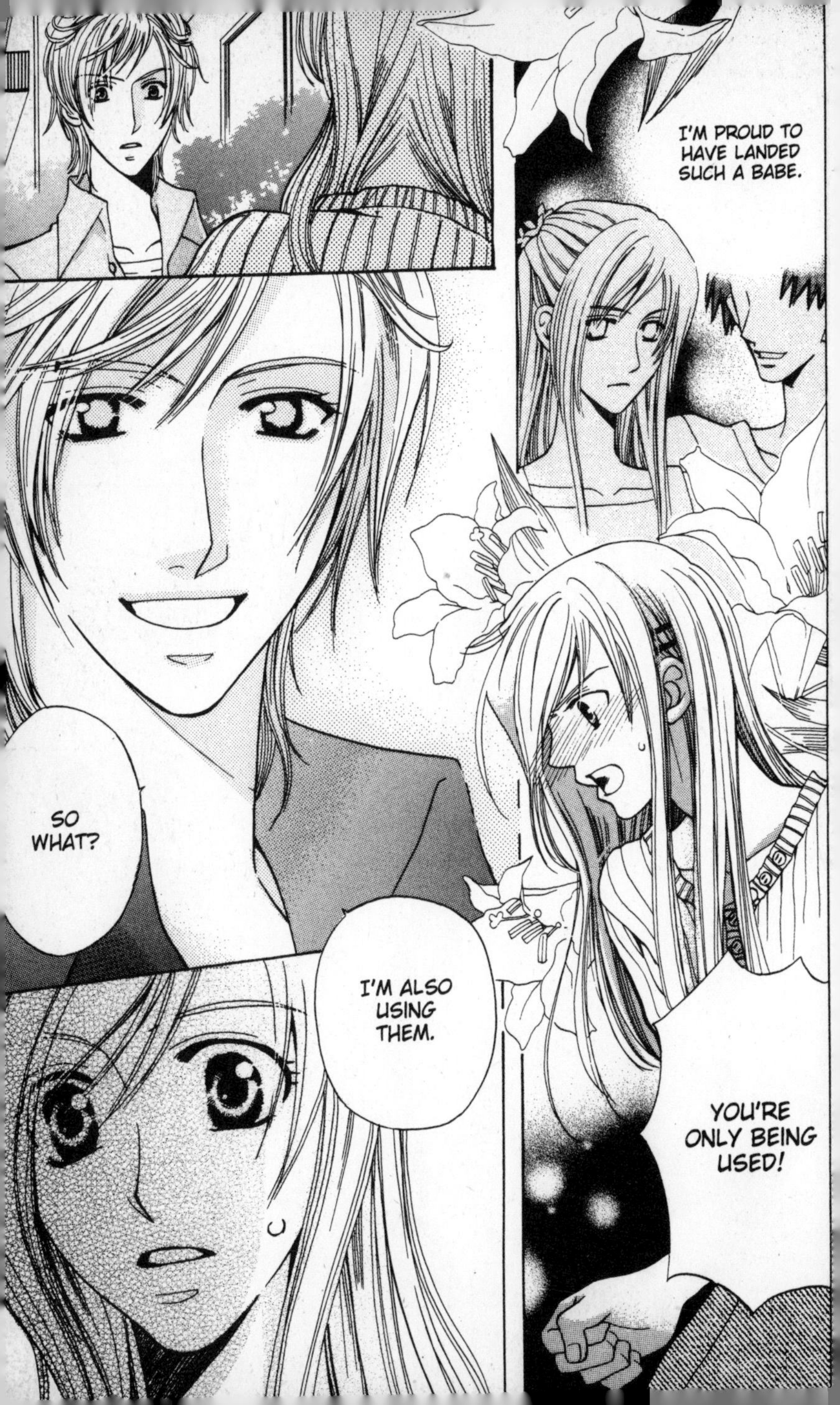
I'M PROUD TO HAVE LANDED SUCH A BABE.
YOU'RE ONLY BEING USED!
SO WHAT?
I'M ALSO USING THEM.

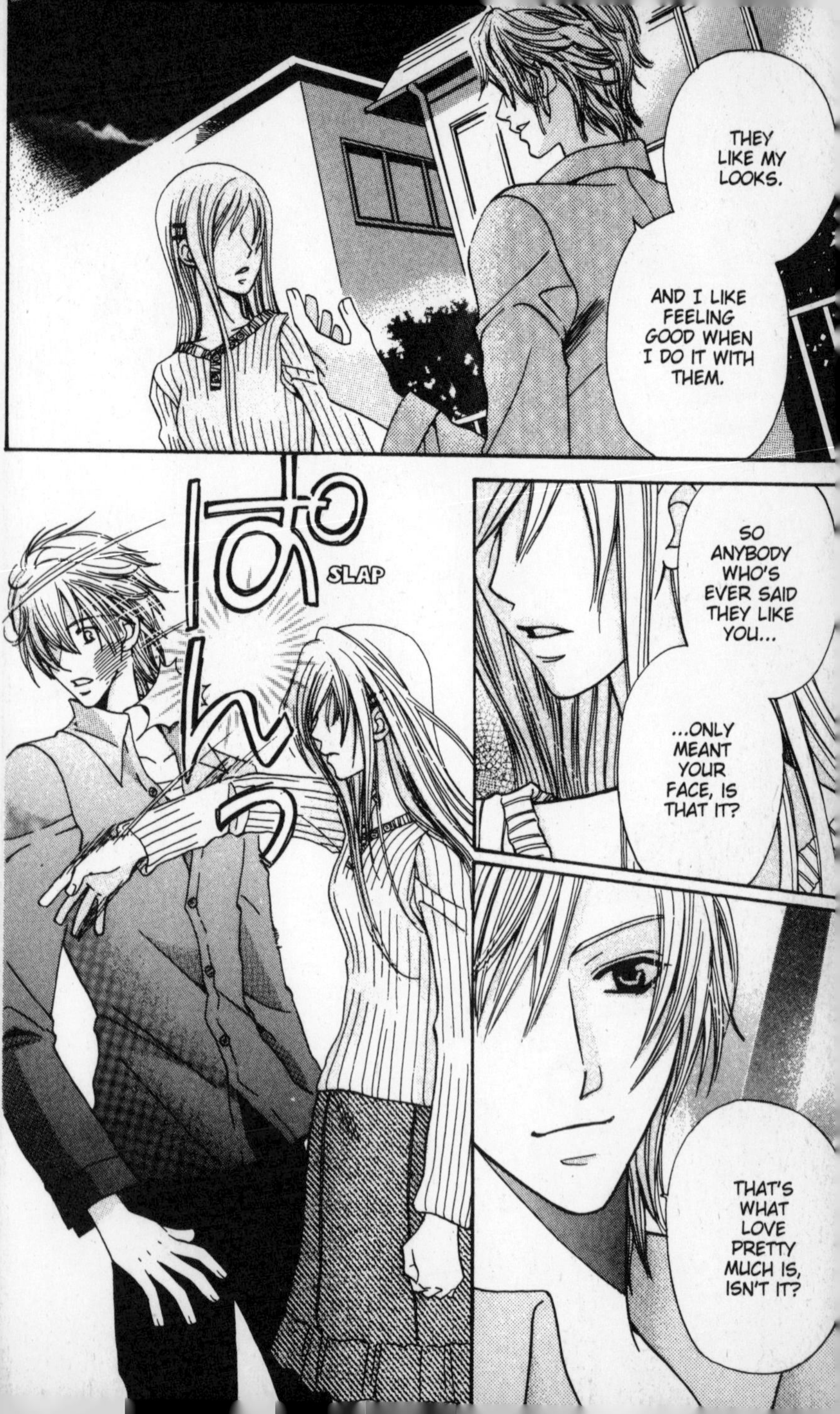
THEY LIKE MY LOOKS.
AND I LIKE FEELING GOOD WHEN I DO IT WITH THEM.
SO ANYBODY WHO'S EVER SAID THEY LIKE YOU...
...ONLY MEANT YOUR FACE, IS THAT IT?
THAT'S WHAT LOVE PRETTY MUCH IS, ISN'T IT?
ぱん
SLAP

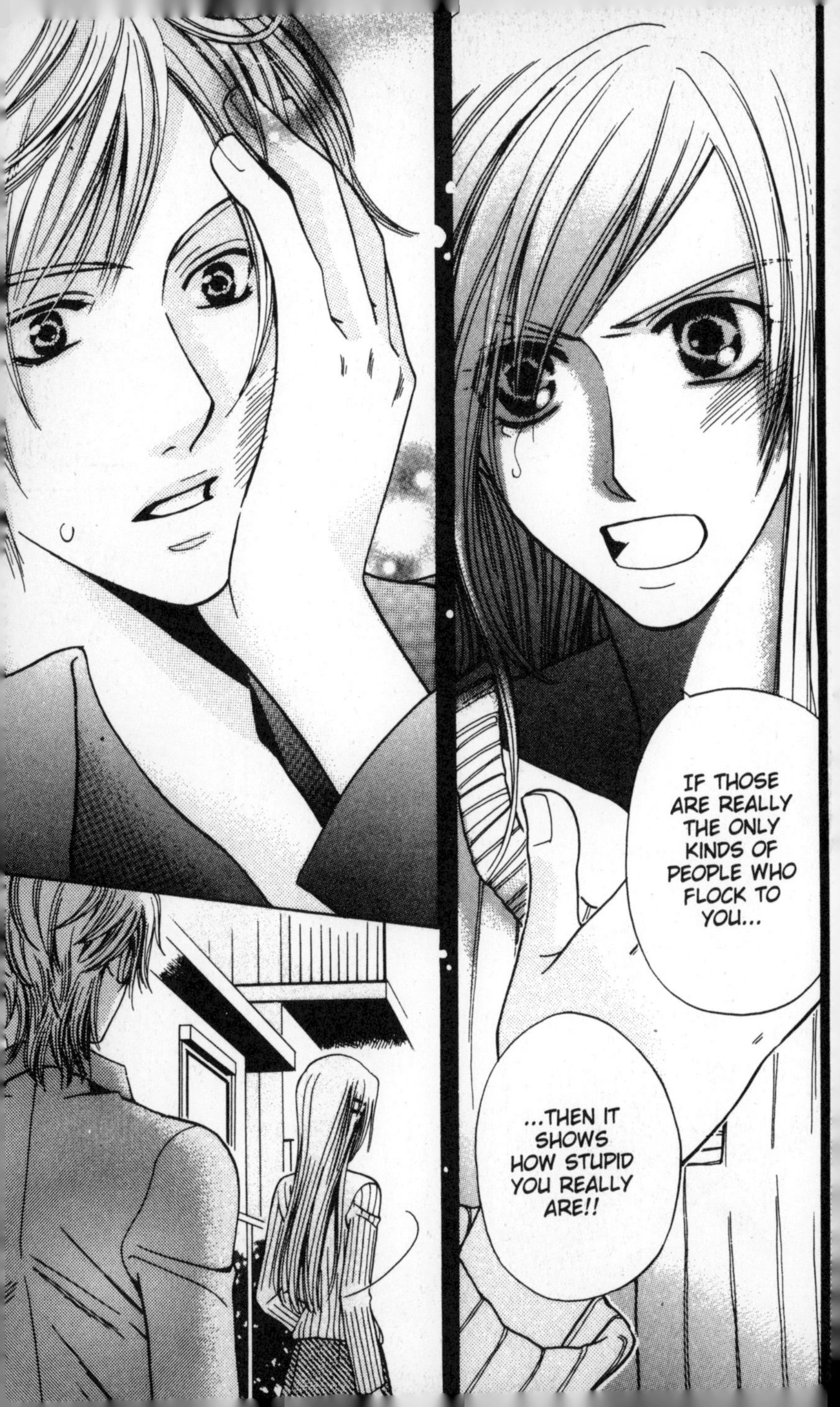
IF THOSE ARE REALLY THE ONLY KINDS OF PEOPLE WHO FLOCK TO YOU...
...THEN IT SHOWS HOW STUPID YOU REALLY ARE!!

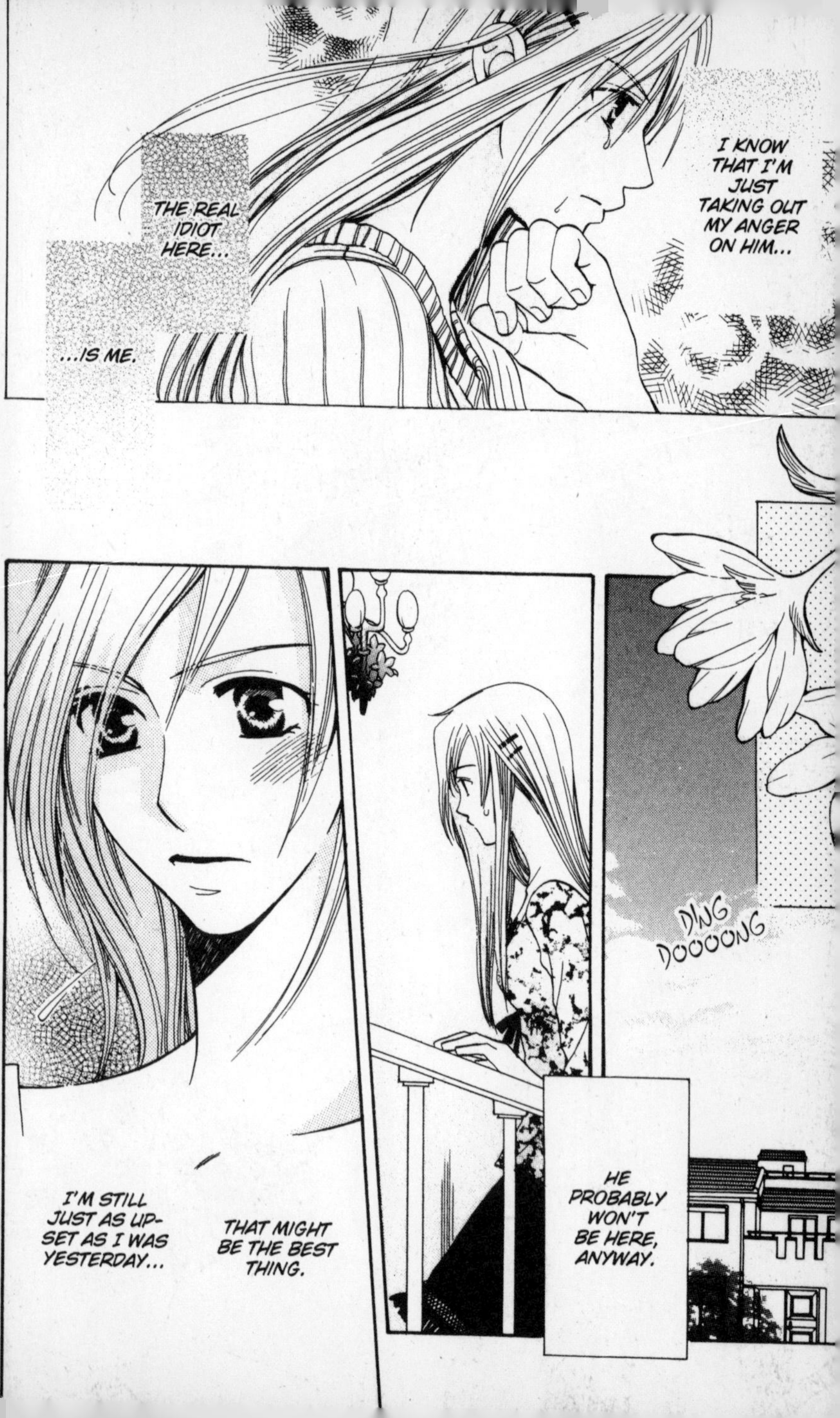
I KNOW THAT I'M JUST TAKING OUT MY ANGER ON HIM...
THE REAL IDIOT HERE...
...IS ME.
DING DOOOONG
HE PROBABLY WON'T BE HERE, ANYWAY.
THAT MIGHT BE THE BEST THING.
I'M STILL JUST AS UPSET AS I WAS YESTERDAY...

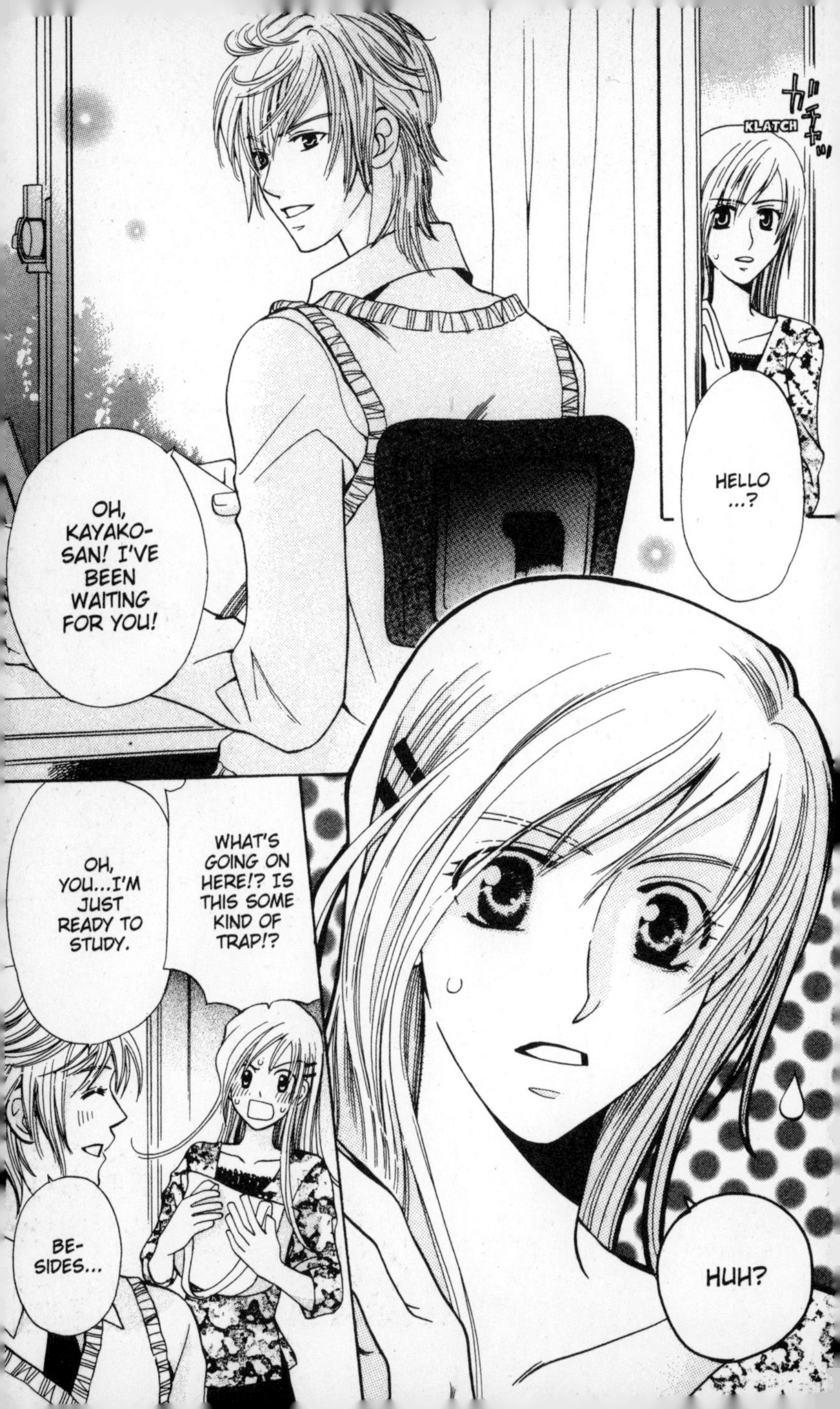

ガチャ
KLATCH
HELLO ...?
OH, KAYAKO-SAN! I'VE BEEN WAITING FOR YOU!
HUH?
WHAT'S GOING ON HERE!? IS THIS SOME KIND OF TRAP!?
OH, YOU...I'M JUST READY TO STUDY.
BE-SIDES...

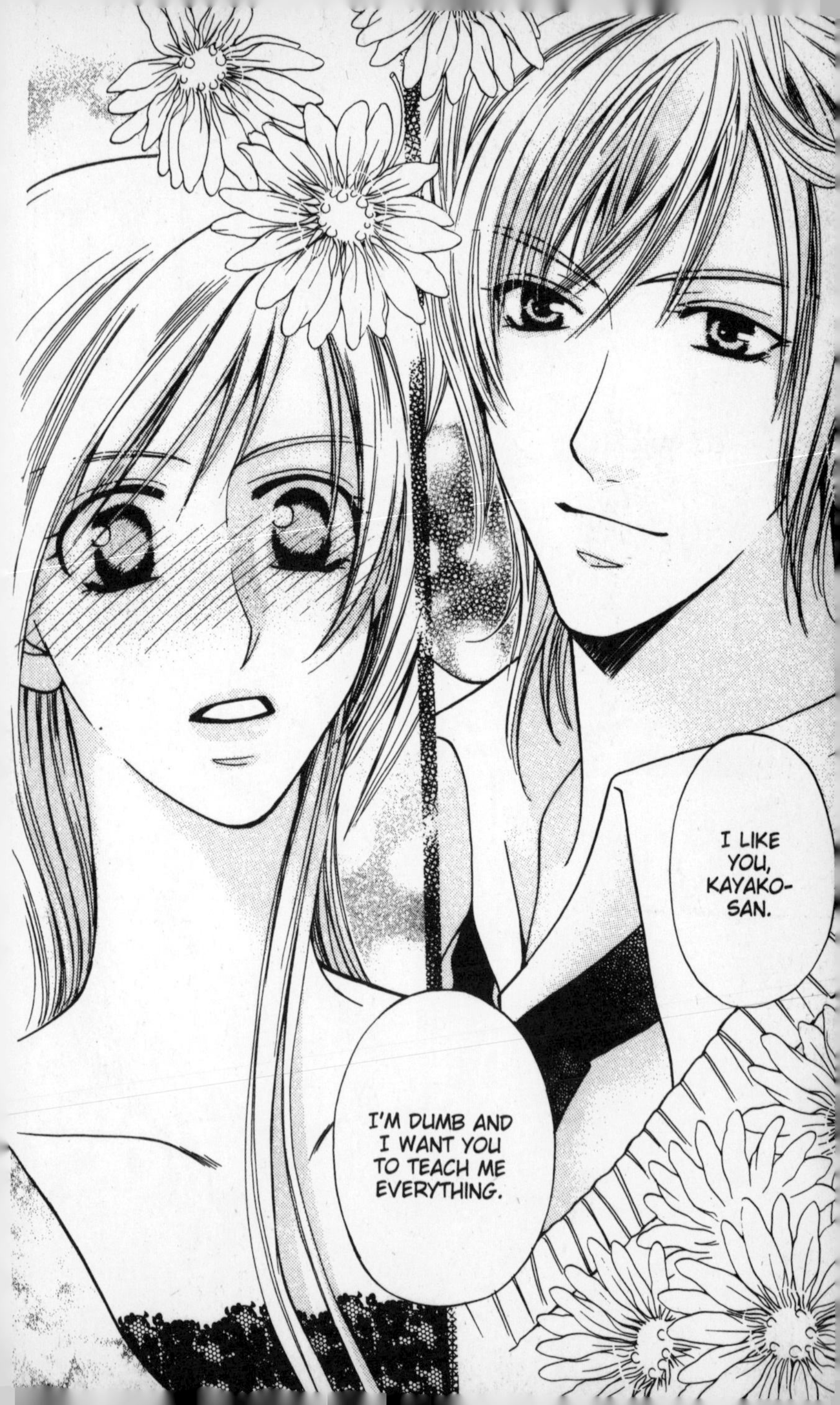
I LIKE YOU, KAYAKO-SAN.
I'M DUMB AND I WANT YOU TO TEACH ME EVERYTHING.

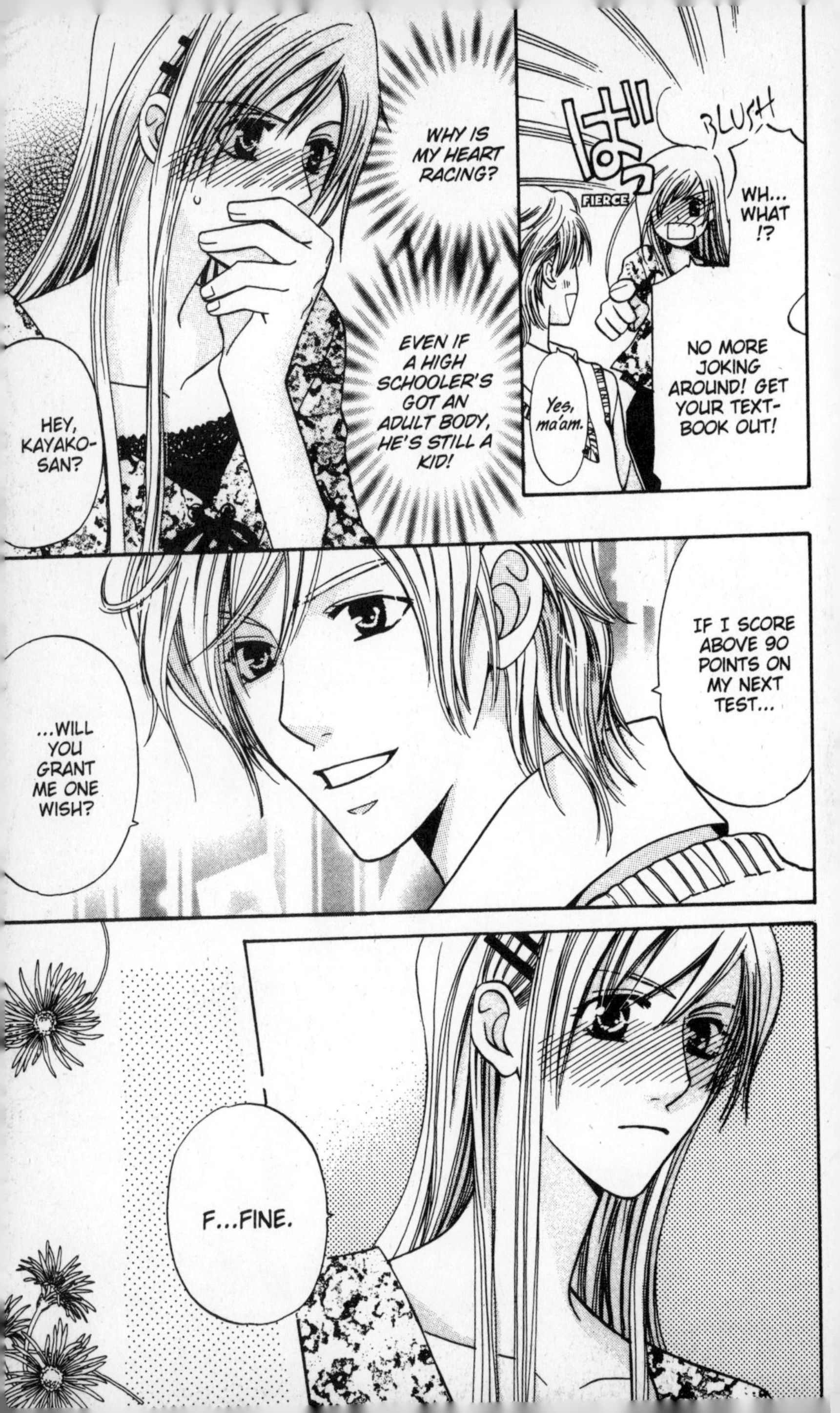
BLUSH
ぱっ
FIERCE
WH... WHAT!?
NO MORE JOKING AROUND! GET YOUR TEXT-BOOK OUT!
Yes, ma'am.
WHY IS MY HEART RACING?
EVEN IF A HIGH SCHOOLER'S GOT AN ADULT BODY, HE'S STILL A KID!
HEY, KAYAKO-SAN?
IF I SCORE ABOVE 90 POINTS ON MY NEXT TEST...
...WILL YOU GRANT ME ONE WISH?
F...FINE.

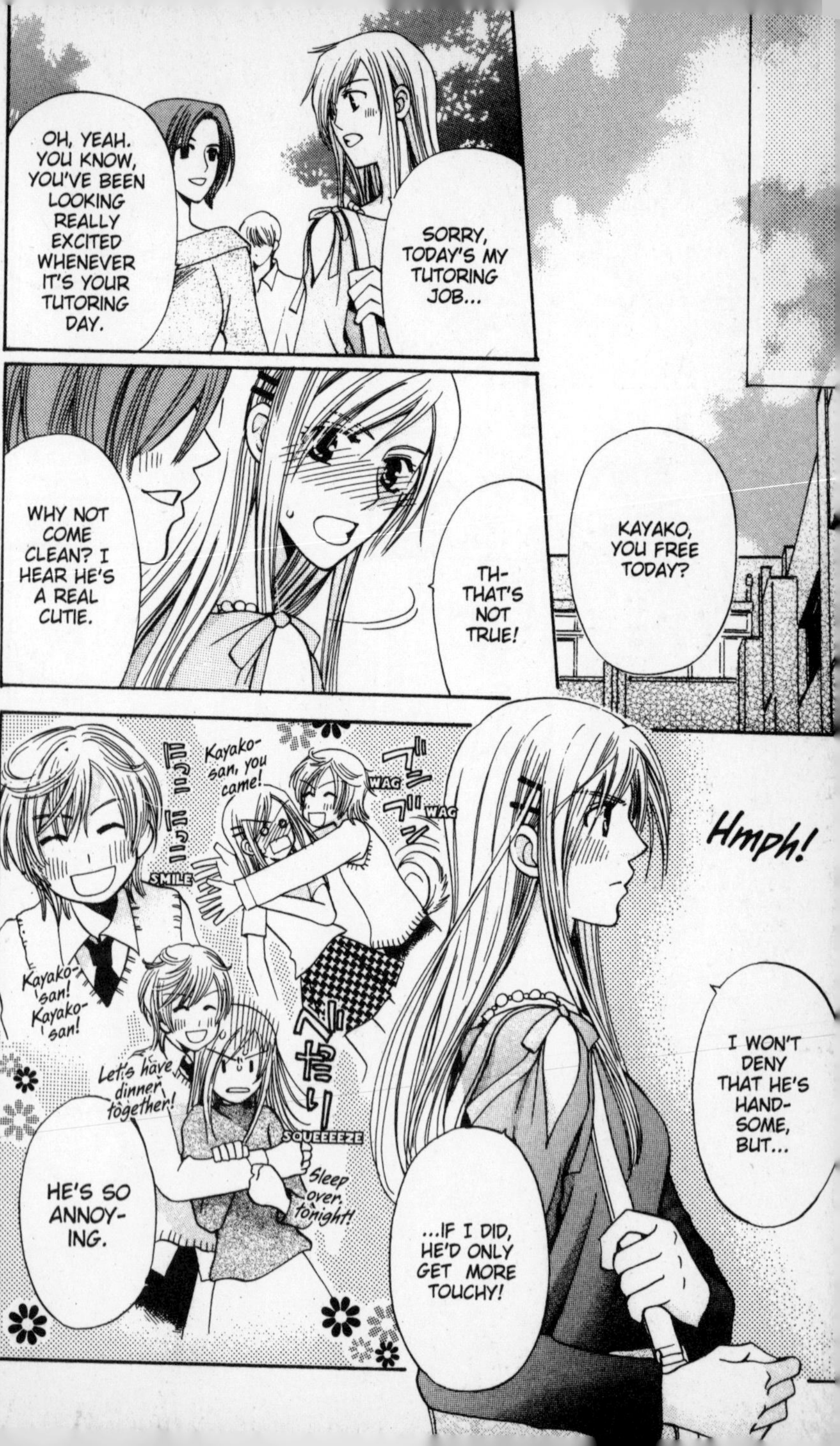
KAYAKO, YOU FREE TODAY?
SORRY, TODAY'S MY TUTORING JOB...
OH, YEAH. YOU KNOW, YOU'VE BEEN LOOKING REALLY EXCITED WHENEVER IT'S YOUR TUTORING DAY.
TH-THAT'S NOT TRUE!
WHY NOT COME CLEAN? I HEAR HE'S A REAL CUTIE.
Hmph!
I WON'T DENY THAT HE'S HAND-SOME, BUT...
...IF I DID, HE'D ONLY GET MORE TOUCHY!
Kayako-san, you came!
WAG
WAG
SMILE
Kayako-san! Kayako-san!
Let's have dinner together!
SQUEEEEZE
Sleep over, tonight!
HE'S SO ANNOYING.

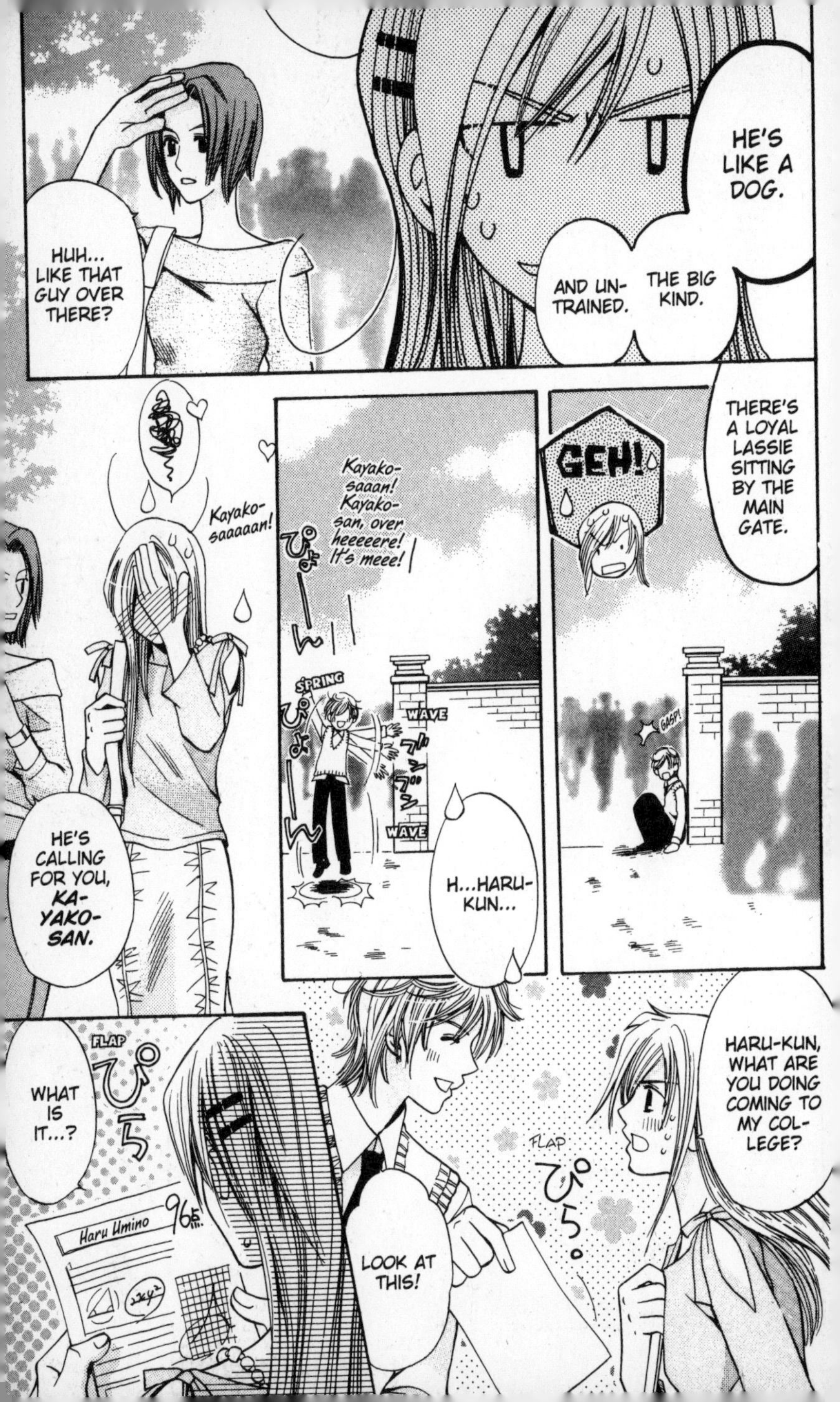
HE'S LIKE A DOG.
THE BIG KIND.
AND UN-TRAINED.
HUH... LIKE THAT GUY OVER THERE?
THERE'S A LOYAL LASSIE SITTING BY THE MAIN GATE.
GEH!
GASP!
Kayako-saaan! Kayako-san, over heeeeere! It's meee!
SPRING
WAVE
WAVE
Kayako-saaaaan!
H...HARU-KUN...
HE'S CALLING FOR YOU, KA-YAKO-SAN.
HARU-KUN, WHAT ARE YOU DOING COMING TO MY COL-LEGE?
FLAP
LOOK AT THIS!
FLAP
WHAT IS IT...?
Haru Umino
96

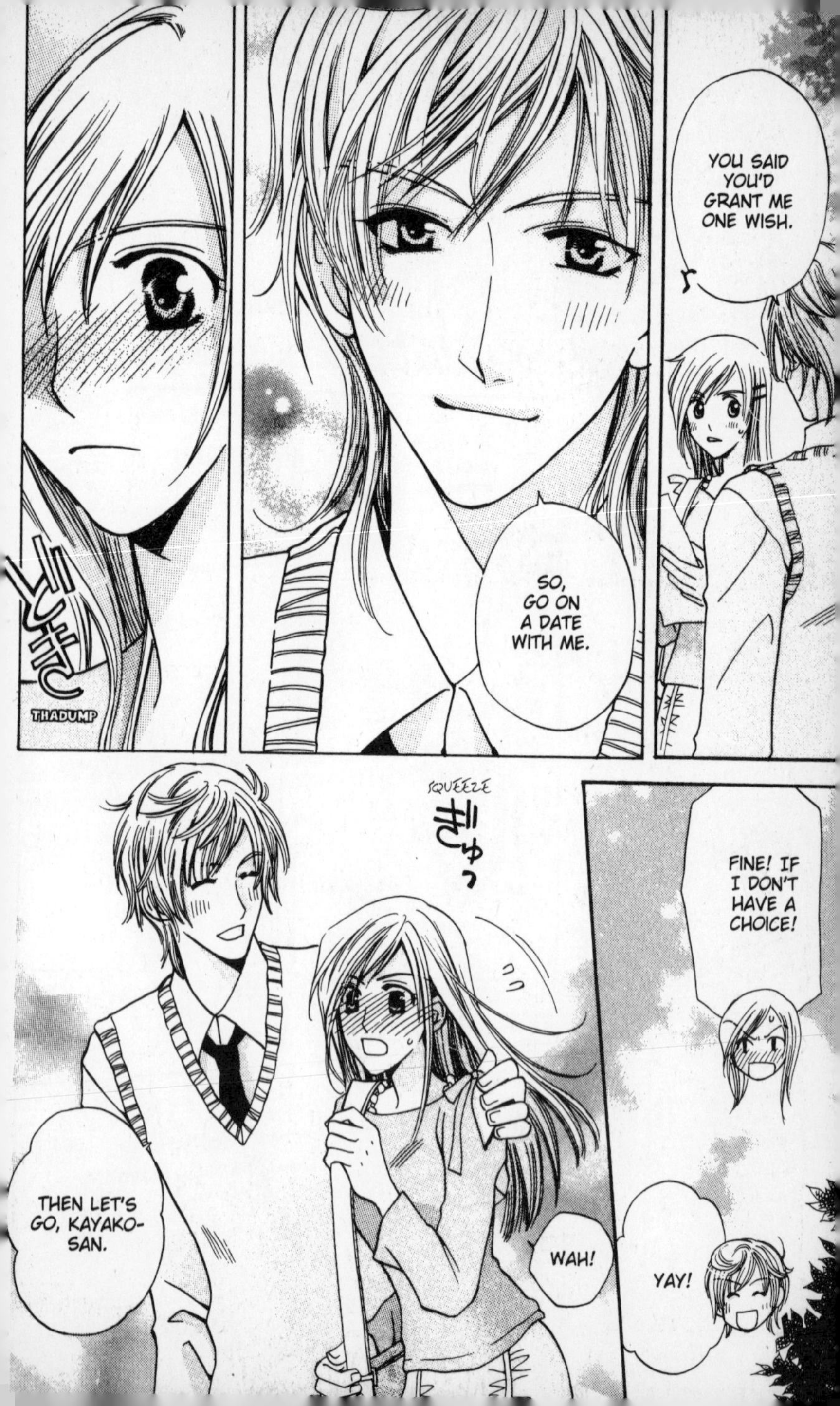

YOU SAID YOU'D GRANT ME ONE WISH.
SO, GO ON A DATE WITH ME.
THADUMP
FINE! IF I DON'T HAVE A CHOICE!
YAY!
SQUEEZE
ぎゅっ
WAH!
THEN LET'S GO, KAYAKO-SAN.

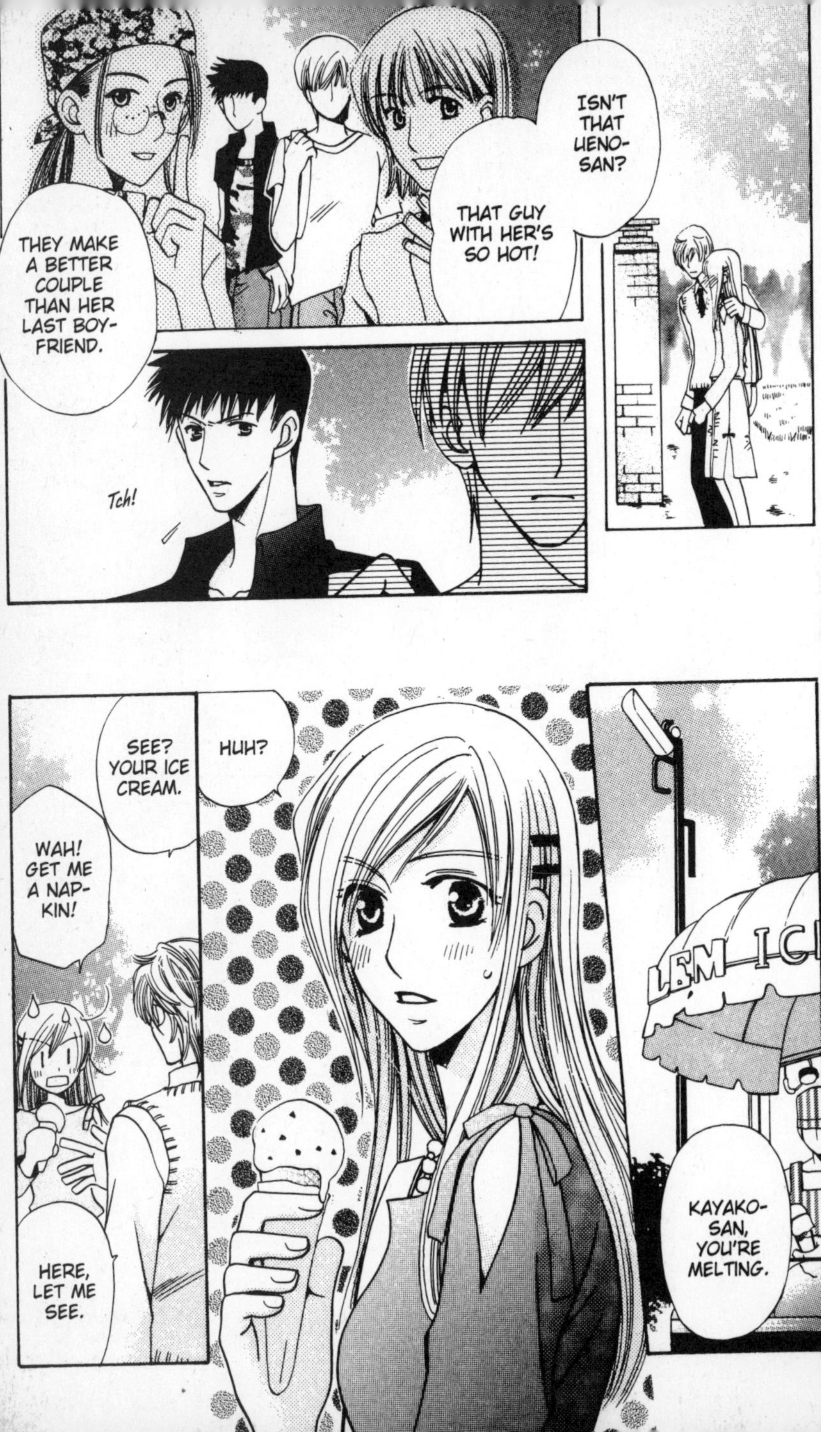
ISN'T THAT UENO-SAN?
THAT GUY WITH HER'S SO HOT!
THEY MAKE A BETTER COUPLE THAN HER LAST BOY-FRIEND.
Tch!
KAYAKO-SAN, YOU'RE MELTING.
HUH?
SEE? YOUR ICE CREAM.
WAH! GET ME A NAP-KIN!
HERE, LET ME SEE.

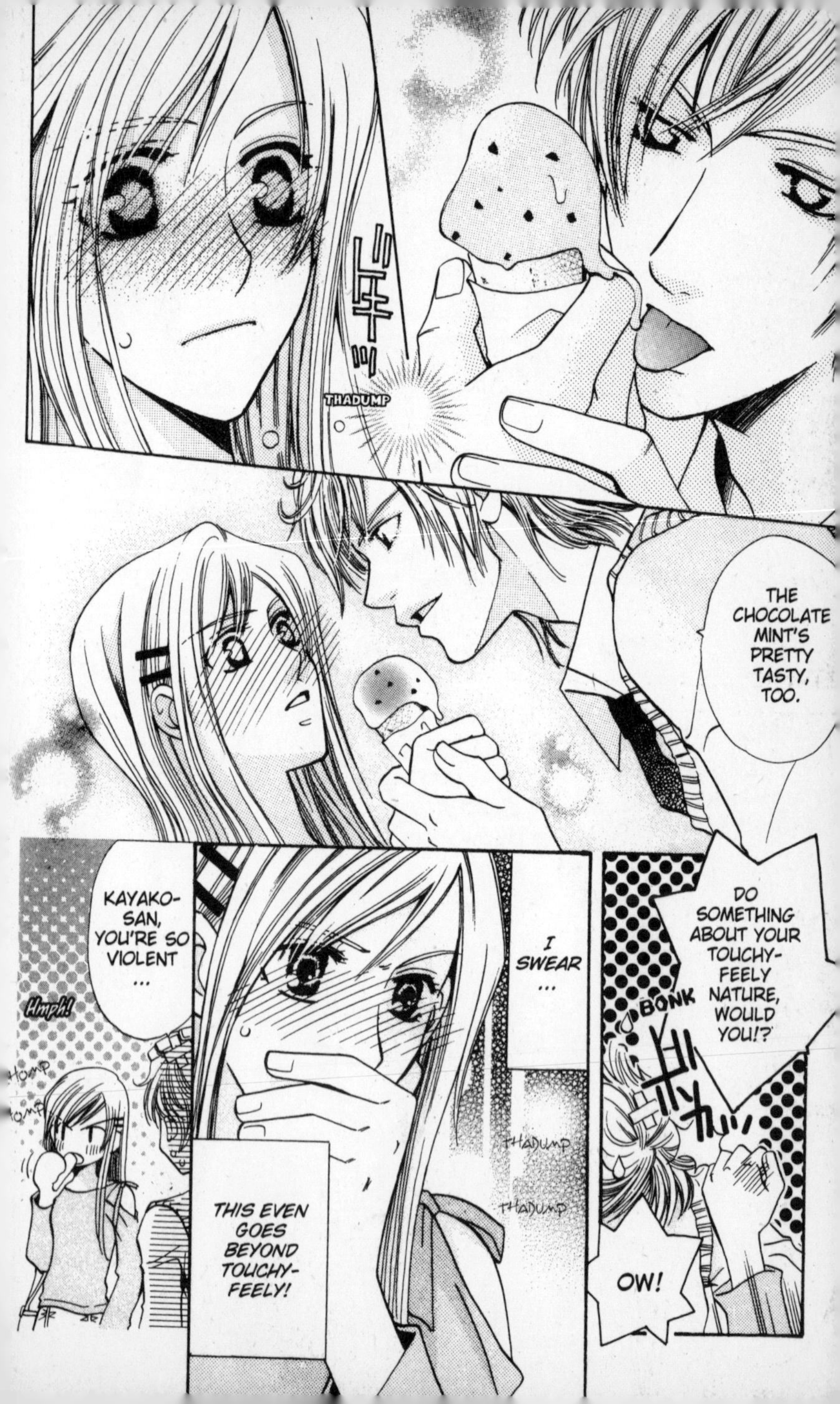
THADUMP
THE CHOCOLATE MINT'S PRETTY TASTY, TOO.
DO SOMETHING ABOUT YOUR TOUCHY-FEELY NATURE, WOULD YOU!?
BONK
OW!
I SWEAR ...
THADUMP
THADUMP
THIS EVEN GOES BEYOND TOUCHY-FEELY!
KAYAKO-SAN, YOU'RE SO VIOLENT ...
Hmph!

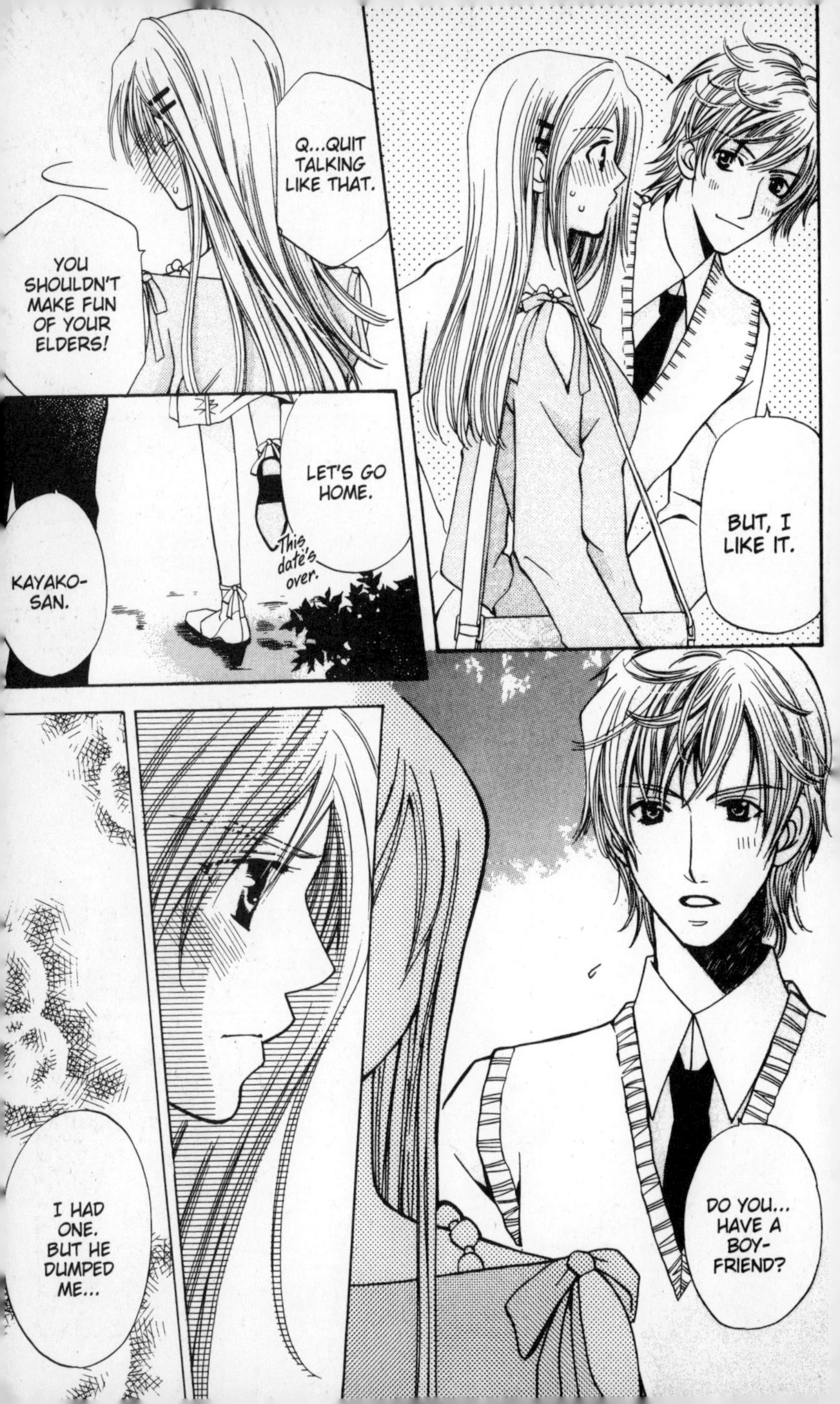
BUT, I LIKE IT.
Q...QUIT TALKING LIKE THAT.
YOU SHOULDN'T MAKE FUN OF YOUR ELDERS!
LET'S GO HOME.
This date's over.
KAYAKO-SAN.
DO YOU... HAVE A BOY-FRIEND?
I HAD ONE. BUT HE DUMPED ME...

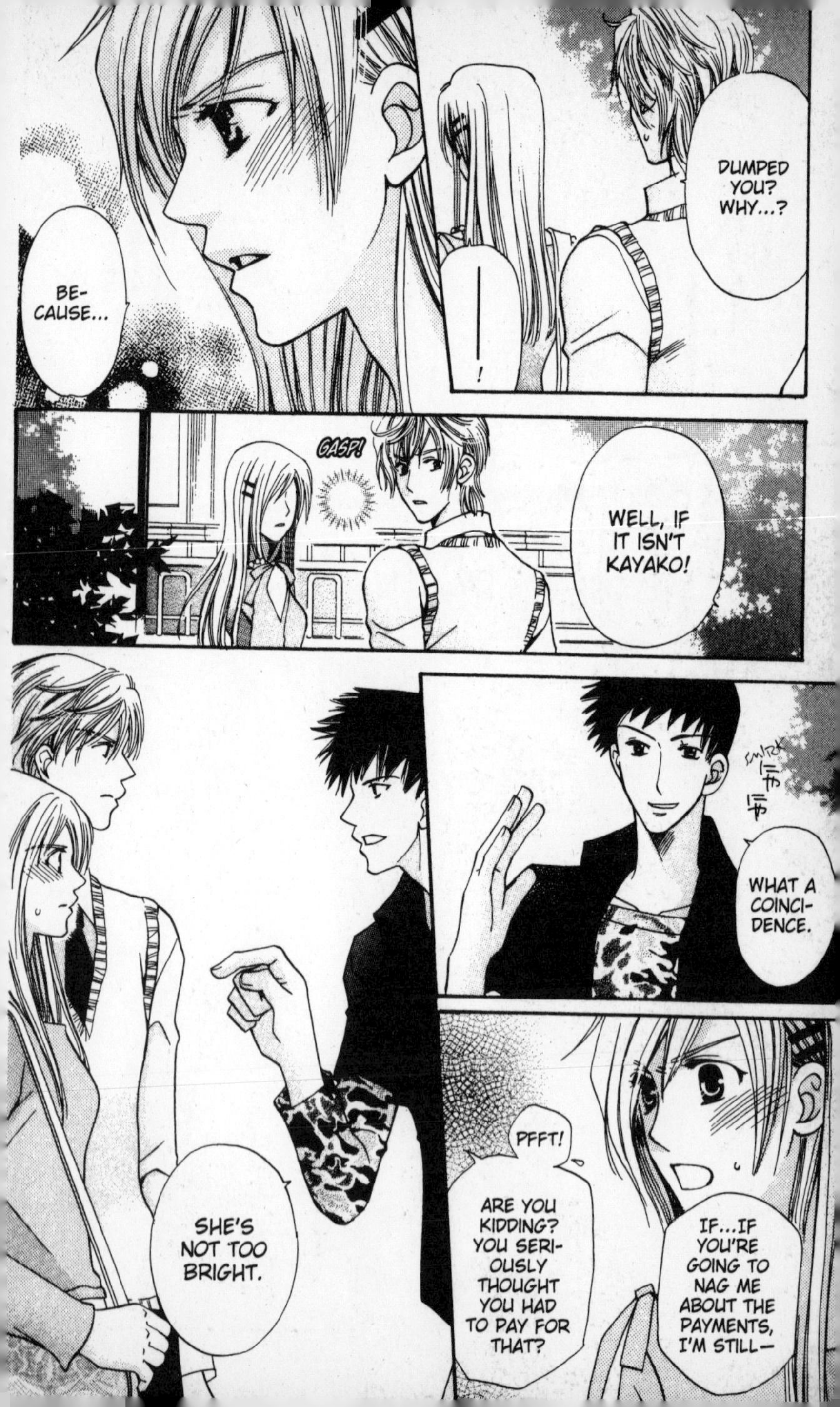
DUMPED YOU? WHY...?
!
BE-CAUSE...
WELL, IF IT ISN'T KAYAKO!
GASP!
SMIRK
WHAT A COINCI-DENCE.
IF...IF YOU'RE GOING TO NAG ME ABOUT THE PAYMENTS, I'M STILL—
PFFT!
ARE YOU KIDDING? YOU SERI-OUSLY THOUGHT YOU HAD TO PAY FOR THAT?
SHE'S NOT TOO BRIGHT.

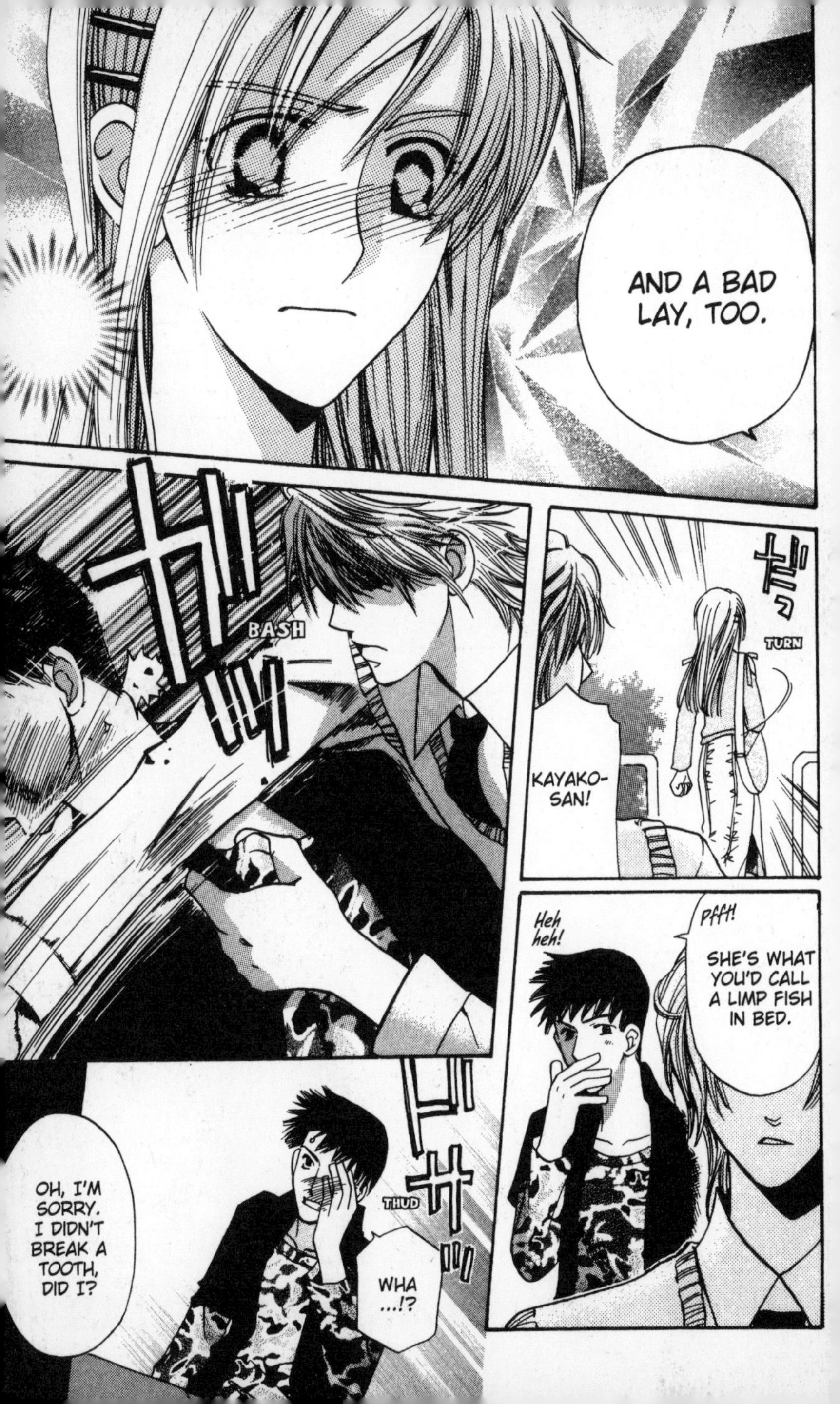
AND A BAD LAY, TOO.
TURN
KAYAKO-SAN!
Pfft!
Heh heh!
SHE'S WHAT YOU'D CALL A LIMP FISH IN BED.
BASH
THUD
WHA ...!?
OH, I'M SORRY. I DIDN'T BREAK A TOOTH, DID I?

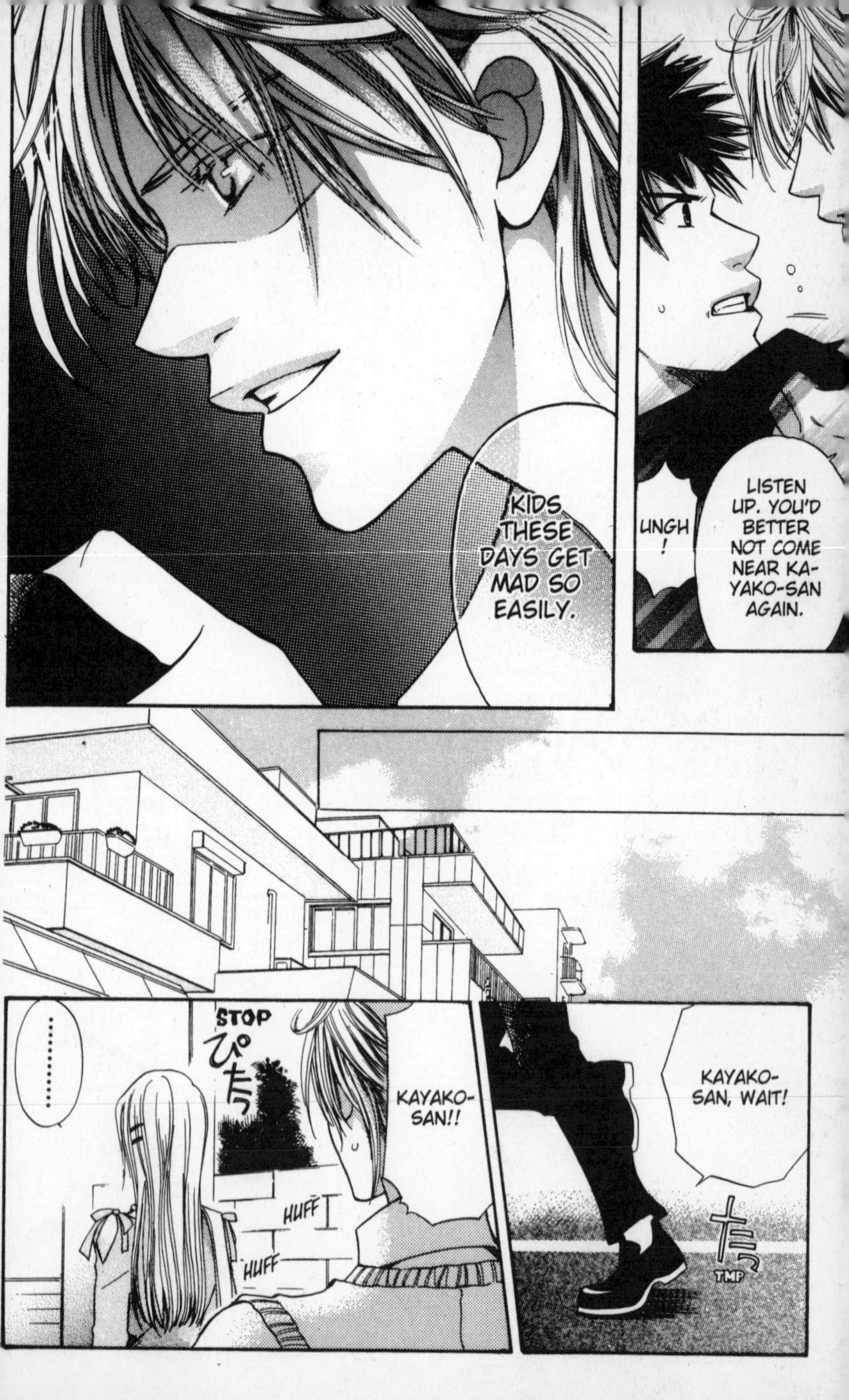
LISTEN UP. YOU'D BETTER NOT COME NEAR KA-YAKO-SAN AGAIN.
UNGH!
KIDS THESE DAYS GET MAD SO EASILY.
KAYAKO-SAN, WAIT!
TMP
KAYAKO-SAN!!
STOP
HUFF
HUFF
......

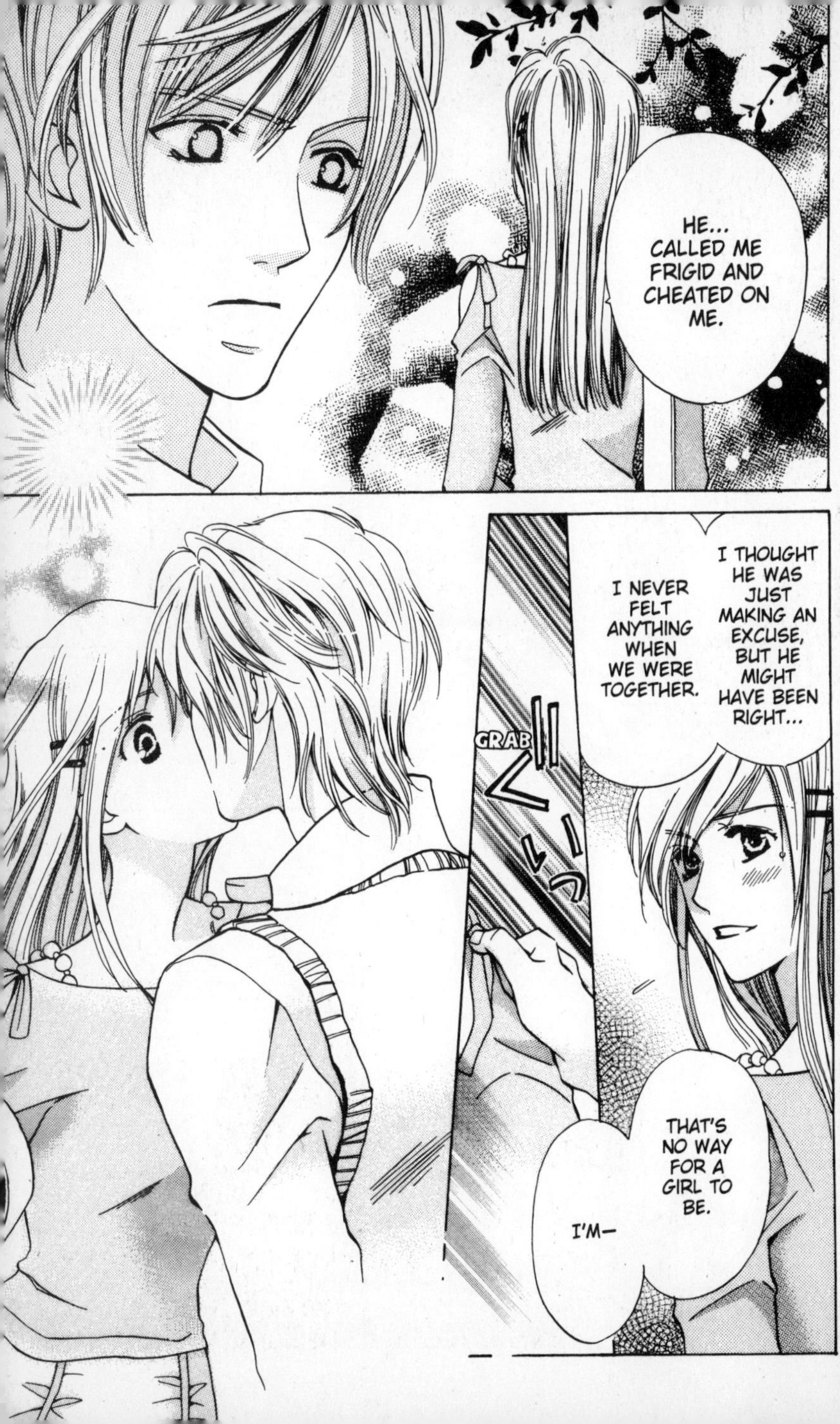
HE... CALLED ME FRIGID AND CHEATED ON ME.
I THOUGHT HE WAS JUST MAKING AN EXCUSE, BUT HE MIGHT HAVE BEEN RIGHT...
I NEVER FELT ANYTHING WHEN WE WERE TOGETHER.
GRAB
THAT'S NO WAY FOR A GIRL TO BE.
I'M—

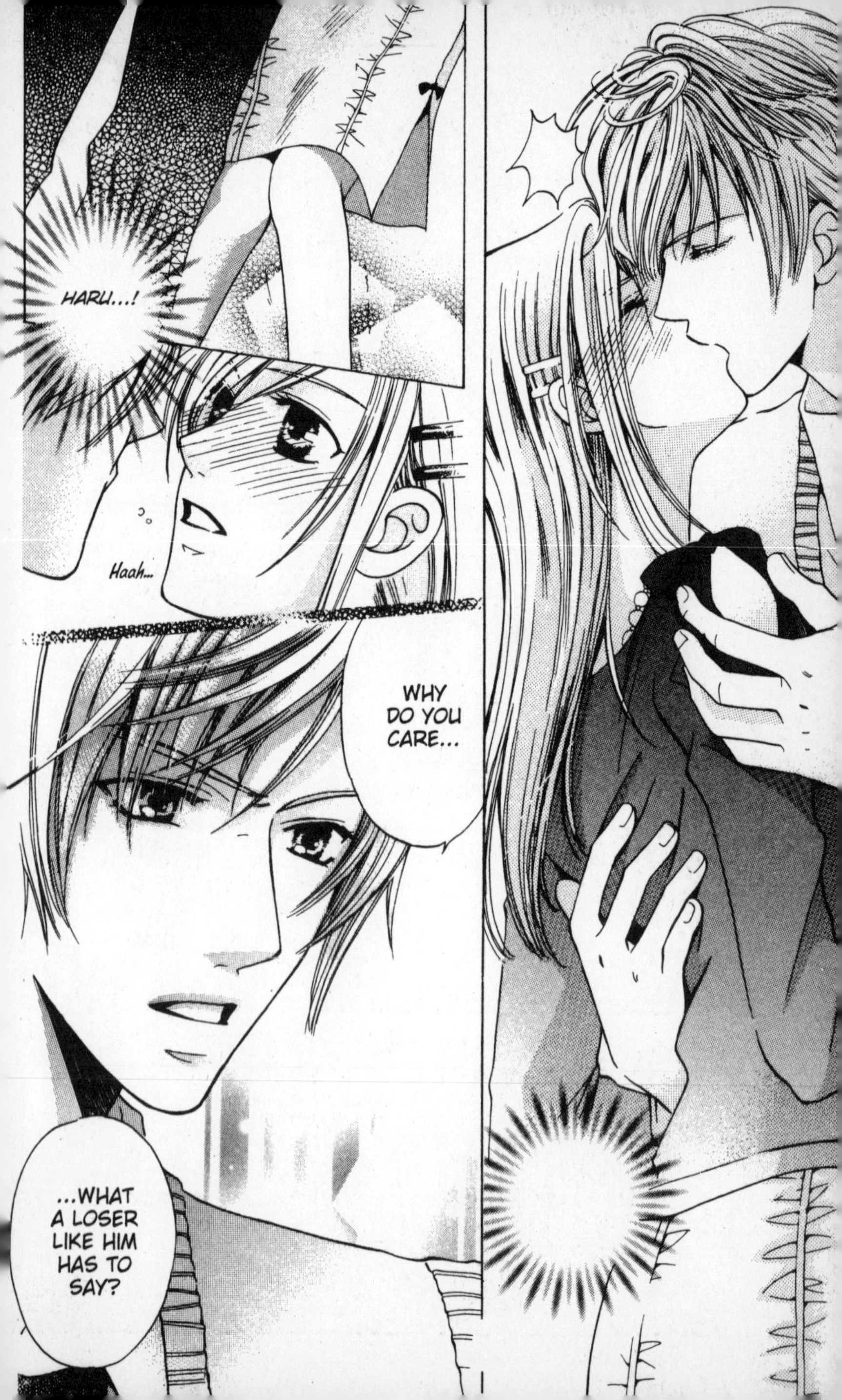
HARU...!
Haah...
WHY DO YOU CARE...
...WHAT A LOSER LIKE HIM HAS TO SAY?

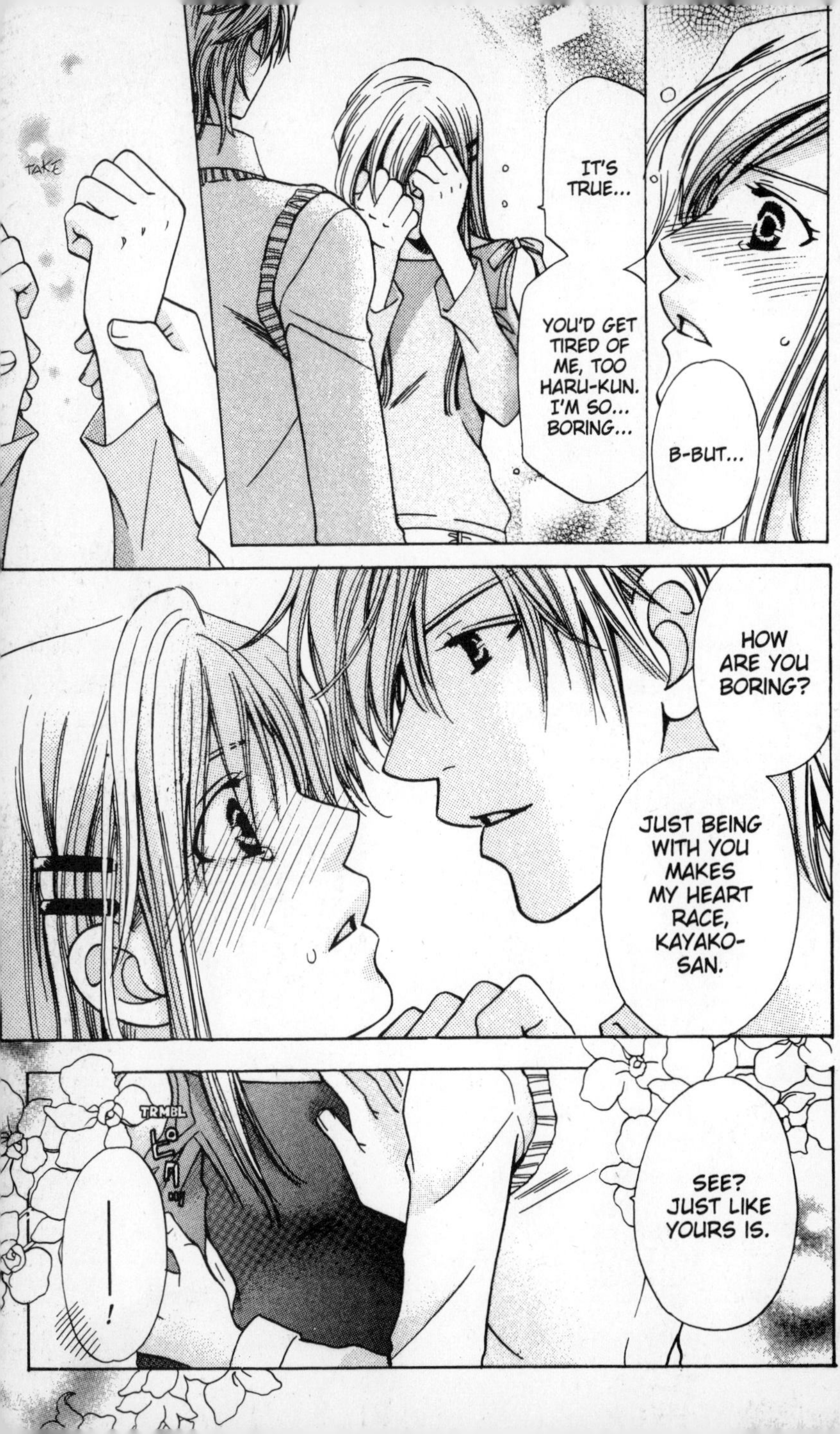
B-BUT...
IT'S TRUE...
YOU'D GET TIRED OF ME, TOO HARU-KUN. I'M SO... BORING...
TAKE
HOW ARE YOU BORING?
JUST BEING WITH YOU MAKES MY HEART RACE, KAYAKO-SAN.
SEE? JUST LIKE YOURS IS.
TRMBL
!

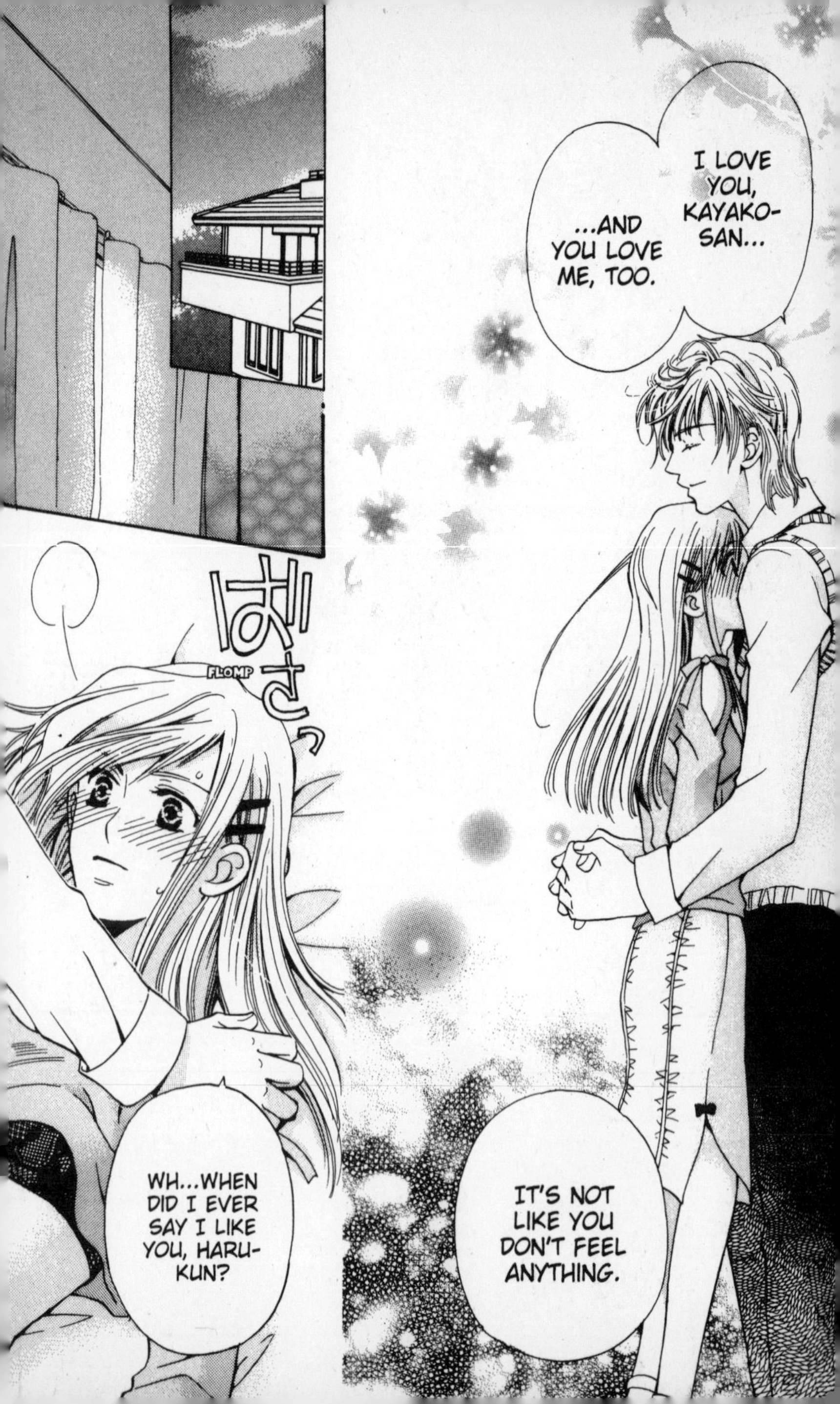
I LOVE YOU, KAYAKO-SAN...
...AND YOU LOVE ME, TOO.
IT'S NOT LIKE YOU DON'T FEEL ANYTHING.
はさっ
FLOMP
WH...WHEN DID I EVER SAY I LIKE YOU, HARU-KUN?

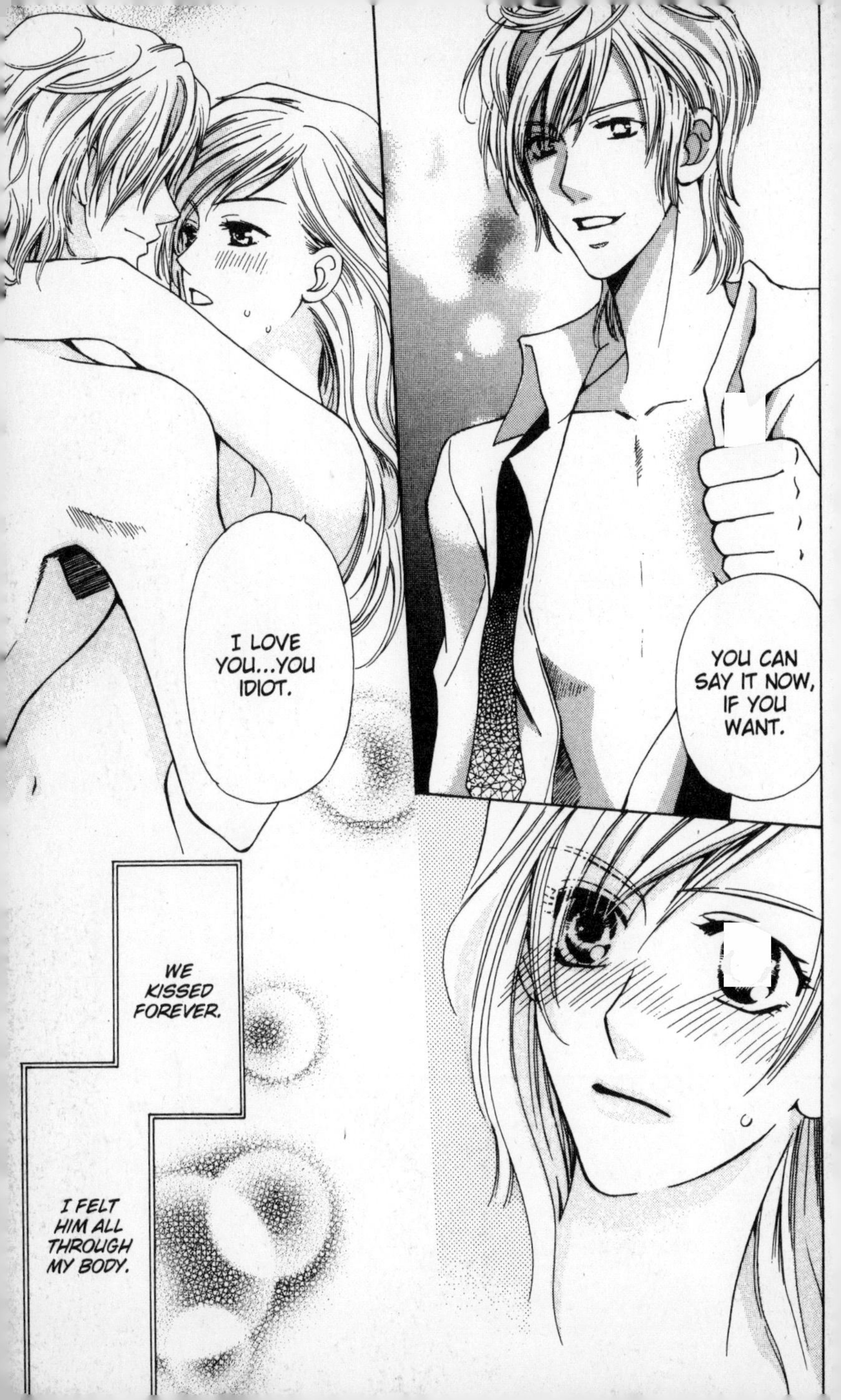
YOU CAN SAY IT NOW, IF YOU WANT.
I LOVE YOU...YOU IDIOT.
WE KISSED FOREVER.
I FELT HIM ALL THROUGH MY BODY.

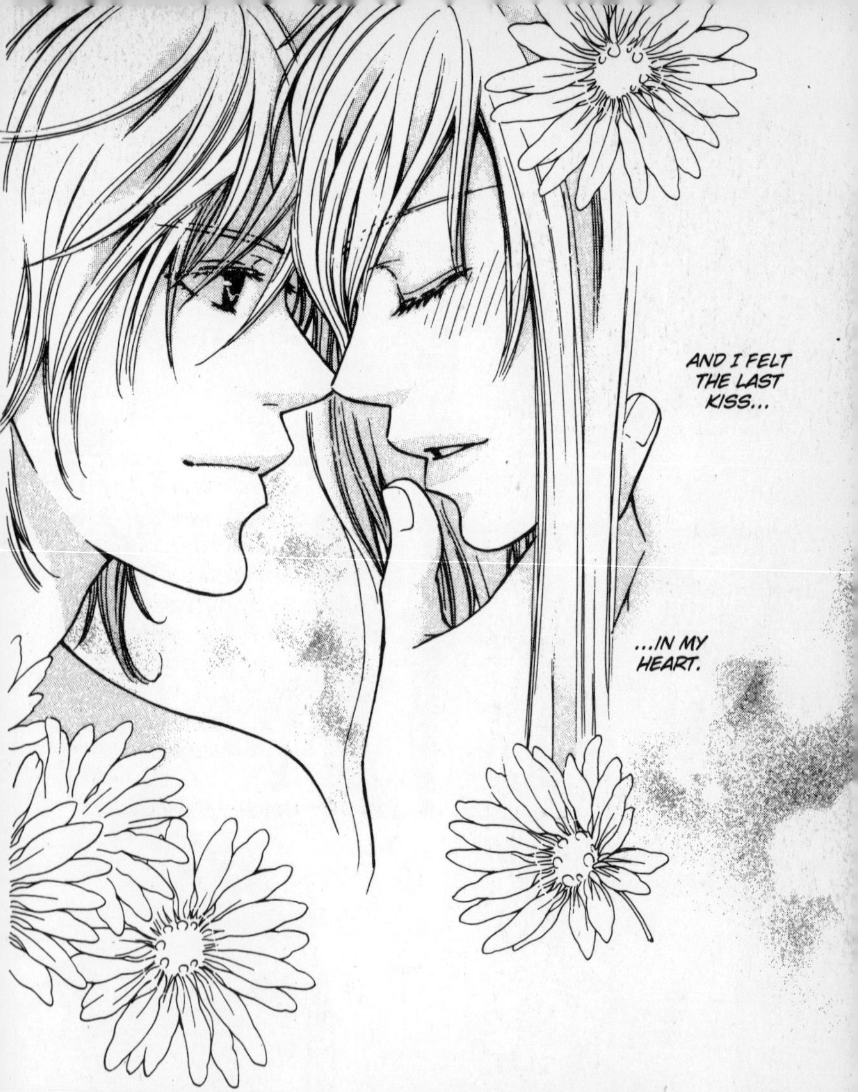
AND I FELT THE LAST KISS...
...IN MY HEART.

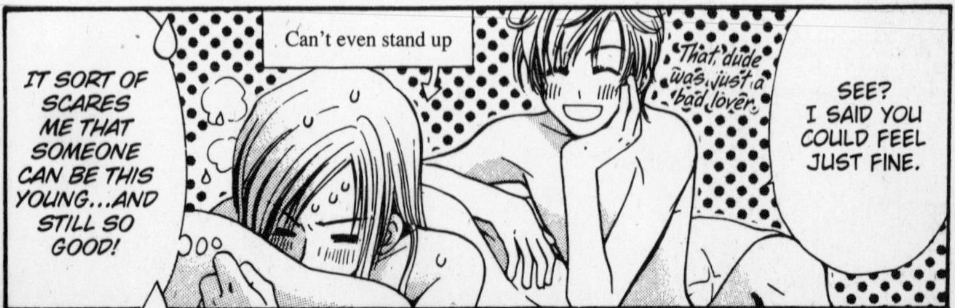
SEE? I SAID YOU COULD FEEL JUST FINE.
That dude was just a bad lover.
Can't even stand up
IT SORT OF SCARES ME THAT SOMEONE CAN BE THIS YOUNG...AND STILL SO GOOD!

NAUGHTY HONEY♥

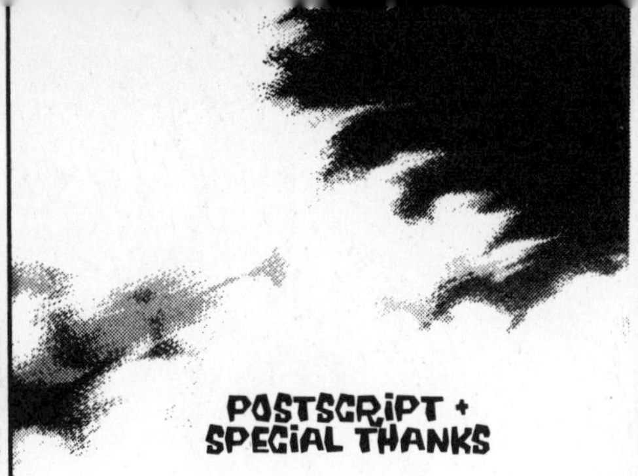

POSTSCRIPT + SPECIAL THANKS

Thank you very much
for reading volume 3 of
"Ultimate Venus"!
And to Kishima-san who
always supports me as my
editor, and Hariguchi-san and
Fujiyama-san who always help
me out with my pages and
stick around with me despite
all my stupid stories: thank
you so much!!

Best regards hereafter, too!

2007. 7.17

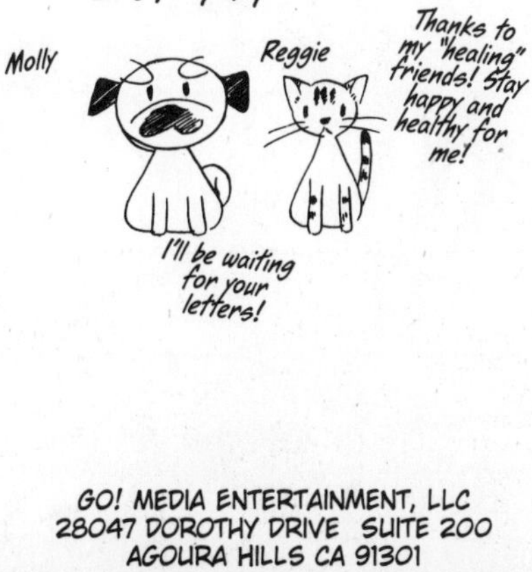
Molly
Reggie
Thanks to my "healing" friends! Stay happy and healthy for me!
I'll be waiting for your letters!

GO! MEDIA ENTERTAINMENT, LLC
28047 DOROTHY DRIVE SUITE 200
AGOURA HILLS CA 91301

ULTIMATE VENUS VOLUME 3 / END

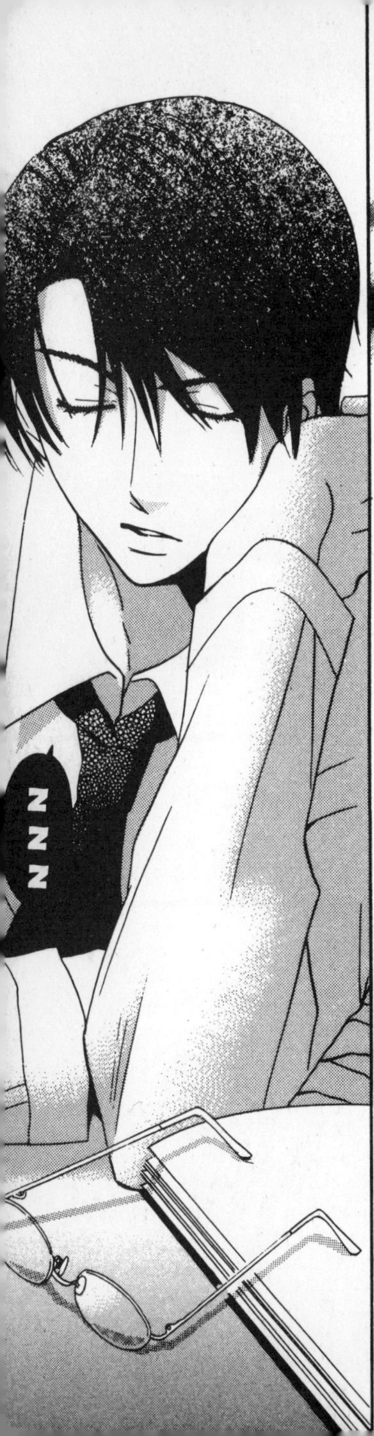
ZZZ

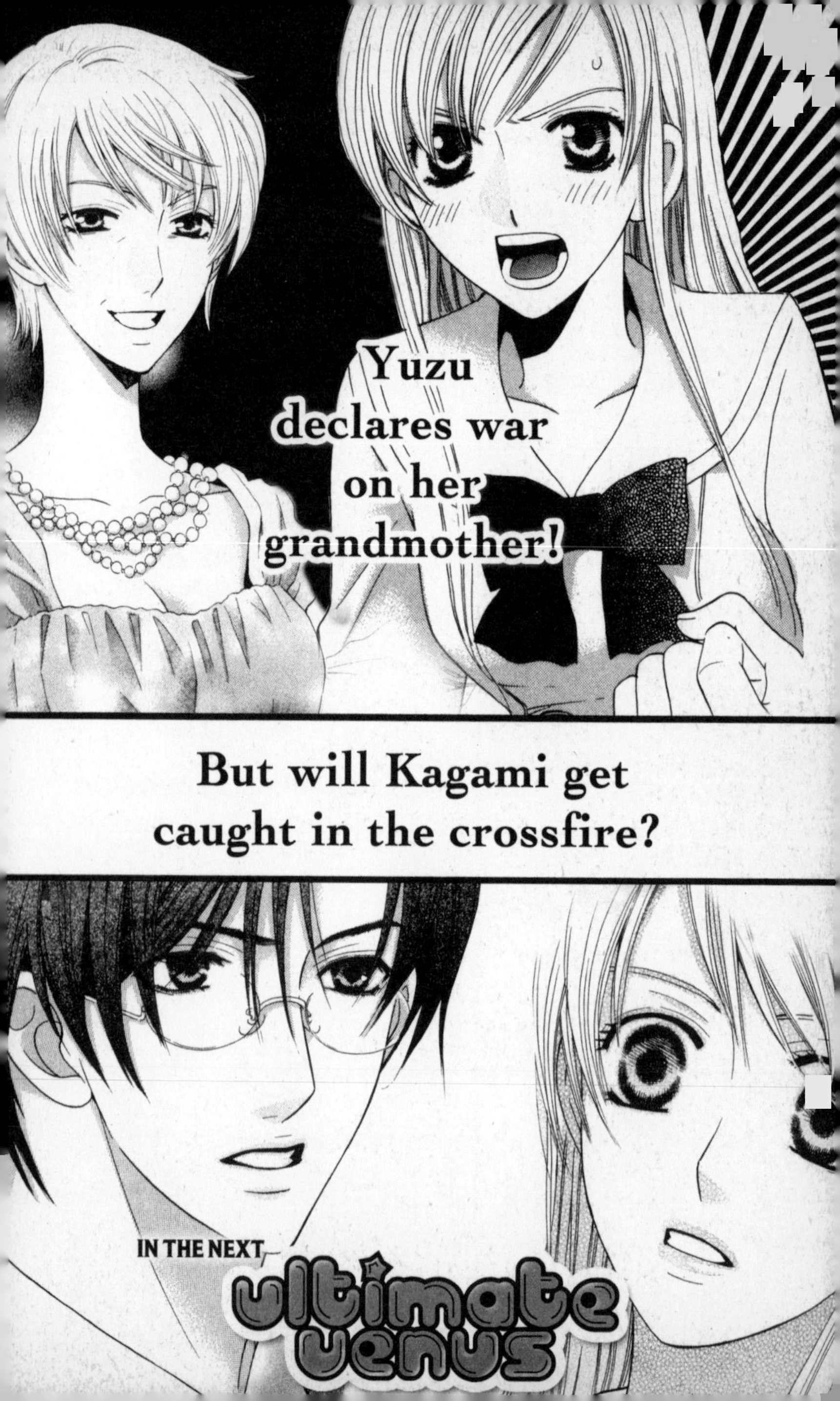
Yuzu declares war on her grandmother!
But will Kagami get caught in the crossfire?
IN THE NEXT
ultimate venus

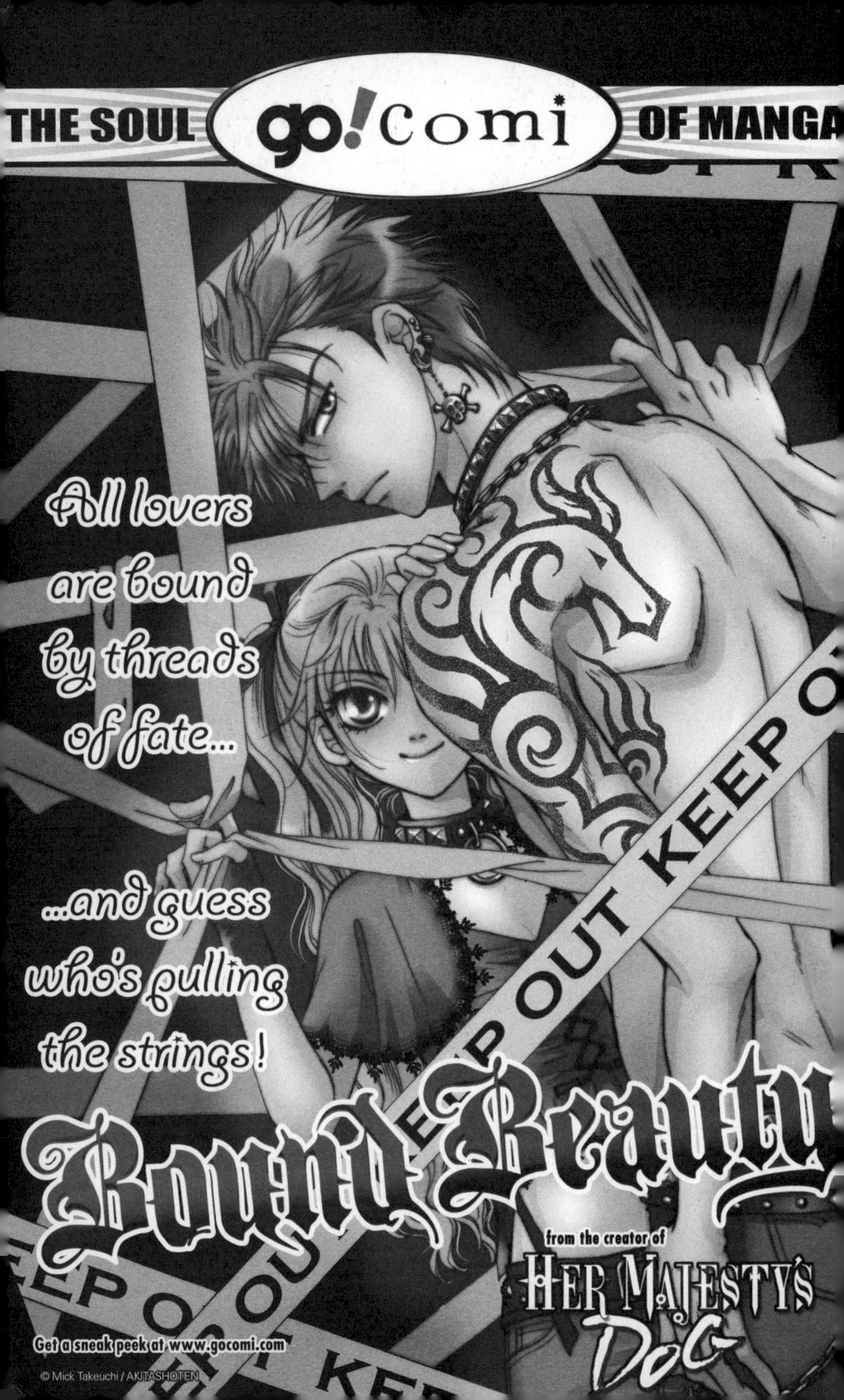
THE SOUL go!comi OF MANGA
All lovers are bound by threads of fate...
...and guess who's pulling the strings!
Bound Beauty
from the creator of
HER MAJESTY'S DOG
Get a sneak peek at www.gocomi.com
© Mick Takeuchi / AKITASHOTEN

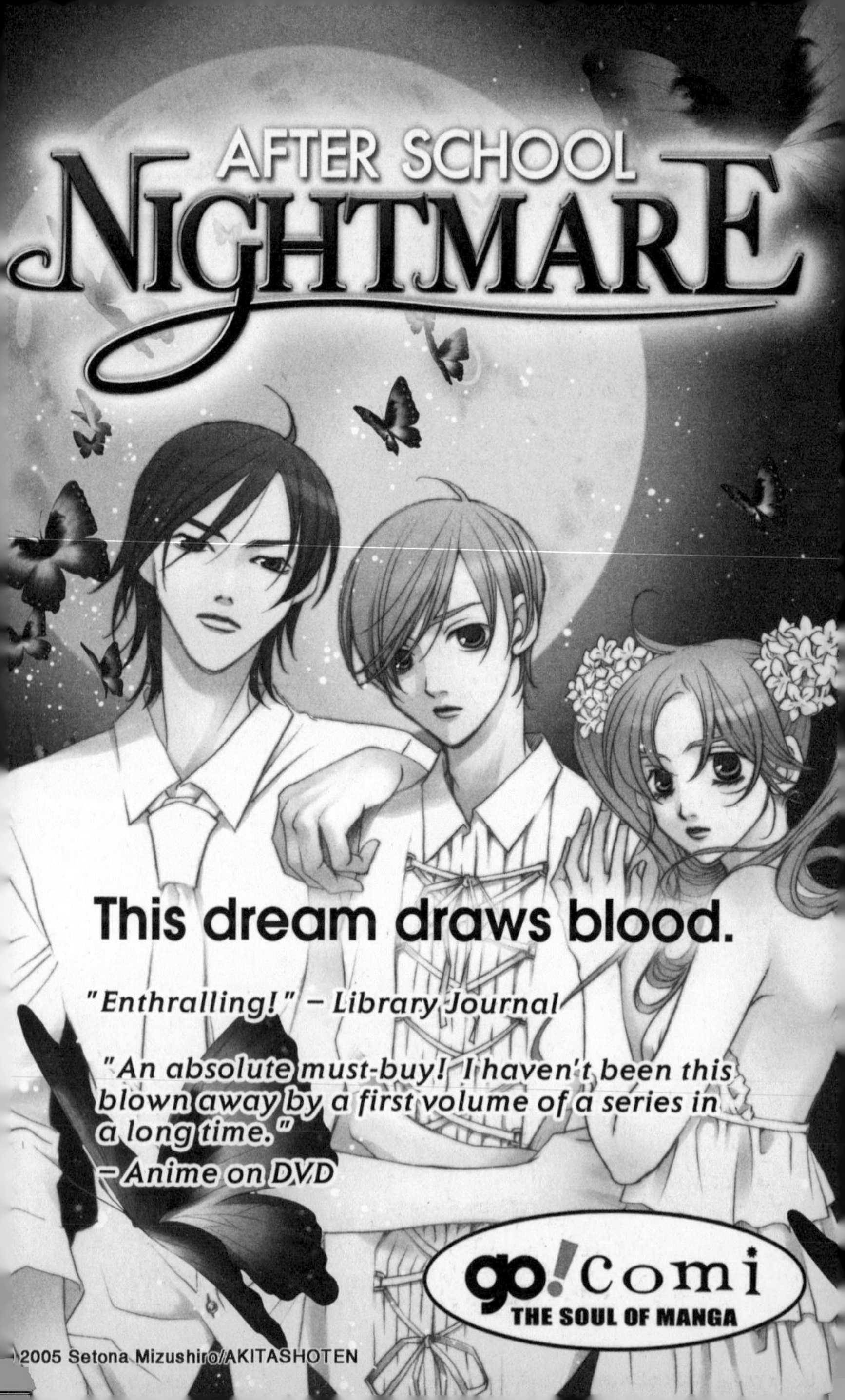
AFTER SCHOOL
NIGHTMARE
This dream draws blood.
"Enthralling!" – Library Journal
"An absolute must-buy! I haven't been this blown away by a first volume of a series in a long time."
– Anime on DVD
go!comi
THE SOUL OF MANGA
©2005 Setona Mizushiro/AKITASHOTEN